Mary Lettington .

THE LAKE & THE CASTLE

Also by Arthur Guirdham

A THEORY OF DISEASE
THE NATURE OF HEALING
CHRIST AND FREUD
COSMIC FACTORS IN DISEASE
MAN: DIVINE OR SOCIAL
THE GIBBET AND THE CROSS
THE CATHARS AND REINCARNATION
OBSESSION
A FOOT IN BOTH WORLDS
WE ARE ONE ANOTHER

ARTHUR GUIRDHAM

The Lake
& the Castle

JERSEY

NEVILLE SPEARMAN

First published in 1976 by
Neville Spearman (Jersey) Limited
PO Box 75, Normandy House, St. Helier
Jersey, Channel Islands

Distributed by Neville Spearman Ltd.,
112 Whitfield Street, London W1P 6DP

ISBN 0 85978 024 4

Set in 11/12½ point Juliana and printed by
Western Printing Services Limited, Bristol
on paper supplied by Frank Grunfeld Ltd, London
Bound by The Pitman Press, Bath

CONTENTS

FOREWORD

This is the story of the Roman, Celtic, and Napoleonic incarnations of a group which has kept together through five incarnations. Some of its members have figured as Cathars in *We Are One Another*. Here they are seen in their Roman, Celtic and Napoleonic rôles. The main characters are new and were only revealed as members of the group in the last two years. For those readers who have not read *We Are One Another* a short summary may be helpful. Clare Mills is the woman who received from the next world a spate of visits and written messages which indubitably revealed her as having lived as Esclarmonde de Perella in the thirteenth century. Her principal discarnate visitor was also identified as Braïda de Montserver. In this present book the latter is as informative about the Roman, Celtic and Napoleonic incarnations as she was about the Cathar.

Clare Mills' father, recognised in the earlier book as Bertrand Marty, reappears in the present work but against the background of other incarnations. Betty, previously my sister Hélis de Mazerolles in the thirteenth century, reappears in a different rôle in *The Lake and the Castle*. So does her twentieth-century mother Jane Butler, formerly Bruna, the Cathar wife of a sergeant-at-arms and burnt as a heretic after the siege of Montségur in 1244.

Kathleen was identified in *We Are One Another* as Arsendis, wife of another medieval sergeant-at-arms and, like her friend Bruna, burnt at the stake on the same day in 1244. This fate was also shared by Jack, yet another sergeant-at-arms, who as Brasillac took part in the siege of Montségur.

I myself have been more than adequately identified in both *The Cathars and Reincarnation* and *We Are One Another* as Roger de Grisolles (or Fanjeaux).

This stark précis is offered merely to clarify the connection

7

between medieval characters and their equivalents in the Celtic and Napoleonic eras. The principal characters appear for the first time. For every member of the group one particular incarnation was dominant. That is why the Celtic incarnation is centred round Annette and the Napoleonic round Marion.

While, in the course of this history, I have identified my characters by the names they bore in their Celtic and Napoleonic incarnations I have, in telling their story, allowed one name to serve one character through their different lives. This is to avoid confusion. The woman known in this life as Betty cannot be saddled with five names in a single record, nor can one keep changing her sex in referring to her. For the most part I have kept to the description which comes most naturally to my mind. In whatever incarnation Annette appears it is easier for me to think of her in terms of her twentieth-century description. On the other hand Braïda is always predominantly Braïda because the incarnation in which she bore this name was the most important for her and for me. For those with a taste for such things I have appended a list of the different names borne by the members of the group in their different incarnations.

The reader may note that the Celtic names have a latin flavour. This is easily understandable. The group which lived in Cumberland in the seventh century after Christ was what was called Romano-British. A good number were products of intermarriage between Celts and Romans. It was also a practice at that time to Romanise Celtic names. Betty, as Brigida, was the most pure-bred Celt among us.

The Lake and the Castle is not only a story of group reincarnation in the so-called dark ages and in the First Empire and the régimes which preceded and followed it. The record of our lives as members of the Celtic Church in Cumberland is of immense importance because of the light it throws on the nature and sophisticated teachings of Celtic Christianity.

This history is inextricably bound up with communication with the next world. Paradoxically it is also concerned with the immense evocative power, at least to members of the group, of certain places on this planet. I never thought that some of the most magical hours I spent as a boy in Cumberland were due to the fact that I had been there before.

8

I refer in different places in the text to my capacity to communicate directly with the discarnates. Until September 1973 I had for the most part relied on Clare Mills to relay information provided by them. From that time onwards I could often speak with them directly provided she was present. Later I was able to function independently to a restricted degree. The process whereby I achieved the capacity to speak, feel and see the revenants was in itself a revelation. It is recorded in the last section of this book.

That I continue to use the word revenants for the non-substantial visitors who instructed me is academic. To call them spirits is highly misleading when what we are dealing with is psyches. Over-use of the phrase discarnate entities seems to me cumbrous and pedantic.

In the table which follows the entry 'unknown' means that the name has not been disclosed. A horizontal stroke indicates that there is no evidence that the individual was alive in that particular incarnation.

Table of Names in Different Incarnations

Roman (4th cent. A.D.)	Celtic Church (7th cent.)	Cathar (13th cent.)	Napoleonic (End of 18th and beginning of 19th cent.)	Twentieth cent.
Cressida	Trubellia	Esclarmonde de Perella	Pierre	Clare Mills
Unknown	Eusebia	Braïda de Montserver	Unknown	Jocelyn S
Claudius	Aurelia	Cecilia de Montserver	Unknown	Annette
Unknown	Unknown	Bertrand Marty	Captain X	Mr. Mills
Unknown	Unknown	Bruna de la Rocque d'Olmes	Unknown	Jane Butler
Camillia	Brigida	Hélis de Mazerolles	Henri A	Betty
—	—	Arnaud Domerq	Henri B	Marion
—	—	—	Unknown	Mrs. Dacre
Blodena	Unknown	Arsendis	Unknown	Kathleen
Cornelius	Davidius	Pons Narbona	Jacques	Graham
Berenice	Mercantius	Roger-Isarn de Fanjeaux	Raymond	Arthur
—	—	Brasillac	Guirdaud	Guirdham
Marcellus	Johannus	Jean de Cambiaire	Unknown	Jack
—	—	Unknown	Unknown	Dr. Simon S
—	—	—	—	Guy

BOOK ONE

The Lake

Chapter One

In October 1916 I walked with my mother on the road over Wythop to Bassenthwaite Lake. Two years earlier a world had died at the height of a burning summer. The death of the world and the passing of summer were written in the silence and the pallid sunshine.

Everything that day had sharper outlines. A crab apple leaned from the hedge towards the valley. The yellow of the apples was clear in the sunshine and sharpened by last night's frost. There were China roses in a cottage garden. Their petals were sheathed in light and their beauty almost audible.

I walked right out of time. It is something I cannot forget. I have known instants, even minutes, as luminous. That day was different. Time and duration were expressed in light.

I know now that I remember that day because, hour after hour, I was out of time. What we remember most are the timeless moments. It is a paradox that memory, the test of our response to the pain of duration, is sharper for the episodes when time is sleeping.

With my mother I left the train at Embleton. The road twisted clear of the muttering stream and the shadow of the trees to the open fell. It was still morning. I saw the lake with the mist dispersed and no clouds above it. Bassenthwaite was very quiet in the first years of the century but its echoes are insistent throughout my story. I have heard them for more than a thousand years.

We went in to lunch at the Pheasant, a long, low building in the shadow of the trees. As far as the inn the road belongs to my mother and to me as I was many centuries ago. Beyond the inn it is three hundred yards to the landing stage. I did not know till the last few years that this stretch of road belongs as much to my father as the road to the inn was my mother's because of my timeless experience with her. I did not know that time dissolves still more sharply on the road to the landing stage.

My father died in 1952. When they told me he was dead I asked them to repeat the message. When I saw him three days after he was dead his Roman profile was more clean-cut than ever but there was no remoteness and even in death he had not attained to indifference. There was life in the room and the air vibrated. As I leaned towards him the vibration and the feeling of life intensified. Something flickered and passed in the air above his face. I had no feeling at that time except that he still existed and that his face was beautiful. I did not believe in spirits. I only felt them in the air. I did not know that what I was feeling was the passing of his soul. Perhaps he had waited for me to come.

After that there was a blankness, a non-realisation that my father had departed. It lasted for years and dissolved in a sudden collapse in a moment on a winter morning.

I see now that when my father was alive he was looking at life and beyond it. He was fully committed to this world and to people in it. He smiled as though he constantly contemplated something fascinating beyond the next corner. His pale-blue eyes were luminous and piercing. His story was written in his eyes. When they were directed fully at the world they were light and shining. At odd moments they were withdrawn and lightless. They were looking within him at some message suddenly scribbled on the retina of the unconscious. When the light went out of his eyes he was drawn to another world and a deeper knowledge. In these moments he was passing back and forward across the formless tundra of time and space.

Twenty years after my father's death, nearly sixty years since I walked over Wythop with my mother, I walked by the lake with the light of day failing and the country sinking to its winter sleep. I walked from the landing stage to the Pheasant. With the fall of twilight the slap of the waves on the jetty sharpened and the lake was dark under the shadow of the mountain. Suddenly, irrefutably, I felt my father beside me. His presence was sharper and clearer than the darkness of the trees and the murmur of lake water in the winter nightfall.

I had known before that my father had come back after death to be with me. There was the woman in the cottage who had never seen him. She was less aware of my presence than that of my father behind me. She described his profile and above all his

14

undeniably direct gaze that saw everything and all things and did not cease to love. She told me that his message to me was that I stood on the shore and should swim in the ocean. I did not pay much attention. I did not feel that I was born for these oceanic experiences. When I think of my father I recall less the inflammatory and anonymous genius of his soul than an ardent and utterly concentrated figure playing bowls on an evening before the old world died. It is logical that I should prefer these parochial and rustic memories of him. He never told me there were other worlds. He knew that truth cannot be verbalised.

For a time I thought that the road from the inn to the landing stage was evocative to me because of my memories of my father. This is the story of how I learnt that it is magical in its own right. It is not actually the road itself but the wood and the hillock adjacent to it. The dead whisper to the living from between the trees. Those who return are as easily identifiable as my father. Those who call and those who hear are on a certain wavelength but the power of recall is located in the place.

Chapter Two

I suppose you could call her a dark horse. Clare was blue-eyed and blonde. She had a clear, pink and white skin and looked unnaturally healthy. She wore the clothes and had the interests you would have expected of her. She loved tweeds, flowers, dogs, going to Wimbledon and watching rugger matches. She liked ballet and traditional landscapes. She worked hard and in her spare time was seriously addicted to fresh air.

She was highly gregarious and her social calendar was congested. I never knew where she found the energy for so much work and so many concerts and lectures. So far as one could judge from her words she lived by a few simple maxims. She was like the wind from the sea. She breezed in and out of people's houses peppering the atmosphere with such simple slogans as "Not to worry" and "Press on regardless". She had tonic qualities. It was remarkable how much better people felt for her visits. She should have been installed in a museum as a pre-permissive model of the outgoing Anglo-Saxon. There was absolutely no nonsense about her. She saw things as they were. She seemed to like most of what she saw because she loved a diversity of creatures.

She concealed herself very well. She was an extrovert but different from others in reaching out not only to her fellows but to the whole cosmos. No one looking at her could realise that her perceptive antennae oscillated through time and space.

Her friend Jocelyn was the widow of an Army officer. She was cast in the same mould as Clare. She was equally vigorous and with the same practical intelligence. She had the same capacity to see quickly to the heart of the problem. She saw both the wood and the trees.

Jocelyn had one daughter called Annette. In 1950, at the age of five, Annette fell off a swing and hurt her back badly. Her mother put one hand where the pain was worst and the other on the solar plexus. At the same time Clare placed one hand on the child's forehead and the other on the nape of her neck. Clare had no idea what impelled her to do so. It did not occur to her to ask Jocelyn why she placed her hands in this particular position. She did not know that they were both practising a healing technique seven centuries old. Whether Jocelyn knew is another matter.

Clare and Jocelyn met often in the house by the downs. In those days the suburb was quiet. It was beautiful in May. The gardens were bright with banners of laburnum. On the wide lawns between the houses, the twisted hawthorns leaned away from the wind of the estuary. When the air was still the scent of hawthorn was narcotic and persistent because of the high houses enclosing the squares. When Jocelyn and Clare met they spoke of many things but only rarely of what was most important. Without sentiment, without surmise, and with little discussion they knew they had met in another life. They never spoke of the when and where. At that time Clare herself had no pointer to another century. Jocelyn never said how much she remembered.

It was thunder and darkness out of a clear sky when Jocelyn went to hospital. She was so healthy and normal that no one could think of her as sick. Of course she was gravely ill. There was an indefinable radiance about her. Such people attract the shadows. If a light is sufficiently intense it draws the darkness towards it. She had an incurable cancer.

She was looked after in one of those nursing homes which make death respectable. In the first spring of the year it was beautiful to go along the mounting roads with the almonds illumining the long grey twilight. In the late spring there was always the plethoric overflow of lilac from the gardens and the flames of laburnums overhanging the pavements. Above the river and with the west wind blowing there was always the feeling of the sea.

It was along this road, with her heart heavy and with her feet dragging with misery, that Clare walked daily to the nursing home. The day came when what was left of Jocelyn looked at her intently from her excavated eyes. There is a kind of love which at certain moments is both selfless and self-disintegrating. Clare fled from herself and from the woman beside her. "I will see you again tomorrow," she said.

Jocelyn's hand closed on hers with the strength and desperation of farewell. "No, not tomorrow. I shall see you again but not as soon as that. It will be some time before I come back to you."

Clare went home through the dignified, unheeding streets. She believed in a life after death and that one day she would see Jocelyn. She told herself this many times going down the street. She persuaded herself that this thought was comforting. She believed also that we come back to this world and that in our next journey we meet those we have loved previously. These thoughts were so obviously consoling that she wondered why she felt so desperate. She went to the garden where she had talked so often with the laughing antecedent of the shadow at the clinic. The agony was the same.

She did not sleep that night. In the empty hours, when the sorrowing are afflicted not only with their own miseries but with the malice of ages, she schooled herself for another visit to Jocelyn. But when day came and she phoned the clinic it was no longer necessary.

In the first days after her death Jocelyn's words came back, "I will see you again but not as soon as that." With the passing of time the impact of her words faded. Clare could never forget Jocelyn. Sometimes when she thought of her the atmosphere seemed invaded for a moment by the echo of her contagious gaiety. She no longer thought of Jocelyn returning. There was another world and other lives in this world. One could not ask more than that.

Before she died Jocelyn had asked her to look after her daughter but Annette was happily married and living at a distance. There was really nothing she could do.

There was nothing she could do about Jocelyn or Annette but there was always something to get on with. She had two days' exhaustion which was all she allowed for a crisis. Even then there was little to show. Her complexion was as clear and her voice as resonant as ever. Only her eyes were different. They were no longer luminous and it was as though the light was turned inwards. She never flagged in her conscientious determination to give other people their money's worth. She had also her father to care for.

18

Mr. Mills was a retired businessman of over eighty. I found him charming. He emanated goodness and several of the people who come into this book were to speak of him later with adulation. When Jocelyn died he deteriorated rapidly. He was fond of Jocelyn and her daughter but no more than he was of Clare's other friends. It became evident to Clare and his doctor that he did not know what he was reading. Sometimes he was unaware of the date and the day of the week and confused the identity of visitors.

It was odd, but at that time not especially significant, that he had spent so much time at Bassenthwaite. He had no connections with Cumberland. He had travelled the world and lived for years in India. It was strange that Bassenthwaite should exert on him a powerful and constant compulsion. It was as though the place had some special message for him.

His mental confusion increased still more. In a man of his age and type this means often that a physical catastrophe is impending. He was stricken with pneumonia and his condition was soon critical. He failed to respond to antibiotics. It seemed preordained that his illness should run its course quickly. Near the end his mind clarified. This is not one of the mysteries but a plain fact and easily understandable. We see with our psyche and as our body dies our psyche sees more clearly. Nevertheless, in spite of his terminal clarity, his last words, clear, firm and confident, were hard to interpret. His last words were spoken to Clare. "Very soon you will be able to heal people."

She did not know what he meant. She knew that what he had said must have meaning because of the clear and undistorting nature of his love for her. She still did not see the significance of his last words when, a few weeks later, a stream of people came to her for help. Night after night she was besieged after her hours of work by people bereaved, agitated and sick. Sometimes she stretched her hands involuntarily towards them and touched their foreheads. A day came when they said that her hands were burning. Later still it was said that a great power seemed to emanate from her. She never connected what was happening with her father's last words.

One night her telephone never stopped ringing. When she took off the receiver there was no answer. When she replaced it the ringing continued. She sat beside it so that she could take off the receiver at the first ring. Nothing at all came through. She rang round her friends to see if they had phoned her. None had done so but when she put the receiver down the phone started ringing again. I had been out that evening and it was late when she rang me. She was strangely agitated and persisted that someone was trying to get in touch with her. I said this may well have been so and that the person involved had failed to do so. After she had spoken to me the phone stopped ringing. I stressed the remarkable idiosyncrasies of the local service.

Next morning she told me that the previous day was the anniversary of Jocelyn's death. She had been reminded of this because that morning she had received a letter from Annette. I was astonished when she said she believed her friend Jocelyn had been trying to communicate with her. I did not think it worth while to discuss the mechanical impossibility of such an explanation. She said also that she believed that I had stopped the phone ringing. I could not see how I could be a substitute for her deceased friend. I knew by this time that Clare had a foot out of this world. I felt that at the moment it was splayed out excessively.

I do not know how one explains the telephone ringing but after that day her life was changed. To outward appearance she remained the same. She was vigorous, vivacious and constantly available. At another level she was living, day and night, a life unknown to others. I have described in *We Are One Another* how she established contact with a discarnate called Braïda de Montserver, who was to become her mentor and guardian angel so that Clare was to say later that she did not know how she ever existed without her. What I did not see, when I wrote the latter book, was the relationship between Jocelyn's death, the importunate telephone and the later revelations.

I have written two books about previous lives. These were the end results of an epic of verification, of taking nothing on trust. I was, in fact, refuting materialism with its own weapons. Now I am writing at another level. I still check and verify but not to the same extent because I am as much concerned with the so-called dead as with the living. The former are lavish in the provision of evidence. I listen with care to those who have

20

stepped out of the envelope of flesh but have retained their individuality, their form and their capacity to communicate. This, in a way, is my Book of the Dead. Nevertheless, I am not concerned only with people alive or passed over. Places, as well as persons, have living qualities. The hill and the wood by Bassenthwaite Lake are as important in this story as any of the characters.

Chapter Three

There is an eternal and indissoluble bond between me and Betty, already introduced as my thirteenth-century sister Hélis de Mazerolles, in *We Are One Another*. We are now concerned with her further adventures. We are back on the road to Bassenthwaite.

Some months after Betty died of a subarachnoid haemorrhage I was fascinated to learn that she had returned from the dead to her mother, and more than astonished to hear that this had occurred at Bassenthwaite and above all on the three-hundred-yard stretch of road between the Pheasant and the landing stage where, the previous year, I had felt my father beside me. Was it just that Betty and her mother, my father and myself, an equal proportion of the dead and living, were congregating at a place we had known and loved? I learnt later that Betty in her twentieth-century existence had never been to Bassenthwaite. I did not know yet that the short stretch of road curving by the lake had its own spirit which drew us into its embrace and wakened our memories after centuries.

I had a phone call from Betty's mother, Jane Butler. "Why did it happen there?" she said.

"Perhaps the same kind of people go to the same kind of places."

I was happy for Jane because she had been to the Pheasant. I was sorry not to be in Bassenthwaite myself. Going down to the Pheasant from the landing stage you could look beyond the poplars in the marshy meadows to the curtain of trees on the fells behind. I visualised this as I spoke to Jane. I did not know that I was looking beyond my childhood to an earlier incarnation. I had no clue that Betty had returned not merely because her mother was at Bassenthwaite but because she herself was inexorably linked to it by the chains of far memory. I did not know that the place was as living as the people who visited it and that the psyches of the living and the dead spoke more clearly in certain places.

I have written elsewhere Jack's earlier history, of how his wife, Penelope, in dying of cancer, had remembered him by his thirteenth-century name of Brasillac, and how he, too, recalled his identity as another sergeant-at-arms who had died at the stake at Montségur. To complete his story we move from another age and another country, from the enigmatic beauty of Montségur to the lake at Bassenthwaite which seems to have no memory of persecution. A few weeks after his wife's death Jack was also discovered to have cancer. He rang Clare with whom he and Penelope had been very friendly when they lived in the same locality. He told her, precisely and dispassionately, that he was going into hospital. It was strange that he should so frankly seek her company after ten years' lack of contact. He apologised for bothering her but said that he simply had to get in touch with her. He was calm and undemanding but gave no reason for his action. It was astounding to Clare that he was so confiding.

The operation which followed relieved his immediate symptoms but he was discovered to be riddled with cancer. After his discharge from hospital he visited Clare. He brought with him some drawings of Cathar girdles of characteristic pattern, of a medallion worn by priestesses who specialised in healing and of a table prepared for the Cathar Consolamentum. It was more clear than ever that he and Penelope had shared a thirteenth-century incarnation. He asked Clare if there was anything else she wanted. She asked for the names of people he remembered from his previous life. It was clear that he was saying farewell.

I was swept off my feet by what Jack said when he next phoned her. He said he intended to visit the Lakes. He had never been there before. His reason for going was that his wife, Penelope, had always wished to go there. He said simply that it had come to him during the night that he should go to Bassenthwaite. He had never heard the name before. He did not know where the suggestion came from. He felt it must have come from Penelope but admitted that he was not aware of her as a presence. Clare asked if he had fixed up to stay anywhere. He said he had made no arrangements but he intended to stay at the Pheasant. He was sure it would be all right. He had not known of the hotel's existence. Like the word Bassenthwaite it had simply come to him in the night. It was interesting that the day before I had been working on a poem that fluttered backwards and forwards between Bassenthwaite and Florence. Clare never revealed to Jack that I had mentioned Bassenthwaite to her.

A few days later he called on Clare on his way to the north. He left with her more drawings and the list of names which Penelope and he remembered. The latter included the same men and the same place names as those recalled by Clare, Jane, Betty and others.

It was beyond any doubt that he had gone up to Bassenthwaite for a purpose. It was part of a design originating from beyond this life. He was following the road trodden by three other Cathars. Clare asked me if there was evidence of any Cathar colony near Bassenthwaite. This seemed to be wholly unreal. There is not a shred of evidence indicating that Catharism ever reached Cumberland. Besides it was not a question of these people being directed to Bassenthwaite and stimulated to remembering their meridional past. They knew themselves as Cathars before they went there.

I could not explain why Bassenthwaite should act as a magnet to reincarnated Cathars. Was there some other link binding Betty, Jack and me together? What was there in common between Jack and Betty? What was the connection between Jack and the child who came to Bassenthwaite from Wythop Fell on an October morning sixty years previously? It seemed to me more important to accept these mysterious connections than to explain them. Of one thing I was certain. At Bassenthwaite Jack would resume contact with Penelope. I also feared he was saying farewell.

Almost a week later Clare had a letter from him. It was as Clare and I had expected. Penelope had returned. He had not seen her but had felt her presence intensely. What was more important was the site of his experience. She had come to him between the inn and the landing stage. He was quite unaware of what others had felt along this stretch of road.

Jack rang Clare after his return from Cumberland. He confirmed what he had said in his letter and that when he was by

24

the lake Penelope was a living reality. He said that being at Bassenthwaite had been a magical experience. He felt Penelope so close that he awaited death without a particle of fear. He said that he did not positively ask for it but that it could "come when it liked". At the end of his life he felt an even deeper peace on the road by the lake than I had known in my own childhood.

He never expressed the slightest surprise that he should have been directed to Bassenthwaite.

Jack returned to his home in the south-west. A few days later he was admitted to hospital and died within twenty-four hours. His son rang Clare to tell her the news. Michael said that his father had died not only peacefully but with positive happiness. It had been as though he was not dying but moving deliberately to someone he loved. He said his father's death had been so happy that he felt no pity for him. He could only feel sorry for himself. In talking of his father's death the boy used the exact words his father had employed in speaking of his mother's passing.

I knew now what kind of people reacted to Bassenthwaite and how they were affected by it. I knew that along that road the dead returned to the living. But I still thought of these reactions as engendered by the people rather than the place. I was unsatisfied by all the explanations I thought of. I had to wait until Annette appeared before I knew the answers. It did not occur to me that the memory of another incarnation was waking.

Chapter Four

Annette came into the story when Jack was on his way out of it. It seems there is a kind of shuttle service between the living and those who have passed over. When Jack was near death Annette was emerging from the sleep of half memory. When Jane Butler died Raymond Agulher, the big Cathar she had called the rugger forward, moved off to console another.

Annette asked Clare's help on a greater issue than a fall from the swing in her mother's garden. She was now twenty-six and was married to a man five years older. They lived in a grimy city. They had no children but were very happy until the day they went to see the doctor. Her husband Guy was suffering from headaches. He was also off-balance and had fallen on several occasions. He was cheerful and uncomplaining and did not feel physically ill. The doctor took the matter more seriously than he did. He arranged a visit to a neurologist who diagnosed a brain tumour. Guy was sent to hospital where the diagnosis of cancer was confirmed by radiology and laboratory investigation. The growth was described as incurable. He was allowed to return home.

Annette wrote Clare to say that she had seen her mother who had told her to ask Clare's help. It seemed that Annette was frequently visited by her mother and accepted her presence as a matter of course. Nor was Clare herself especially surprised that Jocelyn, three years dead, had returned to her daughter. She was only concerned to help Annette who was crushed by the doctor's diagnosis. Clare was also anxious for herself. She wished to keep her experiences secret. She did not think her contacts with Braïda and the thirteenth century would marry well with her life in a provincial town. She was worried as to how she should reply to Annette's letter. It surprised me that she made a special journey to show me the reply she had written. She told Annette that her mother must be referring to the fact that "she did a bit of healing". (By this time she accepted that she was able to do what her father had foretold on his death-bed.) She assured Annette that she would do all she could and asked if Guy could come down to see her.

It was not an impressive letter, nevertheless it seemed that Annette was grateful for it. She rang next morning and said that the night previously she had again been visited by her mother. She could not understand why the latter was dressed in a dark-blue robe with a silver chain round her waist. The chain had a loop which dangled from her left hip. It was evident that her mother's attire was the same as Braïda's. What was more astonishing was that she was accompanied by Clare's father. Mr. Mills was clearly recognisable though his features were sharper than she had known them in life. His hair was black. As she had known him it had always been grey. He was the same height but thinner. He wore a dark-blue robe of the same colour and lines as her mother. Annette did not seem as astonished as she might have been at the appearance of these two visitors. Clare assumed that it was because Annette's feelings were spent in her concern for Guy. Clare and I were astounded that Jocelyn had appeared in a dark-blue Cathar robe. That Mr. Mills had been similarly attired was less surprising. We knew that in the thirteenth century he had been the Cathar bishop Bertrand Marty.

Braïda appeared that night to Clare. She told her that she should either visit Annette or invite her to her house. This was a new attitude on Braïda's part. She had always advised Clare to wait until other people made positive requests. It was odd, too, that she had spoken of Annette rather than of her husband. It was as if she considered there was more to be done for Annette than Guy. The latter's condition had deteriorated and he had been readmitted to hospital.

That day I had a visit from Clare. She was very entertaining and spoke with her usual whole-hearted vivacity. It is a marvel how such people can carry so many sorrows from two worlds. It is not a question of fortitude. What they have is the search-light's ability to sweep from one corner of the horizon to another. Where the beam is directed there is always light. The shadow is always near but when the beam swings towards us we live in its incandescence. Then a cloud crosses the frontier between this world and the next. You feel these people to be moving from you through the cosmic sorrow of the world's ghosts passing.

As she got up to leave the colour drained from her cheeks and I saw her shiver. Her face was contracted and pinched with cold. It was one of those breathless, mild days of August. The leaves were unmoving on the trees. There was no coldness in the air and no menace of autumn. I was surprised when she asked my wife to lend her a cardigan. I had seen her before in moments of depletion. I had never expected to hear her admit that she was denuded of vitality. It was not difficult to know that she was being shattered by the experience she was registering. When Jack's wife had died a hundred miles away I had seen the light extinguished in her eyes, suddenly, completely, as if by a switch.

When she called next morning she was as open and smiling as ever. She talked as factually as always about the things she had seen and the people she had met. It was only when she left the house that she said, "Annette's husband died last evening."

A few days later Annette visited Clare. She stayed the night and they talked for hours. She believed that she would see her husband again. She believed that they had been together before this life. She was certain that people reincarnated in groups. She did not indicate that this was for any special purpose. It was as though she believed simply that love was stronger than death. She believed also that even in this life we do not lose contact with those who have loved us and died.

Clare described her as speaking endlessly and eagerly but without pressure. Considering her recent loss she was astonishingly resilient. There were dark hollows under her eyes and she appeared exhausted. In spite of this she gave the impression of being physically strong. She was forthcoming and said the first thing which came to her mind. She was not only direct but almost precipitate. I assumed that she was pouring out her soul to relieve her sorrow. When I knew her better I realised that it was her nature to speak without premeditation. Clare said that in the depths of sorrow there was something ardent and frank about her. Something within her survived the sudden closing of the door on her husband for whom her devotion was eternal. She felt that he would return but accepted that for the present the silence of death was about him.

28

Before she left Clare told her that the dark-blue robe worn by her mother and Mr. Mills had been worn by the Cathars. She explained very briefly who they were. Annette had never heard the name. Clare told her they were heretics who lived in the Languedoc in the thirteenth century. She was not surprised but not especially interested. She believed in a cycle of lives but was not concerned with any particular incarnation.

Annette rang Clare in a few days' time. She had been asked to dinner by friends in the vicinity. One of the friends had spoken of Montségur and suggested that she read a book called The Cathars and Reincarnation. Annette had never met me or heard my name. She told Clare that she sat up reading the book until the small hours of the morning. She said that her mother had a passion for the name Roger. In turn all the dogs, cats and caged birds in the house had been called by that name. Roger was my name in my thirteenth-century incarnation. It is how I am described in that book.

Next day Annette rang me for the first time. With the first syllable she uttered I was weak-kneed with astonishment. Her voice was identical with Jane Butler's. They were unrelated and unknown to each other. It was also very similar to Kathleen's. The latter was fainter and less vibrating. It is difficult to describe a voice common to three people. It was a deep vibration which began in the throat and seemed lightened by its passage through mobile lips. Annette's voice was stronger than Jane Butler's but then there was a difference of fifty years between them. Annette was Jane on a spring morning three decades earlier and without her sardonic humour.

Annette rang to say how much she enjoyed my book and repeated what she had told Clare about the name Roger. She said that she was sure that her mother had recollections of another life but had never said anything to indicate that she had lived in the thirteenth century. Annette herself had no recollections of having lived before. We talked a great deal about Clare's dead father. She had seen Mr. Mills often in her childhood. "He was a wonderful man, yes, wonderful, and everybody loved him. I was like the rest." She was only repeating what Jane Butler and others had said about him. Annette's contact with him was different because she had lived near him and seen

29

him often. She had felt, at full strength, the emanation I had perceived less clearly in his final years.

Two or three days later Annette rang me again. "It is funny that mummy wears this dark-blue robe and this chain round the waist and the dingle-dangle."

"Where's the dingle-dangle?" I said.

"At the left hip. Why do you ask?"

"I've heard the same thing from other people."

"What interests me more is the medallion. It's hanging from the loop. I can't see the details."

"I've heard of the medallion before," I said. Before Braïda de Montserver had materialised to her, Clare had drawn on paper an inexplicable design of an equal-armed cross with three little T's at the end of each arm. Some months later, when Braïda appeared, she was wearing at her left hip a medallion decorated with the described design which indicated that she had been trained as a healer.

"Do you think mummy was a Cathar? She wears that blue robe."

"It's possible."

"Do you think she practised healing?"

"I wouldn't be surprised," I said. My thoughts switched to Jocelyn and Clare treating Annette in the garden the day she fell from the swing.

"Oh, well, some time I'll ring you again."

I had the impression that she was brooding about the question of healing.

Annette did not brood for long. She rang again in the evening. "I can't stop seeing the medallion. Do you really think mummy practised as a healer?"

"The medallion you describe is worn by another spirit called Braïda whom I know to be a healer. But you'd have to have more to go on."

"Whenever I hurt myself as a child she put her hand on the sore place and kept it still. Sometimes she put the other hand near the sore place. The funny thing was that she never moved her hands. She never rubbed or stroked the sore places like other mothers do."

I pricked up my ears when she spoke to me about her mother's hands. When Braïda taught Clare how to heal she insisted that the hands were kept still at certain fixed points. The latter were determined by the site of the wound or pain and also in relation to certain bony landmarks. I felt that Annette's mother could well be an addition to my growing collection of Cathars.

I was amazed when Annette told me that her mother had brought her up as a Dualist. I found it hard to credit that Jocelyn had given her positive instruction in any creed. I supposed this was because of my own inhibitions about proselytising. I can never missionise because I do not believe in belief. I think faith is a total reaction which occurs when the moment is ripe. We are at a given time open to certain ideas as a flower bud is open to the sun. I cannot believe that any system intellectually expressed can affect by one jot or tittle one's inward evolution. If we are converted by the words of others it is because we are already vibrating to them before they are uttered. Nevertheless it was beyond doubt that as a child of seven Annette had been taught about the Light and the Dark which were synonyms for good and evil. She had been told that the world had been created by the Devil and had taken it as natural. Her mother had used the same simple arguments as I have used so often in writing and in lectures. If the world is Hell it has its compensations. It is beautiful at times and we get through it somehow. If we regard this life as the worst we have to endure the outlook is on the whole favourable. It is clear that even as a child Annette saw it this way and was in no sense depressed by the instruction she received. Nevertheless I was still astonished that in the twentieth century a child could have been brought up as a Dualist. "Did your mother tell you that the good God made the good spirits and the Devil the world of forms?"

"Yes," she answered. "In exactly those words."

It seemed I had to accept that Annette's mother was a Cathar. "Did you ever feel isolated from other people because of these ideas?"

"No. I never discussed them with anyone but mummy until I met Guy."

"Didn't you feel it clashed with the religion you were taught at school?"

"I never thought that the prayers and hymns I heard clashed

31

with anything. Everything mummy told me was a help to me. I wouldn't have got through Guy's death like I did except for what she taught me."

Nevertheless it was strange to think of this child playing in the opulent and narcotic beauty of her garden in summer and carrying in her heart what had previously been taught in the bleached hills of the Corbières, scarred with dark fissures, and beyond the last brushwood at Montségur. I was certain that though Annette had received instruction from her mother she had not been in any sense indoctrinated. Her Dualism was natural and without tension. To her its truths were so inevitable that they did not merit discussion. It was interesting that her mother had never used the word Cathar. Annette had never heard the word Dualism till she met me. She did not know that Catharism was one of its medieval forms.

When Annette rang next she said that for years she had had recurrent dreams of being in an enclosed space battered continuously from without by enormous stones. Montségur was bombarded in this way by two engines of war known as the *trebuchet* and *mangoneau*. Annette did not know that Clare, Penelope and Kathleen had had similar recollections. The next statement pointed clearly to her pre-existence as a Cathar. "I'm a bit worried about something. A word keeps coming into my mind. Is there something called the Consolamentum? I see women led round a room by the elbow by men in dark-blue robes."

I was completely astounded. At that time I was receiving a great deal of evidence for group reincarnation but I was not yet so saturated with data that I could not be excited by this detailed recollection. Surely it was impossible that here was another looking back to the same crucial years, perhaps to the same day, as Clare, Penelope and Kathleen. These three had shared in the same celebration of the Consolamentum before going to the stake. The Consolamentum was the only sacrament recognised by the Cathars. Most people received it on their death-beds. After the ceremony the men were led round the room by the hand. The women were guided by the elbow.

Whether or no she herself had received the Consolamentum it seemed she remembered it being administered to another

32

woman. I wished to question her further but she swept on breathlessly and impetuously. "Is there a passage in the Consolamentum which says make me a good Christian?"

"That could be any kind of prayer," I said.

"It goes on 'and bring me'. My memory stops there."

"I can finish it for you. 'And bring me to a good end.'"

"Yes, that's it," she said.

"But it's not the Consolamentum. It's what a believer said when he met a Parfait. He also bowed three times."

I remembered how months before Clare had asked me the same question in the same way and how I had given her the wrong answer. I had thought the extract she quoted was part of the Consolamentum. Annette had tuned in to this simple ritual as well as to the sacrament. I knew now beyond doubt that we were dealing with another Cathar. I knew it in my bones and with the antennae of perception. The other side of my head required further evidence. "Anything else you remember?" I said.

"I am always seeing meetings in woods."

"You mean in your dreams?"

"Yes, and by day as well. It just comes to me. The people all wear dark blue." She did not know that months previously Clare had seen constantly men and women in blue robes at their meetings in forests.

Annette zigzagged from one topic to another. She asked if salt had any medical importance in the thirteenth century. She said that her mother had always used salt solutions for medical purposes. I told her that salt was rare and important in the Middle Ages. Before the capitulation at Montségur the Parfaits had given salt, with other condiments, as presents to the soldiers who had defended them. Salt, wax and pepper were included in the written messages dictated to Clare by Braïda de Montserver.

"Mummy was a great one for salt. One day when I sprained my ankle she dressed it with a mixture of salt and something else. I can't remember the other thing's name."

"Witch-hazel," I said. A year previously Braïda had prescribed this mixture to Clare who was suffering from fluid in one of the tendons of the right foot.

"Yes, that's the thing. Is salt and witch-hazel a doctor's mixture?"

33

"It was seven centuries ago."

From that moment on I felt at one with Annette. I knew we had re-established contact. It was not merely a matter of being on the same wavelength. We were both vibrating to the same music the chords of which had been struck seven centuries previously. Certainly something was suddenly loosened in the coils of her unconscious. Her recollections of childhood in this life were quickening her recall of another existence. "Yes, I remember that time I sprained my ankle. After mummy had put on the dressing she put one hand on my ankle and the other on my knee. She kept both hands still. Oh, yes, and then I fell off the swing. She and Clare both treated me. Clare put her hands on my neck and forehead. Mummy did my back and somewhere on my tummy." She repeated the story of medieval therapy I had heard already from Clare.

Annette hesitated a little before she continued. "I feel I can talk to you about anything. I suppose it's because you are a doctor. You know Guy and I were blissfully happy. I cannot put it in other words. It was just out of this world. And do you know there were no physical relations between us? I wonder sometimes if this was fair to Guy. One thing I'm certain of and that is it made no difference to our happiness. It's just since he died that I feel at times that I failed him." She paused for a moment and added softly, "Has this anything to do with my being a Cathar?"

There was nothing guilt-induced or self-justifying in her conversation. She was in no sense compensating for past failures. She spoke so gently and simply about her love for her husband that I did not know that we were approaching one of the central points of the story. "Guy and I were so happy that at times it was as if the world was lost to us. Once something happened which I can't describe. We went right out of ourselves and time. You could only call it bliss. What was odd was that we both did it at the same time."

"When was that?"

"It was on our honeymoon."

I could not help reflecting that some quite mundane people feel bliss on their honeymoon. At this stage I was not especially attentive. I felt the conversation to be drifting. I said, "Where did you go?"

34

"To a place in the Lakes."

"What was it called?" I knew what was coming.

"Bassenthwaite."

"And where did you stay?" I did not need to ask.

"At a place called the Pheasant."

"I know it well." I did not think it necessary to ask more questions. "And you had this timeless, being away feeling on the road between the landing stage and the Pheasant."

"But how did you know?" Her voice was youthful and excited. She had not lived so many synchronisations as Clare and myself.

"I have known one or two people who've had similar experiences at the same place."

"There is something magical about that stretch of road."

"What made you go to Bassenthwaite? Did you know the Lakes well?"

"I didn't know them at all. We went there because Clare's father said we would love it. He often went there himself."

I cannot describe my feelings when she spoke of her Bassenthwaite experience. I felt a kind of awe. For me Bassenthwaite had become one of the nodes of intersection of human destiny. But it had been all about me in my childhood, the lake, the jetty, the road past the inn, the waiting on the station on summer evenings, the last view of the mountains as we went back home. Had I lived an amendment of Wordsworth's experience and in the same country? Heaven had been about me in my childhood but I had not known it. Annette was the fourth to have freed her pysche on the road from the Pheasant. And Mr. Mills, who had haunted the place, who had insisted on her going there for her honeymoon and whom everybody reverenced, was different from the common run of men. What was his connection with the road by the lake? I knew he had been a Cathar. After his death he had appeared in the dark-blue robe with his bishop's belt and buckle. I could not accept that Catharism was connected with Bassenthwaite.

The whole thing was too mysterious. I rejected the idea that there had been in the neighbourhood some weird and forgotten form of Dualism. Then an odd thought came into my head. I had heard it surmised that Bassenthwaite was the lake from

35

which Arthur drew the sword Excalibur. I knew that to some, and especially to German romanticists, Catharism is inexplicably connected with the Grail legend and that there is also some shadowy evidence, refined almost to dust by the erosion of time, which described Arthur as a heretic. But I am not a German romantic nor am I competent to say how far theory and legend is an expression of Dualism. I could not persuade myself that to look for Catharism in Bassenthwaite was a profitable occupation. Also by this time I was less intent in searching for written evidence. When I was writing *Cathars and Reincarnation* and *We Are One Another* I dipped eagerly into the necessary sources. It had now become harder for me to practise the refinements of scholarship. In the last two years my course through the libraries has been darting and snipe-like. I follow an irregular trajectory and pick unpredictably for nourishment. This is not from lack of interest. I know that if I wait others will supply the evidence.

I felt that what happened on this road was at least related to the fact that I had lived before and that I loved Bassenthwaite. But I could not attribute other people's experiences spread over years to my own reactions and to the solitary illumination of my love for the place. I was becoming more than ever convinced that these phenomena were attributable as much to the place as the people.

I longed to see Annette. I regretted bitterly that I had never seen Betty. At this time my longing intensified to a gnawing anguish. It resembled the dejection and the cramps of hunger. I was yearning not only consciously but with my viscera for what I had known before. It seemed that, for the moment, I had to be satisfied with hearing her voice. Dualism minimised the importance of the world of form. Perhaps, in the course of life, I had paid too much attention to what can be seen.

Chapter Five

By this time I had an idea that Annette's mother was Braïda. The connecting link was the matter of healing. Clare had recently received intensive instruction in this subject from Braïda. Years before she had practised the same art in Jocelyn's garden. On the day when she had placed her hands on Annette's head she had no idea where the impulse came from. Why had she and Jocelyn, without a word to each other, employed an ancient ritual on an afternoon in summer twenty years before?

The next time Annette rang I asked her if her mother's features were in any way altered since death. She said that she was exactly as she had known her in life. It appeared reasonable to me that discarnate entities should appear to people under the guise in which they were best known. If Clare had known Braïda in any incarnation other than the thirteenth century it was obvious that their ties had been closer in the latter. She and Braïda had studied together the making of medicines and the laying on of hands.* Two years later I learnt directly from the revenants that we see those who return to us in the form in which we have known them best. If they appear at times as in other incarnations it is always for a special purpose.

Annette was depressed because her employer, a disinterested and kindly person who had helped her arrange her modest affairs after Guy's death, had died in a coronary attack. Her mother had visited Annette and told her to ring me. "After all," she had said, "I knew him well." Annette's voice went up an octave as she gave this message. "What did she mean?" she said.

"I assure you that in this life I never met your mother. She must have known me a long time back."

Surely, I thought, this must be Braïda. This was certainly the nearest I had achieved to direct contact with her. She had played

* See We Are One Another (Neville Spearman, London).

an inaudible rôle in moving Kathleen and others towards me. She had never before specifically directed any living person other than Clare to make contact with me. I realised that when people consult mediums they receive messages and specific directions but our rapport with Braïda was not of this type. Clare and I had never tried to contact Braïda or any of her confrères. It was always Braïda who had sought us out. Braïda differed from the spirit guides of many mediums in that she rarely answered any direct questions posed to her by Clare. Knowledge was disseminated tangentially in the course of conversation. It often foretold what would happen in the future but rarely in response to direct requests.

Annette came to see me without telephoning beforehand. On that day I was due to visit my daughter in Dorset. I was feeling unwell that day. I was feverish and tired and my throat was painful. I felt I was unfit to travel but I was seduced by the prospect of the day in the country. Nevertheless as we drove down the hill I felt an almost irresistible impulse to return. My wife stopped the car. "Don't go," she said. "You'll be better at home."

Of course she was right but I did not listen. As Braïda said, I had not yet learnt to follow my hunches.

We drove on to my daughter's. That was how I missed Annette. She called at my house that afternoon, so I felt deeply depressed at having missed her. I did not know that she would leave the country without seeing me.

When Annette rang next she told me that in the last two weeks she had found messages scrawled in her own writing on a writing pad on her bedside table. She had no recollection whatever of having written them. I was amazed that a girl of twenty-six should accept this almost without comment. It was fascinating that she was undergoing the same experience as Clare. There was also my friend at Montségur who had had a similar experience ten years previously. Like her two predecessors Annette had written down the same scriptural references, chiefly to the *Epistles of St. Paul* and more especially to *First Corinthians*. This is understandable because Paul is the interpreter of Christianity in its spiritist aspect. He is more precise than the other Apostles in speaking of bodies corruptible and incorruptible.

38

In her written references Annette went outside the Scriptures. She recorded such names as Plotinus and Porphyry. In this also she repeated the previous experiences of Clare without the slightest knowledge of what the latter had written. Annette threw off these names casually and it was obvious that they meant nothing to her. I think she had become so habituated to her mother's visits that dictated messages from the other world were to her of secondary importance.

The next written item was amazingly specific. She found the number 609 written on her own scribbling block. I have explained elsewhere how the repetition of 609 was a major clue in enabling me to identify Braïda de Montserver.* Now this number came out of a clear sky and without accompanying evidence to this uncomplicated and candid girl in her small house on the edge of an insalubrious city. 609 is the number of the file in the archives of the library at Toulouse which contains most of the references to the Montserver family. Annette had never heard this name before. Why had this girl, uninstructed in the history of Catharism, received this particular message? Was it so that she should contact me and that I could explain to her how it had helped me to identify Braïda? I had the odd idea that we were dealing with an entirely different problem.

Braïda's next visit to Clare was an important milestone. She said that someone younger than us all was making her appearance. I was getting on in years and the others in the group were well in their forties. We were to be strongly reinforced by someone younger and more vigorous. It was amusing that Braïda, from the next world, should be so involved in the practical necessities of this life. The new recruit was quite obviously Annette.

I weighed again the possibility that Braïda had been Jocelyn in the twentieth century. The picture was so different since Annette appeared. It is odd to say so but it seemed more human. For example, it seemed that every night Jocelyn kissed her daughter as she had done when she was living. These homely details are intensely important. Jocelyn, with her blue robe and silver chain, was certainly a Cathar. For centuries Catharism has

* See *We Are One Another*.

been regarded by its enemies and some of its misguided sympathisers as a dour and repressive creed. Some of those most sympathetic to it have painted it as impossibly austere and with a mutilated nobility amounting almost to a perversion. Those who have come back to us, Braïda herself, the chubby-faced Guilhabert and Jane Butler's Raymond, were all in their different ways still deeply involved in the mutations of mood and the changing cloudscape of human sorrow. Even after death they were in touch. We read of emancipated souls returning to earth because of their infinite compassion. The language in which this phenomenon is described is often so lyrical that the experience seems to lose validity. None of these dead Cathars who visited the living were detached from them or struck uplifting ethical attitudes. They were intensely practical and expressed themselves in everyday language. Though described as despisers of the flesh they showed an intense interest in physical illness. Even as discarnate entities they were homely and good-natured.

After death Jocelyn was as motherly to Annette as she had been in life. Was it possible that they exemplified something deeper and more protracted than an ordinary mother-and-daughter relationship?

What I told her about the archives at Toulouse certainly stimulated Annette's interest. She wondered who she had been in the thirteenth century. I said also that I did not think she would obtain any information by direct questioning of her mother. I quoted Clare's experience with Braïda. I said that in their many conversations it had been established beyond doubt that Clare had been Esclarmonde de Perella and myself Roger-Isarn de Grisolles.* But never at any time had Braïda answered point-blank questions as to the former identity of living persons.

In a way I was right though I had not allowed for the ingenuity of the discarnates. Annette rang again the same evening. Her mother had just appeared to her. As I had foretold, Jocelyn had not answered any direct questions as to her daughter's identity. She had circumvented the problem by addressing

* In The Cathars and Reincarnation I describe myself chiefly as Roger de Grisolles. This title, and Roger de Fanjeaux, are interchangeable.

Annette by another name. By now the latter was really excited. "What did she mean by calling me Cecilia?"

"Because that was your name, Cecilia de Montserver." It is recorded that Braïda had a daughter called Cecilia and a son Isarn.

"And mummy?"

"Well, surely she was Braïda de Montserver."

I cannot analyse my feelings at that moment. I do not think any emotion in particular was predominant. I had a sense of inevitability. of being close to reality, of perhaps being closer than ever before. There was plenty to be excited about but the plain fact of the matter was that I was not excited. The girl was Cecilia de Montserver. Her mother *was* Braïda. The latter had appeared to Annette as her mother and to Clare as Braïda. Braïda and Cecilia had been mother and daughter in the thirteenth century and had been reborn with the same affinity in the twentieth. This was my first experience of such a phenomenon. For me at any rate it was something to write about. All I felt was that I was nearer than ever before to the thirteenth century. I cannot explain it. I can only record it. Perhaps such convictions are a substitute for emotion.

I felt closer than ever to Annette and her mother because when Braïda was ill in 1235 she was nursed in the house of my brother, Isarn de Fanjeaux, at Limoux. I knew and loved Limoux. In this life I have been many times down the long road that twists across the river at Alet. The sun beats down between the high, bleached plane trees. I have been on that road in early November with the vineyards afire with the vine leaves turning. This is an old road and in the thirteenth century there was a busy and continuous traffic along it. The road went from the lost culture and the unexpounded secret of Toulouse through Carcassonne and beyond it to Limoux. When she was well Braïda left my brother's house and went along the road to Fanjeaux. Was I with my brother when she lay beneath his roof? Was it because of this that she sent her daughter to me?

Annette made another of her sudden, impulsive visits to Somerset to see Clare. She had hoped to see me but I was out on one of my infrequent evening engagements. I went to a sophisticated party among people who were convinced of their own usefulness. I let myself float on the tide of conversation. I kept drifting back to the sense of deprivation which seemed to erode my breastbone.

Annette rang me early next morning before she set off for home. She was anxious to see me but said it was impossible. She felt obliged to comfort the relatives of her deceased employer. Those I have known who have been in regular contact with the next world have been highly conscientious in this. I am speaking of those in regular contact. I have known a number of those who have made impressive grabs at eternity and who have had no time for anything else. I felt depressed and bitter that once again she had left the neighbourhood without our meeting. Perhaps I expected her to share my sense of deprivation. She never knew how much it hurt me not to see her.

Her next visit was equally disastrous. Once again she came down for the night and once again I could not see her. We had friends whom we had not seen for a long time and who were only staying a single night. I was heartsick that once more by the malice of circumstance I should be prevented from seeing her. I pulled myself together because I believe that, whatever the plane on which we function, will and organisation are asked of us in this world. I arranged that I would await Annette's arrival at Clare's house. This would mean my appearing late for my guests but I thought the situation justified it. I waited alone in the palpitating silence, for what I thought was perhaps the most intimate messenger of destiny. Annette did not appear. She had had trouble with the condenser of her car. She arrived just after I had left.

Yet had I seen her I might have missed the experience which followed after. Perhaps we do not know how much we miss by clinging to the world of form and substance.

Later that evening I had a phone call from Annette. She was staying with Clare who had found her exhausted and depressed. She gave her supper and put her to bed. She repeated the treatment she had given years ago when Annette fell from the swing. Clare had then gone out on a previously arranged appointment.

Annette told me that when she had her treatment she had no sense of being touched. She could not have said where Clare's

42

fingers touched her or even if they touched at all. She was experiencing the complete self-abandonment which can occur between psychic people with the slightest physical contact. I had been prepared for this by a Tibetan lama several summers past on a bleak Scotch upland. I had experienced it myself, a floating above the body sensation, when my knee had been massaged by a woman who had an immense capacity to heal. After her treatment Annette fell asleep. When she awoke she found a chubby-faced man beside her bed. "He was wearing a dark-blue robe and the belt and buckle of a Cathar bishop." From past experience I recognised him as Guilhabert de Castres.

"What did he say?" I said.

"He said I should not hang so tightly to life and that I should let myself be pulled along by it. What does that mean? I just can't understand it." She sounded anxious. It was obvious that his words disturbed her more than his presence.

"I would say he meant that it's no good trying to dominate circumstances. We should let things take their course." It was not impressive but it is difficult at a moment's notice to express metaphysics in words of one syllable. Fortunately in her next question she strayed to more concrete matters.

"What does this word mean? It came through while I was talking to him." She spelled out Mioret. "At least that's what it sounded like. It has something to do with a battle."

"That's easy," I said. "It's the battle of Muret."

"What happened?"

"The combined forces of the Languedoc and the king of Aragon were defeated by De Montfort and his Crusaders. Muret was the real graveyard of the hopes of the Languedoc from the military and political point of view."

I was more interested than she was by this reference to Muret. She rang me late on September 11th. The battle was fought on the 12th in 1213. Annette was less accurate than the others in tuning in to anniversaries but certainly she showed promise. One of the characteristics of our group was the accuracy with which its members reacted by depression, tension, or physical symptoms to tragedies occurring in previous incarnations. Then Annette said something which reverberated more deeply than anything she had said previously. "I've a feeling I've done all this before."

"All what?"

"This talking with the bishop, all this muddled-up stuff about life and time. I have the feeling that once I was trained for something. I don't know if I qualified."

I told her that it was possible that she had received the instruction for intending Parfaites. I said it was customary among the heretical nobility to train one at least of their daughters for the faith. It seemed that she had fallen by the wayside because after all she had married Arnaud-Roger de Mirepoix. As Cecilia de Montserver, she is recorded as one of the women who took part in the defence of Montségur. She is not in the list of those who perished at the stake. This in itself is not conclusive because we have no evidence that the names which have come down to us include all the victims. After I had spoken to her I was certain that Annette had received instruction and been rejected as unsuitable material. More than a year later I heard directly from Braïda and others that Annette had never qualified as a Parfaite, had not been burnt as a heretic and had lived to a ripe old age, dying in the neighbourhood of the Château d'Usson.

My conversation with Annette lasted about forty minutes. While I was talking to her I lost all sense of time. I realised how long I had spoken when I went downstairs and looked at the clock. We had a detailed and factual conversation, we were both registering at full capacity and attentive to environmental details. I had asked her if she was comfortable and warm and if she was still in bed. She had said that she was sitting on the edge of the bed in her dressing-gown.

Annette rang me next morning before she returned to the Midlands. "I'm sorry," she said. "I'm terribly sorry."

"What about?"

"About phoning last night. Was I talking rubbish?"

"Do you really think that what you said was rubbish?"

"That's just the trouble," she said. "I just can't say. I can't remember what I said."

"You're not serious?"

"Yes. A few vague scraps but most of it's forgotten."

My first reaction was clinical. I wished to reassure her. "Look, everything you said was stone-cold rational. It doesn't matter whether you remember or not. What you said was sense."

"It's pretty odd, isn't it?"

"No. Things aren't odd just because you can't explain them. What time do you set off?"

"I must go now."

"Come up before you go."

"I can't," she said, "but I do so want to meet you."

Even with her going that morning I was less heartsick than the previous evening. Last night's conversation had been a substitute for seeing her in the flesh. I could see also the shadow of purpose behind our not meeting. Perhaps it is better that the deeper truths are conveyed to us as impersonally as possible.

When Clare rang later I said, "Do you realise that this girl has forgotten what she said to me last night?"

"She said the same herself. When I got back last night I had to stop her from phoning you again. She knew she had to but she couldn't be certain that she hadn't done it already."

After my conversation with Annette I understood things better. When she had talked to me the previous evening she had been absolutely clear-headed and perfectly orientated in time and place. Yet in spite of all this she was unaware within an hour of speaking to me as to whether she had already done so. There is no question here of mental confusion. This is not a psychiatric problem but a matter of levels of consciousness. These certainly exist and we can pass daily from one to another. In its most undramatic form this phenomenon is a daily experience.

This shift of levels was more pronounced when, during a grave illness, I had a long and rational conversation with a woman I had known for years and whom I did not recognise. This experience was not strictly analogous to Annette's but leans in the same direction. The morning after her encounter with Guilhabert de Castres I regarded it as to some degree similar to what had happened to Clare when she had taken down the written messages. I was to learn later, when Annette repeated the same performance in remembering another incarnation, that we were dealing with a different psychic mechanism.

Chapter Six

It was a blow when Annette told me she was going to Canada. She was due to leave in three months' time. The idea was that a new country would distract her from her sorrow. I longed all the more to see her. It was a further blow when she rang to say she was going to Scotland for a fortnight. I ought to have been happy that, after all her troubles, she was having a holiday. I felt hollow and dejected. The rationalists and Freudians can, if they wish, visualise me as a thwarted sentimentalist weaving senile fantasies round an unseen face. Certainly I was less passive with her than I was with others because I was convinced that she had some special message for me. I did not know what influence was keeping us apart but I resented bitterly my separation from her. I did not know that I would receive immediate and mysterious comfort.

She said that the night before Clare had materialised in a dark-blue robe similar to that worn by her mother, that is to say Braïda, and others I have mentioned. In some ways she was changed. She was short and light and her features were sharper. "But," Annette continued, "she had the same extraordinary eyes, you know what I mean, pale blue and glowing."

Clare had with her a man in his fifties. He, too, wore a dark-blue robe and the belt and buckle of the senior members of the Cathar hierarchy. He was thin in face and body. He was taller than the chubby-faced man but not tall by modern standards. He had Roman features and a prominent nose. His hair was still dark and came down to his shoulders. This man came towards Annette and touched her forehead. She was quite sure that this was not the usual curative ritual. He had not touched the pre-scribed places on the forehead and neck. "He seemed very happy that he had touched me."

"*He* seemed happy?" I said.

"Oh, yes." She spoke in level tones and indeed had no need to do otherwise. She did not know I was depressed about her going to Scotland. "Of course I was glad he touched me but *he* was especially happy."

The description of me as I was in the thirteenth century coincided exactly with that given by Clare and Kathleen who had seen me in dreams and visions. In my first Cathar encounter Mrs. Smith told me that I had changed little in appearance since the thirteenth century. "That was me," I said.

It was astonishing how my heart lightened at what she told me. Last night, while I was sleeping, I had made some shadowy contact with her. It seemed it was enough to make me happy.

She said that on her visit to Scotland she was going to Iona. I told her I had been there, that it was very beautiful but that it had made no great impression on me. I said that possibly it did nothing for me because I was expecting something from it. Montségur was the only place which gave me the atmosphere I had desired and which continued to exercise its influence. I told her that of all other places Rievaulx, which I had visited in 1964, was outstanding and vibrated with indefinable memories.

A week later Annette rang again to describe her visit to Iona. She is a simple, direct person who communicates by emanation. When she is speaking of her own sensations and feelings she restricts herself to a limited vocabulary. When she is describing events she expresses herself precisely and with competence.

In the old part of the church at Iona she had heard chanting and seen a monk with long hair down to his shoulders in something like the modern style. She was very emphatic that he was not tonsured. His robes were darker than those worn by her mother.

After she had visited the Cathedral she sat on a seat by St. Martin's Cross. Here she was visited by her mother. The latter was dressed in her dark-blue robe. It seemed she had adopted this attire permanently. She told Annette that Guy had been a member of the Celtic Christian Church. Annette recalled how, when he was alive, Guy had often spoken of the Celtic Church and said that the priests were allowed to marry. He had never shown the slightest interest in any contemporary religious observance.

Stendhal said, in his *Life of Henri Brulard*, that it was impossible to describe the great moments of life, as when he crossed the

Alps while serving with L'Armée d'Italie. It was clearly impossible for Annette to amplify in words the joy she had received from this reference to Guy. She merely kept repeating "It was wonderful."

After Annette's experience at Iona I wondered if there was any tie between Catharism and the early Celtic Church. No direct link seemed possible. Was there any evidence that the Celtic Church had Dualist tendencies? I knew that Pelagius had, like the Cathars, rejected the sacrament of baptism. I knew that marriage was permitted in the early Celtic Church. This was to some extent a link because, while the Cathars have still an unmerited reputation for frenetic austerity, they recruited their priesthood to a considerable degree from those who had previously been married or who had lived with members of the other sex. I knew also that a belief in the immortality of the soul and reincarnation was widespread among the Celts in pre-Christian times and were basic features of Druidism. Did the Celtic Church reflect these old beliefs?

Annette supplied more information the next time she spoke. Her mother had told her to ask me if I understood "the crosses and the intertwinings". Because her mother addressed questions to me through Annette I regarded the latter as in some way closer to me than others in the group. Preoccupied with this personal reaction I failed to see that the question of crosses and intertwinings was a crucial point in the story and indeed in my life.

The question of crosses was not too difficult. Both the Cathar and the Celtic crosses have equal arms. Typically the Celtic design is an equal-armed cross enclosed in a circle. This is exactly what I saw on a wall by a church at Vals. This is near Fanjeaux, a region saturated with Catharism and the centre of so much activity on the part of Braïda, Clare and myself in the thirteenth century. Many of the crosses described as Cathar in the Languedoc would be regarded by us as Celtic.

The year previously Clare had recalled how she had completed a mandala under the direction of Guilhabert de Castres. She had drawn an intertwined cable pattern resembling that seen on so many Celtic crosses. The effect conveyed by the intertwining is that it is without beginning or end. It symbolises immor-
48

tality. A similar pattern was drawn out by Penelope, Jack's wife, in the last few months of her life. She was sketching one kind of girdle worn by Cathar priests.

On her return to the south of Scotland Annette was feeling happy. She had been transformed by Iona. She thought it would not be long before Guy returned from the dead. In a moment of exaltation she was half-walking, half-tripping along the pavement. Suddenly she slipped. Her ankle was acutely painful. At the local hospital they thought she had broken a bone but it turned out later she had ruptured a ligament. The area was immobilised in plaster but even then the foot was very painful. She was forbidden to put any weight on it. The doctors also supplied her with a pair of crutches.

She had arranged that when she returned from her holiday she would come to Bath to see me. She could not do so because of her foot. At this time she was depressed. I could tell it from her voice. It had lost its ringing tone which gave it a curiously stimulating quality. Vitality had been drained from her because of the unreasoning antipathy of a workmate. Like other contemporary Dualists I have known she was extremely vulnerable to bad atmospheres. She was also suffering from the earnest good intentions of a young man who had always loved her and wished to marry her. This was impossible because she was still in love with Guy who was still living for her. She was not cherishing an illusion but living a reality. She knew that it was unrealistic to think she could be loved again by someone who would make no physical demands on her.

She felt the need to escape from these problems. She was also anxious to see me. She fixed a date to come down to Bath. Still needing crutches, she could not drive a car and travelling on a train would be difficult for her. She was nevertheless so eager to come that on two successive days before she was due she rang to tell us how much she longed to see us.

I have totally failed if I paint this girl as clinging or suggestible. She was not constructing a future but recalling the past. If she felt as I did she would be wondering whether the past was coming nearer. In these matters I had always believed that the more you seek the less you find. Because of this I had had no patience with people who searched for the touchstone of a face to recall another life. But now I was doing this myself. The past was eroding the barrier of consciousness in a peculiarly personal way. I wondered if she felt the same.

When the great day came for Annette's visit to us she went down with gastric flu. I knew by now we would not meet before she went to Canada. It was useless Clare fobbing me off with comforting ideas that it was a full two months to Christmas. I could not accept with my heart and soul that the time was not right for our meeting. I wondered if some maleficent force was working against us. It was beyond reason to believe that the Cathars had prevented Annette seeing me by a painful accident and a sharp virus infection. Kathleen and Marion, the latter an important character who intervenes later, were also to be prevented from seeing me by acute illnesses. Even if the Cathars had wished to interpose themselves between us I knew they were incapable of inflicting pain on anybody. In addition they were constantly urging Annette to make contact with me. I knew well enough by this time that the force of evil can precipitate accidents and is especially efficacious in inducing what we call virus infection. I had dealt with these subjects previously in books and articles. I knew what my old friend, a brilliantly perceptive hospital matron, would have said about it. She had no doubt that evil was a major factor in the causation of disease and particularly of accidents.

But perhaps there was also a wise intention behind my separation from Annette. At least it taught me the unimportance of form. For a long time I had believed that the function of beauty is to lift ourselves to the contemplation of a principle beyond form and substance, to an ultimate harmony transcending the categories of good and evil. I have always sympathised ardently with the Sufi poet who said that the contemplation of human beauty was necessary to us to facilitate our contemplation of the divine. This attitude has always seemed warm and comforting and more adapted to my frailties than the thin air of more impersonal forms of aspiration. The Hindu implication that the world and the people in it are an intricate web of illusion is too arid and demanding for me. Perhaps the hour had come when I was asked to live with my whole being what I had contemplated when I thought of an abstract principle of beauty. I had gone even further in saying that the greatest loves of our lives are either those long dead or those we have never met. Nevertheless it was painful not to see Annette even once.

My wife with her habitual unpretentious wisdom said that, though it may be ordained that I should not see her, or that the Devil himself was contriving to part us, I should resist the malice of circumstance and do what she considered obvious. This was simply to drive to the city in which Annette lived. She said that however much we believe in the fates it was up to us to defy them sometimes. With this tonic and cheery prescription we made up our minds to go the following week. I could not help feeling that if we did so the car would break down or that we would be involved in an accident. In a few days it was clear that our projected journey was unnecessary.

Braïda appeared one night to Clare and told her that the early Celtic Church had existed other than in Ireland, Scotland, Northumbria, Wales, Cornwall and Brittany. She said it was wrong to think of it as more or less exclusively concentrated in the north-west of Europe. There were also pockets in Belgium, the west of Germany, southern France and Italy. This may be no news to the scholars but it was to me. Now these areas are precisely those where Catharism was strong in the Middle Ages. (Cathars were recognised, and treated with relative moderation, in the neighbourhood of Liège in the twelfth century. There was also a strong colony at Cologne. The heresy was as strong in northern Italy as in the Midi. In the latter region it was predominant in the Languedoc and Provence.) Braïda was drawing attention to the geographical distribution of Catharism and its tendency to erupt in Celtic areas. It is well known that its strength was chiefly in the Pyrenees, their foothills and the adjoining plains. This area was strongly infiltrated by Celtic influence and the regions adjacent have always resisted Roman orthodoxy.

Braïda spoke also of the Druids. She said they were referred to by Plato. I knew this well enough but not that the Druids were also referred to in Sanskrit. Braïda said also that the Atlantean civilisation spoken of by Plato was of Celtic origin. She told Clare that it was important to read a book or article written by someone whose name Clare could not spell exactly but which

51

sounded to me like de Nelli. I was quite unaware at this time of Donnelly's book on Atlantis. Certainly it is well known to students of Atlantis. What is important is that Braïda thought fit to remedy my ignorance.

At this time the earlier Celtic theme was predominant. It seemed that Annette was acting as an accessory messenger. She rang to say that she had seen Mr. Mills in the blue robe of his thirteenth-century precursor Bertrand Marty. He had with him a monk dressed in the much darker robe and with the same long hair as she had seen at Iona. The latter gave her a message, "Read about the Isle of Man."

But the next day the Isle of Man and the Celtic Church were banished brusquely from my mind. Annette told me with a schooled absence of emotion that she was leaving tomorrow for Canada. The date of her departure had been advanced abruptly. She had known this for days. She had made a last, short visit to Clare while I was away giving a lecture at Brighton. I was too stunned to be infuriated. She seemed unable to understand how eagerly I would have abbreviated my visit in order to see her. She believed she had behaved with consideration.

Whatever resentment I felt died completely when I heard her weeping. "I don't want to go. Please, please forgive me for behaving like this. I just don't want to go."

It was heart-rending to listen to this solitary and bereft girl weeping her heart out to someone she had never seen. Though she attracted a great deal of affection, except for Clare she had few close friends. She and Guy had lived a wide life within a narrow compass. They meant so much to each other that they had no need of the company of others. She wept to me because in some way we were close to each other.

"Why go if you don't want to?" I said.

"I can't let my friends down. They've found me a job."

"I think if you don't go you will feel worse than ever. Give it a few weeks' trial. If you can't stand it, put your pride and your conscience in your pocket and come back home."

"I feel I have to go."

It was hard enough for this girl bereaved in her twenties to face alone a new life in another continent. I did not know then that it would be harder still and that her life in the New World

52

would be a positive Gethsemane. All I knew was that I was given over entirely to the pity I felt for her. We said goodbye. I went for a walk on the road outside. It was mild October weather. The sun was veiled but the sky was light and the valley was warm with the beech leaves turning. Nevertheless the roadway, the hedges and the fields between them were part of a lifeless and unbreathing pattern. The common features of the landscape were stony and indifferent.

Next morning she rang me from the airport. It was like a voice from the dead and for me there was nothing but joy in its accent. I almost forgot I was losing her for years. She said she was sorry about yesterday and that this morning she felt better. She spoke with determination. It was obvious that her morale was higher but she still longed to stay.

She had been visited the night previously by Braïda and Mr. Mills. They were wearing their dark-blue robes. From now on they were never dressed otherwise. Mr. Mills had a message he wished given to me. "Be careful to note Paulinus and James the Deacon."

It was odd to think of this girl leading me back to the Dark Ages from the brassy modernity and heartless sophistication of London Airport. Before she said goodbye she was silent a little. I felt there was something imploring in her silence. When she spoke again her voice was quieter than usual and she seemed younger and no more than a schoolgirl. "Do you think I will see mummy when I go to Canada?"

"Yes." For weeks now Braïda had told Clare that space was in a way solid but that it could be annihilated by changing vibrations. I had never understood the physics and metaphysics of these statements but I could follow quite easily the general principle. Braïda was preparing us for a physical separation which could be circumvented by astral and out-of-the-body travel.

Annette said goodbye and went for her plane.

What was the significance of Annette's last-minute messages from Mr. Mills about Paulinus and James the Deacon? I found that these were Christian preachers who operated in Northumbria in the seventh century A.D. And the previous message about the Isle of Man from the monk she had seen at Iona? So far as I was concerned this brought things a little nearer home. Manx-

53

men are substantially of the same race as the people of Cumberland, a Norse stock grafted on a Celtic root. I knew that in the Dark Ages there had been considerable communication between the two regions. I did not know that we were getting nearer to the timeless experiences on the stretch of road by Bassenthwaite Lake. Why had Annette's Cathar mother appeared to her at an early Celtic shrine like Iona? Who was the monk Annette had seen at that place? Why was Guy so preoccupied with the Celtic Church?

I had abandoned completely any idea that there was any direct connection between Bassenthwaite and Catharism. It was clear that the Cathars I have mentioned were tuning in also to a Celtic epoch. Could it be that the same people who had regrouped in England today from the thirteenth-century Languedoc had also been together at an earlier period? Were there affinities between the Celtic Church and Catharism? Until Braïda spoke of the crosses and intertwinings I had no idea that there could be any affiliation between them.

Now I recalled that there was in what used to be Northumbria an early Celtic foundation other than Bassenthwaite which spoke clearly to several reincarnated Cathars, myself included.

When I went to the ruins of Rievaulx Abbey in Yorkshire in 1964 I had a mystical experience, not truly describable, in which the whole of history seemed to be reversing past me at an enormous speed as though played back by an enormous and universal tape recorder. The feeling of the world and time revolving backwards was so intense that I felt dizzy. I felt that the stones were alive.

At the time of my visit to Rievaulx I had no knowledge of its history. All I knew was that it had done something to me and that, as I have described elsewhere, my sense of time was dislocated. Two years later I read, in Professor Nelli's *L'Erotique des Troubadours* that Alfred, Abbot of Rievaulx in the twelfth century, had ideas on Platonic love similar to those expressed by the troubadours of the Languedoc and Provence in the Middle Ages. I had thought, and rightly, that my reaction to Rievaulx was determined by my previous existence as a Cathar. So it was, but it was not exclusive to me. It came out slowly and tangentially that, as well as myself, seven of our group of reincarnated

54

Cathars had been to the Abbey. They had all visited it apart from each other. Jane Butler and Betty had been intensely moved by it. Clare strode happily towards the ruins and immediately fainted. Kathleen had heard chanting she described as beautiful in spite of its resemblance to plainsong which she normally detests. Marion, a late recruit who has not yet made her entry, also heard chanting when she visited Rievaulx. It was clear beyond doubt that this place was especially significant for our Cathar circle. The Abbey is built on the site of an earlier Celtic foundation. I had to wait eighteen months after Braïda first switched our attention to the Celtic Church before I knew that Clare and I had a closer identification with Rievaulx, and that, within the Abbey ruins, we are taken back beyond Catharism to something older entwined in its roots. As Braïda and Bertrand Marty said, we must study the crosses and intertwinings.

I supposed that when Braïda steered us back through the Celtic Church to the Druids and Atlantis, she was drawing our attention to the antiquity of Dualism in Europe and the Middle East. There are writers in our day who postulate similarities between Catharism and the Druids. Otto Rahn goes so far as to say that the former reduplicated the social structure of the latter. To him the troubadours, who were contemporary with the Cathars and strongly influenced by them, fulfilled the rôle of the Druidic bards. The Cathar Parfaits represented the Druid priesthood. Much of what he says is completely unacceptable. Some of his intuitions may be described as permissible conjecture. Whatever the answers to these questions it was clear that Braïda needed us to know the antiquity of our Dualist origins. Certainly she seemed to be pointing to a Celtic incarnation.

When Annette had left for Canada I thought often of what she said about her dead mother's visits. What I have learned from these last years is that, once they have disclosed themselves, the dead are in no sense remote from the pains and problems of the living. To me this was very strange. Years earlier I had seen death as the solvent of human ties. For the young and happy it was a tragedy because it separated them from those to whom they were joined in the ardour of young love. Love could not be as strong as death. Death was an agony for those still warm with the fires of individuality. It was less painful for the truly old and the prematurely wearied who saw it as the dissolution of the burden of individuality in some vague state of indivisible consciousness. It was a blank relief for the old in whom the reluctant embers no longer gave warmth.

My views were transformed by my recent experiences. Braïda still demonstrated, across the no-man's-land between psyche and matter, a personal and special concern for her daughter. Before Annette went to Canada she discussed her with Clare. She said that Annette was an unsophisticated type who was not undetermined but who, during the critical issues of her life, would need someone to push her in the proper direction. She tended to lower her head and charge. While Braïda's advice was always direct and practical it taught me also that love, in a personal and specific sense, is so much stronger than death.

Chapter Seven

In her down-to-earth and sardonic outlook Kathleen resembled Jane Butler. She had an added talent for picturesque invective. If she described anybody she could always find a vivid and evocative name for them and her descriptions were often waspish. She had died with Jane Butler in the thirteenth century. They had been among the last to go to the stake. I described in *We Are One Another* how I was baffled by the name Brunasendis which had been dictated to Clare by Braïda and how I discovered later that it was an elision of Bruna and Arsendis, the names of Jane Butler and Kathleen in their Cathar incarnation. There can be no greater sharing of experience than to be burnt alive together.

It was therefore logical that in this life Kathleen should have been devoted to Jane Butler. Though they met seldom she said how close she felt to her. When Jane died in July 1972 Kathleen was convalescing from angina and also prostrated by a domestic crisis. In spite of her exhaustion and depression, and though she had not seen Jane for years, she forced herself to travel two hundred miles to the funeral. She returned completely exhausted. Later, because of her depression and exhaustion, she was persuaded to see her doctor. He attributed her condition to her domestic disturbance and time of life. I knew there were other factors. She was missing Jane Butler acutely. To be separated from the woman with whom she had died seven centuries before was like one Siamese twin being amputated from the other.

Once again I was astounded by the voice phenomenon. At this time to speak to Kathleen on the phone was an uncanny experience. Her voice had always had a remarkable resemblance to Jane's though its pitch and volume were lower. Now it had gained in volume and acquired the other's resonance. Her voice was more than ever indistinguishable from Jane's.

Her voice was not all she inherited from Jane. One night she had had a vision in full waking consciousness. She had been in a

57

dense wood with Mr. Mills. He wore his dark-blue robe and a belt and buckle. It was a little time before she recognised him because his hair was darker and his face thinner than in his twentieth-century incarnation. He looked younger because he had died at an earlier age in his Cathar incarnation. He had with him another figure similarly attired. The latter was taller, wide-chested and more strongly made. He was a sharp-featured, rugged fellow with a taciturn expression. She saw the two men as clearly as if they had been in the room with her. Clare's father spoke to Kathleen. He said that she was to be handed over to this other man. The new arrival was easily identifiable as Raymond Agulher, who had visited Jane Butler for years and whom she had described as the rugger forward. Now that Jane was dead he had transferred his support to the woman with whom she had died in her thirteenth-century incarnation.

Kathleen was visited two or three times by the rugger forward who remained silent on each occasion. It was clear that she felt an understandable and all too human disappointment that he had not spoken. One day she rang to say that she was not herself, that she was highly irritable and saying vindictive and completely unjustifiable things to people she was fond of. She was visited by Raymond Agulher. He still said nothing but gave her treatment. He had put a hand on her forehead and another at the point on her neck prescribed by Braïda and performed by Clare.

The great day came when Raymond Agulher spoke for the first time. He told her that someone else was coming, someone younger than us all, who had a great part to play. (He was speaking at the time when Annette first appeared in the picture.) What was even more striking was that he confirmed her identity. He kept repeating the words "Braïda, Cecilia". This was the night after Braïda had visited Annette and called her Cecilia.

Though in the thirteenth century he was renowned as a formidable debater, in this life Raymond was far better at giving practical advice and information than in dispensing the consolations of philosophy. When he first began to impart concrete information I was too astonished to comment. He told Kathleen to look out for the "crosses and the intertwining". He was repeating exactly what Clare had heard from Braïda and her

58

father. I was less concerned with what he said than with its timing. Kathleen received this message the same night as Annette had heard it in identical terms from Braïda.

Raymond Agulher visited Kathleen and said that Clare and I would discover the connection between the Celtic Church and Catharism and that we should not waste too much time positively looking for proof and searching for sources. The connection would be revealed in due course. This was exactly what Clare had heard previously from Braïda. A night or two later Raymond visited Kathleen and drew her attention to the design on the buckle of his belt. The night previously Clare's father had taken off his belt in order to show her the buckle more clearly. This action was certainly to emphasise that, though the buckle was Cathar, it was also Celtic in its intertwining pattern. It was clear that the revenants were implying that the Celtic Church was also Dualist.

It was obvious that some of the revenants had specific functions. Braïda was Clare's particular and most constant mentor. Raymond acted in the same capacity for Kathleen. Annette was served mostly by Braïda and later by Guy and Mr. Mills. These interchanges were conducted mostly within twelve hours of each other. It was common for me to have a call from Annette in Canada, another from Kathleen in Switzerland where she settled after leaving East Anglia, and another from Clare in Somerset, all within an hour and all describing the same psychic experience. There was no possibility of collaboration between them. I do not know the processes involved in these phenomena. It is hard to comprehend the mechanics of divinity. This is neither blindness nor stupidity but a blunt recognition of the fact that in this life we have no instrument of full understanding. Our attempts to fabricate for ourselves such an apparatus are at best vain and at worst diabolic. I only know that I understand more fully the meaning and purpose of group reincarnation. I had thought of the living remembering past lives and perhaps sharing their memories of rare, illuminated intervals in the Cosmic weather. I did not understand, until I learnt it from Clare, Annette and Kathleen, that in these circles of psychic incandescence a clear pattern evolves from this constant sharing between this world and the next.

On a still, mournful November morning I received an astonishing message from Kathleen. She had been visited by Raymond Agulher who had spoken to her about the Troubadours. He said that they were not only poets and singers of poetry but propagators of the truth. They had spread, mostly surreptitiously and by innuendo, the facts about Dualism. The last statement was vital. To me it was obvious that the Troubadours were immensely influenced by Catharism. To say, as some have done, that they and the Cathars were contemporary but that there was no link between them was like insisting that, though the teachings of Freud came to London in the twenties, the intelligentsia and the medical profession were totally uninfluenced by them. But it was when Raymond said that they were great travellers and came to England that I became excited. He said they had influenced the Lollards. This is an astonishing statement because, in spite of the erroneous tendency to see Catharism as a precursor of Protestantism, I have read in no book that Lollardy was influenced by Catharism. I read somewhere that there were those among the Lollards who rejected the idea of a constructed and visible Church. In this they resemble the Cathars who held their meetings so often in the forests. This was little enough to go on. But I could not forget that two years ago Clare had been beset for weeks by references to the Lollards and to William Wycliff. They came to her by clairaudience and also in the written messages dictated by Braïda. She had no more knowledge of Wycliff than that manifested by the average student who has studied that period for O level. I recalled the persistence with which Clare had returned to the theme of the Lollards and her query as to whether they were in any way related to the Cathars. I had told her that there was no evidence for this supposition.

Nevertheless I could not forget my years' long preoccupation with Ashridge in Hertfordshire as a possible centre of Catharism. Was it suggestive that Mrs. Smith in *The Cathars and Reincarnation* had been similarly concerned with the same place or that Professor Nelli, a great French authority on Catharism, should have been preoccupied with Ashridge and should possess a picture of it? Was it mere coincidence that Annette, who at this time did not know of Kathleen's existence, told me that Guy had always been fascinated by the Lollards? He had also taken a business course at the college at Ashridge, standing on the site of the old monastery said by Todd in 1821 to have been founded to accommodate a heretical sect from the Midi, a statement which incidentally I cannot accept as proven. Annette recalled that Guy had loved Ashridge, had commented on its atmosphere and had been particularly fascinated by the well, the idiosyncratic position of which had influenced me more than anything to believe that there were strange and unexplained factors about the building of Ashridge. Vicars Bell, in his book *Little Gaddesden*, has examined with sympathy the question of Ashridge being a heretical foundation.

It could be that I was looking backwards too much to Ashridge as a Cathar foundation and too little forward to its association with the Lollards. Lollardy was particularly strong in this neighbourhood and many of its adherents were recruited from what we now call Buckinghamshire and Hertfordshire. Ashridge stands close to the boundary between the two counties. Here we must decide whether we believe that truth by revelation includes not only that which is directly a nourishment for the spirit but the truth of history built up from the concrete granules of fact. At this time Braïda told Clare to read Bayley's book *New Light on the Renaissance*. I have indicated that since the appearance of Annette, Braïda had become even more positive and specific in her instructions. She had never used the portentous language of esotericism. For her the truth was something accessible. You reached out and it fluttered in your hand like a captive bird. A year or more ago she had given chapter and verse in her scriptural quotations. It was a strange, almost urgent modernisation of her methods that she should now give Clare the names of more contemporary books. One of the main themes of Bayley's work is exactly that mentioned by Raymond Agulher on his visit to Kathleen. The Troubadours were travellers and messengers of the Word. Many court jesters, after Catharism had gone underground, were carrying on the Troubadour tradition and by their anti-clericalism and Dualist beliefs eroding like moles the foundations of Catholicism.

Another theme of this book is that the Cathars were among the first manufacturers of paper. For centuries after Catharism had gone underground the faith was spread by seemingly inexplicable watermarks which were actually veiled Dualist propaganda. It is significant that to this day Hertfordshire, in which Ashridge lies, is still famous for the manufacture of paper.

I regarded what the revenants said about the derivations of Lollardy as a fascinating sideline. I had no idea that it was an arrow pointing directly at the very heart of a Celtic incarnation.

Kathleen was in so sense a spiritual athlete and had no wish to be a seer or any kind of oracle. Had she had such ambitions her own acid humour would have stood in the way of their fulfilment. At the same time it was obvious that she was yearning to establish deeper contact with someone or something. When Raymond Agulher first appeared she was comforted and transfigured but later the experience was tarnished a little by his delay in speaking to her and by the fact that he only came infrequently and when she was in trouble. Was she looking for someone or something else? Was it that her yearnings in this life were determined by her reactions in another? I had heard often enough that what we are is determined by what we have been in past lives. I had often felt that the case was over-stated. Kathleen was to prove I was wrong.

Like so many things it began with Clare. When I met her on a windless November day with tentative sunshine she was positively effervescent. She had been awakened from sleep the previous evening by her dog barking. It was as it had been the first night she saw Braïda, but instead of a woman in a dark-blue robe she was Jane Butler dressed in a simple medieval dress of some rough brownish material. It was held in at the waist by a kind of girdle. She wore no medallions of any kind. "What did she say?" I said.

"It was really just chit-chat, a kind of after-life gossip. It was wonderful seeing her. It wasn't just that she was absolutely real. That's the same with Braïda. It was just the way she nattered about people like she did in life. It was just as if we'd continued the last talk we had before she died four months ago. She said she was doing nothing in particular, just noting things and especially the colours. She said that in this world we had no idea of the intensity of colour and of how all the colours vibrated. She sent you her love."

I remembered the last time I had spoken to Jane. It was a negative grey day towards the end of June. There was no smell of summer and the air was cold. I was going away for my holidays. She lingered a little as she wished me well. There was no foreboding in her voice but I felt she wished to prolong the moment. When I came back to England she was dead.

The reverberations of what, for Clare, was a poignantly happy, sharp-coloured day were felt a week later. Kathleen had run into another bad patch. She was suffering still from the traumatic months in which she had also been stretched to her limits in moving from one plane of consciousness to another. She had now exhausted herself still further by nursing friends who were seriously ill. Her doctor sent her away to rest. She felt depressed and self-accusatory. She believed she had let her friends down. She needed all the support I could give her. Once again help came when it was most needed. She told me about it at once. One of the likeable things about her was that when she was better she informed you quickly. For most of my life it had been the other way round. "Last night I saw a woman in a browny-green robe. It was a simple affair, taken in by a girdle. She wore no ornaments of any kind."

"Was the colour of the robe more brown than green?"

"Oh yes," she said. "It was brown with a green tinge in it. She was small and thin with a pixy-like face."

"What age was she?"

"Oh, young," she said. "About her middle twenties. Who do you think she was?"

I hesitated before I answered. It was simply that I was afraid of upsetting her. She had felt herself close to Jane in this life, and knew she had died with her seven centuries previously. Was this to say that she could take calmly a visitation from the dead? Was she in a state in which she could undergo such an experience without disaster? But I knew that at this time she was acutely perceptive. If I did not tell her she would discover it for herself. "It could only be Jane Butler," I said. I told her about Clare's experience.

"Yes, I know." As she said it her voice faded to nothing. I felt she was weary but content.

Two or three nights later Jane Butler returned. Kathleen spoke of her quietly as though her appearance was an interesting aside.

"It's Jane all right," she said. "With the pixy-like face. She's a bit different from what she was here but I'm certain it's Jane."

"You see her as you knew her best. You didn't meet often in this life. You saw her day after day for months at Montségur. You lived together and you died together."

Kathleen was wonderfully better after Jane Butler's visit. If you are half living in another century you are better knowing your whereabouts. Bruna had come back to Arsendis. Kathleen had waited a long time but then she had done the same thing before. She and Jane were among the last to die at Montségur.

Once again Kathleen was disappointed that Jane Butler remained silent during her first visits. She did not have long to wait. It was largely through Jane that we learnt a good deal about Kathleen's highly coloured misdemeanours in another incarnation.

Chapter Eight

It is interesting how the different characters in this story enter at appropriate moments. It resembles a play in which the entries and exits are well timed. It is sometimes necessary to go back in time in order to describe the entries. When Annette was leaving for Canada two new actors appeared. I had a phone call from Marion, a woman doctor who was a main figure in our Napoleonic incarnation, and who enters the story some pages ahead. The other actor made a more ghostly entry.

We have to turn back to the day before Annette was due to stay with us before departing for Canada. It was mild and sunny. With the leaves still thick on the hedgerow elms you felt in the air the memory of summer. The menace of winter was not yet here. I was happy in my anticipation of Annette's visit.

Kathleen telephoned Clare. They spoke of everyday topics and Clare had no complaints about anything. Nevertheless Kathleen rang me immediately to say that Clare was very depressed. This was by now an old story. Jane Butler had always been anxious that I should look after Clare and see that she did not expend herself vainly. Kathleen was merely taking on where Jane had left off. Like the voice and Raymond Agulher, it was something else she had inherited from her.

It then transpired that Clare had lost a man friend who it seemed had been devoted to her for years. Graham had died suddenly, at an early age, of a heart attack on a business trip to New Zealand. He had asked her to marry him but she had known that the pleasures of marriage were not for her. Her rejection of his offer had not affected their relationship and he remained constantly and unbitterly devoted to her. She was very fond of him and always felt happy in his company. They seem to have achieved the near impossibility of remaining friends in spite of his undoubted love for her. A week or two after his death she handed me a bulky envelope containing a dozen sheets of flimsy paper covered with angular and spiky handwriting. Her name was written on the envelope. "I suppose he was another," she said.

"Another what? Another Cathar?"

She nodded her head towards the envelope. It was quite unlike her to make abrupt and positive statements without evidence. Her usual technique was to produce first a plethora of data and leave the conclusions to me. I made allowance for a loss which I was beginning to see was far more grievous than I had imagined.

It was quite unbelievable but the history of Betty and Penelope was repeated. Written on the sheets of paper were names identical with those discovered by her mother after Betty's death and by Jack among Penelope's papers. What stuck out a mile were the names of the sergeants-at-arms implicated in the massacre at Avignonet. It was clear that for Graham, as well as for the reincarnated Cathars already known to us, the affair at Avignonet was an intense focus of vibration. There were also a host of names of writers of Dualist or Gnostic tendency. These included Plotinus and Porphyry. Graham's list was very similar to that provided by Betty. New features were his preoccupation with what he called the Alexandrine school and with Basilides, a second-century Gnostic.

On one sheet of paper was a short list of what was obviously favourite reading. It included Kipling's *Song to Mithras* and *A Creed*, by Masefield. The former had been among Penelope's papers. The latter had occurred in a message dictated to Clare after death by Betty. There were also the identical references to Ecclesiasticus and Wisdom of Solomon which Clare had received from Braïda.

In life Graham had not known of Penelope's existence. Twenty years previously he had met Betty on one or two occasions. The rest of the group were unknown to him. As I read through his papers I was less intrigued than one might imagine. He was one more Cathar added to an already sizeable group and he appeared at a date when my interest was directed to the Celtic Church and to other forms of Dualism. I regarded Graham's intervention as a side issue fascinating in itself but not particularly interesting to me. I felt that we had enough information

66

about the Cathars. As I read on I realised that in harbouring this reflection I was both precipitate and parochial. In was clear that Graham was concerned with Dualism as a whole. On the next page it was clearly stated that he believed in reincarnation, in forces of good and evil, and that the world was created by the Devil.

I felt sure that Graham had possessed far memory. What he had written synchronised so perfectly with what I had gathered from other sources in this world and the next. He described a castle on a hill assaulted by stones hurled from engines of war. He was obviously reverting to Montségur and sharing an experience already lived and reported on by Clare, Kathleen and Penelope. Graham remembered that he wore a peculiar jacket strengthened by leather strips. This tied up completely with what Jane Butler had told me of her husband, Arnaud, who was also a sergeant-at-arms and whose name was mentioned along with Brasillac (Jack) and Pons Narbona who had been Kathleen's husband in her Cathar incarnation.

The next paragraph was startling. Graham described how he had been a prisoner in a castle by the sea. This had nothing to do with Montségur which is perched on the top of a mountain. Graham said he had been a French sailor. He had been taken prisoner in a sea battle in which his ship was damaged, capitulated and towed into the harbour. He was taken from the harbour by a small boat to a castle. He had been remarkably happy as a prisoner. He had belonged to a club which believed in the equality of man and universal brotherhood. I cannot dilate on this aspect of Graham's experience till I have introduced Marion who was very enlightening about this later incarnation and who has not yet appeared in these pages. She made herself known to me between Graham's death and the reception by Clare of his notes. The story of our appearance as French sailors is inextricably intertwined with that of the Celtic incarnation. To me, as the natural historian of these phenomena, these intertwinings are fascinating and of major importance but to recount each event in the order of its occurrence would be hopelessly confusing to the reader.

Graham passed abruptly from his life as a French prisoner of war to clear and positive statements about the nature of primitive

Christianity. He described it categorically as a form of Dualism. Its particular antecedents were philosophies of Pythagoras and Plato. In Graham's writings there were also references to Plotinus and the Gnostics whom he regarded as carrying on the Dualist tradition. He said that Dualism was the earliest and best-founded religious attitude. It was something which had always been persecuted but which would never die.

It was unmistakable that Graham had been interested in the many forms of Dualism exhibited in Europe since the decline of the Roman Empire. It was almost certain that he had lived through several incarnations as a Dualist. He had first revealed himself as a Cathar because we were most familiar with this particular incarnation. What happened next was to clinch the matter.

One night I had a dream in which I saw Clare dressed in a robe with a hood. The colour of her robe was so purple as to be almost black. Then I saw the misty outline of a man dressed similarly. The two figures merged into each other. It was not a question of any kind of embrace. It was more like a somewhat faded photograph being superimposed on another. Then the second figure seemed separate again but his clothes were different. He wore a kind of jacket, a bit shorter than tails, strengthened with vertical bits of leather. His appearance had changed too and he looked a more rugged type. The same process was repeated. He and Clare merged into each other like the blurred images of a photograph. This ritual was repeated a third time. On the latter occasion the stranger wore a rough jersey and rather wide trousers like a sailor's. Except for this I cannot remember having ever dreamt of a single member of the group. My psychic contact with them was such as to make dreams unnecessary.

It is not necessary for me to explain this dream because its interpretation is contained in Clare's phone call. She was breathless and excited and could hardly wait to speak. "I have to get it out or burst," she said.

"What is it?"

"Last night I saw a monk in a long dark robe with his hair long. Then this changed to a rough-looking type with a russety complexion. He was wearing a long jacket reinforced by

68

leather strips. Then this changed again to another rugged-looking character in a rough sailor's jersey with widish blue trousers. I know that all three were the same man."

"The second fellow with the jacket strengthened with leather is easy," I said. "It's another sergeant-at-arms from the thirteenth century. I suppose the third's another French sailor. (At this time Clare and I were aware of our French incarnation in the Republican and Napoleonic era.) After what's been going on these last few weeks the monk represents somebody in the early Celtic Church. What do you think the thing means?"

"I think it's the same person in three incarnations."

"And who?" I said.

"Graham."

"Were any of the faces like his?"

"No. I just recognised him."

I know that statements like the last are unsatisfying to the squirrel type of investigator who rolls one factor over like a favourite nut and ignores the whole experience. By now I knew Clare well enough to know that the statement "I just recognised him" was a manifestation of the supernormal perception she had exhibited so often previously. I knew also that we would soon have evidence from other sources and that the pattern was becoming streamlined.

On the following night Clare wished ardently that her father would visit her. In due course he appeared. It was this sort of phenomenon which so impressed me and which underlined my own limitations. I never had the experiences I wanted. It was clear beyond any doubt that my desire for them prevented their appearance. Clare had, more than I, the capacity to summon up aid and consolation when it was needed.

Mr. Mills told Clare that Graham had been the central figure in her vision the previous night. He said that what she had seen was a culminating experience. It was designed to reveal to her that we, who had been together in one incarnation, had maintained close contact in all four.

Who was Graham in the thirteenth century? The name Pons Narbona figured prominently in his papers. It rang a clear bell with Kathleen. It was among the names which returned to her

69

most vividly in the period of heightened far memory I described in *We Are One Another*. That she remembered him well was only reasonable. In the thirteenth century he had been her husband and had been burnt with her at Montségur. What was equally understandable and still more fascinating was that in this life, as a young woman, though she had seen little of him, she had been devoted to him and was desolated when it became clear that his affection was given to Clare. There was no doubt that he was Pons Narbona.

In spite of what I had learnt about him Graham remained to me a shadowy character. I regarded him as someone on the fringe of the group. He had been thrown in relatively late in the proceedings to provide additional evidence that the group had persisted through several incarnations. I did not see that his coming had been prepared for. The matter was clinched by Annette. She rang from Canada in a gale of exultation. The previous night Guy had appeared to her as he had been in life and had spoken to her for the first time. He told her he was very happy. Like Jane Butler, he spoke especially of the intensity and vibrating quality of the colours with which he was surrounded in his world. His next statement put the importance of Graham in perspective. He said that another important contributor was in the process of attaching himself to us. Beyond any doubt this was Graham. He told her that he, Guy, was the monk in the dark robe she had seen at Iona. At the time she had not recognised him. It may be remembered that her mother had given her a clue by saying that in a previous existence he had been a member of the Celtic Church.

Guy told her that in Cumberland where he had lived and worked, the Celtic Church resembled primitive Christianity and that the latter was Dualist. Belief in reincarnation and in forces of good and evil were basic. Christ was not the son of God but one in a line of prophets and sages which began with Pythagoras and included Plato. (Once again, as with others in this group, both dead and alive, we were referred back to classical Greece.) Pythagoras, Plato and Christ spoke from the same basic standpoint. What was distinctive about Christ was that he was a different kind of being. It was for this reason that people followed him and not because his message was new or unique.

70

Primitive Christianity was a religion of emanation. It spread by what one Christian radiated to another and Christ was the principal source of emanation.

Annette said she could not understand fully all Guy had said. This showed up clearly when she referred to his statement that Christ had a special kind of body. "I cannot understand it or remember it all."

At this stage I intervened and offered a stock explanation I have given to several others and which for me was a kind of private litany I reserved for these occasions. "You see, everything in life is a matter of vibration. A thing like a table may look inert but it isn't. In a table the vibrations are so slow that it *looks* inert. In the universe there is every kind of gradation from, say, a block of wood which represents spirit slowed down in matter and, at the opposite pole, somebody like Christ who has a body so spiritualised that he has the outlines of other people but in actual fact is almost immaterial. This is what Christ displayed to his disciples on the Transfiguration on the Mount. What they had taken for a natural man was in reality a spiritualised body."

"But how could you know?" she said. "That's exactly what Guy said and in his own words."

"It's been like that for a year or more. People in this world and the next have said the same thing in the same words." I was fascinated that the Celtic Church should have had similar views about the nature of Christ's body as the Cathars. "What else did Guy say?"

"He said such a lot I can't remember it all. Oh yes, he said that the Celtic Church hated the Crucifix. This tied up with their ideas about the Incarnation."

Guy said that the Celtic Church used equal-armed crosses but that all kinds of crucifixes and rosaries were taboo. It was essentially a very simple religion unsoured by dogma. The Crucifixion was not an essential part of Christianity. It was a great misfortune that it should have ever happened. Like the Cathars the Celtic Church rejected altogether that immense cornerstone of orthodox Christianity, that we are redeemed by Christ's death on the Cross.

Guy said that the idea that the early Celtic Church had

"different kinds of tonsures and fancy haircuts was all nonsense". It was interesting that the Cathar Parfaits also wore their hair long, a little short of shoulder length.

He talked a great deal about Iona and Lindisfarne. He said that Clare would go later to the latter place and also to the Isle of Man and Cumberland.

If I still needed proof that our deepest convictions are given to us by what are called spirits it was furnished by Annette's most recent conversation. I shared my views on the Transfiguration with Guy who had undergone the higher education of death. What struck me most was the repeated expression of this idea that Christianity was a religion of emanation. I had said this for years and sometimes with less evidence than I would have liked. It was a great comfort to know from what sources my ideas had originated. Nor was it just a matter of shared convictions. The very form in which these were expressed was identical with what the revenants had said to others. Now I see clearly that much creative art, philosophy and religious experience arises not in ourselves but in the discarnates by whom we are encompassed. The more we are content to serve only as instruments the greater and more valid the phenomena we perceive.

What was a historical day in my life was completed when Clare came to supper. She told me that Guy had also appeared to her the night previously. She had not the explosive enthusiasm of Annette but it was obvious that this experience had been an intense joy to her. He spoke to her about the nature and beliefs of the Celtic Church. What he said was so identical with what Guy had told Annette that it does not need repeating. It differed only in his relative emphasis of certain points. For instance he expressed himself forcibly when he spoke of the Crucifix which he even described as evil.

It is hardly necessary to add that next morning Kathleen rang from Switzerland. She was combining with Raymond Agulher to make her usual immediate contribution. She had seen him last night. He repeated what Guy had said to Annette and Clare. He left no doubt that the early Celtic Church was unmistakably Dualist and that primitive and early Celtic Christianity were religions of emanation. He disliked not only crucifixes but the Latin form of cross with the lengthened lower arm because this also symbolised the Crucifixion. He loved the equal-armed Celtic crosses which simply and modestly represented love.

Raymond had two additions of his own. He said that the Pauline writings were of great significance to the Celtic Church. This was fascinating because I knew already their importance to the Cathars. I recalled the flood of Pauline references with which Clare had been deluged a year or two previously.* This was because Paul was the prime interpreter of Christianity from the spiritist aspect and conveyed more than any other writer that primitive Christianity was a religion of emanation. Catharism itself was essentially of the same nature and markedly spiritist. What Raymond Agulher was saying was that Celtic Christianity was of the same nature and that the Pauline writings were of equal importance to it.

Raymond told Kathleen that, in the early Celtic Church, *Corinthians* was more important than the other Pauline epistles. She said she did not know whether it was *First* or *Second* *Corinthians*. Readers of *We Are One Another*, recalling the flood of quotations given to Clare previously, will have no doubt that it was the former.

* See *We Are One Another*.

73

Chapter Nine

When I talk of Marion Dacre I can only marvel how the whole process was miraculously designed and how one source of revelation was replaced by another. To tell her story I have to go back on my tracks. She entered my life the day Annette left for Canada.

When Marion first spoke to me I had the shock of my life. I had already observed that Annette spoke with almost the identical accents of Jane Butler but the voices of Marion and Annette were absolutely indistinguishable from each other. This phenomenon in which different people spoke with the same voice was becoming a little eerie.

Marion had been advised to ring me by Clare. They had met years ago but had not been particularly friendly. They saw each other every two or three years. They had a mutual respect but were not especially intimate. Marion was diffident and apologetic. She made it clear that Clare had advised her to phone me. She had been to Iona. Standing in the oldest part of the church a monk had materialised in front of her. He was short with long hair and dressed in dark robes. The cut and length of his hair and the colour of his robe were the same as those of the monk Annette had seen in the identical place. She watched him come and go. When she went to Lindisfarne she saw him again.

On her journey Marion had stopped at Rievaulx. She was enthralled by the atmosphere and heard chanting in the ruins. She revealed more fully her Celtic connections. Some years previously she had visited the Isle of Man and had found it magical because of its abundant Celtic crosses and memorials.

Marion was a doctor dealing largely with children's conditions. She had read a good deal of what I had written. She agreed that certain congenital malformations can only be explained by the attitude of the mother during pregnancy and that many children born as a result of Cesarean section have psychic mothers in whom the maternal impulse is in conflict with the disinclination to imprison other souls in matter. She seemed to have Dualist leanings.

She spoke of her younger patients and especially of those with club foot. In such cases the aim of treatment is to relax the muscles in the neighbourhood of the deformity to enable the foot to move more freely. She said that recently she had been trying a little physiotherapy on her own account. She had put one hand on the deformity and another over one of the knee's anatomical landmarks. What was striking was that she had used the palm of her hand and kept both hands still. Some kind of movement simulating massage would have been more in keeping with her rôle as a doctor. It was clear that she was using the thirteenth-century Cathar therapy which Clare and Jocelyn had practised on Annette when she fell from the swing twenty years ago and in which Clare had been re-instructed during Braïda's visits. Marion had no idea that she was practising a medieval technique.

I wondered if I had seen too much in her Celtic interests and if we were reverting once more to the Cathars. The balance was tilted in favour of Celtic Christianity when, on a later occasion, she switched me over to her mother when I had raised the question of people reincarnating in the same family. Once again I encountered the stupefying problem of the identical voice. On one occasion, after Marion had brought her mother to speak to me on the phone, I was reduced to asking the latter whether I was indeed talking to her or whether Marion had failed to find her and had herself returned to continue our conversation.

Mrs. Dacre was in her late seventies. Though she was soft-spoken and shy, she was also logical and in her quiet way forth-right. Looking back to our first conversation it is obvious to me that I regarded her as one set in authority above me and this in spite of the fact that her affectionate concern for me was evident from the beginning. Why my affection for her was combined with respect and reverence will become obvious in the later chapters.

Mrs. Dacre brought us back sharply to the theme of Bassen-thwaite. She said that her deceased husband's family hailed from Cumberland. I spoke of many of my old haunts and it seemed

she was familiar with them all and above all Bassenthwaite.
She said it was especially dear to her because it was there that,
after his death, her husband had returned to her. "By the lake?"
I asked.

"Yes. Do you know the Pheasant?"

"Yes."

"He came back on the road between the landing stage and
the Pheasant."

We were back again to the unpretentious mild beauty of the
road that curved round the corner by the Pheasant. Along that
road the dead had returned to three people and Annette and her
husband had gone out of time. I felt no excitement but only a
sense of inevitability. In my mind and heart I had come back
home. I had come home through time and in the sense of returning to my heart's recesses. I had returned also, symbolically and
actually, to my own country. I walked through limited and
definable space to the carved stone altars of truth. It was here,
in home country, that I had first heard the murmured accents of
Dualism. Bassenthwaite spoke to me and to others who had
Dualism in their bones. I had been born in this country because
it had a message for me.

With our return to this magnetic length of road it was obvious
that the finger of destiny was pointing again in the direction of
Bassenthwaite. This was all the more clear when she advised me
to go up to Cumberland with Clare whom she had only seen
twice in her lifetime. She stressed above all that we should go to
Bassenthwaite. She said also that I should visit Isel, Uldale and
Lamplugh. She spoke most insistently of a cross I should see near
Lamplugh. Her deceased husband, who had been an authority
on these matters, had been fascinated by it. It astonished me that
she should know this remote area which for me since childhood
had been inexplicably endowed with magic. What was stranger
was that I, so sceptical by nature and so meticulous in my sifting
of evidence, should set such store on what was said to me by so
recent and shadowy an acquaintance. I listened with special
intensity to Mrs. Dacre and did not realise that this was because
of what I owed to her. I did not know that my indebtedness
originated beyond my present lifetime.

All that Mrs. Dacre advised was amply supported from the

76

next world. For weeks I was bombarded by the revenants with advice that I should go with Clare to Cumberland. This was obviously a crucial issue. It was essential that I went with her otherwise I would fail to interpret what I saw. These exhortations were intensified in the latter half of March. It was indicated that we would see a stone which would be for us a transfiguring experience. It would communicate something it was essential for us to know.

This general advice was transmitted from Braïda and Mr. Mills directly to Clare or through Annette and from Raymond Agulher to Kathleen. Braïda also gave specific directions. She repeated what Mrs. Dacre had said about our visiting Bassenthwaite, Lamplugh, Isel and Uldale. She was insistent that we should see the old church of St. Bega at Bassenthwaite. This church, and that at Isel, are small and remote and Braïda had, as Jocelyn, never visited them in her twentieth-century incarnation. Most of all she spoke of the mysterious stone. She said that it would reveal to us how our different incarnations were linked together. Braïda never told Clare the stone's exact whereabouts. All we knew was that it was near Lamplugh. She mentioned the name of the hamlet to Annette but the latter unfortunately forgot it.

I failed to notice that Betty had taken no part in these exhortations. It was months before I understood the reasons for her abstention.

There was every indication that our visit to Cumberland was seen by the revenants, and possibly by Mrs. Dacre, as a watershed in our lives. It may be surprising that I expected little from it. This was simply because in my experience to wish for anything impedes its realisation. I had heard so much of Bassenthwaite from this world and the next that I could not feel it would speak to me even more clearly. My story began with my walking over Wythop to Bassenthwaite Lake. It could hardly be expected that it should reach a climax in the same place. It may seem a want of faith that I could not believe that the fingers of destiny were brushing my forehead. I accepted completely the truth of all Braïda had said to Clare. I had had cast-iron evidence of the accuracy of her predictions. If I could not accept that the sun was up and the harvest near it was because my psyche was impeded by the tatters of my old scepticism.

Apart from this I had for long expected little of this world. It was too much to expect that the experiences associated with Bassenthwaite and its surroundings would continue with me acting as an enthusiastic spectator on the sidelines. The dead had returned to three people on the road between the Pheasant and the landing stage. A fourth had had a mystical experience in the same place. I refused to believe that a fifth would materialise in the same locality to enable me to round off the evidence with precision and elegance. Life simply did not work like that.

Yet going up to Cumberland in mid-April was a turning point. It was as if I had arrived suddenly at the summit of a mountain without having known of its proximity. That is one way of travelling and as good as most others. All my life I had known that to search is to lose and that we sterilise ourselves by our deepest longings.

Chapter Ten

I had concluded from what the revenants and others had said that the object of our visit to Cumberland was twofold. Firstly we would learn more of the affinities between the Celtic and Cathar Churches. In a word we would have further evidence that the former was Dualist. Secondly, we should see some stone of I knew not what shape or dimension which would summarize for us the persisting threads woven into our several incarnations. I considered little the possibility of other more aching and personal revelations.

Something happened the night of our arrival. I went with my wife and Clare along the road from the Pheasant where Betty had returned to Jane and where I had felt, years after his death, the presence of my father. I turned suddenly and went through a gap in a hedge I had never seen before. I had known that country for sixty years but, in the days when I walked the fells, this little hillock by the lake was too undramatic to attract my attention. An old and clearly defined path leads to the summit of the knoll. The hill is enclosed between the lake and the road. The summit is flat and rounded and ringed with earthworks. I will not say that it was here that things began to happen because at that time my perception of individual presences was modest. I can only say that I had walked into a new atmosphere. I was breathing a sharper and thinner air. The place was violently alive. My memory was stabbed by the intensity of the life which radiated from it. I looked through the birch saplings in young leaf to the lake and Skiddaw and the green fells northwards. I had the same feeling of giddiness and of the air vibrating as I had had at Rievaulx ten years before. Once again history was being revealed to me. It was as if an illuminated scroll was unrolling so rapidly that I could not see the details. I belonged to Castle How as I did to Montségur.

Clare wandered about on her own. I knew from a kind of

twilight illumination in her eyes that she was perceiving things intensely. "Do you feel anything?" she said.

"The whole place is alive."

"And that anyone is here?" These days she seemed surprised that I did not see or feel things as quickly as she did.

"No. Just that the place is alive and that the air has a kind of palpitating rhythm."

The next morning Clare rose early and went for a walk before breakfast. She turned left at the door of the Pheasant and walked away from the landing stage. She walked up the road to Wythop which I had descended with my mother nearly sixty years before. My story begins with me walking with my mother and out of time on the road to Bassenthwaite. It takes a huge step forward with the same kind of experience in the same place more than half a century later. It is clear that the radiating capacity of Castle How extends beyond the road between the inn and the jetty.

Graham came back to Clare on the road to Wythop. He was wearing a robe much darker than the dark royal blue of the Cathar Parfait. He told Clare to look for the Mithraic stone. I assumed immediately that this was the stone of which Braïda and the others had spoken. It seemed natural that Graham should add his exhortations to those of the others.

We made our second visit to Castle How at twilight. Though there were other visitors going up the path the place was as alive as ever. Its atmosphere was uncontaminated by the talkative visitors and their bustling semi-humanised dogs. We waited until they had gone. I stood alone on the summit of the knoll. Clare moved restlessly along its periphery. My wife looked at the lake from somewhere down the slope. Suddenly I was aware that Clare had returned and was watching me intently. "What are you looking at?" I asked.

"Don't you feel anything?"

"As I said before, the place is alive."

"But someone behind you?"

"No. What is it you see?"

"Why, Betty. I've felt her all the time but now I see her. You're sure you didn't?"

"No."

"You will," she said. "They have said you will." She seemed very disappointed.

It was fitting that Betty should stand behind me. Her mother had been the first in the group to tell me how the dead returned on the road to the landing stage. Jane had said Betty and I had been very close to each other and that she had relied on me a great deal in the thirteenth century. It did not hurt me that I had not seen her. I felt that direct vision was withheld from me for a specific purpose, that some other inward change was required of me before I could see further. I knew also that no special effort was required of me. All I need do was wait.

I never asked myself why Betty should come to me at Castle How. I accepted now that I had lived before in Cumberland and that at the moment I was on my own territory. It never occurred to me that Betty had lived here too. If she stood behind me at Castle How it was because we had been so much to each other in the Cathar incarnation and that she was still entitled to haunt me.

The hill and the oak wood were magical but to me they were not the main object of my visit. It was another example of how, through too concentrated aims, we pass unheeded places sacred to us. Since my childhood Castle How had been as familiar to me as my own garden. It was characteristic that I should be unaware of its sanctity. The stone spoken of by Braïda and the others occupied the first place in my thoughts.

It may seem cold-blooded but for me everything was secondary to the mysterious stone. This was in part because the build-up was so considerable and also because of my preference for concrete evidence. Mrs. Dacre described it as being near Lamplugh. Braïda, who in this life had never been in Cumberland, was still more specific. What was maddening was that she had mentioned the name of the locality to Annette who in her undiscriminating way did not regard it as especially important. She forgot the name. When I repeated a string of names to her she said that Lorton was the nearest approximation to what her mother had said. It seemed that it rhymed with the name of the site of the stone.

The first evening we went to Isel which again was one of the places to which we had been directed by agents from this world and the next. What I was seeking there was not the Ark of the covenant but the Triskele stone which I had learnt was of ancient and unknown origin. The little church at Isel was out of time and beyond description. Its outlines were modest and what gave it beauty was the torrent of wild daffodils which flooded the paddock between the churchyard and the river. Beyond the paddock was the speed and silence of the cold, swift Derwent.

Because I knew that the Triskele stone was in the church I passed quickly through the porch. I looked to my left as I came to the door. On the wall of the porch was a rough-hewn stone with a circular toothed pattern. I had the feeling of having seen it before. Had I encountered its like in the Languedoc or in a photograph? I could not place it at all. What was odd was that, in the moment when I first saw it, I felt a strange, faint stab in the solar plexus. I could not account for it at all. My thoughts wandered as if magnetised to the Languedoc. I did not know, till months later, that in looking at this stone I was confusing my incarnations.

The Triskele stone itself provoked no reaction. The vital stone was not easy to discover. I could not find it at Lamplugh. All the people I asked agreed on one thing, that a certain local gentleman would surely know. We had a charming encounter in the course of which his wife revealed that in one particular at least her father had instructed her in Dualist doctrines. Our host set us on our way.

When I saw the stone I knew beyond doubt that it was what we were seeking. It was encased high in the wall of a barn in a farmyard. I noticed that as soon as we entered Clare's eyes were raised. She saw it before I did and admitted later that she had always envisaged it as high in a wall. The farm overlooked the cold northern waters of Ennerdale. It was a far cry from the tawny uplands and the crushing heat of the Lauragais to the shadow of the fells reflected in the water. This country of wind-raked copses, with white anemones with bent heads, was another world from the fanged, tenacious contours of the Corbières with young vines twisting towards the light in the sunbaked pockets between the rocks. The more I approached my Celtic origins the more I leaned back to my dominant incarnation in the Langue-doc.

82

A magical, strangely personal emanation of truth poured from the cross set in the wall of the long barn, long as a Viking ship. There had been some traffic going down the twisting lane from the upland country to the dark gash of Ennerdale with its cool waters and the feeling of being at the end of the world. In the farmyard which sheltered the cross there was a silence underlying the turbulence of the years, the winds from the sea and the land winds from the fells. There was the feeling of a quietness which underpinned and outstayed the caprices of memory.

What we saw with the naked eye was to me a marvel. It was all the more miraculous when I examined later the photo shot precariously from a leaning ladder and saw, through a magnifier, the story of centuries written in the fissures and ridges of this steadfast stone. In its broad outlines, where it sank into the wall, it was a Celtic cross. Lower down, on the shaft of the cross, there were the remains of Celtic intertwinings. Within the outlines of the cross there was a circle with twelve teeth. They pointed outwards as if from an inner circle. This sunray pattern was a Dualist symbol and I had seen it among the Cathar relics in the Languedoc. Oddly enough this part of the cross was the same as I had seen in the porch at Isel. There was the clear outline of a rose within the Cathar circle. Since the days of ancient Egypt the rose has been the esoteric symbol of truth. It has carried the same message to different generations of Dualists. It was especially significant for the Rosicrucians who utilised a secret alphabet of symbols in those epochs when the world was incapable of tolerating the mention of Dualism.

Further down on the stone was a clear leaf pattern. It stood out more boldly than the lines and markings in its vicinity. I saw later that the leaf was accompanied by a simple and stylised flower like a tulip. Clare recognised it as identical with the leaf patterns with which she had completed her mandala under the direction of Guilhabert de Castres in the thirteenth century. There was much more to it than that.

I felt from the beginning that the cross was extremely ancient. At first I thought of it as carved in the Middle Ages. This is because for one reason or another the Cathar incarnation was clamouring for attention. I was playing with the idea that it had been brought to Cumberland by some itinerant Dualist in

83

the Middle Ages. I did not ask myself how he managed to transport it. Later it seemed to me that the cross was still older. What I felt most was a peculiar intimate magnetism which seemed to emanate from it. It was almost as if it had a personal message for me.

As well as the outlines I have mentioned that of a dove was discernible on later and closer examination of the photograph with a magnifying glass. This was indubitably a Cathar symbol. I recalled the day years ago when, in a room shaded from the heat and palpitating traffic of Carcassonne, I balanced in my hand a leaden model of a dove picked up from the remembering and reverberating earth of the Ariège. This was satisfying enough in all conscience. There were symbols of the Celtic Church and of Catharism joined together in the same mute but eloquent memorial. This was enough for me. There was also the rose which, as well as being an immemorial symbol of enlightenment, tended especially to recur as a Dualist emblem. For me the stone fell perfectly into place as part of an intricate and immense pattern. It was the tablet of the law towards which the fingers of two worlds had been pointed.

I did not bother a great deal about the simple flower and leaf pattern because it resembled the design with which Clare had completed her mandala in the thirteenth century.* I dismissed it as another Cathar symbol. The stone had withstood for centuries the wind and weather of this desolate cleft in a northern fastness. In its substance it had defied the erosion of time. It could afford to keep a further secret a week or two longer. It was enough for me to have established that, in the tangled brushwood of the centuries, the tough liana of Celtic Christianity and other forms of Dualism had remained intertwined with each other.

What I have described so far are geometric patterns encased in stone. You can recognise the circle as a circle and the rose as a rose. Other shapes are visible when the photograph is examined with a magnifying glass. I do not discuss them because their outlines were faint and their nature more conjectural. Clare was especially preoccupied with the simplified and stylised lily or tulip at the base of the cross. I was satisfied with its thirteenth-

* See We Are One Another.

84

century connections. It was clear that for Clare there was more to come.

We saw the cross on the same day as that on which Graham had appeared on the road to Wythop. That night he came again to Clare. He spoke again of the Mithraic stone. I found this injunction bewildering. The stone I had seen at W——* was ancient enough but I could not think it so old that it had served for the cult of Mithras. I did not pay a great deal of attention when Clare spoke of the Mithraic stone. I woke that morning so intensely depressed that immediate circumstances had no interest for me. Clare did not comment on my mood but asked if I had seen Betty the previous night. She seemed astonished that I had not done so. She said that Betty had been speaking to me during the night and that I had awakened depressed because I could not remember what she said. I did not pay a great deal of attention to this. I could not understand her intense preoccupation with Betty. All I knew was that I was expected to see her and had not done so. The stone at W—— seemed much more important.

We spent the morning wandering through the places to which we had been directed by Braïda and the others. It was a sunny day, the air was still and the earth was waking from the torpor of winter. In the still, unmoving hours of the early afternoon we came to Torpenhow. I was uncertain whether we should go to the church. According to my confused memory of it it was not particularly interesting. I went in solely for the sake of my mother whose antecedents had lived but a few miles distant. Clare and my wife were busy reading the descriptive leaflet and verifying the details. I wandered idly about. I was in that semi-intoxicated mood induced by a warm day in spring when one is soaked in the exhalation of the earth waking from sleep and has no time for minutiae. Clare beckoned to me from the chancel. Above the piscina was a stone decorated by a circle with projecting rays. It was obviously a sun with solar radiations. The leaflet said that this stone had been taken from a Roman site in the vicinity. All I assumed from this was that Graham was drawing

* At the request of the charming and helpful farmer who owns the barn I do not give the name of the village.

85

our attention to a Mithraic symbol to remind us of the age and indestructibility of Dualism. I could not see the connection between the stone at Torpenhow and the eloquent symbol we had seen at W——. It was several months before I learnt that this preoccupation with the cult of Mithras was well founded.

On that particular Sunday we saw how justified was Braïda's contention that, in Cumberland at least, the Celtic Church had built on Druidical sites or at least on those which would have been favoured by them. St. Bega's was isolated by the lakeside and a long way from Bassenthwaite village and had also a stream beside it. The churchyard was circular. When the church was built the land adjoining was covered by a forest. Going down to the church there is to this day a wood, predominantly oak, with a circular clearing ringed by stones. I found it hard to tear myself from the silent clearing in the centre of this wood. It spoke to me more clearly than the church itself but its language was as yet untranslatable.

The site of St. Bega's church is such as would satisfy not only the most toxic addict of the Celtic twilight but also all those acutely responsive to the picturesque. On that Sunday morning I could not give it my full attention. Clare had wandered off alone. She was standing some distance from the church beside a flat stone buried in the ground. She had the far-away look which gave a twilight effect to her luminous eyes and which I had observed before when she was receiving the presages of disaster. I wondered if anything ominous was impending. It had not occurred to me that she might equally be looking at the tragic past. All I was concerned with was that she was withdrawn and that, not knowing she was observed, she was smiling sadly.

That Sunday was a fruitful day. We saw other evidence that Celts had built on Druidic sites. The church at Uldale was a mile and a half from the bleak, wind-tormented hamlet and the churchyard was a deformed oval. Perhaps what fascinated me most was the discovery in three of the churchyards of patches of a rare plant which in my childhood we called Easter Magiant. I suppose this is as near as one can get to the spelling of what is obviously a folk name. The plant is like a small and delicate dock with deep-pink stems. I think it is known in the south of England

86

as bloodroot and that it is some kind of polygonum. It is described in the textbooks as rare and found only in northern pastures. I was fascinated to find it for two reasons. It was one of the constituents of the herb pudding we had eaten at Easter in childhood and which I had never heard of outside Cumberland. It was obviously in the folkloric tradition of spring medicines. I was still more intrigued to find it because I had recently read, in a Cumberland magazine, how an old farmer had insisted that this herb always grew best in churchyards. I thought, with unbecoming realism, of all kinds of theories to explain how Easter Magiant should flourish on the slow decomposition of our mortal remains. Once again I was off beam. I was to learn later that the reason why this plant flourished in churchyards was simpler, pleasanter and more absorbing than my over-realistic physiological reflections.

I had wondered when I saw Clare by the stone in St. Bega's churchyard whether she was anticipating trouble in the future. It came that night. I woke up in the small hours of the morning with an agonising depression and feeling that she was passing through some crisis. She was obviously shattered and exhausted next morning. She was so pale, drawn and her eyes were so lightless that I wondered whether she was fit to make the return journey to Somerset. From what she said it was obvious that this trip to Cumberland had stimulated acute and painful memories. These were in the process of breaking through to the conscious level. During the night she had seen a whole host of faces and figures moving past her. She felt that she recognised them but could not put a name or a period to them. At the same time she felt horribly ill with an agonising pain in the chest. She felt that in some way she was being drawn away from herself to another country. She felt so desperate that she longed to ask my assistance. Not being made that way she limited herself to yearning for the presence of Braïda. The latter duly came, accompanied by Mr. Mills. They told her that she must not try to remember her Celtic incarnation. It would come to her in due course. She denied to me having ever made any conscious effort at recollection. Her father told her that her name in her Celtic incarnation was Trubellia and that mine was Mercantius.

On our way back to Bath we dropped Clare at her home and

took a meal with her. She showed me a little case of coffee spoons her father had given her as a birthday present three years before he died. It was inscribed, "With love, to Bellia." She had never understood why he had always called her by this name. It was becoming clear that Mr. Mills' interest in Bassenthwaite, as shown by his constant visits and his exhortation to Annette that she should go there on her honeymoon, was not only well founded but long established.

On my way back home I pondered again on the date of the W—— cross. At first I had wondered whether some far-wandering refugee from the Cathar persecution had found his way to what for me was always an Ultima Thule. Had he inscribed his beliefs in stone as a testimony to the past and as a veiled challenge to this savage outpost surveyed and protected by the soaring eagles? It was a stimulating thought to think of some solitary creature, his skin cured, his eyes sharpened by the sun and the light of the Languedoc, carrying his faith and his fidelity to this northern wilderness of naked fell and tree-choked valleys. It was stimulating, not altogether impossible but hardly likely. The cross looked older even than the thirteenth century, as ancient, for example, as the crosses at Iona and other relics of the Celtic Church. But how did one explain the varied motifs interwoven in its substance? Could it be that what I had thought of as Cathar symbols were also used by the Celtic Church?

Suddenly I thought of the Lollards. This was not a purely intuitive flash because Raymond had spoken of them a few weeks previously and I recalled how Clare had been preoccupied by them. When she was recording her mysterious messages in the night watches and hearing the voice by day there was a period of weeks when one of her more subtle side channels had pointed in the direction of Lollardy.

The Lollards flourished in the thirteenth and fourteenth centuries. I wondered if the cross could be of this date. It looked much older but I hesitated to claim it as such. I did not regard myself as an authority on these matters. I was prepared to read and examine what came my way but I did not propose to embark on an intensive study of the subject. By now I was able to appreciate the varying rhythms of the system of psychic vibrations with which I was surrounded. I knew that the pace had accelerated and that we had not long to wait before other voices would add their testimony.

It was strange that I, brought up in Cumberland, a tireless walker and interested in history, should have been so indifferent to my Celtic heritage. As a boy I had never registered that Celtic crosses were traditional here. On this visit I had seen at Crosthwaite a score or more crosses of Celtic design dating from the beginning of this century. This at least implies that the Celtic tradition is still alive among the local stonemasons. I suppose, in my youth, my eyes were directed to the far-off hills. I had not yet acquired the sharpness of vision enabling me to see what was on my own doorstep. This week-end was for me a transcendental experience. It is fascinating to me that the country round Lamplugh, which had seemed sacred to me in boyhood, was regarded as a holy place during the epoch of the Celtic Church. The name of the village actually conveys that this was the site of a church. That the stone at W—— should have been so near my birthplace was something beyond belief.

Chapter Eleven

The first evening on my return from Cumberland I had a call from Annette. Her calls were unique. There was a throbbing silence before her voice came over. Then it exploded into consciousness with salvoes of goodwill interspersed with messages from the next world thrown off inconsequentially like sparkling fireworks. It was difficult to think of her as a reed shaken by the wind because the music she transmitted was so full-throated. Nevertheless she was, in the complete sense of the word, a passive transmitter. She had no idea of the importance or otherwise of what she relayed to us. "Does it matter?" she would say. "Does it really matter? Oh, it does, that's good."

When I mentioned it to her she recalled immediately that W—— was the name by which Braïda had described the cross and which she had previously forgotten. She was quite unable to realise the tensions, the surmises and the discomforts of the false starts I had made in chasing this stone up and down the wide purlieus of Lamplugh. She wasted no time discussing Celtic relics. She was more concerned with Clare. She insisted that she had been ill and wished to know all the details. I told her what I knew of Clare's experience the previous evening. "Oh, there's much more to it than that," she said. "I saw mummy last night. She told me that Clare had been very ill indeed. She had actually passed over. I can't tell you exactly what she said because I don't know what she meant but it seems that her psyche passed over and stayed too long outside her body. Is psyche the name and does this make sense? She was given some kind of choice, to go on or come back. She didn't want to come back, to this world I mean, but mummy said she did because it was necessary to help you with your writing. This doesn't mean you need coaching in writing but without her you wouldn't get the information you need. Anyway she's better now. Mummy said her time hasn't come and she has lots to do."

I was relieved by Annette's last two sentences because I had failed in my attempt to persuade Clare to ring her doctor. It seemed to me that while her symptoms were psychically induced they were also to a significant and grave degree physical in nature. As such they were outside my province. Annette was now more concerned with Clare's future. She said that her experiences the night previously had been a necessary prelude to her learning more of her Celtic incarnation. The stream of faces she had seen in the night were of people she had known from that epoch.

Three days later I met Clare. Braïda had revisited her after a longish interval. She spoke of the crosses we had seen in Cumberland. She said that these were basically Celtic but that those at Isel and W—— contained emblems associated with other forms of Dualism. This was above all true of the cross at W——. This was, for us, the most important symbol we were ever likely to encounter.

When she said that the stone at W—— was connected with the Lollards it was odd how casually I received this information. A few years before I would have seized on it avidly and explored every possibility arising from it. These days I took it in my stride. Was I becoming blasé? Was it merely that what had once been a rare adventure was now a commonplace? Was it that in these days the pieces of the jigsaw were shuttled into place with such speed and dexterity? All these explanations were true but insufficient in themselves. I had known for some time that another factor was operating. I was not surprised that Braïda should express this idea about the Lollards because I was convinced that it was she who had put it in my head in the first place. I knew from my congested experience of the last three years that when we seem inspired it is merely that we are receiving more freely. What seem our better achievements are not our own and we should take no credit for them. They are hints whispered in the ears of our psyche by those who love us and love is an aspect of wisdom which is in itself the echo of a long memory.

When Annette next rang me it was to say that she had taken to heart my jocular criticisms of her forgetfulness. She was less inclined to mingle memories of past incarnations with details about transatlantic cooking and excessive central heating. She had no means of regulating what poured in on her from the next world. She made a determined but unsustained effort to relay it in proper sequence. She had seen Guy the night before. He told her that Clare and I had seen a cross which was important because, "It contained a bit of everything." He bore out the conclusions which I had made tentatively, even timidly, because I could never regard myself as an authority on the subject. I do not know that I need have been so timid. Despite my lack of scholastic qualifications I had access to sources of information not available to the savants.

Guy seems to have expressed himself tersely. Was he aware of Annette's genius for bubbling parenthesis or had she herself remembered that, apart from her psychic accomplishments, she was a first-class secretary and, faced with a matter of business, could express herself easily and precisely? Anyway he said simply and clearly that the cross was Celtic, that the circle and stem were Cathar, that the intertwinings were Celtic and represented immortality and that the rose was the age-old symbol of truth. It seemed from what he said that the rose was the earliest in origin of the symbols depicted. He confirmed, what I had thought, that the ten points round the disc were Cathar but added to my surprise that they were also Roman and Mithraic. They represented the rays of the sun which symbolised the God of light and goodness.

I could not savour to the full what Guy had said because of another item which Annette quoted. Her matter-of-fact citation took my breath away. "He talked a lot about a flower and a leaf that had to do with French prisoners in the Napoleonic wars."

This was the simple flower and leaf pattern which Clare had recognised as part of the mandala she had completed in the thirteenth century. More significantly I knew already that it was a symbol associated with our life in the Napoleonic incarnation because by this time, as we will see in the later chapters, much had been revealed to me by Marion and her mother. What baffled me completely was that the Napoleonic wars were centuries after the date of the cross. "But look," I said. "I know your mother implied that all the incarnations were represented in the W—— stone, but surely she meant all the incarnations before the Cathars, or for that matter before the Lollards?"

"What Guy says is always true."

"I'm certain it is," I said, "but how do you explain that some-thing about a Napoleonic incarnation is contained in a stone at least six centuries earlier?"

"Don't ask me, I'm not clever. I'll ask Guy. He knows."

My sceptical questions were not very intelligent. What I failed to see was that a medieval symbol could still be in use six hundred years later. In any case Annette had no need to ask Guy.

A week later I had a call from Marion, still waiting in the wings to make her entry. She confirmed beyond doubt that this emblem had been worn by the French prisoners at Portchester in the early nineteenth century. Her mother also confirmed its con-nection with France. I will leave the evidence till I tell Marion's story. In the meantime I can only repeat that the W—— stone contained symbols from all my known incarnations.

Chapter Twelve

I had no need to think of the Lollards because I was purposefully reminded of them. I had the usual rapid confirmatory call from Kathleen in Switzerland. Raymond had visited her and said that the stone had been put there by the Lollards. He did not say when they had obtained it or who had made it. I was by now accustomed to this confirmatory evidence from the other side. It was as though Raymond and Kathleen were a branch of some cosmic exchange operated by Braïda and Annette in Canada. Throughout the whole of this period no letter or telephone call was exchanged between Annette and Kathleen. They never met except for a few hours when Annette found herself a day and a night in Switzerland on a business trip.

The telephone call from Marion's mother, Mrs. Dacre, was far more significant. She did not ring because she wished to discuss stones in Cumberland but because she felt I was worried. So I was and she knew the cause. My wife, whose illness is woven into the pattern of my story, was feeling particularly unwell. The fact that the Lollards came only second on the agenda in some way made the evidence more telling.

Mrs. Dacre asked me if I had seen the stone at W——. I said I had and that it was one of the few things in my life which had lived up to and surpassed my expectations. She had said before that her husband had been fascinated by it. She now told me he had believed that it was in some way concerned with the Lollards. What she said astonished me. It was as though some object which had been scrutinised by the naked eye, was now being put under the microscope.

Mrs. Dacre herself had no great knowledge of Lollardy. She asked me if the name Wycliffe meant anything and if Oxford was the centre of the heresy. It is a matter of historical fact that at one time the religious life of Oxford was virtually in the hands of the Lollards. I think it is the only time in Oxford's long

94

and varied history that it was swept by a religious heresy. (There have been plenty of secular equivalents.) This preoccupation with Wycliffe and Oxford had come to Mrs. Dacre recently. She said that when the heresy had been clamped down on at Oxford one of Wycliffe's most ardent supporters had gone off to Scotland. He had halted in the neighbourhood of Carlisle and had arranged for the transport of the stone to its present site. "If you can find the name of the man who went to Carlisle you would be near to completing the story of the stone." This information had not been acquired by Mrs. Dacre by study. I do not know how much it derived from her own or her husband's intuitions.

She told me that Mr. Dacre, who died a few years after the Second World War, had devoted what life he spared from his business to the study of memorials of the early Celtic Church. He was not in the least a person prone to conjecture. He would have had little use for a good deal of the speculative literature devoted these days to the Celtic Church and allied subjects. He was a man given to hunches but, unlike the majority of such types, he never rested until he had proved his intuitions by examination of all the documentary and other evidence. In instructed circles he was recognised as an authority in spite of the fact that he never wrote an article or gave a single lecture on the subject. He was permitted by the savants and curators of museums to examine at length their most precious documents and exhibits because in correspondence with them he had proved the immensity of his knowledge. He had studied the factors common to the designs in the Book of Kells, the Lindisfarne Gospel and the Book of St. Chad at Lichfield. He had classified in his mind and explained to his wife the different designs in Celtic crosses. Those originating in England and Ireland were more closely interwoven. A broader pattern was favoured on the Continent. This latter statement was particularly fascinating to me. What Mr. Dacre had said was born out by what I myself saw in Croatia. He had also informed her that the addition of animals to the designs indicated Viking influences and, generally speaking, a later date to the crosses.

It fascinated me that this successful businessman, devoted to the restricted circle of his wife and only daughter, should have been such an authority on the Celtic Church. Was he, too, guided by an insistent far memory? Was his marriage to Mrs. Dacre, highly psychic and with undoubted far memory, another example of the pieces of the jigsaw fitting together? There was also the fact, revealed later in this book, that his wife, his daughter Marion and I had been closely associated in an incarnation passed chiefly in the first half of the nineteenth century. Was it surprising that later it became clear that in this life I was related to this family and that we both derived from the bleak, deserted country with gaunt hamlets and piercing visibility which begins north of Bassenthwaite and rolls by green fell and undulating pasture to the market town of Wigton?

Mr. Dacre had insisted always that the barn at W—— had been a religious meeting place. The cross had been inserted high in the wall to prevent its defacement. Clare had the same impression immediately she saw it. In the last analysis it is not a matter of Mr. Dacre and herself drawing the same conclusions at different times. In these affairs she and he looked in the same direction from the central, vibrationless node of the timeless experience.

Chapter Thirteen

After our week-end in the middle of April until early in May things began to move steadily in the direction of the Celtic incarnation. A good deal of this was achieved by the intervention of Guy who spoke of it much on his visits to Annette. On one occasion he told her that the two days' depression I had recently suffered was due to something which happened in my Celtic incarnation. This was the first evidence I had that anything in that incarnation could still affect one in this life. On another visit he told Annette that she, too, had had a Celtic incarnation. I asked her what she had looked like but, before she could answer, I said, "Stop, I'll tell you. You had auburn hair and green eyes. They were really green not hazel. They were rather witchy. You had the pale but not pasty skin that goes with that type or at least that type as I see it."

"How on earth do you know? That's just how Guy described me but actually I have seen myself like that for some time past."

"Compared with the average for that period you were rather tall."

"Yes. Do you remember what my name was? It's rather pretty."

"Aurelia," I said without a moment's hesitation.

"But how do you know?"

"Why bother? All I can say is that I have had the name and description in my mind for years."

My memories of Annette as Aurelia were sparked off by a visit to Sorrento and Rome a dozen years ago. Driving down a road which plunged between the rocks to the winter sea I thought of a girl called Aurelia. She had rich auburn hair and her eyes were deeper than sea green. She was beside me often and for months. I dismissed her as a kind of fantasy companion. This was not enough. In my novel *The Gibbet and the Cross* the heroine

97

Andrée foreshadowed the coming of Annette. She was a healer, was regarded as a witch, damaged her left ankle and was the target of a mob. The novel was published in 1971. It was revealed in 1973 that the above-mentioned items were true of Annette in her Celtic incarnation.

At this time Guy from the next world gave Annette a mass of information which she was only able to relay in fragments. It was a thousand pities that she was not so made as to keep a diary. This was too much to expect from one who scarcely ever wrote a personal letter. At that time I feared, quite needlessly, that if I tried to convert her into a scribe I would have inhibited her experiences. I know now that this would have been impossible but certainly the effort to do so would have created a problem for her. She lived two lives. In one the antennae of her psyche were floating uninhibited in the palpitating media of the next world. In the other she was a highly competent secretary. I felt that if she tried too hard and too quickly to close the gap between the practical and the intuitive sides of her nature she might produce obsessional symptoms. It is interesting that later she passed through such a phase.

Guy told Annette that the Celtic Church was primarily concerned with healing. Very often the herbs and potions were distributed from the Church itself or just outside it. The immediate environs of the church were often used for the cultivation of herbs. Then he mentioned something which, in its intimacy and commonplace nature, reverberated within me more powerfully than other more dramatic disclosures. He said that among the herbs used was one which resembled a rather delicate-leaved dock, with conspicuous pink stems. We were back to the Easter Magiant which was part of my regular spring diet as a boy. Guy said it was pounded up, boiled and made into a potion. What followed was more interesting. He said that young nettles and hawthorn leaves were also used as medicinal herbs. All these three plants were constituents of the herb pudding we were given as children. I cannot remember that any other vegetables were included in it. It seemed that what was traditional and part of my life as a child in Cumberland was based on the principles and practice of early Celtic therapy.

Clare was booked to go for a holiday with a friend to the

98

Isle of Man and the north of England. Guy instructed Annette as to what crosses Clare should see on her holiday. He was particularly anxious that she should see the cross at Maughold in the Isle of Man. He said that at Lindisfarne she would see a stone which would be of immense importance to her but that she would not realise its full significance. Guy, Braïda and Clare's father all said that she would not react to the full to what she saw on her holiday because she would be accompanied by somebody not on the same wavelength. I assumed that this would be the sole explanation of her failure to comprehend fully the stone at Lindisfarne. I did not know that much depended on what I saw on my own holiday. My wife and I had arranged to visit Yugoslavia. She had always longed to visit the Adriatic. I myself wished to see what I could of the Bogomil Tombs.* Guy told me through Annette that I should visit Trogir and Solano. He added that without Clare I would not perceive the significance of all I saw.

As a matter of fact I did better than I expected. In Croatia and on a trip to Bosnia I saw something similar to what I had observed in Cumberland the month previously. I saw equal-armed crosses enclosed in circles. There were also numerous patterns of stars similarly enclosed. Some of the stars radiated from a central circular focus and resembled daisies. I saw inter-twinings very similar to those on the Celtic crosses in Cumberland. In some of these the inwound cables were broad and gave the impression of being plaited. A striking feature of the Yugoslav patterns was that often the intertwinings ended in circular whorls.

I was ravished by the squares of Trogir which, even though beset with early visitors, emanated an atmosphere of silence and seclusion. I suppose Guy had directed me to this exquisite back-water because it was associated with the Dualist heresy and is said to have been one of the centres from which the Languedoc was missionised. I felt a stab of recollection in a small ninth-century church huddled in the shadows of bigger buildings and built from pillaged Roman columns. Above the porch outside

* The Bogomils were Balkan Dualists who preceded and outlived the Cathars.

99

there were simple designs enclosed in circles similar to what I had seen in Cumberland. I left Trogir and the fourth-century Christian cemetery at Solano with the feeling that, because of the absence of Clare, I had failed to perceive much I would have found enlightening. Had I been capable at that time of direct communication with the revenants I would have learnt more but it was not until August of the same year that I achieved a modest competence in these matters.

In spite of my limitations I gained a great deal from my visit to Yugoslavia. It was comforting to know that while in Dalmatia I had lived in an atmosphere liberally charged with Dualism. As I penetrated into Bosnia I was as near to the heart of the heresy as I had been in the Languedoc. The sight of the chalky white Bogomil tombs, themselves evocative of bleached bones, was unforgettable. They lay untended, unenclosed and on a piece of waste land. There were isolated tombs across the road from the space where the monuments were more congested. It was evident that at some time a track had been driven through them and the indifference of man added to the erosion of time and the rigours of the weather. One tomb struck me with an impact which was almost physical. On one face there was a crescent at one extremity and, at the other, the pattern of a star. Had the star been in close proximity to the crescent I would have assumed we were dealing with a Turkish emblem. I felt immediately that this was a Dualist pattern. It was really pre-cipitate to do so because the design at the left extremity was a star. I learnt only later that such designs symbolised the sun and its radiations. To me, it was immediately, and perhaps illogically, a symbolisation of the sun and moon, of light and darkness, of good and evil. I can only record that it spoke to me insistently with the silent eloquence of the stones and crosses I had seen in Cumberland.

My next total reaction was to a simple pattern of straight lines surmounted by crude circles. It recurred on several of the tombs. A month previously I had seen these on a building we came on by accident. Driving along a narrow lane in Cumberland we saw over the hedge a small ruined building, high in proportion to its width, isolated in a field and distant from the nearest village. When we entered it we found it was Ireby Old Church. The designs on one of the outer walls were the same as we saw on the Bogomil tombs.

I have described the two items which aroused in me a personal pang of recollection. In actual fact the most dramatic design was that of a man with arms outstretched and wearing a kind of skirt. This was repeated on more than one of the tombs. I had seen a similar memorial three years previously at the Yugoslav exhibition in Paris and also in a book illustration.

When we returned to England Clare brought me the spoils of her expedition to the Isle of Man and Lindisfarne. She had been enchanted by the Celtic crosses and sights in the island. Maughold spoke especially to her. She amassed a comprehensive collection of photographs, postcards and illustrated pamphlets. I was not unduly excited to see again the intertwinings terminating in concentric whorls which had struck me in Yugoslavia. Perhaps this would have been instructive to someone more erudite than myself but intertwining motifs are not uncommon and I was not unduly excited by them. What really astonished me was to find repeated the male figure dressed in a skirt which, because of its crude, wide-armed welcoming gesture, I had thought absolutely characteristic of the Bogomils.

There was still a surprise to come. Clare had been swept off her feet by the atmosphere at Lindisfarne. She spoke of it as she had done of Montségur. After she had seen the former she said, and with truth, that life would never be the same again. It was clear that Lindisfarne had had a similar effect on her. Had she lived there some time as she had at Montségur? With one exception the details and contents of Lindisfarne had little effect on her. "Only one thing struck me," she said. "There was a tomb in the museum with a star and a half moon on it. I wondered if it meant anything." She searched among her mass of material and produced a picture which reproduced, as on the Bosnian tomb, the outline of a star and the crescent clearly separate from each other. The accompanying leaflet suggested that it represented the sun and moon and drew a dainty comparison with life before and after the Christian revelation. To me it was one more representation of the light and dark which is the basis of Dualism.

I had never realised that a Slavonic cemetery could produce

101

Dualist symbols similar to those in Celtic countries. I had read somewhere that the contact between the Eastern and Celtic Churches had been much closer than was generally imagined. I had never expected to see the evidence with my own eyes. When Braïda was instructing Clare by written messages she had deviated at one time towards the Balkans. Among the names Clare had found written by her bedside were Solano and Trogarium. The latter was the ancient name for Trogir. Braïda had succeeded in demonstrating that the roots of Dualism were not only deep but spreading. It is hard to define the emotion I felt when I learnt that what I had seen in Bosnia was also to be found at Lindisfarne. There was first a general feeling of sharing something which was universal, ancient and indestructible. I had no clue at all that what I had seen was a more specific signpost to my own past.

After Clare's return from the Isle of Man and my own from Yugoslavia Annette was unusually active. She had seen Guy frequently during our absence and since our return. It was as if he had followed our footsteps and checked our progress and that she was reporting on it. He had told her that many of the star-shaped designs I had seen represented the sun. The age of a proportion of them could be told by the number of points on the stars. Some of the earliest, dating from the days of undiluted sun worship, had an even number. The Mithraic symbols were either even or uneven and acted as a bridge between the early sun worshippers and the later Dualists who affected mostly an even number of points. He said that the significance of the designs on the tombs at Solac and Lindisfarne was identical. They represented the sun and moon as the old analogy for good and evil. He said also that he and Clare had worked together at Maughold.

Jane Butler appeared also from the shadows to say that Clare had been a priestess at Maughold.

Annette confirmed what Mr. Mills had said previously that Clare's name in her Celtic incarnation had been Trubellia and my own Mercantius. She also produced as an isolated item that Graham's name had been Cornelius and he had to do with the cult of Mithras. Naturally I saw this as another memory from the Celtic incarnation because this was much in evidence at that time. I assumed that Graham was still influenced by the cult of

Mithras even as a member of the Celtic Church. In actual fact Annette had got her lines crossed and my own interpretation was faulty. She was harking back to Graham's still more distant past. It was in his Roman, frankly Mithraic incarnation that Graham had been called Cornelius. In his Celtic incarnation he was known as Davidius.

Chapter Fourteen

This story would be incomplete without reference to Annette's appalling pathological saga. She shuttled in and out of the portals of death in a way I have never known equalled. It began in the early months of 1973. She was walking down the street in the Canadian city in which she worked. She tripped over some inconsiderable projection in the pavement. It was a repetition of what had happened to her in Scotland the previous autumn. On this occasion she had, too, an equally disproportionate consequence to a trivial accident. She sustained a severe fracture of the tibia. The fracture was low down on the left side and within centimetres of the ruptured ligament for which, in Scotland, she had been encased in plaster and supplied with crutches. The doctor who examined her and diagnosed the fracture found that the bone ends were out of alignment. He attempted to readjust them and checked what he had achieved by X-ray. He told her that the displacement had been corrected. She had found the manipulation excruciatingly painful and had been considerably shocked by it. She was fitted with a temporary plaster and crutches. That evening Annette was visited by Clare and her mother. The former put one hand at the site of the fracture and another on the inner side of the knee. Braïda put one hand under Annette's foot and enfolded her big toe with the other. Annette said that she had not slept and had spoken all night with Clare and her mother. To know how long she had been awake in the presence of such visitors was a new experience for her. During most of her episodes of altered consciousness she had no sense of duration. When, in the early days of our acquaintance, she had spoken to me of Guilhabert de Castres, she did not know how long we had talked or even if we had done so.

On this occasion Clare had no knowledge of having lived an out-of-the-body experience.

The doctor saw Annette next day. He removed the temporary

plaster and repeated her X-rays. He was astonished by the result and remarkably frank in his observations to Annette. He told her that the previous day he had not succeeded in realigning the bone ends. He had abandoned his attempts to do so because he considered she had suffered enough. Nevertheless he found that, during the night, the separated fragments appeared to have slipped into place of their own volition. He realised that this was impossible. He also noted that the ugly swelling had subsided to a degree he would never have anticipated. He told Annette that there was something miraculous about the whole proceeding.

Doctor Paul was exceptionally gifted. He realised immediately that Annette's make-up was unusual and that her response to treatment would be influenced by it. He ordered another X-ray in the course of a few days. This was not orthodox procedure as he was by now satisfied that the bone ends were perfectly aligned. He was astonished to find that callus formation had already begun. The healing process was far away in advance of what could have been expected. His reaction was twofold. He decided that Annette was the target of healing influences independent of the orthodox procedures of medicine. He also believed that she was a potential healer in her own right. It was extraordinary that a young doctor in a new, pioneering, positively materialistic country, and on the staff of a world-famous hospital, should have slipped immediately outside the frontiers of orthodox medicine in assessing the make-up of Annette. That he was right was revealed by specialist evidence. Braïda appeared to Clare and told her that Annette's duty was to be a healer but that before she embarked on her career she would suffer some unavoidable tribulations. Out of respect for our feelings she did not enlarge on their nature.

When Annette had left for Canada the previous autumn I had felt a sense of acute deprivation, because I knew we had been intimately connected in an earlier incarnation and because I was deprived of the sight of her in this. Always I had thought of her as she had been in her Cathar incarnation. Now I wondered whether we had known each other in yet another life. Certainly we seemed to be drawing closer together for she rang me to say that I had materialised at her bedside while Clare and Braïda were treating her leg. Since my last appearance in this role she had seen a photograph of me. It seemed I had changed little since my Cathar incarnation except that I was paunchy and my hair was white.

During one of her phone calls I asked her if she thought that the two accidents to her left ankle were an echo of something which had happened in a previous incarnation. "Oh, yes," she answered, "I remember *that*. I was running down a hill away from a mob. I caught my foot in a thick strand of bramble or bryony or something. I fell an awful clatter and my ankle was badly damaged."

"Why the mob?" I said.

"They thought I was a witch."

"Why a witch?"

"Because I was always making potions. Because I practised healing." The whole thing was coming to the surface.

However much we seemed to be on the verge of a new enlightenment we were actually moving into the shadows. At the end of May she ran into a patch of depression which was clearly attributable to her memories of the massacre at Avignonet in the same month in 1242. The other members of the group were also acutely affected. Annette suffered from her own far memory and also from the depression she picked up from the rest of us. She pulled round at the beginning of June. When she rang me from London en route for Germany she was joyful and loquacious. I was also happy because there was a prospect that she might be able to visit Bath on her return. At this stage she was flying up and down the world with her boss as his confidential secretary.

Next day I woke up in the middle of the night acutely depressed and with a feeling that some disaster was imminent. I fell asleep again. When I woke for the second time I was in no better shape. Going downstairs to breakfast I felt in my nostrils the sweet and pervasive odour of balsam poplar. The whole atmosphere was penetrated by it. Balsam poplar was the odour by which Braïda announced herself when she had no intention of materialising. She had adopted this stratagem to communicate her presence to Clare when the latter was surrounded by people and when Braïda did not wish to reveal herself visually. I wondered what was portending.

106

Three days later we had Clare for drinks and dinner. She had one of her absences in which she appeared to be looking into the distance but in which, at the same time, the light seemed to drain from her luminous eyes. This is a phenomenon which at first sight could be mistaken for *petit mal* (minor epilepsy) but which I know from experience is not an interruption of consciousness but its direction to another plane. Next morning I had a phone call from Annette in Brussels. Her boss had driven her the day previously to the field of Waterloo but she had felt so ill she had not descended from the car. On her return to Brussels in the evening she fainted some time between 7.00 and 7.30. It was during this period that Clare had suffered from her "absence".

Annette rang next day to say she had arrived in London en route for New York. She was now feeling a little better but still seedy. I told her that if she felt ill she should stay where she was. She felt sick, exhausted and generally ill. She had vomited on more than one occasion but had had no pain to speak of. I wondered what she could be suffering from. I imagined she was unused to the rich food and good wines of the exclusive restaurants to which she had been taken by her boss and that also she had been exhausted by too much long-distance flying. The latter can be toxic to the psychic. It dislocates the time sequence in people already liable to slip from one century to another.

The next day my wife complained of a pain in the abdomen. This had been brewing up for a few days but had not been of any intensity. That day it was worse and she looked grey and exhausted by it. In addition she had waves of nausea in which she changed colour and half fainted. I had the usual lugubrious thoughts which afflict doctors these days when their wives have abdominal pains. My most cheerful diagnosis was a variety of intestinal spasm. I thought also of a gynaecological condition. The pain was on the right side. The abdomen was distended especially that side and I wondered if she had a rapidly expanding ovarian cyst. She had had her appendix removed at the age of sixteen.

Clare laid one hand on the painful area and the other at the point recommended by the Cathars in the neighbourhood of the right knee. The hand on my wife's abdomen was vibrating to a degree that was almost audible. I wondered if the healing processes were operating with increasing intensity or if this indicated there was a lesion of ominous significance beneath her fingers.

On returning home Clare heard her phone ringing as she went upstairs. She rushed to it and took down a cable from New York. Paul said that Annette had had an emergency operation for appendicitis. I did not connect my wife's symptoms with Annette's condition. There was no reason for me to do so because my wife was not a member of the group and not liable to pick up one of its members' symptoms. In addition she had had her appendix removed. This constituted some impediment to her feeling pain in the organ afflicted in Annette's case.

It soon became clear that the cable Clare had received was merely a formal and dutiful report of an emergency. A little later I had a call from New York from someone I had never met but who knew Annette and was aware that she phoned me often. Jesse said that Annette was desperately ill. The appendicitis had only been a courtesy title for her condition. She had had a ruptured appendix abcess which had given rise to a severe and widespread peritonitis. She was barely conscious. It was clear that she was not responding to antibiotics. From the contemporary clinical standpoint the outlook was black. I clung to the hope that someone, in this world or the next, would intervene on her behalf. I knew they had the capacity to do so but was it inexorably traced in the pattern that Annette's days were numbered? I slogged away at my daily tasks and jumped in my skin when the telephone rang.

I felt for Annette as though I had known her all my life. It made no difference that I had never seen her. I did not ponder at all the pitiless irony of the situation by which I was, it seemed, to be robbed of someone close to me for seven centuries and who seemed to be departing without my having had a moment's sight of her. In those days, which, as I recall them, seem only half real, a nightmare dream in another life, I had no thought for anything other than Annette's predicament and her isolation in another country.

That night Clare was visited by Graham. He said that everything was being done by the doctors and that he, Clare and myself had also been with her. I noted dimly that this was my first contact with him. I was only concerned that I had been with Annette. Braïda reported to Clare that she would soon be completely unconscious.

The day following there was another call from the girl in New York who had phoned previously. Annette had gone finally into coma. By every reasonable standard the end was near. Further comment in the case was offered by Mr. Mills. He visited Clare and said that Annette was suffering from this illness because "something had to be freed in her". It was often like that before a new revelation or a big step forward. Annette had an important rôle to play in this life. Mr. Mills was repeating what Braïda and Raymond Agulher had said when they told us that someone new and much younger was being added to the group. Mr. Mills said that Annette could not fulfil her predestined function without the enlightenment and fresh insight conferred by her illness. I could not believe that we would have been informed of Annette's importance to the group if it had been ordained that she should die. Clare also saw Braïda. The latter said that she would not be returning to Clare for some time because it was necessary to stay with Annette who would deteriorate still further before she improved.

From the very beginning of Annette's illness other members of the group who had not met her had picked up the SOS signals emanating from her. Marion's mother Mrs. Dacre, destined never to meet Annette, rang me the day she was operated on to say that she could not get me out of her thoughts and that she knew I was greatly troubled about someone.

The most agonising moment of this vigil at a distance of 3000 miles was when Dr. Paul rang Clare to say that Annette was now passing into an even deeper coma. She had no near relatives in the world. He wished to know what funeral arrangements should be made. He himself thought that she should be cremated and her ashes sent to England. To hear this kind of message over the transatlantic phone was a shattering experience for Clare. It is profitless to imagine the feelings of Dr. Paul who was by now devoted to Annette.

Next evening Clare came to supper. She asked me if I could detect a very sweet smell in the room. She said it resembled the perfume of roses, something, she said, like Ena Harkness. I had done so for a few minutes at intervals. She perceived it continually. I knew by now that one of the discarnate entities was present. They announced themselves sometimes by smell and particularly when it was inopportune for them to materialise visually. Clare said she was aware of Graham but could not see him. Perhaps he thought me too underdeveloped to benefit from seeing him.

Suddenly Clare leapt up from her seat, her face and eyes radiant, and said "Annette is going to get better." She insisted on leaving immediately afterwards. I knew by now that these precipite departures meant further revelations. She arrived in time for a call from New York. Dr. Paul said that Annette had rallied from her coma but as yet she did not recognise anybody. He said that the change was miraculous. He admitted that when he had rung previously about the funeral arrangements she was regarded as actually sinking.

Next day Graham appeared to Clare. She confirmed that he had been with us the previous evening when we perceived the smell of roses. He said that Annette was doing well. He was more specific about her future than Braïda and Raymond Agulher. He stressed that she would fulfil her destiny in the rôle of healer.

He also spoke a good deal of oak trees. He said the oak had always been the symbol of light and goodness. He went on from the discussion of oaks and acorns to the Celtic incarnation. He said that he, Clare and I had been priests. We had lived during the period when the Celtic Church was becoming Romanised and cluttered up with ceremonial. We three made a group devoted to a predominant degree to healing. We were practitioners of an old tradition in virtue of which we functioned more as healers and sages than as priests. When we had entered the priesthood there was little in the way of ceremonial and sacraments. The sermons were not centred round ethical subjects but designed to create a certain atmosphere and encourage a particular attitude towards life. They were concerned with the indivisibility of consciousness and of the common life we shared with animals and plants. As far as possible Clare, Graham and I had continued the traditions. We gave lectures rather than sermonised and our themes were liberally sprinkled with analogies from nature.

I had an unforgettable experience on an overcast and torpid Sunday morning in mid-June. When the phone rang there was a long delay after I removed the receiver. Then I heard a voice with an American accent saying gently but firmly, "Now only for a short time." Then I heard a husky whisper. It was as though a weak voice was whispering from the depths of a cavern that gave back no echo. "Love to you and Aunty Mary," she said. "I am full of drips and what have you. I hope to come to the U.K. soon. Thank you for all you have done to help me."

I cannot remember what I said to Annette. The whole experience was too astounding for description. It occurred less than a week after the discussion of the arrangements for her funeral. It was truly like a voice from the grave. I felt deeply for her in spite of the fact that the whole experience was dreamlike. It was astonishing to me that the doctors allowed her to put through a telephone call when she was still so completely drained of vitality. I had unkind thoughts about transatlantic medicine and the exhaustion imposed on patients by the new enlightenment. In this I was entirely wrong. The whole length of her *via dolorosa* Annette was managed not only with skill but with exceptional insight by her doctors. They sensed immediately that she was no ordinary girl. It was clear that from the beginning Dr. Paul realised that her relationship with me was unusual and that I was neither an ageing satyr nor a bland and succulent father-figure made to a recipe of Freud.

In the next week Annette rang two or three times. They were short calls but they acted as lifelines. I could not understand why, in this no-man's-land between life and death, she preferred to ring me rather than Clare. She had made no bones about her veneration for the latter. It was clear to the whole world that Clare meant more to her than anyone else. She turned to me because we had spoken together on so many subjects in previous incarnations. She had been as inveterate a natterer in her Cathar and Celtic lives as she was in the twentieth century. One of the doctors who was to look after her later told me that he was sure that when she was critically ill she preferred to talk to me rather than to anyone else. At this stage in her life the influence of the past was stronger than that of her affections in the present.

While Annette was gradually and painfully fighting her way back to the half-life imposed by her great weakness there were significant events on other fronts. My wife's pain in her right lower abdomen intensified. A consultant was called in in due course. I had the greatest respect for his skill and humanity. I considered him the most competent and understanding in the region. After he had examined her we discussed several alternative diagnoses. These included gynaecological conditions like ovarian cyst and adhesions from a repair operation performed on my wife many years previously for a uterine prolapse. He also considered the possibility of referred pain from a gall bladder. The consideration of these alternatives was only to be expected from a doctor as competent and conscientious as my colleague. What baffled me was his preoccupation with the scar of her appendix. He pointed out that, though the pain tended to vary from day to day in its distribution, it was apt to concentrate round the lower third of this scar. He wondered if there were adhesions in the appendix area. He suggested tentatively that she might have strained these in the course of gardening. In spite of my admiration for him and gratitude to him—he had looked after me admirably when I was gravely ill—I found this preoccupation with the appendix pernickety and academic. I did not see that, at some level of consciousness, he was seeing more clearly than I. My wife was duly X-rayed. All the pictures revealed was a partial leakage of a valve in the intestines. I translated this finding as excluding all possibility of pain arising from the appendix scar. Was it likely that she looked so pale and tired and that she should feel suddenly sick and collapsed because of a lesion connected with an ancient scar?

Across the water Guy appeared regularly to Annette. Sometimes he came with her mother and sometimes with Graham. The latter was coming more and more into the picture. I did not see it at the time because my attention was concentrated mostly on the female revenants. The latter recognised this distinctive trait in my character. The plain fact is that the Mother Goddess means more to me than the masculine deity. Though I myself have an excess of male logic I prefer to be guided by female intuition. Guy repeated to Annette what Graham had told Clare about the Celtic Church. I found Clare a better witness. In what she received from the revenants Annette lacked the capacity to distinguish between important and minor issues. Or was it merely that she had become so accustomed to talking to Braïda that she regarded what she heard as of everyday significance?

One message from Guy appeared to be of particular importance. He told Annette to ask me "If I remembered the ring". I expended a good deal of energy wondering if he referred to the kind of ring I had worn in my Cathar incarnation. Annette rang again next day. Guy had revisited her and reproved her for her carelessness. The ring he had mentioned was a circular clearing in a forest in which I and others had practised healing. I was convinced that this was the circular clearing in the wood I had seen when I had visited St. Bega's church in April. We were steering as confidently as ever in the direction of Bassenthwaite. In the course of the next two weeks the issue was to be settled beyond doubt.

On the other side of the water Graham's visits became more frequent. I had told Clare that I thought that, in the Celtic incarnation, she and I had been of Romano-British rather than purely Celtic stock. I felt we were the offspring, I do not know how many generations back, of Roman soldiers or administrators intermarried with the original population. Both Graham and Braïda confirmed that this was so. This leap in the dark on my part is not necessarily to be ascribed to intuitive gifts. I knew well enough by now that what I had thought my brighter ideas were implanted in my mind by Braïda in particular and, on special occasions, by Guilhabert de Castres. Graham also confirmed that the Celtic names of Clare, himself and myself were Trubellia, Davidius and Mercantius respectively. Braïda had also been a priestess in the Celtic incarnation. Her name was Euse
She was much older than the rest of us.

Graham was chiefly occupied in visiting Clare but at this ti he insisted on closer contact with me. At this time Jane appeare to Clare and told her that the visits of the revenants were determined to a large extent by which incarnation was looming uppermost. One day Clare visited and gave me treatment for an attack of bronchitis. (It had been foretold by Braïda that for a year or more I would be subject to this condition when I was depressed.) She laid one hand on the apex of one lung. She held my thumb with her other hand. On previous occasions when having treatment, I had felt in my skin the sensation of heat and tingling and had seen and felt her arms vibrating. These phenomena were almost always accompanied by a feeling of deep relaxation. On this occasion, after two minutes, I felt myself invaded by a force so powerful that I could hardly tolerate it. It was as though I had been placed too close to a battery emitting rays I was unable to support. At the same time I felt a kind of curving arc of pressure on the back of my neck. This was accompanied by a sensation of deeper, more penetrating heat. "Is anyone else giving me treatment?" I asked.

"Yes, Graham. Where do you feel it?"

"At the back of my neck."

"Where else?" she said.

"Is his other hand on my forehead?"

"Yes."

"I don't feel it so well."

She moved away. I was scarcely aware of the lost contact with her hands. The deep, penetrating heat continued at the back of my neck. I felt his other hand more distinctly on my forehead. Then I felt a sudden burning and a heavy pressure in the solar plexus. I said, "Has he moved one hand again?"

"Yes. Where?"

"Above the solar plexus."

I lay in silence for I do not know how long. The heavy pressure and deep heat of his hand were above my heart. "Has he moved it over my heart?" I said.*

"Yes."

I was aware when Graham left us. There was no longer the feeling of a great and palpable force vibrating in the room. It was as though the wind had fallen.

My depression had gone when I awoke next morning. My cough had almost disappeared. When Clare rang she told me that Graham had visited me last night but that I had been unaware of it. He had paid me this extra visit because it was

* Compared with that of the other revenants Graham's touch was particularly heavy.

the anniversay of Waterloo—this was a side glance at the Napoleonic incarnation—and also because I was reacting by my depression to something tragic which had happened in the Celtic incarnation. Certainly his visits had dispelled my *cafard*.

After that I was visited frequently by Graham. He treated me on several occasions and I was aware always of the weight of his hands and of the heat and strength which emanated from them. I learned from him, sometimes directly, sometimes through Clare, how the laying on of hands had varied in the Celtic and Cathar incarnations. In the former the priests had laid one hand above where the disease process was manifested and the other on one of the great nerve plexuses, the cervical in the neck, the solar in the pit of the stomach, and the lumbar in the small of the back. This interested me because this method seemed in some way based on Hindu lore. The Celtic system appeared at first sight to differ radically from the Cathars. In the latter the hand not over the affected area was placed on certain bony points. This had always puzzled me. It seemed more rational that the position of the hand should be determined by proximity to the nervous or circulatory systems which permeated the whole substance of the body, the one through its nerve channels and the other by means of its arteries and veins. Then I saw that in actual fact the Cathar technique was merely a refinement of the Celtic system. Near the selected bony points all the great nerves arising from the plexuses came nearer to the surface. It was merely a question of the level at which one trapped the available energy of the nervous system.

At this time there were two themes which preoccupied Annette. These were centred round Loweswater and Bassenthwaite. Before our excursion to Cumberland in April Braïda had indicated that Loweswater was very important to me. She now returned to the theme and Guy seconded her efforts on his visits to Annette. The latter remembered living in a hut and sleeping on a bed of moss and bracken. She recalled that she wore a simple and shapeless gown made of some kind of sacking. She said it resembled hessian. It was a green-brown colour with a simple U-shaped neck. She remembered how she found it uncomfortable against her skin. She was constantly busy preparing potions. She prepared these in a cauldron over a perpetual turf fire. She was a healer and differed from her fellow practitioners in that she prepared her potions fresh for each patient and did not keep stocks of each. She gathered the herbs as required and made frequent trips to the lake to replenish the cauldron with water.

I asked her if the lake was Bassenthwaite. She said that this was impossible because she had stayed a fortnight at the Pheasant Inn on her honeymoon and would have known immediately had it appeared again in a vision.

She remembered a tall woman, at least tall for that age, with black hair down to her waist and a very wrinkled face. At the second showing she recognised this woman as her mother. The latter was very fond of her daughter but did not live with her. She regarded her as disorganised and messy and considered that she did not feed herself properly. Her mother made food for her and brought it to her.

Annette's mother disapproved of her freelance healing. Medicine was very much a preoccupation of the priesthood but Annette did not see things their way and practised on her own. She loathed the new rituals introduced into the Church and was very much up against the authorities. Her mother would have preferred a more compliant daughter. She looked after her to the best of her ability but would not live with her.

Annette's hut was in a wood where a path from the fells descended to the track by the lake. There were other dwellings about a mile away. When she spoke of the hut in which she lived I felt sure I knew its location. I have described elsewhere how, in my boyhood, I was always obsessed by the house by the lake at Loweswater and how, to me, all my life before I went to Oxford could be symbolised and compressed in a summer morning spent sitting on the jetty farther down the road. It was on the path ascending from the road by the lake and going past the house that I had my experience of the force of evil. On a fine summer day, with no menace in the air and no ripple on the lake, I was stabbed by panic through the solar plexus. I bolted back to the road by the lake. Half a century later I was told, by the owner of the house, that twenty years previously a horse had bolted at that point and killed its rider. It was fascinating that Annette had lived so near to the place where I had panicked in my young

116

manhood. I still regarded my fear on that occasion as a sword thrust from the Cosmos. I did not know that I was personally involved, that I was hearing the echoes of an old disaster.

In a few days Annette had remembered everything. She had been descending the path from the hills when the mob came towards her from the thick bracken already rusty with September. She ran towards her hut with the fell on her left, a few clumps of birch on its lower slopes. To the right was the forest and below it the wood and lake beyond. She was running desperately but still ahead of the pack when she tripped over a thick, twisted stem. She had mentioned this incident in an earlier more fragmentary recall. She fell headlong and felt an excruciating pain in her left ankle. She was unable to rise.

I had called at her hut and found her absent. I heard the baying and chattering of the pack and ran through the trees and came to the path. I saw her lying on the grass. She was pallid with fear and her eyes were blazing. The mob held back when they saw me. I was dressed in my priest's robes, dark purple with a hood. As a priest, even though a variety becoming rapidly discredited, I still had some authority over them. They respected me for the worst possible motives, as a purveyor of magic. I pulled Annette to her feet. She could only stand on one leg. I supported her injured side as she hopped towards the hut. As we entered there were yells and imprecations outside, then an audible rumbling of hate and afterwards the sound of receding footsteps.

Talking to her over the phone to Canada I asked her why we had been left unmolested inside the hut. "We were safe within four walls," she said. "They believed I was a witch and that in my house I could put the 'fluence on them."

"Why did they think you were a witch?"

"Because I went about healing."

"I thought the Celtic Church rather specialised in healing."

"So they did but they didn't want anything to do with me. I was out on my own. They had started a lot of ceremonials and sacraments and I wouldn't have anything to do with it. I expect I was obstinate. You know I still am." (She was right in this. There were times when her devotion to some particular *idée fixe* could be exasperating.) "They didn't like the way I made up my

117

potions fresh. They thought that was really witchcraft. The others gave them the medicines out of stock as it were. Of course there was one particular priest who egged them on. He had it in for you. Wherever you went he followed after and said the dead opposite."

"Was he a pale, fanatical-looking fellow with a triangular face?"

"Yes. Have you seen him too?"

"Did he have a sharp, nasty profile like a bird of prey and a wiry thatch of very black hair?"

"How did you know?"

"About three years ago I scribbled rapidly a story of a woman addicted to the cult of Mithras and martyred by a mob inflamed by a Christian priest. This was obviously the fellow I saw. It seems I got the incarnations mixed up. My story was set during the decadence of Rome. This fellow was operating at Loweswater in the seventh century A.D."

"That's funny. Guy is always telling me that Graham has had to do with the cult of Mithras."

"Why are you so sure that this took place at Loweswater?"

"I have seen myself many times running down this track and it is always the same, the fell to the left, the wood to the right, a hut in the wood and the track below the house and the lake by the track. There was also a flat stone on the road where I used to sit looking at the lake. It was the place Guy and I picnicked the day we went to Loweswater on our honeymoon."

"Did you actually fracture your ankle at Loweswater?"

"I can't remember. I know it was bruised and painful and horrible to look at and that I couldn't walk on it. You were frightfully skilful."

"What did I do?"

"You put your hands on it and dressed it with some kind of lotion soaked in a kind of moss." (This would be the staghorn moss which so excited me as a child and which was used as an absorptive dressing for wounds as late as the beginning of the First World War.)

"Your left foot seems to be your weak spot. In this life, within a few months, you have been twice on crutches for trouble with your ankle."

118

"I am a bit of a clot. Uncle Mills used to always tell me to pick my feet up."

I did not know that we were far from finished with Annette's left foot.

"What happened after I had dressed your ankle?"

"You got Guy to see me."

"Did he live at Loweswater?"

"No, near a little hill by another lake."

"I expect it was Bassenthwaite."

"Why?" she asked.

"Because we cannot get away from Bassenthwaite. You had to go there for your honeymoon. You went out of this world on the road by the lake. So many other people had odd experiences at the same spot."

"I expect mummy will say something about it sooner or later." (In this she was completely right.) "Anyway I went away with you, Guy and Clare to a place on a hill. There was some sort of building where they practised healing."

"We won't have to wait long to know," I said.

There was no doubt in my mind that, when I bolted down the path that summer afternoon, I was reliving Annette's experiences as a fugitive. Not only this but when I stayed in the house by the water in the early 1970s I was afflicted by a sense of impending horror. I suppose you could call it an anxiety depression except that I only felt it when I was in the house or its vicinity. It stopped immediately I was clear of the modern plantation on the road to Kirkstile. It never afflicted me while I was out wandering the country by day and only descended like a suffocating curtain when I returned to the house in the evening. This was one of those cases where one's emotional responses are permissible as evidence. My childhood and boyhood reactions to this place fitted in perfectly with Annette's story. There was the house, more silent than ever in the years at the beginning of the century. There was the jetty on which I had sat as a boy watching the shadows of the pines lengthen on the water and the somnolence of afternoon unfolding like a cloud around the hunched shoulders of Melbreak. A few minutes from the decomposing and deserted jetty was the path descending between the green fells. It was strange that I, an omnivorous explorer, had

119

never walked the few paces up from the road except on that single occasion when the past went through me like an arrow. It was clear that in my childhood and early boyhood I had been armed to withstand the experience.

I told Annette what had happened to me in my late teens. "Isn't it strange," she said, "but how nice to know we knew each other even in those days." At this stage she had a childish way of personalising everything. I suppose it was in part the effect of her grossly debilitated condition. Her life at this time was being lived in compartments. There was, on the one hand, the everyday, spaced-out and organised monotony of a flagging convalescence and, on the other, a torrent of memories sweeping through the channels of her unconscious. The dam of her inhibition had yielded at last to the eroding force of her varied diseases.

Annette broke off her recollections of Loweswater to ask after my wife. For some weeks now she had looked forward to talking to her. It was odd how excited she was to speak to a woman forty years her senior and whom she had never met. She referred to her automatically and without self-consciousness as Aunt Mary. I told Annette that my wife was still suffering from the pain in her right side. "She gets this because of my appendicitis and all the trouble that followed it."

I was not sure that Annette was right because she and my wife had not shared an incarnation. In my experience with this group it was this fact which, more than any other, determined whether people acquired each other's symptoms. "You really think that?" I said.

"Yes, I do, but I didn't think so at first. It was mummy who told me that Aunty Mary was suffering for me."

"If Braïda said so it must be right."

What Annette had remembered through her own far memory of Loweswater and her ignominious departure from it was confirmed to her later by Braïda and Guy. Clare heard it also from Braïda and Graham. I learnt a good deal of what we were like at that time. Annette, as Aurelia, with her deep-green eyes and her auburn hair illuminated by red lights, was a striking figure. She was in her early twenties. She was a controversial, uncompromising person. In some respects her resemblance to herself in

120

this incarnation is almost laughable. She displays in some matters an undeviating obduracy unaccompanied by any great show of truculence. It is merely that she hurls herself at the first available, and often highest, fence and seems surprised when she comes a cropper. On issues important to her she says the first thing which comes to her head and what she says is frequently outrageous. At these times she could be written off as lacking in flair but your truly tactless person is often an egocentric. Annette passed, as many do, through a self-centred phase after her disastrous illnesses but no dyed-in-the-wool egocentric could attract the love which she evokes from a diversity of creatures. One of the doctors who looked after her during her five months' spell in and out of one of the major hospitals of the New World told me that, in whatever state of dilapidation she returned as an in-patient, the staff were ridiculously happy to see her again.

When Annette first knew us in the Celtic incarnation Clare and I were just over thirty. Clare had the same luminous eyes as in all her incarnations but their colour was different. It was hazel instead of blue. According to Annette's description I was "dark-haired, rather chubby-faced and not very tall". Graham was tallish for that period. He had broad shoulders but was slimly made. He was a good-looking fellow with dark hair, blue eyes and a sombre expression. Guy was shorter and fair-haired. Braïda was round about sixty. So far Betty had not come into the picture.

There was additional evidence that the path descending towards the road at Loweswater was ill-omened for our group. Annette recalled her experience on it in midsummer 1973. In the autumn of the same year Clare provided equally varied but more ugly evidence. Braïda had warned Annette a few days previously that Clare would soon have an unpleasant experience. She said that she hoped she would not be alone on this occasion. The day before the event Braïda appeared to Clare and told her that she should be sure to see me the following day. She was ensuring that Clare should not be alone during her ordeal and also that there should be a witness of it.

During Clare's visit her eyes closed suddenly. Her expression became blank and her trunk sagged forward. She slithered face downwards from the couch to the floor. In my younger days I would have said this was the kind of minor epilepsy where there is a transient interruption of consciousness. The patient does not necessarily fall but sometimes does; there are no convulsions. The position Clare assumed on the floor was a natural consequence of her fall. Then I noticed that her back began to twitch. I had no fear of a major convulsive disturbance. Her legs and arms were not rigid and her body was not generally spastic. It was merely a localised twitching of the muscles across the centre of her back. I did not consider the type of epilepsy called myoclonic, which is accompanied by isolated muscle contractions, because the position of these twitching movements was not characteristic. A little later each tremor of her dorsal muscles was accompanied by a positive ducking movement of the back. It was as though she was flinching from a fusillade of blows. Her breath quickened and became heavy and her face congested. When she opened her eyes, her pupils were large and dark. "There are lots of horrible people coming at me," she cried. "They are beating me with sticks."

She presented for all the world the appearance of a person emerging from an epileptoid disturbance. One could have said, erroneously, that she had suffered a complete interruption of consciousness. What she had experienced was the direction of consciousness to another plane, in this particular instance to another age. It was not the first time I had seen her, or was to see her, in such a condition. When she had returned to everyday consciousness she told me the story. She had been descending the path from Mosser between the hills at Loweswater. Although she had never been up the path she described the surroundings perfectly and in greater detail than Annette. Actually there were a few details of the scene which came to me directly, between her attack and her description of it. I saw that the bracken was turning colour and the season was early autumn. It had also been raining. There were runnels of water at the sides of the path.

As she descended the path Clare had been set upon by a mob emerging from the wood to the right and from thick bracken and bushes on the fell to the left. She had been knocked down, kicked and beaten with sticks. As they withdrew, her attackers threw stones at her and left her for dead. She had, in fact, suffered a worse fate than Annette and in the same place. She was something over thirty at the time and may not have been so mobile as Annette and so unable to escape from her persecutors.

Clare was rescued by Graham. He had been visiting Annette and knew that Clare had been going to talk to the people of the valley. He carried her to Annette's hut and once again the people desisted because of his authority as a priest. They were not aware of the degree to which Graham was upsides with the authorities and out of favour with them. They also recoiled at entering Annette's hut. To trap her outside was one thing. To enter within the orbit of concentrated black magic was quite another.

The circumstances which provoked the attack on Clare come under two headings. The effect of the Romanisation of the Celtic Church was to reduce the emphasis on healing. It had formerly been regarded as of such importance that Guy had been able to tell Annette, on one of his visits to her in Canada, that Christ was primarily a healer and had wished the anonymity which goes with the calling. The Evangelists used his power to heal and his gift of emanation to facilitate the dissemination of his teachings.

The swing to Rome involved an intensification of sacraments, ceremonial and the practice of the liturgy at the expense of healing and the simple discourses derived from analogies with nature. It was indeed suggested by the ultra-Romanised clergy that healing was a form of witchcraft. They wished to denigrate anything which could be thought occult and which could be considered as competing with the strong magic of the Holy Sacrament, with its insistence on Transubstantiation and the rationed bestowal of the body and blood of the Saviour. To the Rome-trained new entry the bestowal of grace, transmitted by the magic of the sacraments, was the perquisite of ecclesiastics specially trained to offer salvation in graduated doses. This was entirely different from the Celtic conception of healing as a manifestation of the total force of goodness, disseminated liberally in nature, and acting totally on the sick and suffering through people who functioned as passive instruments because they were born with a certain constitution.

123

The Romanised clergy were also inclined to regard healing as witchcraft because so many of those who practised it were women. In Cumberland there were as many priestesses as priests and, as we shall see later, Betty was the authorised leader in her region. In my story I record three assaults on women healers by mobs inflamed by the priesthood. No male priest suffered in this matter. When, later, I was knocked about by ordinary hoodlums on the road to Lindisfarne, they were instigated by the relatively innocent motive of loot.

Our part in this fluctuating state of affairs is simple to define but was difficult to live. To Clare, Graham and myself healing was our chief function. We paid lip service to the new order but were separated off from its principal practitioners who were steadily and inexorably taking over in Cumberland. We were out of favour and there was literally no future for us. Guy was more acceptable to the authorities because he was not particularly interested in healing. (During his many visits to Annette since his death in the twentieth century I can only trace his having given her healing on a single occasion and then only one of its most basic forms at a time when she was agitated.) It was a great comfort to us that Betty, first and foremost a healer, was still in a position of authority.

When I asked Braïda if at this time there was positive persecution she said very firmly, "Yes." It was limited mostly to the cold-hearted expulsion of devoted priests of the older persuasion or to hot-blooded excesses committed by the rabble at the instigation of the Romanists. Certainly there was no recognised torture or burning at the stake. The standard of education in the Dark Ages did not permit the refinements of the rack and stake which, centuries later, were inevitable components of the international theocracy dictated from Rome. The old faith was on the way out in Cumberland in the middle of the seventh century and we went out with it. Isolated pockets of resistance existed until the beginning of the eighth century.

Clare had a clear recollection of the immediate precipitating causes for the attack on her. I had recently delivered some sort of oration in the locality. She could not recall my subject. What she remembered was that a day or two after I had spoken the pale, twitching, triangular-faced priest had addressed an audience in the same place and contradicted everything I had said. After he had delivered his address he hung about in the neighbourhood. Clare had also conducted a meeting of her own. She had spoken of the nature of good and evil. The audience had been conditioned by the priest to misinterpret the import of what she said. She sealed her fate by speaking also of the old Celtic deities. She had said that it was sad that the Church had dispensed with these natural intermediaries between God and man. She had said also that there were hierarchies of different orders of development between us on this earth and a God transcending time and space. The Romanised priest, when he was not frothing at the mouth with indignation, described these ancient gods and goddesses as evil and pagan and, worst of all, as lacking in power compared to the Roman god with his accessible and potent sacramental magic and the supreme blood sacrifice of his only son. Probably the priest's main motive for instigating the attack on Clare was his hatred of women and above all for women as priests. This attitude is still with us.

The path where Annette and Clare were attacked goes from Mosser to Loweswater. I only saw once the church in the former place. This was at least fifty years ago. I have retained from my single visit a recollection of great sanctity. I have written somewhere that perhaps the church at Mosser was a focus of goodness which attracted the shadow of evil. Perhaps we are concerned with a more specific factor. Did Clare preach her sermon at Mosser?

The day after this lacerating experience Clare told me that Graham and I had visited her the previous night. The former had appeared in his dark-purple robes as a Celtic priest. I was dressed in the deep royal blue of the Cathar incarnation. He had given Clare the Celtic form of healing using the great nerve plexuses. I placed one hand on each big toe. This treatment was employed because she had complained of loss of power to move her legs after the beatings she had endured. In my out-of-the-body form I had spoken to her of the controversial issues which resulted in her ordeal on the road from Mosser. I said it was a great pity we had abandoned the Celtic conception of many gods and that to me the doctrine that monotheism was a great spiritual advance was fallacious. The idea of a supreme being was understandable but we needed other entities to make contact with him. It was interesting that, in this life, I have only recently caught up with what I believed in my Celtic incarnation.

Annette phoned the same day to pass on a message from Braïda. The latter had said that Clare's experience the previous evening was not ordinary far memory but an intensification of it. There was a difference between remembering something and reliving it. It would be necessary for Clare to undergo other similar experiences. I thought it was a gruesome prospect. Now I understood clearly why in ancient Greece and elsewhere the oracles and particularly the female prophetesses were regarded as epileptics. I had seen how Clare's insight into the past had been accompanied by an amended state of awareness which, to a doctor as well as a layman, could appear as a total loss of consciousness and which could justifiably be regarded as epileptic. I had heard her cry out. Certainly it was not the strident screeching of the epileptic induced by spasm of the larynx, but the whole picture gave me an understanding of how, in ancient times, epilepsy came to be regarded as the sacred disease. Surely this was because many of those with insight into the past and future retreated for varying periods from ordinary consciousness.

After the attack on Clare we went off to Bassenthwaite. I did not know whether this was merely a temporary measure but I am inclined to believe that from that date we installed ourselves in and around Castle How more or less permanently. Certainly the latter site was the heart and centre of the Celtic Church in that area of Cumberland. Before I describe our life at Castle How it is necessary to return exclusively to Annette because it was through her sufferings that we learned much about our life at Bassenthwaite.

Chapter Fifteen

After Annette came back from the grave following her peritonitis she passed through a long period of fluctuating convalescence. It was very natural that she should be extremely weak after her experience and her doctors were not greatly disturbed during the first two weeks after she was resurrected from her coma. During this time she was affectionate, grateful and remarkably cheerful. Later she was forced to admit that there was no life in her. As the weeks went by it became clear that she was still very feeble. She could not walk a hundred paces without being completely exhausted. Two features of her condition were paramount. She had a marked anaemia. This was understandable in that while in hospital and during and following her peritonitis, her food intake had been negligible. Secondly, she had a cough with expectoration and was recorded as running a temperature. She was given antibiotics and the response was sluggish.

It was heart-rending to hear from her that she was due to return to the operating theatre for a bronchoscopy. She was dreading this unpleasant proceeding. She rang up, soberly and quietly, but hoping desperately to receive from me some impalpable injection of courage. It was discovered that she had had a pulmonary embolus, very evidently during the period when she was comatose. A pulmonary embolus is the lodging of a clot, similar to that which gives rise to coronary thrombosis, in the pulmonary artery. This is not a common condition at the best of times and is pretty catastrophic in a girl in her twenties. As a result of the embolus it was discovered that she had sustained a collapse of the lobe of one lung. This means that this lobe was airless and out of function. The medical authorities were still unsatisfied. It was consoling that the attention she received was unremitting, humane and immensely skilled. Annette indicated that they now wanted to "take a bit out of my chest or something". What they were contemplating was sending a small section of the lung tissue for microscopic and other examination. What they clearly had in mind was the possibility of cancer. With one side of my being I did not worry about this but there were times when I felt that her medical history, without blemish before the death of her husband, was becoming such a nightmare of pathology that anything at all could happen to her. The biopsy was performed and was found negative to cancer.

Slowly, reluctantly, the chest symptoms withdrew. It was reasonable to anticipate that by now she had turned the corner. She had her emergency operation for her ruptured appendix in June. We were now in late summer. She was still listless, weak and incapable of dragging one leg after the other. Her anaemia persisted. At first I considered that a certain reduction in her blood count was inevitable. Dr. Paul began to telephone Clare with details of Annette's blood count. I found his recital chilling. Sixty per cent indicated a conclusive and debilitating anaemia. I still believed this could be a result of her general condition and at one time wondered if she was being over-investigated and told myself it would be better if she was left alone to recuperate in her own time. This attitude, only briefly sustained, was completely unjustified. Her count fell below 60 per cent with the stimulus of blood transfusions. When you introduce three pints of blood into a person's circulation without a sizeable and sustained improvement of the blood count you are up against something serious. On September 1st the count had fallen to 48 per cent.

At this time Annette rang to say that her mother was giving her regular treatment, putting a hand on her left side over her lower rib. Braïda continued to do this every night. It was evident that she was giving treatment to the spleen. It was that, together with the clinical symptoms. which clinched for me the diagnosis of splenic anaemia.

It was atrocious and unthinkable that this girl only approaching her twenty-eighth birthday should be afflicted with such a condition. The doctors hesitated before making the diagnosis. The point at issue was that the spleen did not seem to be sufficiently enlarged to correspond to the classical picture of a splenic anaemia. This caution was all to the good. Doctors who hesitate before embarking on surgery are always to be encouraged. This

128

generation is suffering too much in body, heart and pocket from knife-happy surgeons. Annette was sent off to the country to sit by the wooded shores of a lake in the hope that some improvement in her general condition would lift her blood count and obviate the necessity for an operation. This was a forlorn hope at best but absolutely justifiable and a tribute to the intelligence of the doctors. It is always good to know when a physician believes that to ensure the harmony of the whole is of benefit to the patient's individual symptoms. It should be remembered also that Dr. Paul, as well as the surgeon who operated on Annette for her appendix abcess, realised that there was something unusual about her and that her rallying from a state of deep coma was at least near miraculous. I was quite convinced that Dr. Paul at least had a similar attitude to my own. He hoped that Annette herself would pull something out of the bag or that other agencies, and particularly Clare, would intervene on her behalf.

So we come to the early days of September with Annette's morale remarkably high and her medical outlook disastrous. At this stage I knew from what she told me during her phone calls that she was remembering her past lives vividly and comprehensively. Braïda and Mr. Mills had said that the function of her first illness, the appendicitis followed by peritonitis, had been to release her recall of past incarnations. Now a whole succession of maladies was doing this with a vengeance. In these first days of a Canadian autumn she was remembering the Castle at Portchester and her Napoleonic incarnation. By the second week she was recalling Bassenthwaite. Perhaps she was stirred by the proximity to wood and lake water. One day she was sitting looking over the lake. She took a few steps and tripped over a stone. She fell not particularly heavily on the not especially hard earth of the forest. In falling she banged her head against another stone. It was the destiny of this strong-muscled, athletic girl to sustain disproportionate damage from seemingly trivial accidents.

Before discussing further the consequences of this particular fall we should remember that, in the course of twelve months, she had been for weeks on crutches and in plaster for a ruptured lateral ligament and, on the second occasion, for a fractured tibia after falling in Edinburgh and Toronto respectively. She was now to be relegated once more to the same treatment.

On this occasion the damage she sustained was twofold. She had a swollen, painful and badly bruised left foot. (It was always the left foot which was affected.) X-ray revealed that she had fractured one of the small bones called metatarsals. What the surgeons were more concerned with was the swelling and horrible bruising of her left temple. All this necessitated her return to hospital, a calamitous end to a rather forlorn venture designed to make her feel a little better.

She rang me from hospital. She described what they had found in her foot. "It's painful but not too much bother," she said. "What I can't understand is that they keep on asking me if I have got a headache or if I feel giddy. I haven't got a headache at all."

"They must have some reason for asking."

"Well, yes. My forehead on that side is absolutely black and blue. It's a fearful sight."

"They have X-rayed your head?"

"Yes, but they can't find anything. But they keep on talking about concussion. They just can't understand that I don't feel concussed. I cannot feel concussed just to oblige them. They are far more interested in my head than in my foot and, after all, I have broken a bone there."

"Do you feel absolutely nothing the matter with your head?"

"No pain at all. All I have is a feeling that I have ricked my neck low down on the left side but it only hurts if I move it."

In England Clare was groping her way through her working hours with an excruciating left-sided migraine which began in her left temple, the site of Annette's bruising and discoloration. The migraine began the previous day. She had also a pain low down in the left side of the neck. I discovered later that the onset of her symptoms coincided exactly with the time of Annette's fall.

I noted that Annette's accident occurred either on the anniversary of, or within a day of, her fall the year previously in Scotland. I cannot be absolutely precise because of a slight confusion of dates in my diary for that period. This, and other matters, were settled conclusively the day after Annette's phone call.

I was sitting with Clare when Braïda appeared. For a month now I had been able to recognise the identity of the revenants and interpret their conversation when Clare was present. Braïda said that Annette's fall of yesterday coincided to a day with another fall in her Celtic incarnation. Once again Annette was the victim of a mob. This time the fracas occurred near Castle How, in the flat land where the road curves round to Armathwaite Hall. Annette had behaved with the same impetuousness she showed in her present incarnation. She had been chatting indiscreetly to the villagers about the forces of good and evil. This was a dangerous subject for her to discuss because of her reputation as a witch and as a practitioner of the evil eye. She followed this up by saying that the priest who had inflamed the mob against her at Loweswater was the incarnation of evil. The mob closed in on her. She ran away towards Castle How. She was stoned en route and was badly hit on the left temple. It was swollen, hideously discoloured and also cut. She remembered being treated with some kind of alga, a livid green weed which grew in the stagnant water between the rushes. The rushes and sedges are still visible looking forward and to the left from the landing stage.

It was clear, as it had been on several recent occasions, that Clare had taken to herself Annette's pain. The vulnerability of the latter's left foot, and Clare's ability to accept the symptoms arising from it, were still operating six months later. When one of Annette's doctors was in England in March 1974 he mentioned her in the course of a phone call in which we were discussing the origin of diseases in previous incarnations. I said that I considered Annette's fractures in this life to stem back to her exploits in her Celtic incarnation. A few minutes after putting down the receiver I had a call from Annette. She said she had fallen again, that her leg was swollen and discoloured but not painful. Later that day I mentioned this to Clare. "Do you want to see mine?" she said. Her left ankle was discoloured and markedly swollen. She was positive that she had not fallen and knocked against anything.

With this fall in the wood in Canada Annette was well and truly back at Bassenthwaite and in her Celtic incarnation. She had returned to her seventh-century habitat partly in virtue of

131

the sufferings she had endured. As these were not yet over it is well to describe them before recording more of our life at Bassenthwaite. By now, with her blood count desperately low and there having been no sustained response to several trans-fusions, Annette's medical advisers were seriously considering the removal of the spleen. It seemed that they had made up their minds in a great hurry but it is now clear that they did not let her know until the last moment to spare her worry and to lessen our anxiety this side of the water. The reader will be surprised at the amazing consideration shown to Clare by some of the Canadian doctors in charge of Annette. None of these had met her. At first they regarded her as their patient's nearest relative. They were later disabused of this idea.

I spoke to Annette one day in mid-October. She was very tired and resigned to the operation. She said, without self-pity or emotional display, that she didn't care which way it went. She had little to lose in parting from this world. In the next she would at least be in more permanent contact with Guy and her mother.

It was by no means cheering to be this side of the Atlantic and to contemplate the plight of this girl isolated from her friends and against what, in spite of the kindness she had received, was an alien background. It was a compensation that at this time Clare and I received a good deal of comfort from the revenants. When Graham was present one evening I said to Clare that it was some time since he had last put his hands on me or reinforced her own efforts when she gave me treatment. Clare smiled when Graham said, "If he still needs proof." I was re-ceiving treatment at that moment for sinusitis. Clare's hands were placed slantwise across my skull. I felt another deep warm pressure above the protuberance at the left side of the occiput and at the base of the left thumb. Graham's treatment was again recognisable by the heavy pressure of his hands.

On the day of Annette's operation I went for a walk in the park. It was well into October and the leaves were turning. It was a mid-morning affair in Canada. In England we waited on a mild late afternoon, to see if Annette would live or die.

Graham and Mr. Mills were present with us from the begin-ning. I realised that their main function was to comfort Clare.

132

Betty came in later. She was equally concerned to support me. She stood at my right hand, the position she adopted always unless there was some specific reason which prevented it.

The first exchanges were banal and comforting. I would have closed my ears to them had they not come from the revenants. They said Annette would survive and that actually she would be out of hospital quicker than we imagined. What was significant in the light of this book is that they were insisting that we should take her as soon as possible to Bassenthwaite.

Suddenly I felt unaccountably tense. This was significant because for some time I had felt absolutely no charging of the atmosphere when the revenants were present. I felt also that in some way I was being drawn out of myself. I had had this experience before. I remembered particularly the occasion when I awoke from sleep with a feeling that my soul was being dragged from my body. This sensation had been felt above the solar plexus. It left me hollow and empty and with the feeling that my intestines were knotted up to impede the flight of the soul from my body. This description is palpably crude but I am trying my best to record it as it was. On this, the evening of Annette's operation, the site of my disturbance was entirely different. I felt as though what was vital in me was being drawn through the top of my head. This was a new experience for me and I anticipated that it was something rare and I had no idea of its nature.

I missed the significance of what the revenants were saying. I was too concerned with the phenomenon itself. I was too outside myself. It was as if my soul had departed to meet itself. Clare interpreted for me what the revenants were saying. Annette was with us in the room. She had come with Braïda. The latter had been with us little recently because she had been comforting Annette in Canada.

It seemed that in extreme circumstances it was possible for a human being to summon aid by projecting him or herself through space in an out-of-the-body experience. I was well aware that we can quit our bodies in order to comfort the afflicted but I had no idea whatever that they could come to us. Had I not experienced what happened I would have said it was impossible. My first thought was that one cannot induce out-of-the-body

133

experiences by an act of will. I knew later this reaching towards me was not willed by Annette. What I learnt next provided the explanation. We heard from Graham that Braïda had come with her. This was not a question of two people being joined in an out-of-the-body experience. Clare and I had shared such exploits. Braïda was already dead. In her astral body she had drawn Annette's etheric body from her and brought her to me.

I began to understand a little more why Annette, scarcely conscious, had asked to speak to me when she emerged from her coma after her peritonitis and why she wished me above all others. I accepted that this was because we had been close to each other in several incarnations. Braïda now added that, apart from these considerations, there was another bond between us. Our deepest contact had been in the thirteenth century when I was desperately ill with pulmonary tuberculosis. The situation was now identical though our rôles were reversed. In my Cathar incarnation she had been a young woman and I had been an old man on the point of death. She was now half over the frontier and I was sitting in comfort in a room in Bath. Our ages were practically the same as they had been when we talked together in the thirteenth century.

I was so absorbed by the extraordinary experience of Annette being drawn to me that I did not realise its full significance. I looked at Clare's face. It was pale and still and her eyes were focused somewhere beyond the room. I asked her what was the matter. "Things aren't going so well," she said.

At that moment I was with Clare in the operating theatre. Annette's heart had stopped beating. It was being massaged by the surgeon through the diaphragm. Somebody else was giving her an injection. It appeared to be coramine. I could not understand this because coramine had gone out of fashion in England as a heart stimulant. I could not think of Canadians as more conservative in these matters than the English.

Time was suspended that autumn evening in Clare's house in Somerset. It is useless trying to describe the most critical moments in our history. All I can say is that what seemed like an eternity on one plane was registered as something of small duration on another. I did not stay the whole time in the operating theatre. When Clare said that the operation was finished I was very surprised it was over so quickly. Dr. Paul telephoned us later. Annette had been two hours and a quarter in the theatre.

We learnt that when Annette was taken from the theatre she was a little better but her pulse was still weak. It was obvious that her condition was still critical.

Betty was nearer to me than ever before. My contact with her was almost physical. She sat on the bed and I felt as though there was an exhilarating coldness around my body. Sometimes it clung like a sheath. At this time a soft, feathery film appeared to be circulating just above my skin. I felt a light, moth-like movement on the left temple. She was kissing the side of my forehead. That day she was being especially comforting. I assumed it was because of the ordeal I had undergone in being present after my fashion at Annette's operation. It was also two years to a day since she paid a last visit to Bath, left a small present for me and walked out of my life without our meeting.

The surgeon rang Clare to say that the operation had been a close-run thing. The spleen was much larger than had been estimated but the heart had been the main problem. Annette's blood pressure was very low. The next few days would be critical. Dr. Paul rang later and gave more details. Annette's heart had stopped beating and had required massage through the diaphragm and an injection of coramine. Her low blood pressure was causing concern. Next day we had a visit from a doctor friend of mine. I had previously described Annette's case to him. In spite of the fact that he is a consultant practising in a temple of orthodoxy—he is sited in Wimple Street—he said that the etheric spleen was more important than its physical counterpart. Braïda shared this view. She continued to treat Annette as she had done before her operation and before the surgeons and physicians had made a positive diagnosis of splenic anaemia. She placed a hand over the now absent spleen and another in a position prescribed by the Cathars.

That evening my wife and I went to dinner with the aforementioned consultant and his wife. We had hardly sat down before I noticed that my wife's face was grey and drawn and her cheeks excavated. She looked as though she was in great pain and markedly toxic. She was still suffering off and on from the symptoms she had had since a little before Annette sustained her

135

ruptured appendix. She had been a little better recently and I had hoped that the morbid process was on the wane. She rallied a little when the meal was over. When we returned home I had a call from Dr. Paul to say that Annette had slumped dramatically. Her condition was intensely worrying because of her frighteningly low blood pressure. I worked out that Annette's collapse had coincided exactly with the time and duration of my wife's shattering and toxic appearance in Bath. This sort of thing was to continue until Annette recovered. My wife was a barometer in which the fluctuation in Annette's condition was recorded. At first she suffered from attacks of pain and depression during Annette's relapses. Later, as the latter grew stronger, my wife was freer from pain, more cheerful but excessively tired. The revenants said that, when Annette was acutely ill, my wife's symptoms followed the course of her worst phases. When Annette turned the corner, as far as her physical condition was concerned, she drew on what was left of my wife's strength and at times left her completely exhausted.

Four days after the operation I had an attack of rapid emptying of the stomach. This was an old affliction of mine. I had learnt that it was often a sign of someone in trouble drawing on me. This morning was a pretty sharp attack and accompanied by faintness and tremors and other symptoms indicating that my blood sugar had fallen. I was obliged to go into a restaurant for an unwanted cup of coffee as an alibi for filling myself up with sugar. I recovered quickly enough by the time the sugar was diffused through my blood stream.

At 2.00 p.m. I had a more startling experience. It differed from what I had felt during Annette's operation in that I had no preliminary feeling of tension. I had a sensation of extreme tightness on the vertex of the skull. The area of tension contracted. I had the impression that a restricted portion of my scalp was being drawn up as if by a magnet. Once again I felt as though my psyche was being drawn from my body but this time through a kind of tonsure of tension. I had at the same time a headache and a pain at the back of my neck. I wondered if this meant that there was some variation in Annette's condition.

Clare came to see me that evening. Braïda and Graham

136

appeared almost immediately. Braïda said that Annette had had a much better day. This was because Clare and I had been to see her. We had visited her at the exact time at which I had felt these sensations in my head. Clare also had a clear awareness of being detached from herself and felt that she had undertaken some out-of-the-body experience.

Braïda said that what I had just felt was different from what happened when Annette's condition was critical in the course of the operation. On the latter occasion she was so far over the frontier as to be almost in her astral body. On this later occasion, still tethered in the flesh, she had drawn me towards her by the greatness of her needs. It was the exercise of Annette's will which had made this a painful experience for me and had resulted in a headache, in my case not a common symptom. The rapid emptying of the stomach which I had suffered earlier that morning was merely a sign that she was drawing on my reserves.

Annette telephoned me less than a week after the operation. Her voice was faint but firm and she spoke with greater precision than usual. She was nursing her depleted resources and making sure she made the most essential points. She said that in the last few days Clare had visited her frequently and that she felt herself to be growing stronger with each visit.

We heard from Dr. Paul that both he and the surgeon considered her recovery miraculous.

There were several alarms in the month of October. On one occasion when I was with Clare she ceased talking and changed colour. I knew that her mind was wandering but in a specific direction. Graham appeared to us and said that Annette had had a poor patch today. These episodes were repeated. Clare continued to tune in desperately to Annette's sudden relapses. Dr. Paul reported from Canada that in these attacks her blood pressure fell to an alarming degree and it was feared that she was having a series of internal haemorrhages.

Over a period of days I had had a succession of phone calls from her. Her manner had changed so completely that I was bewildered. I was too astonished to think in terms of any psychiatric category. I merely wondered, in colloquial phraseology, what had got into her. She was hypercritical of all the people

137

who had looked after her and of the doctors who, it seemed to me, had treated her with consummate skill and astonishing consideration. They were foolish and did not know what they were doing. Those who had done most for her were described as rank incompetents. I was sure that this was an outcome of complete exhaustion. She was not convalescing from a single major operation but from several dangerous and almost mortal maladies which had followed each other in the space of four months. Neither could she be said to have recovered from her splenectomy. It appeared that her internal bleeding was a true bill. It seemed to be the final straw she was unable to support.

I met Clare on the morning of Guy Fawkes' day. She looked astonishingly dilapidated. Normally she is a person who does not show her inward stresses in her outward appearance. This day her face was pale, her eyes dull and what was more significant she put up no cheerful façade when I asked what was the matter. She had passed a horrible night. There had been another crisis and Annette had had another operation. At this stage in the proceedings I did not ask her if she had heard this from Braïda or her other informants. At this time she was tuned in with little intermission to what was happening in Canada. Annette herself had said four days previously that Braïda had informed her that Clare was capable of seeing her past by pure far memory and without the intervention of the revenants. It was clear that she was now a searchlight with beams switched in all directions. Past, present and future were equally illumined. She pierced through the clouds of space.

Clare rang later to say that Annette had been taken to the theatre after undeniable evidence of internal haemorrhage. She was bleeding from a small artery the point of which was cauterised. Before the operation she had been difficult and mulish. She had refused to go to the theatre and had only capitulated after every kind of intercession.

From now on the situation deteriorated. The day after her latest excursion to the operating theatre Annette announced that she would be back in England in a few days' time. This would have necessitated her crossing the Atlantic with her stitches in situ. I told her as gently as possible that this was absurd. She was quite incorrigible. She said that those in charge

138

of her were incompetent and foolish. I argued that it was impossible that all those whom she admired so much could have been transformed overnight. She treated my sober reasoning as though it was the feverish ramblings of a sick child. I reminded her of how much Dr. Paul had done for her. She dismissed him along with the rest. It was painful to compare this shrewish volcano with the girl who had wept when she bid me goodbye before she left for Canada. I could not blame her for it. This was not a question of my being one of that non-existent species, the dispassionate psychiatrist. It seemed to me academic to judge the conduct or classify the symptoms of one who had suffered more than should be asked of any human being. It seemed to me that in her over-excited condition she was more vulnerable to fatigue. I thought that her access to the telephone should be restricted. I had reverted to the idea that perhaps those in charge of her were a little too New World and emancipated. My opinions were transmitted by Clare to Dr. Paul. The latter conferred with his colleagues. They decided that while what I said was acceptable in principle they felt she should not be cut off from her friends in England. Above all she should be allowed free access to me. I was astonished at the trouble they took and the conclusions they came to. In my last years of practice in England I had not often encountered such personal consideration for the patient on the part of the pundits. At the same time Braïda stated very clearly to Clare that it would be monstrous to exclude Annette from contact with me.

The next bulletin about Annette came directly from Braïda and Graham. They appeared immediately one evening in November as soon as Clare and I sat down together. Annette was worse. She was negativistic, refusing food and rejecting her former friends in a manner which was out of keeping with her nature. I knew that this negativism and regression was not schizoid. It was impossible that an impetuously open person like Annette could ever be so withdrawn from reality as to merit the name. She was so different from her old self that I wondered whether, in her state of physical depletion, some evil entity had possessed her. Braïda read my thought immediately and said that she had been entered not by one but by several such beings.

Two days later we touched rock bottom.

Annette blamed both the living and the dead for her predicament. Clare was a dullard and she even rejected Braïda. She was speaking with her own voice but only a shrivelled fraction of Annette addressed itself to me. The experience was shattering and I longed to detach myself from it but I could not evade the lance-thrusts of pain from somebody who had suffered in such a short time from such a garish kaleidoscope of horror. Braïda had said that it was her destiny to heal. It seemed part of her apprenticeship and compassion that she should suffer every variety of human agony. For nearly five months she had lived unremittingly in the hands of the surgeons and physicians. She had passed through the grey-black nightmare with astonishing resilience. Now her mind creaked like the stretched ribs of an overstrained instrument. That day she was to see a psychiatrist.

When the call from Canada was cut off my head swam in a vast dark tide of relief because I had escaped from the tension generated by her. Then I was troubled because I thought of her gazing alone from the hygienic vacuum of the hospital across three thousand sea miles and the wider ocean within her mind. Then the phone rang again. She spoke with the same abusive detachment. Then, quite suddenly, she wept. Her weeping was at first almost silent. A thin trickle of sound was followed by a suspension of breath in which she felt herself abandoned and wandering the void at the end of the world. Then the weeping stopped and the silence was total. I was bound by a head-bursting tension and a cord drawn tightly round my solar plexus. Then the weeping returned and died away in a strangled goodbye.

I wondered what in God's name the psychiatrist would make of her. The prospect was terrifying. I saw her visited by a gimlet-eyed, twitchingly repressed Freudian who would seize on her unsexual ecstasies with her husband and ascribe the whole thing to repression. In her present condition such therapy could induce her disintegration into a thousand fragments.

Braïda said that later Annette would descend into a trough of depression. I was afraid lest this tendency should be accentuated by treatment.

I knew well enough that it was no good talking about this kind of thing to the majority of doctors. I considered that the prospect of there being any psychiatrist in Canada likely to recognise Annette's psychic potentialities across the barrier of her symptoms was thin indeed. There was one ray of hope. It was the surgeon who had done the splenectomy and the later cautery of the bleeding point who had insisted that Annette see a psychiatrist. He had no interest in psychiatry and no special love for the species but he was peculiarly insistent that she must not be sent to a Freudian. I have never known a surgeon lay down the law in this manner.

I dreaded Annette's reaction to the idea of seeing a psychiatrist. When I spoke to her the situation was not so bad as I feared. She was hypomanic that morning and in a blistering and elated ill humour. "They think I am crackers. Well, let them." She then discharged a fusillade of unmerited abuse at her circle of friends. Annette was in the mood in which she saw herself as an island of lucidity in a mad world. Then suddenly she collapsed. "Something gets inside me and says things for me. It isn't me. What can it be?"

I had not the slightest intention of discussing what got inside her on the transatlantic telephone. I had my own ideas on the subject. I needed to be near her to manage her according to her minute-to-minute reactions. I wondered whether the psychiatrist would be a merchant purveying pills and electric treatment or a mechanised behaviourist.

She rang after his first visit. I asked a number of emollient and semi-imbecile questions. "Was he nice? Did he help you?" I thought that as the faculty was out of favour with her I had better detach myself as much as possible from my professional skin. Annette replied to my questions with glittering irony. "He was so stupid that when I said he had helped me he actually believed me." So far, so bad, I thought.

Whatever the psychiatrist's qualities I could not help feeling sorry for him. That Annette did not want him was the least of his troubles. He was suddenly confronted with an unusual phenomenon. Annette rang me round about midday. She was in a state of exaltation, laughing uproariously at the world's stupidity, rejoicing in her own dazzling insight and favouring me with a position at her side on the high peak of her buoyant unreason. In the early afternoon she rang me again. She had collapsed in three hours into a state of abject depression with intense self-accusation. She was evil and unworthy. She had hurt her friends. I implored her not to blame herself. I hammered at her that her self-accusation was unfounded and a worse symptom than her depression. I feared she might be suicidal. I knew that my reassurance was of little avail and that in the depths of depression patients are impervious to reason. They need a presence beside them to share the pain. I was four thousand miles away. I should have known by now that where there is fusion of psyches one is always present. I was to learn later from Annette that at this time I visited her often and that she found my visits a comfort. It is strange that, travelling in our psyches, we can bring consolation to others when, in our own personalities, we are distracted by our fears for them.

Graham and Mr. Mills were an immense comfort. They visited us regularly and told us Annette would come to no harm. Braïda herself told us the same on her infrequent visits. At this time she was mostly with Annette in Canada.

My first clue that something was happening was when the psychiatrist, whom I will call Dr. Charles, rang Clare to say that he had been very frightened by Annette's sudden plunge from exaltation to depression but that he felt the latter would not last long. It was odd that he had put himself out to ring Clare whom Annette described as her aunt. Certainly Dr. Paul had encouraged him to do so. It was nevertheless remarkable that two busy men should concern themselves with making and keeping contact with someone living in another country and whom they had learnt was no relation to Annette. He told her that he did not believe this was an ordinary manic-depressive condition. He deplored any tendency to put a name to it. He said he believed that Annette was exhausted and that in her depleted condition she had acted as a magnet attracting to herself malign entities. I was dumbfounded that an orthodox and distinguished psychiatrist at one of the great hospitals of the New World should commit himself to this degree to a woman he had never met. When he spoke to Clare of the nature and implications of Annette's condition she noticed not only that his views were identical with my own but the very words in which they were expressed were my own phraseology.

This identity of views on the big issues was remarkable

142

enough, but what was even more astonishing was the similarity of subject and its expression in highly specific detail. One day in November Braïda spoke to me of the autumn colours which were magnificent that year and remarkably persistent. She said that there were certain precious stones which reduplicated the emanation of these colours and which should be worn by some people at this season. Amber, cornelian and moss agate were beneficial because they produced in late autumn the colour of the sun in midsummer. Within a day Kathleen telephoned from Switzerland. She had heard the same homily from Raymond Agulher. I was not unduly surprised. I had become accustomed to Raymond's confirmatory evidence. What took my breath away was when Annette, by now very happy with her psychiatrist, told me that he spoke to her about everything under the sun and very little about himself and that that day the subject had been autumn colours. He had said that these were reproduced in certain stones and had she thought of wearing moss agates, cornelians or amber?

It is unnecessary to go into detail about the conversations between Annette and her doctor. At this time in England, Graham in particular and to a less extent Braïda and Betty, were talking a great deal about touch and colour. This was not just a psychological discussion about the relationship between different senses. Dr. Charles spoke of how touch could be a transfiguring experience and how it could evoke the perception of particular colours. It was obvious that he was putting in simple terms to Annette what Graham was expressing to me in such detail that at times I found it difficult to follow.

It seemed to me that Dr. Charles had been directed to Annette. But did this explain his extraordinary choice of subjects when he discussed these things with her? In forty years of psychiatry I had not discovered a doctor who discussed with his patients, to their evident benefit, the virtues of the topaz or the cornelian. I wondered whether he was picking up anything from me by telepathy. This inevitably plays a rôle among the psychic but here it was not an essential feature of the story. The whole operation was directed by Braïda. What struck me as one of its most remarkable manifestations was that the surgeon should have been so insistent that Annette was not sent to a Freudian. Braïda

143

admitted that she herself had transmitted this idea. She had also directed Dr. Charles to speak of jewels and autumn colours. For some years he had been thinking of possession as an explanation of certain psychiatric conditions. She had canalised his thoughts so that he spotted this factor immediately in the case of Annette.

The directions given to Dr. Charles and others in Canada were not transmitted through me. The fact that he and I spoke in identical language is not to be explained by any telepathic interchange between us. We both derived it directly from Braïda. This did not surprise me at all. I had been convinced for two or three years that such of my thoughts as counted for anything were, in the main, given me via Braïda and Guilhabert de Castres.

All things considered, Annette recovered speedily. This was due to a large extent to Dr. Charles' passive and unassertive management of her. She went on a holiday to consolidate and gained enormously from it. She had hardly returned when she was readmitted to hospital after being involved in a motor accident in which she suffered from severe concussion and a friend was gravely injured with a fractured skull. Once again Clare responded to Annette's concussion with a severe headache. This was by now *vieux jeu*. The result was that once again Annette had little pain in the head and few symptoms of any description and fumed at being kept in hospital. What was more significant was that Clare had a swollen and discoloured left ankle. She had suffered no trauma. When Dr. Paul next rang her she asked him to look at Annette's foot. He discovered she had sustained a ruptured vein near the left ankle.

Somewhat later Annette had the fourth episode with her left foot which I have already described in which the pain and swelling were accepted by Clare. This persistent proneness to accidents, occurring in one of her type when mentally or physically depleted, is one of the manifestations of evil. We have to regard Annette, battling with her diversity of disasters, as a reflection in microcosm of the battle in the macrocosm between good and evil. Dr. Charles himself, when I first spoke to him long after Annette had passed the high watershed of a psychiatric illness, expressed the same opinion in almost identical terms.

We have to look at Annette's medical history on different

144

planes and from numerous angles. It was part of a pattern she had to complete. I am convinced that she would not have suffered in this way had she not gone to Canada. Braïda and Graham had insisted that the vibrations of that part of the world were hostile to her. The fact that it was an expanding materialistic country also came into the picture. The latter factor stood in particular relation to her blood condition. Nevertheless, seen from another angle, she had to go to Canada to acquire these illnesses. Through the latter the insight into former incarnations had been released. In addition the impulses to heal had to be freed by the separation of psyche and personality which had occurred often during her various illnesses. The latter had also filled a more specific rôle. She had suffered from serious surgical, orthopaedic, medical and psychiatric conditions so that she should be acquainted with every kind of agony and should acquire a wide range of insight into the sufferings of others. After she had recovered from her acute psychiatric illnesses she passed through a stage of self-absorption. This was a final clinging to the self of her personality before practising the healing expected of her by Braïda and her confrères.

As Annette struggled out of the coils of her separate illnesses my wife's depression lifted. What remained was a disheartening weariness. As Annette gained strength my wife grew weaker. In some way I was reluctant to connect the vagaries of Annette with my wife's condition. It seemed too much like a certain kind of story. In any case it was not my original observation. It was a fact observed by Braïda who brought it to my attention. My wife had been Annette's mother in her Celtic incarnation.

By the time Annette returned to work she had embarked on her healing career. She treated a distraught widow and an acutely agitated mother after the death of a friend of Dr. Paul's in a motor accident. She used the same manual technique as her mother and Clare had applied to her in the West Country garden two decades before. This was a tough assignment for a girl expressing for the first time outside her immediate circle an impulse to heal which, as we will see in Book Three, had been first manifested sixteen centuries previously.

Chapter Sixteen

Apart from her released capacity to heal, Annette's main gain from her long, pitched battle with disease and accident was a wider knowledge of her Celtic incarnation. When her attention had been first directed towards it by Guy he had spoken of the mysterious ring the significance of which neither Annette nor I had first appreciated. It later became evident that this was the clearing in the wood near St. Bega's which Clare, my wife and I had noticed on our visit to Cumberland in April. The whole experience of walking past the wood to the church was unforgettable. The place is in some way alive. The past lives in the present as notes vibrate in a sunbeam.

Braïda and Graham appeared several times to Clare and spoke of the circle and how we had made speeches and held services of healing in the clearing between the trees. Graham and Betty were assiduous visitors at this time because for him the Celtic incarnation was undoubtedly predominant, while Betty was the senior member of our community in Cumberland. It was also an important incarnation for Annette, who in its course first practised her healing on an intensive scale. She relayed to us what came to her from Guy who had been a senior priest ranking above Graham and myself in our simple hierarchy in Cumberland.

The manner in which our activities were revealed to us was of immense importance. The separate items poured in from widely divergent sources and within a limited period of time, usually twenty-four hours or less. There were days when I had hardly replaced the receiver after a call from Annette in Canada when I was called again by Kathleen in Switzerland, by Clare in Somerset, by Marion in the North and by her mother in the Home Counties, each offering the same clear memory. One or two members of the group occasionally produced details not recounted by the others. This synchronisation of data was perhaps more noticeable in the Braïda–Clare and Raymond–Kathleen combinations. The circumstances of these telephone calls were such as made collaboration between the participants impossible.

Kathleen's process of recall was slower and more painful. For several nights she had had what she called a vivid dream which could well have been a vision. She saw a long, narrow lake with a hut on its far shore. The hut was roofed by a thatch of reeds and stood very close to the shore. Going inland from the hut was an oak-wood with a clearing surrounded by a ring of stones. If you looked across the wood from the hut you saw a mountain with a classical shape and a conical summit. It was a bit like Vesuvius. Anybody knowing Bassenthwaite will recognise that she is describing what can be seen looking from the church of St. Bega's towards Skiddaw. She saw in her dream the identical scene visited by my wife, Clare and myself the previous April. Kathleen's slower elevation of memory to the conscious level was accompanied by a stunning attack of migraine. She had suffered from this malady on other occasions when she was recalling events from past incarnations.

Kathleen had never visited Bassenthwaite. Annette had stayed there for a fortnight but had never seen St. Bega's and was unacquainted with the far shore and the clearing.

Annette remembered the services in the clearing. The sermons were of major importance in the Celtic Church. It is tempting to draw analogies with the Presbyterian reverence for a good orator but such comparisons would be unjustified. The contents of the so-called sermons would be as unacceptable to a good Calvinist as to an earnest Catholic. It was obvious that the sermons themselves differed totally from what is implied in the current meaning of the word. It was not the practice to take a text and build from it a fabric of ethical exhortations. Neiher did they refer to current events and draw moral conclusions from them. Discussions built on simple objects and functions were common. The significance of such simplicities as having a meal together was expanded into evidence of love. Most of all the speakers—the description seems more appropriate than preachers—spoke of the phenomena of nature and drew their analogies from them. When talking to the simple they would describe water as sacred and not something to be taken for granted, because it quenched our thirst

147

and nourished the fields and so provided sustenance for us. At a higher level they spoke of the healing or noxious effects of plants in nature. There was good and evil in the vegetable kingdom as in all manifestations of life.

One of the most fascinating items was recalled by Graham. What he told us was common Celtic belief and had also been the subject of several sermons. The nature and function of different kinds of trees were of particular interest to the Church in Cumberland. It need not concern us so much that, to them, the oak was a symbol of goodness, tenacity and steadfastness. Oaks endure a long time and are obvious candidates for symbolism of this nature. What was more significant was the broad division into good and bad trees. The elder and the mountain ash were regarded as especially beneficent. Certainly the elder has been regarded for centuries as protective and friendly. It is interesting that in this life Mr. Mills adored mountain ashes and could not live without one in his garden or in close proximity to his house. Perhaps in this he was reliving his former incarnation in Cumberland. There are places in the latter county where the mountain ash is very common. As for bad trees, one can understand that the elm would acquire an undesirable reputation because it drops its branches when they are burdened with leaves in summer. But why was the alder a tree to be avoided? Why was fir healthier and more beneficent than spruce?

Although these generalisations as to the nature and value of trees are interesting they are far less so than some of Graham's more detailed and specific statements. The aspen was to be avoided by the nervous. The poplar was suspect because it accentuated the previous mood of the individual. The tense became more agitated, the depressed more miserable and the happy unduly elated. The ash was not actually toxic but depressing. The birch and larch were beneficial to melancholics and especially in autumn.

I asked the revenants whether in this life we retained the capacity to react to trees as many had done in the Celtic incarnation. They said that those on a certain wavelength, and especially if their perceptions were reinforced by far memory, could still do so. I asked what were the effects of flowering shrubs, like Japanese cherries, unknown in Celtic times. They answered that

148

the effect of these on the beholder depended on his own attitude towards them. If this was one of love they received back, in healing vibrations, what they themselves had given in love.

This concern with nature was not a sideline but something deeply interwoven into the texture of Celtic Christianity. The latter was more sophisticated and cosmic than its Roman successor. It saw man against the background of nature and not as an isolated molecule separated from a jealous and possessive God by a no-man's-land populated by entities of modest significance. We were bathed in a stream of vibrations all of which were significant for good or evil. As well as trees the Celtic preachers were concerned with stones and particularly anxious that their flock should not think of them as dead matter. They were especially interested in semi-precious stones and the vibrations arising from them. The latter differed with the colour of the stone. Their constant theme was that life was a vortex of vibrations, that nothing is dead, that a stone is pulsating with energy though the rhythm and amplitude of its vibrations are not as obvious as the currents in a river. What they were concerned with above all was the indivisibility and indestructibility of consciousness. They believed fervently in what is expressed in what has become my favourite quotation, that God sleeps in the stone, dreams in the plant, wakes in the animal and lives in the man.

The whole aim of Celtic Christianity was not only to see a unifying pattern in nature but to recognise a purpose in the cosmos and to perceive that we are bathed constantly in its influences. I asked Betty whether, having lived in the twentieth century, she thought that there was any special profundity in what she had learned and meditated in the Dark Ages. She said that no one could deny that the increase of knowledge in this century was stupendous. Generally speaking, what was worth retaining was expressed in writing and through other media and was available to all who cared to look for it. What had been passed on orally in Celtic times was far more comprehensive and sophisticated than we imagined. The basis of what she had learnt was much more mature than anything available to the majority in the present age. (What she and especially Graham revealed to me of the vibrational basis of existence and of the process of creation is beyond the scope of this book.)* She told me how, at Bassenthwaite, she had studied astrology and practised meditation. It was beyond doubt that the stars influenced our make-up and temperament but the degree to which they influence our destiny has been exaggerated by the credulous in the present age. When she meditated she adopted no particular posture or technique. Mr. Mills discussed this further when he recalled how he and I climbed Skiddaw every year on the twenty-first days of March and September. We went up before dawn and stayed on the summit until after sunset. I asked him if we remained silent all the time. He said we talked very little but that sometimes we spoke to each other and that our conversation had not broken the thread of meditation. It seemed that in those days we were so much more perceptive that we did not need to practise rigid and concentrated techniques. It is clear that throughout our lives we had a greater and unenforced awareness. It is sad to reflect how much we have lost.

The Celtic Church's attitude to nature was crystallised in its attempts to canalise the primary energies of good in order to disperse the force of evil. I was told by Guilhabert de Castres that such places as Avebury were sited so as to draw in the vibrations of evil from the surrounding region and to neutralise them by the beneficent energy circulating between the stone arteries of such ancient sites. This was followed up by a call from Annette in which she told me that Braïda was insistent that I should go to Avebury with Clare before my imminent visit to Surrey. I had planned to spend a day or two in the latter county because it had been indicated by Braïda, Raymond and others that by so doing I would recall still further my Napoleonic incarnation. Annette reported Braïda as saying that I should go to Avebury to "charge up" before my visit to Surrey.

On a day in late October I duly presented myself at Avebury with my wife and Clare. There is no point in recording in detail my reaction to the different stones. One in particular was icy to the touch even though it was exposed to the full sunshine of October. This struck me all the more because the amethyst I was given by Clare and which intensifies my powers of recall and my

* See The Great Heresy, to be published by Neville Spearman Ltd.
150

capacity to write is positively glacial. The more perceptive I am the colder the stone. This may be news to those interested in healing because the first stages of this process are often accompanied by a sensation of heat. In healing and in psychic experience generally there is also a beneficent coldness differing from the spine-piercing chill induced by evil entities and atmospheres. It is significant that in this coldest of all the stones I felt a humming vibration which seemed to lift my fingers.

I stood on one flat stone. Even through the soles of my shoes I felt more vibration than I had experienced elsewhere through my naked hands. I felt also a tugging sensation as though I was being drawn into the earth. Braïda materialised and said that this was because I was a Piscean. In some ways my feet were more perceptive than my hands. She said I would have felt the vibrations still more had I come in March. Their effect was potent enough during the week-end which followed.

In the wood near St. Bega's at Bassenthwaite there is a stone which is of special significance for me. Braïda visited Annette one night and the latter passed the information on to me at the first opportunity. The stone stands near a tree which is in the line of succession from one damaged in some way. The story was later amplified by Mr. Mills and Graham. The stone and the tree were so sited as to provide the most favourable atmosphere for the preacher. In the course of a meeting there was a thunderstorm and the tree was struck by lightning. There was a repercussion of this incident in the twentieth century. As a young undergraduate I climbed Ullock Pike, a small fell projecting from the face of Skiddaw, with a former schoolmaster. Going up the fell we were caught in a thunderstorm in which the lightning flailed down on the rocks round us with the noise of the swishing of whips. Until that day I had no fear of thunder or lightning. Afterwards I was afraid, not at all of thunder but certainly of lightning. My particular fear was that I would be blinded by it. The revenants confirmed that my fear on Ullock Pike was an echo of what I had experienced in the wood below many centuries before. They also agreed that my fear of losing my sight from lightning was tied up with the dread of blindness I suffered in my Napoleonic incarnation when both my eyes were stricken with iritis.

From her long flirtation with death Annette gained a wealth of detail about her Celtic incarnation. She had one particular flashback in which she saw me preaching. My appearance was not impressive but it seems that my powers of elocution were considerable. It was irritating to learn that I had put up a rousing performance but that she could not recall the subject matter.

At one stage she was particularly importunate in asking me what I knew of the rite of marriage in the Celtic Church. It transpired later that she was diffident about acknowledging that she had lived together with Guy without any noticeable preceding ceremony. I thought that a feeling of guilt about her physical relations thirteen centuries previously was a shade excessive. It seemed that it was common for priests in the Celtic Church to live with their women. Betty told me that the difference between this and the concubinage which characterised the Roman Church at certain periods of the Middle Ages was that by and large the Celtic priests stayed with their women. Only rank outsiders ran two at a time. Annette, with a becoming diffidence not altogether in keeping with her breezy nature, indicated that Clare and I had lived together at that time. I gathered later that Clare had known this for some months but had left me to find out for myself. Graham and Mr. Mills confirmed that we had set up house together. My memory for this interlude was not entirely obliterated. When the revenants recalled this for me I was able to tell them where we had lived. I said it was in the rather marshy land adjacent to, or including, the garden of the Pheasant. Betty said later that this was about fifty paces down the road turning right from the door of the inn. Mr. Mills said that its site was in what was now the garden.

I asked Clare if there had been any ceremony before we had set up house together. She remembered some simple celebration involving the breaking of bread and the sharing of salt. It was certainly a modest affair.

At first sight it may seem odd that those who were to reincarnate as Cathars should be living together without benefit of clergy. Why were the seemingly easy Celts transformed into the austere Cathars? The discrepancy of attitude is less than it seems. Both the Celts and the Cathars rejected, possibly partially in the former and wholly in the latter, the sacrament of marriage. This is not to say they were hostile to the intention and rightness of the marriage state. In addition the Cathars preferred to recruit Parfaits from those who had lived together as man and wife and had experienced the pleasures and deceptions of the flesh.

Chapter Seventeen

While Annette certainly contributed her share to the recollection of our life in Cumberland there came a stage when Betty took over. In the seventh century Annette had been taken by Guy to Bassenthwaite when she made Loweswater too hot to hold her. It was obvious that the main centre of activities was Bassenthwaite but this statement is not sufficiently specific. From the time that Betty, from beyond the grave, took over from Annette as our chief informant we were specifically centred on Castle How. I could see now—I would have been more than blind had I failed to do so—why in this life Betty returned to her mother on the stretch of road which winds round its base. The site of their reunion had nothing to do with her love for her mother. The latter had been drawn to Bassenthwaite because it was here that Betty had lived her most important incarnation.

Betty showed us that her remembrance of Castle How was complete and intimate. She spoke of a certain point in the circle crowning the summit where the magnetism of the place was at its maximum. I said to her, "Surely that's the place where you appeared behind me and were seen by Clare when we all went to Cumberland in April. She told me she could see you behind my shoulder." She said I was right and that a stone altar had stood in that particular spot. The water from the spring had been blessed there. Graham said the water had special properties because it flowed under Castle How before emerging from the earth and therefore transmitted the healing vibrations from the little hill. He said that Castle How was sited at the confluence of vibrations from the sun, the earth, the water from the lake and from the spring underlying the hillock. It was because of these factors that it had been chosen as a centre of healing. All the revenants as well as Annette, Clare and Kathleen describe it as a centre of healing.

The company lived in small huts on its lower slopes or on

the flat land enclosed by the road curving towards Dubwath.

What do we know of Betty in her life at Bassenthwaite? We know her appearance, her origin and that she was head of the community. We know that in spite of her elevated position she was of heretical tendencies. She leaned to the cosmic philosophy of the old Celtic Church and believed above all that healing was its primary function. We have to go to December 20th, 1973 for further clues.

I was visited by Clare on the evening of that day. Braïda and Graham appeared at once. They talked a great deal about touch and of how the vibrations emanating from people of psychic disposition could be focused and concentrated by jewels or transparent semi-precious minerals. Then Braïda changed the subject. She said that the 20th December had been a bad day in the Cathar incarnation. Those responsible for the disposal of the treasure on the second expedition from a besieged Montségur had been refused shelter for themselves, and co-operation in disposal of the treasure, somewhere on the route to Château d'Usson.* I did not ask myself why Braïda had zigzagged suddenly towards the Cathars in the middle of her Celtic interlude. She and the other revenants were prone to these abrupt changes of subject. Today there was an obvious intention behind the reference to the Cathars. It became clear that the 20th was a bad day for others in charge of treasure. Suddenly I saw a river and a bridge. The river was fast-flowing and broken into eddies by the stones in its bed. I looked to the east and saw through the trees the lake from which the river emerged. Then there came into focus the country to the west. It was undulating and wooded and there was the feeling of moving away from the mountains. There was woodland ahead where the road crossed the bridge, and above the treetops, the last green fells and, inclined to the east, the outline of a mountain. I knew that I was looking at a primitive antecedent of Ouse bridge which spans the Derwent soon after it leaves Bassenthwaite lake on its way past Isel to the sea.

I was sitting on a horse and looking down the river. I held a spare horse by some kind of bridle. I was waiting for a boat to

---

* It was here that at least some of the Cathar treasure was ultimately hidden.

come up the river. In this life I have never seen any kind of craft on the Derwent. Those who have seen the speed at which it flows will recognise that a rowing-boat could not move against the current. I never saw Betty step out of the boat but I have the impression that she came by water in some kind of craft and not by a track on the bank of the river. Three months later Graham told me that in those days the river bed was deeper and the current slower and that it was navigable by coracles.

Betty had come from the Isle of Man by way of Workington. She had brought a manuscript from a monastery in the island. Was it Manghold where Clare had at one time lived as a priestess? The manuscript was destined not for anyone in Cumberland but for the monastery at Lindisfarne. At this time the latter adhered more closely to the Celtic tradition. It was nothing like so Romanised as the Church in Cumberland.

I asked Braïda about the contents of the manuscript. She told me that it was a forthright and unmistakable statement of Dualism in its most absolute form. It stated the three basic articles of belief which later were to be the credo of Catharism in the Languedoc and Northern Italy in the thirteenth century. There were two principles, good and evil, in the universe from the beginning and persistent to the end. It was accepted as true that the psyche reincarnates and that the world was created by the Devil.

There was some kind of scuffle at the bridge. A handful of men emerged from the trees to the east. Stones were hurled at us but the nearest I was to receiving injury was when a branch fell from a tree somewhere near my shoulder. I think it was detached by one of the stones. I do not know if the triangular-faced priest was present on this occasion but the attack was instigated by him because he knew of the existence of the manuscript and wished to obtain possession of it. He failed to do so. At different times Braïda and Betty said that in every incarnation there was someone personally concerned with accomplishing our ruin. In the Celtic incarnation it was this particular priest. In our lives in Rome we were plagued by another fanatic of the same vocation.

This affair of the manuscript given to me by Betty and which I hid successfully while we remained in Cumberland is one of the most gripping of all my memories. This is because the issue, totally forgotten except by Clare and myself among those still living, was absolutely vital even though it was played out against a small and remote background. In the Celtic Church at that time there were those who adhered to the old Dualism and who resisted totally the encroachments of Rome. There were others who, still believing in the two principles and in the fact of re-incarnation, were prepared to concede that the world was made by God and not by the Devil. To the full-blooded Romanisers every aspect of Dualism was repugnant but believing that the world was created by the Devil was total anathema and to be expunged from the records as soon as possible. For the time being they were prepared to do a deal with those Dualists who still believed in the two principles and reincarnation but who were prepared to be accommodating on the creation of the world. This latter single issue was creating a schism in the Cumberland Dualists. This is interesting enough in itself but what is absolutely fascinating is that here, in Cumberland in the seventh century A.D., they were living in advance the cleavage between Catharism absolute and *Mitigé* which split the Dualist forces in the Languedoc to some extent but to a greater degree in Northern Italy. The latter region had even separate centres of instruction and practice for the two varieties. *Mitigé*, which was prepared to site the fall of man on this earth rather than earlier on in cosmic evolution, could be adjusted to Catholic doctrine on the fall. Nicetas, a Dualist bishop from the Balkans, was invited to the Languedoc in the twelfth century to give judgment on this issue. He opted for the absolute variety of Catharism. It is fascinating that Betty and I did the same thing at Bassenthwaite in the seventh century.

The Romanising opposition settled the issue in a convincing and practical manner. Incited by the same priest, Betty was murdered by a mob on the flat land below Castle How, between the lake and the curve of the road leading to Bassenthwaite village. The rabble had been previously instructed that she was a witch. This was a free translation of her function as a healer. That she was a woman priestess and was also faithful to the Celtic gods as well as to Christ told also to her detriment. This horror was later revealed to me in detail by Clare in a trance

157

experience to be described in Book Three which records my more intimate contacts with the revenants and especially Betty.

Betty was buried by the lake at St. Bega's. I have described how on our visit the previous April Clare had wandered away from us and out of time and had looked across the lake at the mountains opposite. She was smiling and alone and not with us. She was standing by a flat stone sunk in the ground. Betty lies buried beneath this stone. She said so herself and Braïda, Graham and Mr. Mills have described also the horror and the hazard of that night when we said goodbye not only to Betty but to Castle How and set off on the journey to Lindisfarne which marked the end of the old Celtic Church in Cumberland.

At this time, autumn 1973, I learnt more of why the road to Wythop and Bassenthwaite speaks to me in such unmistakable accents. On that day sixty years ago, when time was dispersed on my walk with my mother, I was moving within yards of an object which has been of crucial importance to me in this record. When I go back to Isel I am still closer to my past. I was sitting with Clare on a September evening when Mr. Mills appeared in his robes as Bertrand Marty accompanied by Guilhabert de Castres. The latter's visits were always of special importance. They were usually concerned with philosophic matters beyond the reach of the others, except perhaps Graham. This evening was a rare occasion in that Clare had told me beforehand that the revenants wished to see me.

In the course of the interview we discussed the atmosphere of places and regions. They told me that that in Cornwall was mixed. Places originally sacred had acted as a magnet to evil and left a suspension of malevolence in the atmosphere. Provence, where my love of the Midi first awakened, was a positive battleground of good and evil. The two forces confronted each other with their maximum intensity. The Languedoc was relatively uncontaminated and on the side of the angels. Alsace and Brittany were also good regions. It seemed that in England the country around Bassenthwaite had the best emanation I was likely to find.

Then we switched over to crosses and symbols. I saw on the wall a St. Andrew's cross. At this time this was a sign that we were dealing with a Celtic incarnation. Often when Braïda appeared she carried a St. Andrew's cross and wore not the blue of the Cathars but the dark-purple robes and the characteristic head-dress of the Celtic priestesses in Cumberland. I then saw, and received instruction on, a variety of crosses. Cathar and Mithraic symbols were the most discussed. I did not comprehend fully that the revenants were impressing on me the continuity of symbols throughout several incarnations.

I could feel that the conversation was flagging and that they were waiting for me to see something to which my eyes were closed. Suddenly I thought of the cross at W——. I did not think of it by deduction as the theme and consequence of what Mr. Mills and Guilhabert de Castres had said. I saw the cross as I had seen it that cloudy day in April in the plunging valley by the quiet lake. On that day, though enigmatic and eternal, it seemed to me that in some strange way it was talking to me. Now when I saw it its message was intensely personal. With my inner eye I saw the church at Isel, the daffodils in the churchyard shaken by the inaudible vibrations of the swift river, the small dark porch and the stone in its wall resembling the head of the cross at W——. I called sharply to the revenants that I knew these crosses. They nodded and I could see that the purpose of their visit had been achieved.

I recalled that I had worked with those who had made the crosses. I had been a spare-time stonemason. The stone at Isel had been a practice run for the more complicated emblem at W——. Both crosses had been made from a quarry a few miles distant. When they were completed the two stones remained where they had been made. Then I remembered that, during our time at Castle How, when the persecutions intensified, we tried to smuggle the complete and better stone from the area. Starting from Isel we came to the valley between the Embleton and Wythop fells. We crossed it somewhere near Brathay Hill. At this point we were attacked by a mob issuing from the woods. The triangular-faced priest was still on the warpath. I was struck by a stone in my left eye which has been a vulnerable point in four incarnations. (I was to suffer a similar but graver injury in a few days' time.) To this day the valley between the Embleton fells and Wythop is sodden in places and especially during rainy periods. In those days it was thickly wooded and positively marshy.

159

We struggled with the stone across the valley and up the slope towards what is now the road which skirts Wythop Fell. Fatigued by breasting the slope we dropped the stone. It buried itself deeply in a marshy puddle and we were completely unable to dislodge it.

All this much I saw and remembered with the eye of memory. By September 1973 I had reached a stage where at times I needed no longer to be prompted by the presence of the revenants or the touch of Clare. The subsequent history of the stone I had from Guilhabert and Mr. Mills. It lay for centuries until it was discovered by a party of itinerant Lollards one of whom recognised its significance. He saw that it was a compressed version in stone of the long history of Dualism. By some means or other it was carried to the neighbourhood of Lamplugh and inserted in the wall of a barn which was used as a place of worship. Clare had always believed that the barn had been a centre for religious meetings and this had been confirmed by Annette who had heard it from Braïda on one of her visits.

When I walked with my mother that other-worldly day in October 1916 we passed very close to where the stone had lain. It may be that many of us need talismans. Those who hear the gods directly are very few. There are still some who can hear the murmur of the source of all things. In this world the voice of the universal consciousness is no more than a whisper. It is perhaps better to talk directly through the individualised spirit within us, to the central vibrational centre where the emanation of truth is at its maximum. But I am not concerned with what is better or worse. I can only accept what I am capable of. It is enough for me that I speak through my psyche to the past and that on that day with my mother, the sun deep gold with the morning haze lifted, the wild apples yellow on the hedgerow trees, I was near to the stone I had seen at its birth and which still spoke to me thirteen centuries later. We know less through the psyche than through the spirit but what I have learnt is enough for me.

I heard later from Braïda and Graham other reasons why the fell road from Embleton over Wythop is sacred to me. There is another upright stone below the road where Graham himself presided over healing sessions in the days when he lived at Embleton before going to Castle How. He had a little hut in the corner of what is now the churchyard at Embleton. Small wonder that when I wrote my short piece, "I Cannot Close the Door on the Senses" for *The Science of Thought Review*, I had in mind the road from Embleton which leads over Wythop where I walked with my mother to another world.

Before they parted from me Guilhabert de Castres and Mr. Mills reminded me of how much in my lives I had worked with stone. In the Celtic incarnation I had made models other than crosses. I had fashioned for myself a not very perfect representation of a dove to which I was very attached and which I always kept beside me when I was working. Later, in the thirteenth century, the dove was to become a Cathar symbol. I learnt later from Mr. Mills, at a time when my osteo-arthritic thumb was being treated by diathermy, that I had acquired this tension in my chisel hand in the seventh century. The hypothenar eminence below my right thumb was swollen and far greater than that of my left hand. I acquired the same distortion in the eighth century after decades of chiselling stone. They told me that if I returned to Isel the condition of my thumb would improve. This was proved true in July 1974 after which date the pain and swelling in my hand diminished. The revenants also reminded me that in my Napoleonic incarnation I had not only built stone walls, as we shall see later, but had modelled at least one girl's head which they described to me as having plaited hair and a Phrygian cap, the latter a Mithraic symbol. It seems that in my preoccupation with the working of stone, which extends over a thousand years, I am always concerned with Dualism.

Chapter Eighteen

Betty's life and death at Bassenthwaite in the seventh century illuminated for me my own love of the place because she and I have been so close to each other for nearly two millennia. My addiction to the Pheasant, which has endured since childhood, is explained by the fact that if I look through its front windows I can see the road which winds round Castle How where Betty lived thirteen centuries ago and where she returned after death to her mother and Clare. When I look eastwards from the inn I can see where Clare and I lived in the Celtic incarnation.

From the beginning of this book it has been evident that all roads lead to Bassenthwaite. But if this meeting of paths is comforting to recall in the twentieth century our departure from Bassenthwaite in the seventh was a long agony. Late in 1973 I knew we had set off for Lindisfarne and that our dispirited cavalcade had consisted of Guy, Clare, Graham, Annette and myself and a little band of lay supporters. We were essentially the non-Romanised remnants of the Bassenthwaite community.

I was carrying the precious manuscript entrusted to me by Betty. I kept it to myself because I knew that its contents were not for general consumption. I do not know the exact route except that we passed through Gilsland. In my early childhood I went there with my parents. I remember the river plunging through the trees, the current straddled by the line of boulders and the well where my father drank the water and looked as though he believed in its properties. Braïda told me that when we went through Gilsland in the seventh century the water was held to have healing powers.

Some while after Gilsland we were attacked by an itinerant band of robbers. It was terrifying when this wave of ragged hoodlums spilled over us from the trees but in retrospect it was a light experience compared with what Betty had suffered at the hands of the mob in Bassenthwaite, their hate engined and accelerated by the priest's malevolence.

Those who attacked us somewhere in what is now Northumberland were influenced by no more than loot. Clare, Graham, Guy and I were wearing priests' robes. Annette was not a priestess. She was too independent, too much a slave of her own impulses, to adhere to any kind of organisation. We had considered that our vocational dress would be a protection in the wilds where the Romish antagonism to us was not yet known. When our attackers saw that our cavalcade included priests they pulled up in their tracks. They recoiled still further when Graham raised aloft the model of the dove I had made at Isel and which I had brought with me. They considered it some kind of magic symbol and retreated precipitately. My already damaged eye was severely injured by one among a fusillade of stones, hurled by the more recalcitrant in the process of retreating. I had to lie up somewhere on the road to Lindisfarne. Because of my injury Clare and I arrived at that place later than the others.

All this, and the fact that after a time I had been expelled from Lindisfarne, I knew at the end of 1973. On a confirmatory visit to Cumberland in July 1974 I learnt the details of our journey and our last years. Before this trip I had been told, directly by Braïda and indirectly through Annette, that we must visit Lanercost and that an equal-armed cross would be important to us. She did not indicate that the cross was at Lanercost. We were also told to visit St. Bees, the place at which St. Bega had first set foot on the soil of Cumberland. Graham impressed on us that we should revisit Castle How and spoke of the spring just below the summit.

The first place we visited was Castle How. A year previously I had known that it was alive and haunted but I had had no specific perception of Betty. Now she returned to us and I saw where thirteen hundred years earlier she had sat and meditated. We saw where Mr. Mills had been similarly occupied. In this life honeysuckle had been his favourite flower. It had grown at the spot where he had meditated in the seventh century. It was flowering here in 1974. Across the road a rowan tree grew at the site of the hut in which he had lived. He told us that some trees and plants are sentient and transmit to a long line of

163

descendants the memory of those who have known and loved them.

We could not find the spring of which Graham had spoken. We thought we would find a stream emerging from the lower slopes so we descended towards the landing stage. We saw and heard nothing. When we returned to the summit we heard the tinkling of a stream. We still saw nothing but followed the track of the sound of water. It led us to a circle of saturated ground at the foot of a tree just below the summit. In those days the spring had emerged from this place and had since gone underground. As well as Clare and I, my wife, who asserts that she is not psychic, heard clearly the unmuffled singing of the long-buried stream. That morning she was close to her Celtic incarnation and perhaps to her daughter Annette.

At Loweswater we saw the stone by the lake where Annette and Guy had picnicked on their honeymoon and where, in the seventh century, she had drawn water from the lake. There was a cluster of stones in the vicinity. Some were grooved and curiously shaped to a degree that could not be explained by weathering or artefacts. They had been shaped to pound roots and to collect the juices expressed from them. One was grooved for this purpose. The drainage channel was covered by a protective overhang. These worked stones were to me alive in that my hand felt warm and my skin tingled at the point of impact with them. I understood better what Teilhard de Chardin meant when he described how, as a boy, he could feel the life vibrating in metal.

We went to St. Bees as Braïda and the others had suggested. As a boy I had played cricket there and in later life I had once visited the headland on a fine afternoon with the west wind blowing. The Priory was unknown to me. Yet it was not the church itself but the sloping green above it which spoke most clearly to me. I paused at a certain spot where my normally cold feet felt warm and tingling. I noticed these sensations all the more because they seemed to give more life to my glacial extremities. I felt a curious resonance inside my head. It was as though my voice was in some way resounding within my skull, as though its echoes were reflected backwards in a closed space and excessively amplified. This is what it felt like to me but Clare's sensations were different. She told me that the volume of my voice was in some way enormously increased. She withdrew to the maximum distance permitted by the grounds of the Priory. I would estimate this at over thirty yards. She asked me to use my ordinary speaking voice which I am told is much quieter than the average. At different points and always at the maximum distance from me she could clearly hear what I said except along one axis where a shrub was interposed between us. I dropped my voice to a half-whisper and was still audible. I continued to be aware of the resonance within my skull.

Braïda, who had joined us, told me that on several occasions in the seventh century I had preached at the spot on which I was standing. The audiences were considerable and were recruited from a wide area. Because I was in the open air it was always necessary for me to speak in a loud voice. With Braïda present I was able to recall, and she to confirm, a particular sermon in which I had spoken of the powers of good and evil in relation to disease. (It is interesting that this has become a preoccupation of mine in recent years in this life.) On this particular occasion I had spoken particularly of "states of decline", that is to say of tubercular conditions, and also of obsessional states which I did not describe by that name but referred to as forms of possession. I also ascribed epilepsy to the latter process. I am sure that my present preoccupation with these subjects is not something recently engendered in me but the resumption of old interests from previous incarnations.

Clare did not tell me that, at St. Bees, I was talking in a strange, harsh language, different from the Languedoc she heard in the accents of Braïda.* It is clear that I was speaking the Celtic language of seventh-century Northumbria. I heard this from Annette after my return from Cumberland. Once again Clare had preferred that I should, as much as possible, learn at first hand by direct revelation.

In the grounds of St. Bees' Priory we discovered the Easter Magiant which, among the revenants, Guy had been first to mention as a healing herb, though Braïda, Graham, Betty and Mr. Mills had in turn spoken of it. We had found it the year

* The capacity to interpret unknown languages has been discussed in *We Are One Another* (Neville Spearman, 1974).

previously in the churchyards at Isel and St. Bega's. Now, in 1974, we discovered it also at Castle How and St. Bees Priory and near the fashioned stones by the shore at Loweswater where we had constructed our simple houses. We were now directed to Lorton by Braïda because it had been a great centre of healing. I felt there was some specific purpose in this particular advice. This was revealed when we discovered the Easter Magiant growing in great profusion in the churchyard. The Easter Magiant* became a reverberating theme for us in the course of 1974.

While staying at Bassenthwaite another link in the chain was more securely forged. In April 1973 Braïda told Annette that at Fellgate I had found evidence that in this, our twentieth-century life, I was related to another member of the group. It became clear later that this was Marion Dacre. In visiting Fellgate in July 1974 I heard more details of the decline and fall of the house of Dacre and that the home farm had been administered by a man bearing the same name as my grandmother. Braïda confirmed again that the two families were related.

One day at Bassenthwaite when Clare was late coming downstairs I went to her room and found her lying face downwards on her bed. Her face was engorged and she was muttering to herself in thick, dragging accents. She was obviously in a state of trance. She was reliving the transfer of the W—— stone from Isel to Wythop. I heard details I had not gathered when speaking recently to Mr. Mills and Guilhabert de Castres. In the skirmish at Brathay Hill the shaft of the cross was broken. If one examines it resting in the wall at W—— one sees that the shaft is foreshortened. This mutilation of the cross did not depress us unduly because the essential symbols were preserved.

In the course of her trance Clare muttered two incomprehensible statements in which I heard references to a stone at Lanercost and another in one of the transepts at Lindisfarne.

A day or two later Clare, my wife and I set off for Lanercost. We arrived at the Priory during a brief calm poised uncertainly

* I have read more than once that the herb in which I am interested is called Easter Mangeant and that the second word derives from the French "to eat". I am sure the Cumbrians of my generation will bear me out that the n was never pronounced. I cannot accept for a moment the French derivation.

between deluges of wind and rain. The atmosphere was indescribably peaceful. It was as though the emanation of the priory had quietened the elements for us. I came through the ruins to a wall with two stones which attracted my attention immediately. One was decorated with an equal-armed cross and the other with a sculptured hand. Clare suggested that I should touch these stones. When I did so my hands felt warm and were tingling with the vibrations they detected in the stone. All the stones near by were cold and dank. At this time Braïda materialised. Stimulated by her presence I recalled how I recuperated at Lanercost from the eye injury I had sustained in my brush with the mob at Brathay Hill. While at the Priory I had carved two stones as a thank-offering for my two weeks' shelter and also because I was bored and needing occupation. Allowing for the hostility of time and the weather the carvings are not well done. The explanation is simple. At the time my impaired vision prevented me from producing work of any quality.

Lanercost's most valuable lesson was that something one has worked with or possessed centuries ago can induce far memory. I suppose one can regard this as a specialised aspect of psychometry. What I learnt at Lanercost was emphasised equally strongly at Lindisfarne.

We went to Lindisfarne on July 6th, 1974. Once again the stones were speaking. Near the chancel I found one with the beginnings of an equal-armed cross chiselled roughly upon it. This stone, and the one adherent which was uncarved, were warm and tingling. All the surrounding stonework was cold with shadow and the sea wind. I knew once again that I had alighted on something with memories for me.

As I walked round the ruins it seemed to me that the atmosphere varied in different places and sometimes abruptly. In places it was positively evil. I persist that there are areas in the ruins which are sinister for me. Going towards the well at the far extremity of the outer court we found the atmosphere wholly beneficent. I recalled with Braïda and Clare that the original settlement had been sited here. We spoke of the occupations of the community. Healing was a major concern and the preparation of potions went on continually. I saw Kathleen plaiting dry reeds to use as roofs. We had dry bracken for bedding.

167

I did not recall my exact state on arrival at Lindisfarne. I knew from what direction Clare and I had come, that I had needed her assistance and that I could not see clearly. Following my arrival I was given a potion by Clare which she had carried with her but had not used until I had reached our resting place. I remembered clearly how warmly we were welcomed.

There was a gap in my memories and I came to the day when I dug a hole in the earth floor and buried a manuscript wrapped in some kind of animal skin. With the passage of time I spoke to two or three people of its contents and message. One of those in whom I confided was indiscreet. That I possessed a secret document became known to a Romanised priest of malevolent disposition who harboured a grudge against me. By watching my movements he discovered the whereabouts of my manuscript and dug it up. He was outraged to find that it contained the clear statement that the world was created by Satan. He showed the manuscript to another senior and influential monk who was not personally antagonistic to me but was fiercely opposed to the idea that the world was created by a lower entity. The influence of these two was enough to turn the majority of the community against me. The Abbot himself, a cheerful, round-faced fellow, was not inimical to me or my ideas but was obliged to bow, for diplomatic reasons, to the will of the majority. With Clare, who supported me, I was expelled from Lindisfarne. We left by a path which, in the seventh century, went diagonally from the well across the lawn of what is now called the outer court.

But before dealing with our departure in disgrace it is necessary to recall the happy days when we were received in Lindisfarne. I have to record events in this order because I did not know the details of our reception till five days after our twentieth-century visit to Lindisfarne. On July 11th Annette rang from Canada immediately on waking. She said, rather inappropriately, "Didn't we have a wonderful time last night?" and was astonished that I had not shared her experience. She had had a vision of watching, with Graham and Guy, the arrival of Clare and myself at Lindisfarne. We had been expected a long time before and they were afraid that something had happened to us. They sent out ponies and a litter to bring us in. She said very positively that I could not see at all and was being led by Clare. It seems

168

I was "very tatty". Everybody busied themselves getting a hut ready for us. Annette was particularly positive that we laid down to rest before we had a meal with the other refugees from Cumberland. When she made her phone call she was still bathed in the happiness we had shared at this meal.

Annette described the settlement exactly as I had seen it when I sat with Clare on the edge of the well in the outer court.

I said to Annette that I wondered if Kathleen would ring. Annette then recalled, as Clare and I had done by the well at Lindisfarne, that Kathleen had been a thatcher, that she had made the particular roof which crowned our hut but that she was not concerned with the construction of the walls. Within ten minutes of Annette ringing off I had a call from Kathleen. She said she had had a remarkable vision the previous night. What she said coincided exactly with Annette's contribution. She emphasised that I was quite blind on arrival. She added one interesting item. She described how Clare gave me a sedative draught and said that, after I had fallen asleep, Clare treated me by some variety of the laying on of hands. When I awoke I could see a few dim outlines. It was this which made everybody so happy during the meal which followed.

After this flash-back to the joys of our arrival at Lindisfarne it is necessary to revert to the agony of our departure from it. I had to leave unfinished the design I had intended for the stone still marked with the equal-armed cross. (At Lindisfarne as in other places I had continued to work with stone.) I had personally chosen two pieces of stone as suitable material for sculpture. One remains untouched to this day and stands above the stone with the equal-armed cross. Both these stones were thrown out by the priests of the settlement after my departure. They were regarded as contaminated because they had been in the hands of a heretic who insisted that the world had been created by Satan.

I was expelled from Lindisfarne. What was worse my manuscript was destroyed as the work of the devil. Of all the failures and abject shortcomings of my five known incarnations this was the most disastrous. Clare went with me on my exodus from the abbey. Graham stayed on. He was largely but not entirely of my view. In any case healing rather than doctrine was his main preoccupation. After the death of Betty, Guy was the senior member of our group. He was sympathetic to me, a confirmed if by now secretive Dualist, but not convinced of the necessity for absolute Dualism. Annette stayed with him. She was devoted to him and could not forget how he cared for her after she suffered from the mob at Loweswater. Clare stuck to me. We were both to be Parfaits in the thirteenth century and Provençal sailors in the nineteenth. Though we did not meet in this life until I was well past sixty I think we can claim for ourselves a creditable record in mutual loyalty.

This was the end of our Celtic Cumbrian group. Dejected as we were when we left Cumberland we did not believe that our unity would disintegrate rapidly. I do not blame those of us who stayed on at Lindisfarne. I was bitter at the time because I have never been able to divest myself of my personal reactions. Certainly none of my friends from Cumberland were instrumental in my being turned out with Clare in the bitterness of winter with the snow falling thickly. The explanation was the same as it had been in Cumberland. Lindisfarne itself was becoming rapidly Romanised. The history books record what prodigies were achieved for Christ by this and that saint and how the unification of the Church was necessary and what it did for England in the Dark Ages. So many of those described as saints were as hard as flint and, once their own intellectualised theology had been questioned, inflexibly uncharitable. The Venerable Bede himself refers to the enlightened Pelagius as though he were a noxious microbe. What was lost with the suppression of the Celtic Church was a truly scientific concept of the cosmos which has not been recovered and a religious and philosophical attitude properly based on states of awareness and contacts with reality. What we gained was a theology fabricated by the congested minds of pedants and established as truth by systematic persecution.

What we suffered and what illnesses Clare contracted on the road to Rievaulx is material for a study of the origin of symptoms in past incarnations. It snowed throughout our journey. I have always hated the snow. It is well enough when out of reach on an alpine peak with a cloudless and torrid blue sky above it. It is a misery descending from a low grey sky, more miserable still when it weighs down the trees and muffles the earth and deadens the footfalls. It was snowing also when I took refuge in the hovel when I met Puerilia in my Cathar incarnation. Snow recalls the past for me and I endure it badly. My eyes refuse to focus. I feel sick and swimmy.

We found our last refuge at Rievaulx. We were welcomed there. We worked as healers and did not talk much of our deepest beliefs. The old faith lingered, however surreptitiously, longer at Rievaulx than Lindisfarne. For years I was convinced that my response to Rievaulx in this life was due to the resurgence of my Cathar memory. The medieval Abbot Alfred had had Platonic ideas of love very similar to those expressed by those among the Troubadours of the Languedoc who were disguised mouthpieces of Catharism. I see now that there was an additional explanation and that the impact of the place was more direct and poignant. When, in 1964, I felt dizzy and out of time I was back in the seventh century beating at the door and asking for entry.

In this life Clare visited Rievaulx alone and many years before she met me. She fell in a dead faint as soon as she entered the ruins. Perhaps in the seventh century she collapsed on arrival. Certainly she took to her bed immediately afterwards and was gravely ill.

I could add much more about our Celtic incarnation. Some small details are etched more sharply in my memory than the major issues. This is so particularly where they are concerned with Bassenthwaite and its immediate environment. It also applies to herbs and, with overwhelming emphasis, to the Easter Magiant I had eaten as a child in my herb pudding. Betty said that in her day it grew by the churches at Isel and St. Bega and that she used it as a medicine. Graham added later that I would find other herbs she had used still growing at St. Bega's by the churchyard wall which faces the lake. He mentioned penny-royal and a form of lichen with a peculiar circular growth and a curled edge, and a distinctive variety of fern. I found all these at St. Bega's in July 1974. What was more striking was that, during this visit to Cumberland, I so frequently found Easter Magiant in places frequented by the group in the Celtic incarnation. This herb was to become a preoccupation of the last member affiliated to our Celtic group.

171

I have said how Dr. Charles was so deliberately directed by Braïda when he was treating Annette. In March 1974 I spoke to him for the first time. I had known through Clare that his views on psychiatry were remarkably identical with my own. Even thus warned I was not prepared for the astonishing similarity of our phraseology. He said he had been equally astonished by the same phenomena as exhibited by Clare and myself. This is to be explained to a large extent by the fact that the three of us were fed with ideas from Braïda. There was still another factor at work. Betty and Graham told me that Dr. Charles had shared with us a Celtic incarnation in Cumberland. He had not been a priest but an ardent supporter of the community. He had lived in a hut to the left of the gate leading to the church at Isel. In July 1974 Clare saw him in the churchyard and also standing by the Derwent in the shadow of a tree. Later that year, unprepared by any evidence from us, he described the setting of Isel, the swift-flowing river and the settlement as it had been in the seventh century. As time went on it was evident that his far memory was deepening. He said that in his Celtic incarnation he had worn a dark-purple robe but had not been a priest, thus bearing out what Betty and Graham had said previously about him. He said he had been a scribe and had sat in at a momentous conference the procedure of which he remembered clearly. One of the items on the agenda was the rejection of the belief that the world was created by Satan. He remembered the aged representatives of the old Celtic Church who were anxious to meet their Romanised confrères half-way and who had no conception that their opponents were incapable of doing likewise. What was clear to Dr. Charles in his seventh-century guise was that the main aim of the younger Romanised clergy was to ensure the ultimate expulsion of women from the priesthood. They were careful not to make this too obvious at this particular session and were happy to hasten slowly. All I heard from this distinguished doctor, working against the New World background of a Canadian city, coincided exactly with what I had gathered directly from the revenants and from Clare.

It was part of the pattern that Dr. Charles should appear in the picture as Annette's doctor because to the latter her Celtic incarnation was by far the most important. It was also logical

172

that he should renew contact with Clare because she, too, had in the Celtic incarnation practised the healing which was her main interest. That the psychic contact between Clare and him remained unbroken was shown by the extraordinary effect on him when he first rang her from Canada to report on Annette's condition. He had been exhausted that day and suffered from a headache. After his telephone call he found himself descending the steps of his hospital without a headache and like a two-year-old. Both he and Dr. Paul testified on numerous occasions to the extraordinary rejuvenating effect they experienced after speaking with Clare on the phone. One should bear in mind that at this time they had never set eyes on her. They were to see her later in the year.

Dr. Charles told me that his mother had been born in Cockermouth, that is to say eight miles from my birthplace and a lesser distance from the house of my mother's ancestors. With the last words uttered on her death-bed his mother told him that, should he become ill, he should return to Cumberland and eat the Easter Magiant. It is one of the regrets of my life that, once again, I failed to see someone who had become not only important in my life but a genuine friend. He died in the late autumn of 1974 after a series of heart attacks. In his last phone call to Clare he said that one of the things he was most looking forward to seeing on his next visit to the United Kingdom was the Easter Magiant I had transplanted from Castle How to my garden and which, against all the odds, was still flourishing.

The story of our Celtic incarnation begins and ends at Bassenthwaite. The dead appear to the living because we all shared a common life between the inn and the landing stage. We meet again because of our memories of each other and because the same earth which nourished us in other days is still magnetic for us. After thirteen centuries we still feel its deep pulsations.

BOOK TWO

The Castle

Chapter Nineteen

As I have said, Marion came into the picture on the same day as Annette departed for Canada. It was also Trafalgar day. I did not know at the time that this date had a certain significance. Marion spoke first of the Celtic cultural centres she had visited. The day came when she steered sharply into another century. She said that off and on for years she had seen the ghost of a sailor. To understand what she saw it is necessary to go back a number of years—I cannot be exact—to a sunless and low-skied afternoon in summer. As I walked through my bedroom the full-length mirror seemed unusually congested. I stopped and looked into it and saw two faces. The one nearest me was infinitely more compelling. His face was striking and unmistakable because of its square shape. It was also peculiarly high-coloured. The red of his cheeks was deeper than the pink seen in northern countries and especially so above the cheekbones. Elsewhere the skin of his face was a dark biscuit colour. He had dark hair, dark eyes and he held himself with a strange and characteristic combination of relaxation and watchfulness. What intrigued me more than his features was his expression. It struck me at once that here was a basically good-natured fellow but who was essentially realistic and without illusion. Whenever his security was threatened he would beyond doubt get his blow in first. He belonged to the strike first and apologise afterwards school. At the time I saw this apparition I had no active interest in the psychic or in reincarnation but I knew instinctively that this fellow was me and that in addition he was a sailor and a Frenchman. All I noticed of his attire was that he wore rather wide trousers.

I had far less time for the other face behind me. It was that of a man in late middle age and intensely depressed. His face was unnaturally pinched by the depth of his depression. He had also a finicky and bureaucratic appearance which was in some way agonising. I knew that this man, too, was me. It was curious that

177

for years I never allowed myself to think about him. The agony of his face was too evident and he seemed also to be in some ways a poor specimen. I learnt later that I had been too hard on myself.

When Marion described her ghost I knew I was moving deeper than ever into the labyrinth of memory. Someone else was coming towards me through the narrowing tunnels of the unconscious. She spoke of the features which had struck me so many years previously, the absolutely characteristic square face, the peculiar high colour, the dark hair and eyes. Her voice was flat calm and she spoke very slowly. She never hurried when she talked. It was as if she were giving her measured opinion of a difficult case which interested her. When I asked her what kind of man he was she replied in the same voice that it was not easy to put into words. I could not wait any longer. I threw overboard my reluctance to condition others by supplying data before they were ready for it. After all, I was speaking of something which had followed me down the centuries, of a self which existed before my lifetime. I spoke of the sailor's good nature, his watchfulness and the half-reflex truculence which was never far below the surface.

"Yes, that's him exactly." I had never heard before, I would rarely hear again, the sudden sharpness and excitability which shattered the harmony of her measured voice.

Now I drew near to what I had seen in a dream for years. The dream was always the same. I moved near the sea through the shadow of trees. It was early autumn. The leaves were golden and the sea was still. I moved furtively from tree to tree, feeling the beauty of the day and the menace of hostile country. I walked at the edge of an inlet of the sea. I waited for a boat to enter the inlet. It never came or at least the dream always stopped before the boat appeared. I felt that this bitter-sweet dream— the trees were so beautiful but I felt myself hunted—was deeply interwoven with my life as a sailor.

For the last two years the impression had intensified that I had come to this country on a special mission. I had been landed from the sea and, when I hid among the trees, I was still waiting for a boat to sail in towards the shore. Though this impression was deepening I had not yet learnt to trust my hunches.

I had assumed that Marion would follow Annette in leading

me from my Cathar towards my Celtic incarnation. We were now on another tack. Where and when had I been a French sailor? There were one or two pointers from the past.

When I first went to Oxford the beauty of the South meant little to me. What I needed of a country was hills and the sea and clear swift rivers. From the fells near Bassenthwaite you could look across the rolling, wind-bitten country and across the Solway to the hills of Scotland. In the rivers you could see the flickering shadows of trout scarcely moving against the current. I was disappointed by my first sight of the country round Oxford, above all by the slow, turbid river tugging soundlessly at its banks. All that changed when I went to London as a medical student. As often as I could I escaped to Surrey. I loved what to others was suburban country, the commons, the brick villages, the miniature heaths with their pines and birches, the deep-cut lanes dark with yew and holly and the sudden smiling cornland beyond the hedges. To this day I am haunted by the village of Shere. I see it either in the glow of summer or in the silence of night and with winter descending slowly upon it. What, as a young medical student, I loved from the moment I first saw it is as precious to me as ever. I am also deeply moved by the country of heather, high commons and warm hamlets where Surrey, Sussex and Hampshire meet. For a reason I never attempted to analyse this latter area has always been associated in my mind with the Napoleonic wars. Against the background of war this half-veiled, unpretentious country was for me more intimate and domestic than ever.

In May 1972 I stayed two nights at Haslemere. I had arranged that Clare Mills should telephone me there about a business matter she was arranging for me. I was surprised to find that she had had an unheralded visit from Jane Butler. The latter also spoke to me on the phone. She said that she felt she had little longer to live. I was positively agitated after this conversation which occurred in the evening. My disquiet was still present the morning afterwards. I walked outside after breakfast to stretch my legs and dissipate the tension. I stared at a wall at the edge of the garden and at the long, low building at right angles to it. I was in one of those moods when anything on which your eye alights has a hypnotic effect. I did not know why I chose the wall. I did not know it had had a still more compelling effect on someone else. Suddenly I felt more intensely than ever the irrational connection between this country and the Napoleonic wars. Then I was presented with the still more astonishing thought that I had been a prisoner of war in this locality. As the day wore on I rejected the idea and accused myself of sentimentality. Nevertheless I had gained something from my visionary flash of myself in this region in the early years of the nineteenth century. Whatever it was it had swept away my tension.

For as long as I can remember I have been fascinated by the Napoleonic wars and by Napoleon himself. In this I may well be sharing the reactions of other immature characters but I do not think so. I disclosed my allegiance at too early an age. I cannot have been more than five when I was taken to the theatre in my home town in Cumberland. I cannot imagine what induced my parents to be so unfashionably indulgent. The play included a scene in which Napoleon said farewell before he was sent to St. Helena. Though at that age I was unentangled in the coils of history I rose in my seat and cried out loudly, "It isn't fair." I did not know what the audience thought of my unpatriotic criticism of the Establishment. One of the landmarks in my early childhood was a book called *Wellington and Waterloo*. In this I was reading, from the other side of the fence, what was vital to me. To this day I cannot read peaceably the story of Quatre Bras. I cannot remain in my chair when I read of the misunderstanding between Napoleon and Ney.

I forgot my feelings at Haslemere until a cold wet Sunday in June. Morale was at its lowest. I counted lugubriously the sunless weeks of a wasted summer. I had a telephone call from Jane Butler. She had been in hospital and was still suffering a great deal of pain from a fractured hip. In her usual courageous way she turned her back on her symptoms and spoke about other subjects. She asked me if I had any evidence of an incarnation other than that in the Languedoc. I said I had vague intimations but did not specify the epoch. I asked her the same question. Her reply astonished me more than her Cathar memory. What she said was less dramatic and verifiable but it excited me because my own far memory in the Napoleonic wars was nearing the

180

surface of consciousness. "Yes, I was a man," she said. "I was a French sailor. It was during the Napoleonic wars."

She did not think it odd that she and I might have known each other in an incarnation other than in the Languedoc. She accepted without difficulty the idea of a group keeping together through several incarnations. We spent little time over these theoretical possibilities. She was a person whose life had been governed by presented evidence and her contempt for theology and metaphysics was obvious. We went on to discuss more tangible matters. "Has Clare ever told you how she and Betty used to play hour after hour with boats and imagine themselves cabin boys?"

"No."

"And how her father used to spend hours with Clare on one knee and Betty on the other telling them stories of Napoleon?"

"No."

"Then ask her some time."

I asked her a few hours later. "Yes," she said. "We used to play a lot at being sailors. Let me see, I was Pierre and Betty was Henri."

"Why the French names?"

"Search me. Do you know I have never thought about it? One thing sticks in my mind—Jane knitted us sailors' berets with little red pom-poms."

"Why the French Navy?"

"What do you mean?"

"Didn't you know that French sailors have red pom-poms on their berets?"

"No, I can't remember ever having seen any. Another thing, my father used to talk to us for hours about sea battles."

I had been in all day and felt restless. I suggested we should walk a little up the road. It was a wild evening for June but in a way beautiful with the branches streaming backwards from the wind-bent trees. My mind had switched away from the Napoleonic era. Suddenly I heard very loudly the creaking of a ship's timbers as it rolled in high seas. Surely my imagination had produced it from the wind and the whining branches. I asked myself how I could feel the strained timbers of a wooden

181

man-o'-war when I had never been in a sailing ship. I told myself I was influenced by suggestion.

Later that evening I had another telephone call from Jane Butler. She was a conscientious and grateful soul. She wanted me to know how much better she felt after our earlier conversation. I changed the subject by saying, "Of course you know that our talk this afternoon was well timed for old Bonapartists. Today's the anniversay of Waterloo."

"Good Heavens, is it really?" She was far more moved than when she admitted to being Bruna. When she had spoken of her daughter as Hélis de Mazerolls she had seemed almost detached. I suppose that she had lived for years with the Cathars and the thirteenth century had become a second home. Certainly she was more excited by the emergence to light of nearer but possibly more cloudy memories.

Because I had just returned from my walk with Clare Jane's next remark was arresting. "Tell me, has Clare ever told you what happens when she hears stairs creaking?"

"No."

"She goes out of time. She hears the creaking timbers of a wooden ship. Hasn't she told you about her dread of cannon balls?"

"Not cannon balls, stones. What you are thinking of is the stone-throwing machines at Montségur."

"No, it was also sea fights."

Next morning I asked Clare if creaking timbers in an old house provoked any reaction in her. "Oh, yes, sea fights," she said. "I was going to tell you last evening when you turned the corner just above your house."

"Why didn't you?"

"Should I? Did I need to?"

My question was superfluous. I should have known already. It had come to me in my clearly audible perception of the ship's strained timbers.

Next morning I had a telephone call from Kathleen. The day previously had been heavy with domestic troubles but towards evening she had felt fortified because Clare materialised in the room with her and was clearly visible. She said also that a short phrase kept repeating in her mind. "I have the will, pray God for

182

me that He gives me the strength." She asked me if these words could be part of any Cathar prayer. I could not immediately recall the sentence. Later I discovered that it is part of the Consolamentum. Though I have referred to the text of the latter several times in writing this book I cannot claim to remember in detail this long office. Kathleen does not read French and has no books about the Cathars. I know of no English translations of the Consolamentum.

After Kathleen had told me of her experience the previous evening I asked her if she had even been specially attracted to the sea. Her voice sharpened when she said, "Why do you ask me that?" and went on to tell me that, when she was younger, she had sought a maritime career as a secretary-purser in an ocean-going liner. This was a rare and curious choice for a girl of that epoch. She had also said that she remembered vividly Clare's hour of triumph as a schoolgirl. Her essay on the life of a cabin boy in a warship was read aloud to her form as a model of how such things should be done.

Later that summer Clare spoke to Jack while he was in hospital. She asked him if he had felt any particular attachment to the sea. He reacted violently and said it horrified him to the degree that he could not bear to go near it and had never swum or bathed in it. He said that he was sure something awful had happened to him at sea.

To me these maritime experiences were not cast-iron evidence of another incarnation but they counted for something. At this time I was satisfied that a circle which had formed in the Languedoc in the thirteenth century had reappeared in England seven hundred years later. My visit to Haslemere and my conversations with Jane and Kathleen took place in the summer of 1972 before Annette appeared on the scene with her Celtic memories. It seemed to me possible that this group could have formed up again in the French Navy in the Napoleonic wars. To me the evidence was no more than presumptive. I had no idea that I would later be provided with data as detailed and convincing as the dovetailed items in my Cathar experience.

Chapter Twenty

Though Marion was to be the fulcrum round which the Napoleonic incarnation was balanced she did not act immediately in that capacity. She had said that she would attend a lecture I was giving. Before it began I waited for her. I knew she would not come but it was necessary to go through the motions. In this life we do what we should. In the next we know why we did it. It was odd to wait for someone who had seen my ghost. It was not disturbing or even exciting. When you accept that you have been in contact with someone in a previous life you have no time for the more palpitating aspects of reincarnation. I was merely sad and empty when she did not come. It seemed that my lot was to listen to their voices. I longed for the sight of a face. The Dualists, I thought, were teaching me a lesson. They were tearing away the final tatters of my lifelong preoccupation with form. What they required of me was a more complete surrender to the invisible. They asked too much. I am unable to live on earth the full implications of Dualism.

Mairon rang me a few days later. She had been unable to come to my lecture because of a virus infection. She had a strangled and fruitless cough. She spoke factually and with detachment about her symptoms. She obviously felt worse than she admitted. She asked me, in the same level tones but with more contrived detachment, what a sergeant-at-arms was. Here was still another returning to Avignonet and Montségur. After I had answered she continued, "Did you mention the name Arnaud during your lecture?"

"Yes." I had ended my lecture with the mention of his name. I had originally planned to cover more ground but had gone into greater detail than I had intended. The last event I had mentioned was Jane Butler calling for her thirteenth-century husband Arnaud when she came round from the anaesthetic. "Does this name mean anything to you?"

184

"Yes."

"Since when?"

"About six months ago." For several people the first months of 1972 were a time of revelation.

Within the next few months it was made clear by the revenants that Marion had been Arnaud in her Cathar incarnation. When she next rang she was ill with phlebitis. By now I understood that, in those with far memory, severe illness can be related to increasing insight. Clare had begun her recurrent dreams when her life was threatened by diphtheria. Betty had written and drawn her recollections of Avignonet when convalescing from scarlet fever. There was no doubt that Marion was following the same pattern. Her illness had coincided with increasing far memory. First she noted a deep-blue haze in the atmosphere. She defined the colour with great care. "It is not the dark blue we mean by navy blue. You could call it French navy, say a deep royal blue." This coincided with Clare's description of the robes and colours worn by Braïda and her father. "At first the blue haze occupied the whole room. After some time it cohered in the shape of a robe tied by some kind of girdle. The latter was silver and not entirely uniform. There was a kind of loop at the left hip."

Marion described the Parfait's uniform in almost the identical terms used by Clare and the others. It was bewildering that members of this group spoke often not only in the same voice but used the same words. It was as though the same oracle was speaking through them yet all spoke from their separate standpoints. It is more important to record these things than to explain their mechanism. The latter, too, will be revealed to us in time, but only when we have acquired a more refined form of consciousness. Perhaps we must wait till death. In these matters to analyse too much is like looking for micro-organisms without a microscope. Intense "scientific" searching induces a kind of spiritual myopia. When you approach the high levels of truth you cannot reason your way into its substance.

It was obvious that for Marion the tuning-in process was intensifying. The Cathar vein was by no means exhausted. Like Clare and others before her she had visions and dreams of men and women in dark-blue robes meeting in forests. It was characteristic of her that one day she changed the subject abruptly. "In your book about the Cathars you never said positively that you were a Parfait."

"Not in so many words."

"You preached and taught," she said. "You were more important than you thought." After she had spoken I felt she was withdrawing from me. When you are close to people but have not seen them you become very sensitive to the inflections of their voices. "I don't claim any detailed knowledge of the thirteenth century," she continued. "Of course the sailor is different." Now she was talking more rapidly and her voice was lighter. "I remember him absolutely clearly."

"We must have known each other before."

"Yes," she said. She made no other comment.

I knew in my heart of hearts that she and I had been sailors in the Napoleonic wars. Of course I would never in speech or in writing have referred to this as an established fact. One may go by hunches but it is still undesirable to present one's intuitions as evidence. But by now I knew from the first days those I had met in another life. It was in part the general atmosphere that emanated from them. It was distinguishable even though I had not met them in the flesh. It was perhaps a proof that our perceptions are more accurate without the impediment of matter. And then of course there was always the feeling of another piece fitting into a pattern.

When she next rang she was happy because a friend had given her a copy of a magazine which had printed some of my poems. She said she had been particularly moved by one poem.

You watched me sleeping
Across the centuries.

You soothed my pains in this world
Because your own were distant.

Come for me in the end,
I would feel the distance
Between myself and my own sorrow.

When she described her reaction to this poem her voice was more controlled than ever. It was obvious that she was stirred

186

by it because we had known each other before. It was equally clear that there was nothing burning or demanding in her memory.

Then Marion switched over abruptly and inexplicably to Portchester Castle. I had never seen it and knew little about it. She had visited it earlier that year. Looking downwards from the keep she had seen a number of men materialise in the green enclosure. They were dressed in a variety of rough clothes worn at the beginning of the last century. Among them was the sailor she had come to know.

"You must go to Portchester," she said.

"What will I find there?"

"You must go and see."

It was curious that in some ways her methods resembled those of the revenants. She would not respond to certain kinds of direct question.

It was curious that Clare also spoke of Portchester. I had not known that she had ever been there. It appeared that she had visited it earlier that year. She said it had a wonderful atmosphere and urged me to go there. I was not enthusiastic. I disliked being prepared for the atmosphere of places. In the past so many have left me cold. She said that I would find it interesting because it had housed French prisoners in the Napoleonic war.

Finally I said I would go if she would accompany me. It was obvious that something had attracted her attention. I had no confidence in my ability to find it if I went alone. She said it would be better if I went without her.

"What is it you found at Portchester?" I said.

"I'll tell you after you've been there. If you see it, well, you see it. If you don't, you've lost nothing."

Marion was far more insistent than Clare about Portchester. Every time she rang me she asked if I had been there. I longed to know what was in her mind. I knew it was no good asking. She was one of those who live alone and austerely with their far memories and who do not condition others.

One day I spoke to Marion of my dream of the trees, of waiting for the boat and of the feeling of moving in hostile country. "The leaves were golden. Is that right?" I said.

"It was autumn."

"Do you remember a line of trees?"

"Not a line, just trees."

"I don't know if I came on a mission or was picked up from a wreck." I wanted her to answer for me. The silence in some way was resounding. Time itself was a slow pulsation. "Well, I can take it I was a prisoner of war?" I continued.

"Yes."

"And at Portchester?"

"Yes."

"Somehow there is nothing painful about it."

"We were happy," she said briefly.

"But I didn't stay there all the time," I said. "I feel I was loaned out, that I worked for someone. I have this feeling about the country round Haslemere where Surrey, Sussex and Hampshire run into each other."

"With me it is only Hampshire."

After I had spoken to her I felt curiously light and detached from myself. I realised that I had put into words the unshaped and inaudible memories of decades.

At this time I obtained a few books and pamphlets about Portchester. I learnt that at the end of the eighteenth and the beginning of the nineteenth century the Norman keep had been adapted for the lodgment of prisoners of war, the majority of whom had been French. The prisoners had also lived in hutments enclosed by the outer walls of the castle. It appeared that there were numerous graffiti on the walls. It came to my mind that Clare had found these inscriptions of great interest. Her responses to my questions were so deliberately evasive that I felt my conjecture was correct. I wondered if I had left somewhere on the castle walls any record of my stay at Portchester.

On a still day in December my wife and I went out to lunch in the village. It was very pleasant to hear the conversation of our hostess's mother. She was a Breton woman with a taste for history. Listening to her I could visualise her country, the gorse scattered thickly in the sheltered hollows and the hard-stoned, sharp-angled houses confronting the wind and the menace of the sea. It was especially fascinating when she spoke of her great-grandfather. He was a French officer taken prisoner at Trafalgar who subsequently died with the rank of admiral. When she

188

went to school in England she did not know that he had been a prisoner of war in the vicinity. She found later from the family papers that his parole had extended to roads and crossroads near Bedales and which were familiar to her.

I listened intently and unaware of the passage of time because it was a question of French prisoners in England. It was so beguiling on a grey afternoon darkening to mist, that I lingered on until early evening. The gulls flew inland above the river. The estuary was twenty miles off with two cities in between. Nevertheless there was always the feeling of the sea because of the Breton woman and because of the admiral who had been a prisoner. It was quite out of pattern for me to arrive before lunch and to linger until evening. We did not leave until darkness had fallen.

We did not leave until after Marion and her mother had left Clare's house. They had rung her at lunch time and said they were coming. There was no deep pain but a sense of sickening futility. They came directly from the French wars and our hostess's mother was a kind of herald. They came, they went, I was doomed to miss them. It was either the malice of circumstance or something good required of me and beyond my doing. I could not endure that the messengers passed so close to me that I could feel their breath on my forehead.

The Dacres had not come to Bath to talk about the Napoleonic wars. Mrs. Dacre, who had seen Clare only once previously, nevertheless insisted that she could cure Marion who had not yet recovered from her thrombo-phlebitis. Clare feigned ignorance and asked for instructions. She was anxious that as few as possible should know her gift of far memory. Mrs. Dacre told Clare where to put her hands. The latter placed one at the site of Marion's phlebitis and the other on the knee at the appropriate landmark. It was obvious that Mrs. Dacre also knew the details of the Cathar laying on of hands. Marion felt much better that evening and still better the next morning. Though a doctor she submitted unquestioningly to the treatment and expected nothing but good from it. Had Mrs. Dacre, as well as her daughter, lived in the thirteenth century?

When Mrs. Dacre next rang I spoke of the group of people who had reincarnated in England after being together in the

thirteenth century. By this time I was less grudging in my communication with others. I took Braïda's advice and followed my
hunches. In any case it was impossible not to be completely
forthcoming with Mrs. Dacre. There was something about her
which inspired me to confide in her. In addition it was ludicrous
to imagine that I could condition her. Her voice was firm, imperious and curiously unwavering. If I had to describe her in a
word I would use the teeth-gritting adjective "queenly" and this
in spite of the fact that I knew she was shy. My relationship
with her was entirely different from what I felt with Marion.
The latter felt deeply the bond between us but appeared to me
loath to admit it. What was between her mother and myself was
unspoken but conscious and intensely human. If it arose in the
past it was simply and warmly felt in the present.

Of my group of names none meant anything to Mrs. Dacre
except Perella. Perhaps Clare, as Esclarmonde de Perella, was the
only individual she remembered from the thirteenth century and
this may have explained her otherwise unaccountable confidence
in Clare as a healer. We spoke again of Cumberland, of her
husband's home near Kendal and of how her father came from
the savage and haunted country near Wastwater. Then she spoke
of her mother who was French and a native of Carpentras. I have
always loved this town. It is beautiful to leave the torrent of
traffic for the quiet of the rue de Vignes. I had stayed there once
with my wife. The house opened blindly on the quiet street and
enclosed a courtyard with a shady tree. We wandered by day
beneath a sky deep-blue and swept clear by the Mistral. It was
lovely to return to the house at evening under the low, clear
stars.

It was significant that Mrs. Dacre had roots in Provence as
well as Cumberland. I had been reincarnated in the latter region.
When I visited Provence before the Second World War, I had
come to life as never before and the impressions of that first visit
are etched deeply and ineradicably in my memory.

It was obvious that our shared loyalties were not limited to
Cumberland and Provence. There was still another country she
loved. Indeed it seemed to me that in our loves and loyalties we
had followed each other up and down the world without ever
meeting. She spoke of her daughter's experience at Portchester.

190

It was clear that it was as important for her as for Marion. Then she said how she herself loved the country round Haslemere. As she spoke to me I felt close to that domesticated and comfortable but still beautiful region with its sudden exhilarating open spaces. It was interesting that she and I, inured to the rugged contours of Cumberland, should feel so deeply for this gentle, hooded country.

I had been moved when she spoke of Haslemere. I held my breath as she continued. "There is a wall there which is important to me. Five years ago, when I was looking at this wall I began to see life differently. It began to have a much deeper significance for me."

"Where was this wall?"

Her voice diminished to a whisper. "It was in the garden at G——."

It was in that garden at Haslemere and looking at the wall that I had my deep and final conviction that I had been a French prisoner in that country. I had looked at the wall with an inexplicable anguish the morning after Jane Butler had phoned me. Jane was the first of the group to tell me that she had been a French sailor at the time of Napoleon. I had seen how places could activate the psyche of those with far memory. The dead had come back on the road at Bassenthwaite. The voice of the past was ringing in the air in the ruins at Rievaulx. Now a garden wall with no known history had acted as a fuse to ignite two people. The wall leads me back to a castle by the shore. The castle points to the sea and ships, to myself as I was in another epoch.

"It was by the wall in the garden at G—— that I first knew for certain that I had been a French prisoner."

"It's very interesting," she said. There were times when she spoke as soberly as her daughter.

From that moment a curtain descended inside me. I became positively reluctant to work out who I was in the nineteenth century and what Marion and her mother were to me. Certainly I was eager to know but I was unwilling to exercise my mind and turn the mystery into a problem. There was no active effort of repression. The change was at a deeper level. I have passed from scrutiny and verification to passive recording and a little interpretation between the main events. Now I can only write what happened. I know that the explanations will be given later and that when they happen they will seem like events. I have less need than before to think things out. This is not a reaction of fatigue. Certainly I am tired because so much has happened so quickly. In the last year the tide of memory has battered away at the crumbling breakwaters of my old inhibitions. It is all like a kind of war. Things happen quickly. One does well enough to keep a record of events.

Chapter Twenty One

The pressure on me to go to Portchester was considerable. I showed a praiseworthy inertia in confronting my destiny. I have never been an impassioned hunter of the psychic. I myself have been the quarry of experiences and forces I have not fully understood.

One feature stood out significantly. There was a consensus of opinion that I should not go without Clare. Marion and her mother were tirelessly emphatic. Annette gave me the same message from Braïda. Clare insisted I should go without her. I knew that she was partly right but I felt a little exasperated. Nobody knew better than I did the evils of conditioning. But did she understand sufficiently the uselessness of my looking for things? I had found from past experience that in my case searching precluded finding. I asked her one positive question. "Are there any scribblings on the walls of any interest to me?"

"I think so." She was deliberately casual and I had neither the desire nor the heart to press her further.

In the middle of January 1973 my wife and I set off for Portchester. I was exhausted that morning and did not think the occasion propitious. My heart lightened as we traversed the squalid respectability of Fareham. The approach to Portchester was detestable. The coast was scarred with housing estates of a hygienic and garish mediocrity. It was less supportable than the intimate squalor of the slums or the brick towns of Lancashire squatting ungainly beneath a sulphury sky. Towards the castle there was a little haven of Georgian houses. The traffic diminished as we went towards them. The castle was beautiful. Despite the length and height of its walls, and the solid dignity of its Norman tower seen behind the trees, there was something delicate and legendary about it.

When we arrived after midday it was closed until early afternoon. We walked along the landward aspect of the castle, towards the tongue of the harbour which goes deeply inland. I felt impelled to walk the whole circuit of the outside wall. Because we had to return to Fareham for lunch I stopped short of the Water Gate. I was particularly anxious to see it but felt it could wait. When we returned after lunch I was bristling with energy and had forgotten my exhaustion of the morning. We went in at the Land Gate. We saw names of French prisoners scrawled on the walls to the right of the entrance. We went straight towards the keep because we knew it had been occupied by a large number of French prisoners. Before we entered the keep I visualised the form, width and substance of the steep wooden walls leading to the dormitories. They were exactly as I pictured them. I did not set much store by this. They were obviously modern and had been laid long after the prisoners had departed. Nevertheless it amounted to something. Nothing I had seen or read in the books I had consulted had prepared me for the shape of the steps.

The first thing noticeable about the prisoners' quarters was that there was no atmosphere of depression or horror. My wife was first to make this comment. This was significant because she has a dread of prisons and dungeons and is always depressed by them. To me to be in the prisoners' quarters was like shrouded sunshine. It was not merely that there was no bad atmosphere. The ambience was positively cheerful. Marion, in her monosyllabic way, had looked back with happiness on her incarceration. Portchester had never been a civil prison. In the mid-eighteenth century it was converted for use for prisoners of war. During the Napoleonic wars the treatment of the inmates was in marked contrast to the horrors inflicted in the disease-infested hulks.

I had gone to Portchester with the idea that I would find easily some relevant inscription. At this time I had received so much data from this world and the next that I expected the evidence to fall into my lap. There was a positive cloudburst of inscriptions on the first two floors of the keep. It was worse than looking for a needle in a haystack. What I was actually looking for was some approximation of my own name in this incarnation. It may seem absurd but such was my intention. This had crossed my mind for no tangible reason in the course of one of my earlier conversations with Marion. Clare had also hinted vaguely that something like my name was on the wall. She had given me no further instructions. I failed altogether to find anything relevant among the swarming maze of inscriptions on the first two floors.

I stayed a long time in the Norman tower. I went up and down the steep stairs on several occasions. Since my illness in 1968 I had never taken so much hard exercise with so little fatigue. When I looked at the view from the keep I felt suddenly that there should be a Martello tower to the east. There was none in sight and I felt I had been cheated. Perhaps it had been destroyed in the years between.

We walked round the grounds inside the walls. We walked to the foot of the tower where the escapees and other malefactors had been put into solitary confinement. We did not go in because the way was barred with scaffolding and there were notices saying that entrance was forbidden.

When we went out by the Land Gate I knew that from every reasonable point of view the expedition had failed. I had recognised nothing that had related to my incarceration in the early 1800s. It was as Braïda and others had warned me. I had gone without Clare and failed. I myself had been in favour of submitting wholly to the guidance of Braïda. Clare had always adapted the latter's advice to fit her own contemporary requirements. I had no doubt that hers was the more mature attitude. She lived to a greater degree out of time than I did but was prepared more to acecpt the disciplines of this world. I was more willing to hand myself over to the other world because I was less acquainted with it than she was. Perhaps I was reaching too strenuously for an experience which had been denied me.

Nevertheless the expedition was a success because my heart widened with love for this place. In the quite recent days when I wrote *The Cathars and Reincarnation* I would have rejected this as evidence. I had come now to accept that love is an eloquent witness. I knew that from now on Portchester would be for me like Montségur, Rievaulx and Bassenthwaite. It was one of those places with a capacity to transport me beyond this world.

Before we returned we walked once again on the path outside

the castle towards the Water Gate. Now I knew instinctively that we should go beyond it to the as yet unvisited path along the south wall. My wife intervened and said, "You've done enough for one day. We'll come again."

I accepted what she said in the same way that I knew that I should go beyond the Water Gate. My two reactions seemed to contradict each other but I believed them both to be right. I had the feeling that I was not yet ready for something.

We had hardly got home when Clare telephoned. She had a bloodhound's instinct for arrivals and departures. "Well, how did you like it?" she said.

"Wonderful. The whole place was beautiful and had a beautiful atmosphere. There isn't an awful lot I can say about it. I felt much better, much stronger physically, for being at Portchester."

"I'm delighted. Of course if you'd gone past the Water Gate you would have seen something you'd have recognised."

"What was it?"

"Perhaps you'll feel it next time. I am sorry you couldn't find the inscription. It's in the first room you come to at the top of the stairs. I suppose it's difficult to see but I spotted it immediately."

I had hardly replaced the receiver before Marion rang. It was strange that this severely self-disciplined woman should be so happy because I had loved Portchester. After all, I had seen nothing of specific importance to me, or, come to that, to her. Then she made a statement almost identical with that of Clare. "If you had gone on past the Water Gate to the path by the south wall you would have seen something you would have recognised."

"What would that be?" I said.

"Perhaps you will see next time."

"There was nothing depressing about the Castle."

"I told you we were happy," she said.

Marion's mother rang next morning. She was even more delighted than her daughter that I had visited Portchester. It was strange that this elderly dignified woman should find such happiness in the reactions of someone she had never met. "Did you walk on the path by the south wall?" she said.

196

"No. I went along the inlet but not as far as the Water Gate."

"If you had gone on further you would have seen something of great interest to you."

I felt little exasperation that I had failed to reach the Water Gate. I was still enveloped in the total serenity of Portchester.

Chapter Twenty Two

A month later we went with Clare to Portchester. The sky was grey and it was less sunny than on my first visit. Nevertheless there was the same lightness of heart and the same feeling of the castle sleeping behind the trees and the somnolence of an endless summer. We went to the lower dormitory in the keep. On my previous visit I had spent most of my time on the floor above. In the dullness of a mid-winter afternoon the inscription was less immediately visible to Clare than when she first saw it on a day in July with the sun overhead and the light falling on the writhing mesh of writing which covered the wall. The inscription "Guird" was heavily eroded by time but still discernible if you looked obliquely across it with your back to the light coming in at the door. I could not tell how the name terminated. I was not greatly impressed by this inscription. It was hard to see except for a person with sharp eyes and a flair for unveiling written patterns.

We stayed only a short time within the walls of the castle. I was anxious to get outside. There was nothing oppressive in the atmosphere. It was as serene and harmonious as on my first visit. It was merely that I wished to walk outside the walls as soon as possible. After all I had been told insistently enough that I should do so. Once again I went from the car park and along the north wall towards the tongue of the inlet inserted from the harbour. This time we reached the Water Gate. I knew I had been through this gate before. I turned to Clare, "Which way were you taken in as a prisoner?"

"Through this gate."

"How did you get there?"

"There was a battle at sea. Our ship, not yours, was crippled and surrendered and was towed into the harbour. Henri, that is to say Betty, was with me. You remember I told you that when we were young she and I used to play at being cabin boys. We were taken off the ship and herded together in small boats. They were terribly crowded. The sailors were a rough lot and shoved us about until the boats were crammed full. One struck me across the ear. I remember absolutely clearly how terrified I was. Then we went in at the gate. The men at the gate asked us a few questions."

"Such as?"

"Just who we were and where we came from. They didn't take a lot of interest."

"What language did you speak?"

"I cannot remember but it must have been French. I didn't speak any English."

"Were you still very frightened at the gate?"

"Terrified. As soon as I got inside things were better."

"I also came through the gate," I said. I saw the neutral, immobile faces of the people who passed us through.

"Yes, the sailor prisoners were brought in small boats from the harbour. I came ashore just opposite the gate. You weren't with us. You were not in our ship. You were brought in another time."

"Did you know me while I was a prisoner?"

"Of course," she said. "You were a considerable figure among the prisoners."

"I am certain I was not an officer."

"You weren't, but you were still important. In a way you were looked up to."

"Why? I cannot think I had a beautiful character."

"No. It was something you had to do."

We went on past the Water Gate and turned right on the path by the south wall of the castle. I had read that in the first years of the eighteenth century there were hutments with prisoners inside the wall. In the light of day I felt the shadows of the past. It engulfed me like a cloud. I needed guidance through it. It irritated me that Clare had walked on ahead. I stopped in my tracks and called to her to wait. I hoped she would return to where I was standing. I was rooted to the spot and reluctant to leave it. She disregarded my call and moved away from me with unusually small and fidgety strides. Her expression was shut-in and her features blunted. I wondered if she sensed and resented my irritation. "Where did I escape from the castle?" I said. It was a peculiar question because I had never learnt from anything or anybody that I had escaped from prison.

"From the place where you are standing?"

"And you?" I said.

"I escaped from there too. There was a tunnel under the wall from the hutments."

"Who were you with?" I said.

"That's just the trouble. You see I escaped once and was immediately recaptured.* Betty, that means Henri, was somewhere about. I don't think she was there the second time. It keeps coming back to me but not absolutely clearly. I know for certain that we escaped a second time. At the second attempt there were three or four people and you were one. I knew you had a letter you wanted taken somewhere. I was here with you." It irritated me profoundly that we kept on walking. After we turned the corner and left the south wall her manner was easier.

"You were recaptured," she said.

"It was in the autumn. The leaves were turning."

"Yes, it could have been autumn."

"How old was I?" I said.

"About thirty-five. Some time after that you went on parole. You had finished something you had to do."

"How long was I on parole?"

"I can't say. I know you did not stay long in Portchester, I'd say, perhaps eighteen months. You didn't come back after you went out on parole. The last thing I recall about you was that you were lying on the grass. I saw that again last July."

"What was I doing on the grass?"

"You were going on parole. You were waiting with a lot of others to be taken off to where you were working."

"Were you ever on parole yourself?"

"Henri and I were allowed as far as the village but no further. It was something to do with our being so young. We were in our early teens."

"By Henri you mean Betty?"

* A year later she relived the first escape in which she never emerged from the tunnel. She was engulfed by debris from its falling roof.

200

"Yes. He was a fattish boy. He doesn't ring a bell in the second escape. Perhaps something will come."

We did another circuit of the outside walls and went in again at the Water Gate. After a hundred and seventy years I felt the tension at the gate and saw the expression of the people who interrogated the prisoners. They were informal and unsmiling but no more forbidding than the average passport officer on a cross-channel steamer. I was ready to leave the castle because I wanted to go to Southsea. I had been told that in its castle there was a list of French prisoners of war. When we were walking towards the Land Gate exit I felt an irresistible impulse to go back to the main building. My wife and I went into Assheton's Tower. It was here that prisoners who escaped and were recaptured were punished by solitary confinement. At the time of our visit it was forbidden to enter but the custodian said we could do so. I noticed no inscriptions on the walls. This was because Clare had not accompanied us into the tower. While my wife and I were within it she beamed encouragingly at us across the scaffolding. This was unusual because she is an intrepid character with great physical courage. My wife told me afterwards she felt that Clare was too frightened to enter. I did not notice her agitation.

As we left the castle I tried hard to locate the line of trees I had seen in my dream. There were trees along the west face of the castle between the keep and the village. They were much too young. My attention was riveted by a tongue of land curving westwards to the right of my point of escape. It was now a suburban wasteland and covered with scrub and low bushes. Perhaps at that time it had a line of trees. The main theme of my dream was the trees gold with autumn and waiting for the boat to loom up round the point. It irked me that I could not find the line of trees. I seemed unable to accept that in a century and a half they could well have been felled.

I had always known that in my dream I was on a mission in enemy country. I had assumed that it referred to my first capture. I had seen myself landing in hostile country to perform some mission and be picked up again. Now I was not so sure. Was I looking back to my escape from Portchester and my subsequent recapture? The predominating theme in my dream was awaiting

201

the boat. It did not occur to me that the boat had not failed us. My dream had stopped before it came round the point.

As a means of identifying the prisoners Southsea was a wild-goose chase, but I was amply repaid when I looked across the Solent from the castle ramparts. Strung along the coast was a line of Martello towers. On my first visit to Portchester I was absolutely convinced that there should be at least one tower lying eastward. It had disappointed me that it was not visible from Portchester. When I saw the forts clearly and the sea between the mainland and the Isle of Wight, the feeling of recognition was even more definite than at Portchester. These forts were in some way related to my mission.

On our way back home Clare was quiet but happy and seemed very tired. It was obvious that it had been a fruitful experience for her but that she was a little shattered by it. I did not ask her any questions. I did not realise that at that time and during the next day the field of recall was widening and deepening. I accepted already that she did not divulge what she knew until it was in my interest to know it. She gave me no opportunity to exercise my powers of imagination or my capacity to visualise. What she revealed to me was all the more convincing because it came at times when a pattern was being completed by others who were not in contact with her in the worldly sense of the term. This interlocking of evidence was to be especially revealed in the Portchester story.

She offered one small item of information on the return journey. "I remember I used to make things with bits of bones. I wasn't very good at it and gave it up quickly."

The French prisoners at Portchester were wonderfully skilled at making model ships with fragments of bones. One can say that this is so well known that the knowledge of it could have influenced her memory. There was more evidence to come about the prisoners' hobbies.

Two days after my trip to Portchester I had a sharp pain in my left eye. In the last couple of years I had from time to time had crops of styes on the eyelid of this eye. I felt this was something different because the pain was sharp, lancinating and more in the substance of the eye itself than merely in the eyelid. I could not see that a stye was forming. Neither my wife nor

I could detect anything except some inflammation of the eyelid.

At lunch-time the same day I had a call from Marion. She told me that her mother was suffering from a corneal ulcer in the left eye. I thought the pain in my own was too sharp and deep-seated to be explained by a stye. Marion said that her mother's eye condition had started to improve and that the pain was less. The improvement occurred at the same time as I felt the pain in my own left eye. By now this kind of thing had happened too often for me to pass it off as coincidence. I had found from experience that the picking up of other people's symptoms was a creative and curative process which occurred in times of intense psychic activity. This healing activity was an essential component in the complex mechanism of psychic synchronisation. In two days' time Mrs. Dacre's condition was radically improved.

After we had spoken of her mother I told Marion of my second expedition to Portchester. After my first visit she had been undemonstratively, almost unemotionally happy because I had liked the atmosphere and felt stronger for it. Now, when I told her of my experiences, she responded baldly and briefly. I don't know what she felt like when she talked to me. My own attitude was always that of someone with less knowledge than she had. I approached her as a young subaltern submitting a report to a senior officer. It is quite possible that I created a completely different impression. I am only saying what I felt like. I asked at what point I had escaped. "Along the path by the harbour. At the place where you said you stopped."

"Was I alone?"

"No. There were three others."

"Were we waiting for a boat?"

"Yes."

"And it came?"

"It came all right."

"Did I go out to it?"

"No. You were here on the bank to see the mission was completed."

"What was the mission?"

"You and I were landed somewhere a good deal east of Portchester. Our job was to investigate the shore defences. We finished what we had set out to do but were captured afterwards.

Inside Portchester you drew a sketch of what you had seen. The whole point of the escape was to dispose of your drawing. It was taken out to a boat which came round the point. There was a go-between linking the prisoners and the garrison. A young cabin boy called Pierre swam out with your sketch in a leather pochette. He was young and active. You and I were considered too old and unathletic."

"How old were we?"

"Well over thirty."

"And the expedition was successful?"

"Completely. That's why we were so happy."

"I suppose after we were recaptured we got solitary confinement."

"No, not you and I. They took the odd view that we were too old to be a menace in such an effort. They regarded us as being misled by this young boy called Pierre."

"What happened to him?"

"He was put in a cell in the tower."

"It seems rather hard if I was responsible. Did we worry about it?"

"Good gracious, no. We had done what we set out to do. Why should we worry?" It was interesting to hear this conscientious and scrupulous doctor expressing such a cavalier disregard of ethics. She was obviously able to live better in her other skin than I was.

"What was your name?"

"I can't say, really." She answered slowly as though she had some inkling. She was so made that she could not say anything based on supposition.

"Was it Henri?"

"It rings a faint bell but I couldn't be sure."

"Do you know my name?"

"Guirdaud," she said promptly.

"And my Christian name?"

"I have no idea. You were never known except by your surname."

It was only natural that I was preoccupied with how I had thought in my previous life. I wondered if my opinions on men and matters had been similar to those of this incarnation. But most of all I wondered if I, who am hostile to what in political circles we know as the forces of progress, had been a Republican or Bonapartist. I could not credit that in those days I had been anything other than the latter. One thing was certain—I had no regrets for the old régime. "I wonder what our politics were in those days?" I said.

"I have never been interested in politics in this life or the last."

"I put all this about 1804."

"It could well be," she said. "I am not interested in dates."

I felt more sure about my dream. It seemed inevitable to me that it must refer not to my first capture but to my attempted escape. Why should my own far memory, and that of two others, be concentrated on the path by the harbour?

On the same day as Marion rang I had a call from Kathleen. She had been visited by Raymond. He said that in the next week or two Clare would be remembering a great deal more. In these days, if Braïda and Raymond predicted anything, it was not long before it was implemented. Once again I had not long to wait.

Next morning Kathleen phoned again. She had gone for a prolonged stay to Switzerland but had thought it urgent to ring me. "I have just rung Clare," she said. "What she said was so extraordinary that I felt I had to ring you. I gather you have been to some place called Portchester. It seems that when you got to some tower or other she felt positively awful."

"My wife noticed something. The gist of the matter is that Clare was shut up there for trying to escape."

"I see. But what follows is really peculiar. She said that you and she went along the path by the water. She felt she could not stay with you."

"She certainly walked on ahead."

"That's because she felt she had to get away from you. She said that if she had stayed with you she would have had to jump in the water. Was that some kind of obsession?"

"Not really," I said. "She had never had it before and she won't again."

"But what does it mean?"

"That in a previous life she swam out from the point on the path where I stood. She was taking a message to a boat." I told her the story rapidly and briefly.

"But why did she want to get away from you?"

"Because I was in charge. I had to see that Pierre did what he had been ordered. Perhaps he got cold feet at the last moment. Perhaps Clare remembered being afraid. In any case there is no need to worry, the water is shallow. It must have been much deeper in those days."

After Kathleen had rung off I telephoned Clare. "I have just had Kathleen on the phone. Why didn't you tell me all this stuff about wanting to jump into the water?"

"I just couldn't at the time. It seemed so utterly stupid, so completely mad. And then the thing only came back to me later that evening. I mean details like the bag I carried. It was a soft leather thing pinched in at the top by some kind of band and the letter was inside it. Why do you think I had to jump in the water to get away from you?"

"I know from Marion I was there to see you did what you were told. When it came to the point it seems you didn't like it. What I would like to know is who was the fourth man."

"Was there a fourth man?"

"Marion says so. You were Pierre. I was Guirdaud, then there was Henri. I don't think this means Henri the plump cabin boy, that's to say Betty. I'm absolutely sure now that it wasn't Betty. I am sure Marion Dacre was the Henri in the escape party," I said. "Who was the fourth?"

"Don't you think it was Graham?"

"Why ever should it be?" I thought she was shuffling the pieces into place at the instigation of an uncharacteristic senti-mental impulse. Graham had loved her for twenty years. She still longed for him to be included in the company.

"Don't you remember his notes about a castle by the sea and a lot of sailor prisoners interested in some kind of club devoted to universal brotherhood?"

"I remember well," I said.

"He talked also about saving bits of bones from his meals to use for carving."

"Now that you mention it I remember."

"Don't you recall that he wrote about making a mechanical toy which worked when you turned a handle?"

"Yes. I'd forgotten. It is odd that only two days ago my son

206

gave me a book—only just published, mind you—with an illustration of such a toy made by a French prisoner in the Napoleonic war. What is all this leading up to?"

"Well, he spoke also of a boy called Pierre. He had visited him a lot in a cell in the tower."

"Yes. I *had* forgotten that."

I felt strongly that Clare was the boy Pierre who had been shut up in the tower and that Graham was the fourth man in our escape from Portchester. The next day Annette rang from Canada. She had one or two considerable worries on which she needed advice. Her problems were carried like swansdown on a gale of boisterous good nature. She was living the happy months before her succession of grave illnesses. It was only at the end of the conversation that she remembered she had a message for me from her mother. Though she had been described by Braïda and Raymond as the white hope of the twentieth-century Cathars she was remarkably insouciant in transmitting messages from the other world. She rode through the cosmos on a light rein. She said that her mother had quoted four names, that they had to do with Portchester—Annette only recalled the name of the castle with difficulty—and that I would know what to make of them. The four names were Raymond, Pierre, Henri and Jacques.

I met Clare the same day and mentioned Annette's message. She said that my name must have been Raymond because I was in charge of the escape and this name appeared at the head of Annette's list. We knew she was Pierre. We were pretty certain that Marion was Henri. We had no more than a couple of minutes' conversation on the subject but I knew from recent experience that the truth would come cascading in on us in all directions. Mr. Mills and Braïda appeared in the course of the next two days and told Clare that Graham had been Jacques and had kept her company in the tower at Portchester.

Round about this time I was walking in the street when I saw myself dressed in a long skirted overcoat in the fashion of the early nineteenth century. The overcoat was light grey and there was a cape attached to the shoulders. I wanted to cry. My eyes were wet but I managed to avoid weeping openly. I knew I had been given this coat by a kind and understanding man I worked for and who had won my heart by this simple gesture. I knew this occurred against an English background and in the country and in the particular region I had loved as a medical student.

I was deeply moved by this experience but soon afterwards I told myself that this was the result of sentimental hindsight and a capacity to visualise. I did not regard it as a significant phenomenon. A year ago Braïda had said to Clare that if, by now, I had not learnt to trust my hunches I never would. It appeared I was still dragging my steps.

Mrs. Dacre rang four days after my visit to Portchester. She was happy I had been there again. Almost immediately she said something which astonished me beyond measure and made me feel the closeness of the tie between us. "Why did Miss Mills move away from you when you were walking along the path by the harbour?"

I did not ask her how she knew. By now I had reached the stage where these commonplaces were no longer necessary. I had not yet described this incident to Marion. Mrs. Dacre did not know of the existence of Kathleen who had tuned in to this affair. After I had answered her question I asked her what had been near to my heart for some time but which I had been reluctant to put into words. It is a strange situation to recall, with someone you have never met, a link established more than a century previously and never really broken. "And you," I said, "were you my employer?"

"Yes."

"At that time you were a man."

"Yes, I wouldn't have been overseeing your activities if I had been a woman."

"What did I do?"

"You started as a general worker on the land. I found you loved building walls. You were very good at it and in the end you did nothing else."

"I feel it was round Haslemere," I said.

"It was. There was a wall you built at G—— but you built many others. I owned a good deal of land in that neighbourhood."

"Had my name any likeness to my present one?"

"I can't remember." It was a measure of Marion's reticence that she had never communicated her recollection of my surname to her mother.

208

It did not occur to me to ask Mrs. Dacre about my Christian name. After all, in Portchester itself I had always been known by my surname. "How long did I stay with you?"

"A long time," she said. "A matter of years."

"Did I go back to France?"

"I cannot remember. You worked for someone else, too."

I felt suddenly deflated. I could not bear to think I had left her. I limit myself to recording rather than explaining my sensations. I did not mention my vision of the grey overcoat.

When I told Clare of my talk with Mrs. Dacre she said she had always wondered if I had been a builder.

"It's your feeling about walls," she said.

"Have I such a feeling?"

"But of course, you love them. You don't like open gardens with views. You like to be shut in. What's the thing you are always saying about a horse that has been out all day loving a dark stable? Mary tells me that when you are abroad you always like a room looking slap on a wall or on what you call a well— I suppose you mean some kind of courtyard. In your own house you prefer the view at the back looking at the wall, whereas everybody else raves about the view from the front window."

"That's true," I said. "When you said I loved walls I thought you meant just bricks and mortar and mixing them together."

Talking of walls set me thinking of the wall at Haslemere and the country itself. Fifty years ago I had been ill and lost a great deal of weight in a short time. I went off to Bramshott to recuperate. It lies on the main road to Hindhead a few miles from Haslemere. I arrived weak and spent in the late afternoon. I had had little to eat for days. I immediately went out walking. I began in the woods at Waggoner's Wells. I walked rapidly for more than three hours. In those days I regularly averaged four miles an hour. I must have covered at least eleven miles. What was interesting was that I, who in those days had a good sense of direction and a sharp eye for the contours of landscape, became completely lost in that domesticated and almost suburban countryside. Certainly I was walking through woods but this was small beer for one who had spent so much of his time roaming the empty fells of Cumberland. I remember clearly my fears as twilight deepened and I could not find the road. I wondered if on that walk I had stumbled on my old haunts and was disorientated by the resurgence of a demanding but unconscious memory. Twenty years after this experience, just off the road where I started my walk, I had my second attack of Menière's disease. My first attack had been a month earlier and coincided with Clare's sudden obsessive impulse which took her for the first time to the Cathar country and with Mrs. Smith's first experience of far memory. In 1954, unknown to myself I was tuning in to my Cathar incarnation. Was I, in the early 1930s, having an upsurge of my Napoleonic memories? Was I treading ground sacred to me in my last incarnation?

The next event was a call from Marion. I asked her if she recognised the list of names quoted by Annette. Like Clare she agreed that I was in command and that my name was Raymond. Pierre was certainly the name of the cabin boy. She accepted her own name as Henri. She had no comment to make on the name Jacques.

Once again the fates intervened to prevent contact between myself and someone else on the same wavelength. I had planned to stay a couple of nights with a friend in Surrey in order to visit Mrs. Dacre. The latter fell ill with a throat infection. She was taken off to be nursed by Marion in the latter's house. The next day was the anniversary of the truce at Montségur. I awoke feeling worse than I had done the two previous years. I did not think this was entirely attributable to my Cathar memory. I was suffering more acutely because the Napoleonic incarnation had broken through the surface of consciousness. It is possible that this heightened perception of one incarnation increased my sensitivity to the buried chords of another.

Later in the day I was cheered by a call from Mrs. Dacre. Her throat was much better. She was concerned to know how I was. It was obvious that she was aware that I was under the weather. If she had known that Clare had walked away from me on the path by the harbour on my visit to Portchester, she could register the cruder earth-tremor of my depression.

I asked her if the names transmitted by Annette from Braïda meant anything to her. As long as I live I shall not forget her answer. "I can certainly say that Raymond meant a lot to me."

She added immediately, calmly and without a tremor, "Had I had a son I had always intended to call him Raymond."

I felt an indefinable and almost luminous happiness. It was as though my level of awareness had suddenly lifted. I was looking at the world from above a cloud.

"Our years together were very happy," she continued. "You worked for someone else just before you came to me. Then you stayed with me until you left the country."

I felt incredibly relieved when I heard her words. I had hated the idea that I had worked for her and left her for another. If this sounds sentimental I can only say that those who would so describe it have never shared my experience.

Next evening I had another call from Marion. Her mother's throat was much better but she was acutely ill with a chest condition. She had a pain in the chest, a racking cough and a high temperature. The doctor had visited twice that day. Marion said that beyond any doubt her mother had pulmonary congestion. I realised that she was under great pressure. She spoke in her usual slow, measured voice but admitted that she was very worried. Once again she was anxious to give her mother treatment according to the principles she had half-discovered for herself when dealing with children with congenital deformities. I reminded her that Clare was a great authority on these matters. It sickened me to think of Mrs. Dacre ill and anguished and that I was separated from her.

Next morning I had an early call from Marion. She said that the change in her mother was miraculous. She had had a perfectly peaceful night, sleeping profoundly and undisturbed by any pain in the chest. Even though she appeared to be sleeping so deeply she told Marion that she was aware of hands sweeping over her body and taking her pains away. It would have been pleasant to think that I had, during the night, made an out-of-the-body trip to my old employer, but I know that Clare was the agent of her recovery. The morning after the latter's etheric excursion Mrs. Dacre's temperature, which had been 104°F the night previously, was down to 99.4°.

Mrs. Dacre sent a message for me through Marion. She said that some people see into their past lives when seriously ill and with a soaring temperature. I knew that children with high temperatures and described as light-headed are often so occupied. She said that she had had a vivid dream the previous night. She and I had been together in the yard of a long, low farm. It was a cold morning and she, or rather he, had given me an overcoat. She described the latter as long, skirted, grey and with a cape attached to the shoulders. She was very anxious that Marion should emphasise how much she remembered the greatcoat and how fond she had been of me. I remembered, calmly and un-emotionally, my own previous vision of myself standing in the open and receiving the grey coat from my employer. I was less emotional than on the day of the vision when I nearly wept in the street. I felt calm and a little stunned. It was odd to feel that the I which accompanied me in my daily tasks was linked with something which was freed from time.

The doctor who visited later that morning agreed that Mrs. Dacre was miraculously better. She had a few mild bronchitic signs but none whatever of pneumonia. Next day Marion rang again. Her mother had intense pain at the base of one lung and the doctor had diagnosed pleurisy. Once again Marion practised the laying on of hands. Two days later she rang again. Her mother was very much better and had merely a cough and some signs of bronchitis.

Whenever I spoke to Mrs. Dacre it was a kind of beauti-ful truce in what was a thrilling but exhausting campaign. Although these communications from the other world were filtered through Clare I still found them exhausting. I would not have been without them for the world and I don't know how I existed in the wintry, unsignposted days before these things began. But I knew how enfeebling it is to live at the same time on two planes of consciousness. With Mrs. Dacre there was always a feeling of peace and rest. I may have worked hard in my previous incarnation but there is also the memory of roses on a porch and an endless afternoon in the heat of summer, in a dark cool parlour with a deep-ticking clock and the branches un-moving outside the window. It was reinvigorating for me to talk to Mrs. Dacre and to resume contact through her with her nineteenth-century predecessor.

At this time there was a concentration of attention on Port-chester. In his nocturnal visits Mr. Mills stressed to Clare how

Graham, as Jacques, had cared for her in Assheton's Tower but he did not specify in what way. My conversations with Mrs. Dacre were also centred around Portchester. I told her that I found it difficult to see what part Dualism had played in our Napoleonic incarnation. I described how Graham had written of the brotherhood he belonged to in Portchester. "I suppose that at that time there were all kinds of young men's clubs devoted to liberty, equality and fraternity. I wondered sometimes whether it could have been something to do with the Freemasons."

"But Portchester was riddled with Masonry." I had never heard her before speaking so rapidly and with such vivacity. "Marion has always said so. You should ask her yourself. I've not spoken to her about it in detail. You should also ask Clare."

"Why Clare?"

"She would know all about it." I was astonished that once again she should regard Clare as the supreme authority even though she had only seen her twice in her lifetime.

"I know nothing about Masonry," I said. "I know people like Mozart and Tolstoy were taken by it but to me it is inextricably associated with plump businessmen playing with ritual."

"There is no likeness between the Masonry practised at Portchester and the stuff you get nowadays. Also it wasn't like Masonary practised in Europe at that time because there was no ritual."

"Did the Portchester variety have Dualist tendencies?"

"Yes, it was what was left of what had been inherited from the original Freemasons of the Middle Ages who were also Dualists."

I had heard this before expressed as a theory. Mrs. Dacre's firm affirmation never struck me as theoretical. I knew I would hear more about this subject. I had learnt by now that it pays to wait.

"What interests me more than anything is how the Napoleonic incarnation is related to Dualism. It seems a long march from the pacific Cathars to an imperialistic Emperor. But I think sometimes that Napoleon recognised more clearly than other great men of action the war between the good and evil in his own heart. He was certainly preoccupied with these matters. He said that no man had ever risen to power and had committed so few crimes. I find it nauseating when people compare Napoleon to Hitler and Stalin. You can put them all in the same political category as dictators but the difference between Hitler and Napoleon is too simple for the intellectual. The former murdered seven million Jews. Napoleon was an emancipator of Jews and Protestants. Napoleon was intelligent enough to know, like the Dualists, that all earthly hierarchies are evil and that, to achieve any good on this planet on the political level, you have to exercise the evil of power for the achievement of goodness and justice. Does this sound extravagant? I feel like a lawyer making a case."

"I don't think you are," she said. "Dualism isn't necessarily pacific. It depends on how it is slanted.* In some ways I think that Napoleon was Europe's last chance."

A week later I had a call from Marion. I spoke of the outline of the flower I had seen on the cross at W——. I did not discuss its provenance, nor did I say how puzzled I had been when Braïda and Guy insisted that this ancient stone included a pattern relevant to something as recent as the Napoleonic era. I merely described the form of the flower.

"But that was the emblem worn by some of the people at Portchester," said Marion. She spoke factually in her usual level tones and without the slightest trace of excitement. The deeper she felt things the less she showed her feelings.

"What sort of flower was it?" I asked.

"A simple kind of lily. It was not like a fleur de lys. It had no bits hanging down the sides of the petals." (I thought this was a good enough confirmation of my description of the flower as a cross between a tulip and a straight-up lily). "Some of these emblems were destroyed on the way to Portchester."

"You mean the sailors wore them?"

"Quite a number did. Some of the sailors made up for the loss by carving the emblem on fragments of bone. I remember somebody carving on a wall but I have no idea whereabouts in the castle." I had no idea that this last remark of Marion's was specially significant.

"What did the emblem stand for?" I asked.

* This is very true. The early Paulicians were a warlike lot.

214

"The people who wore it belonged to some kind of secret society. It was an emblem of a sort of Freemasonry. I cannot remember a lot of detail but I do recall a bit about the meetings. It sounds odd if I say they were something like prayer meetings but it is the nearest I can get. There were always readings from the New Testament. We never read the Old. Afterwards we discussed different passages. It seems silly to say so, but I imagine it was something like the Quakers. What was preached was always simple. There was no ritual and little theology."

I was intensely interested by what she said. The sailor Freemasons were following the Dualist prescription of treating the Old Testament as the biography of Satan and avoided it literally as they would the Devil. What impressed me was the earnest atmosphere which seems to have presided at these sailors' meetings. From Marion I had an impression of a handful of men with a social conscience laboriously instructing their less privileged brethren. When I read the history of the castle I discovered that many of the illiterate sailors who entered Portchester were instructed by their more cultured brethren and could read and write when they left.

"Did these meetings have any political aspect? I have an idea that they had some political aim."

"They did undoubtedly. They were definitely Republican or Bonapartist. They were totally against the Bourbons." It was obvious that her memory had quickened in the past few weeks. She had said previously that neither in the last incarnation nor this had she any interest in politics.

It is recorded that, in 1814, during the Hundred Days, the Legitimists sent an emissary to the prisoners at Portchester to tell them they were free and that the Bourbons were restored. From 7000 or 8000 prisoners not a man could be found to raise the Bourbon flag.

I should say that in my present life I have never wavered in my dislike of Freemasonry. When as a young doctor I was invited to join I refused immediately, in spite of the fact that I am by nature a person who hates to refuse anybody anything. My reaction to this invitation was to wonder that anybody could waste so much money on a secret society preoccupied with ritual. I have not been impressed by what I have seen of British Masonry.

Many of its exponents have seemed to me self-satisfied and un-necessarily prosperous. At the same time I have never been able to stomach the paranoid antipathy shown towards Masons by some kinds of Catholic in modern France. I cannot accept that French Masons are at the bottom of every revolutionary impulse in Europe. This seems to me ludicrously out of date. English Masons are an obviously different kind of animal. Those I have met were quite painfully devoted to the status quo. I am prepared to believe that our island has modified Masonry as it has other continental ideas and movements. There is something in the native air which slows the metabolism.

The Masonry we are concerned with at Portchester differed both from the liberal esotericism which preoccupied people like Mozart and what satisfies the florid and often imperceptive *commerçants* I have met in this life. There is a world of difference between imprisoned sailors reading the Gospels to their illiterate confrères and the comfortable exponents of the profit motive. Once again one of the main divergencies is over the question of ritual. True to the Dualist tradition the French sailors practised a simple creed which dispensed with ceremonial and theological complexities. I remembered how Mrs. Dacre expressed herself with unusual warmth when she compared the faith of the Port-chester sailors with that of the modern British exponents of Masonry. She described the former as uncorrupted and simple and the latter as saturated with ritual and therefore, in her eyes, beyond the pale.

Later that day I was visited by Clare. I asked what had hap-pened to us after our imprisonment in England. It was character-istic of this astonishing person that she had refrained from amplifying the history for me. What she told me that evening she had known for a few months. She had not enlightened me because at this time she hoped against hope that I would learn for myself. In addition she waited always for evidence to flow in first from other sources. She limited herself to completing the pattern for me. One can call this a superhuman exercise in self-control but I think such a description would be erroneous. It was part of her passive wisdom.

She said that after she and Betty had been released from Port-chester they returned directly to their native Provence. I went

216

back to the same region but not with them and not at the same time. I never went back to the sea. I lived a clandestine existence disseminating propaganda against the Bourbons and also spreading the tenets of Dualism. Once again, as in all the previous incarnations known to me, I spent a good deal of my time up against the authorities. It is not difficult for me to trace my foibles and obsessions in this world to my insecure and hunted existence in the seventh, thirteenth and nineteenth centuries. I am moulded by the fact that I was a heretic in two incarnations and a spy and a professional agitator in another. What I endured in these previous lives explains my present make-up more convincingly than any of the current theories of psychiatry.

That same evening I spoke to Clare of the poet Mistral and his house at Maillane. She had always wished to go to Provence and I spoke about it that evening. I mentioned Mistral because I was speaking of the tradition of poetry among the working classes in the Midi. Until that evening she had never heard the name of Frederick Mistral. (She knew that there was a north wind of that name.) She said that Mistral and his school had in their own way revised and continued the work of the Troubadours. She said also that great poetry, untainted by any conscious reference to any religious or philosophical system, is one of the principal vehicles of Dualism, that scattered in its substance there are Dualist references because poetry is the best medium for spreading, in disguised form, what people cannot swallow undiluted. I was startled by this statement. I had not credited her with such an insight into the functions of poetry. When an individual is open to direction from the cosmos their opinions and viewpoints are not their own but derived from some ultimate source of wisdom transmitted by beings on another plane of consciousness.

That evening when she left I picked up Ford Madox's Ford's *Provence*. I wanted to read again what he said about Mistral. I opened it at the page in which Ford describes the persecutions of the Bonapartists after the return of the Bourbons. Some of the worst efforts of the Legitimists occurred at Nimes, Avignon and Tarascon. I remembered my dreams spread over years of a quarry near a road, white in the sunshine, somewhere in Provence and I thought near Nimes. In my dreams the quarry was a place of refuge. I did not know what were its particular associations for me. I only know that when I first visited Nimes I was so depressed that the recollection of it is still like recalling a nightmare. I remembered also the emotions I felt when I first saw Provence. The whole experience was magical. I felt the life in the soil. The sunlight was different and the air vibrated. The castle and peach orchards were not something seen for the first time but the coming to life of old dreams. I mention in *The Cathars and Reincarnation* that my thoughts were first directed to the Midi by reading Ford's book. I described the author as an insecure guide. So he is. When he talks about the Cathars he is clearly unaware of their earlier roots and of the ultimate potential of their teachings. But certainly he acted as a catalyst in that Provence was for me a key to a timeless experience. Was something other than my Cathar past awakened by this country of tenacious herbs rooted in the crevices of sunbaked rocks? I could not get away from the fact that, though my memory of Catharism awakened in Provence, I lived my life as a Cathar in the Languedoc. Was it possible that, in the parched heathland in the neighbourhood of Nimes, my mind recalled a nearer incarnation?

Annette rang from Canada next day. She spoke at great length, a bit forgetfully and in no kind of order. The evening previously she had been visited by both Guy and her mother. The former had gone into great detail about his Celtic incarnation. Braïda had covered a wider field. Annette delivered a crucial message from her in characteristic form. "Mummy said that what you and Clare were talking about last night was right. Does that make sense?"

"Hardly. We talked of many things. Was it about crosses?"

"I don't think so. Anyway not specially."

"Was it to do with poetry?"

"Yes, that's it. I've got it. Let's see, what was the name she used? I always thought it had to do with a wind but there was a man—"

"Was it Mistral?" I said.

"That's it. Mummy said he was a kind of return to the Troubadours. Does that make sense?"

"Go on," I said. She was saying something capable of arousing the appetite of all who loved the poetry, folklore and tradition

218

of the Midi. She was like a careless merchant unaware of the gold hidden in her bales of merchandise.

"I think she said there are bits of Dualism in Mistral. Certainly she said that great poetry is often Dualist. How did she put it? Oh yes, it's a good way of doling out in bits what people cannot take as a whole."

She was talking the same language as Clare and I assumed that both of them had been similarly instructed by Braïda. I learnt later that Clare had been informed by Graham. "What else did your mother say?" I said.

"Oh dear, you do want to know a lot." She pronounced the 'ou' in you and the 'o' in do like a French 'u'. This transformation had occurred in the last few weeks. She was unaware of the change in her voice. In Canada she had had no contact with French Canadians. Even had she done so this would not have been relevant. Her French pronunciation was completely metropolitan. "Oh yes," she continued, "mummy talked about you. She said you had written poetry with hidden meanings."

"In the thirteenth century my predecessor Roger was addicted to poetry."

"I am sure she was not talking about that."

"Certainly I have written poetry in this life but I can't remember contriving any hidden meanings."

"She wasn't talking about this life. She meant the last time you were here."

"You mean when I went back to France?"

"Yes, but it started before that. When you were at Portchester you belonged to some kind of secret organisation. It had something to do with Masonry. When you went back to Provence you belonged to some underground society. It was Dualist. It was also against the government. You said a lot of what you had to say in poetry with double meanings. The meetings were political. The Dualism came out mostly in your writing."

She was repeating to me what Clare had said to me the previous evening. In more specific ways I had been prepared for this phone call. Just before Annette rang I had brought *Calendau* and *Mireille* from my study. These are Mistral's works in Provençal with a French translation. Why did I buy the former more than thirty years ago? My French was negligible and my

Provençal non-existent. The second-hand copy of *Calendau* is decorated by Mistral's signature and a dedication from him. *Mireille* was given to me by Martine. It is rising thirty years since she came to see us. I have only seen her once in the years between. I recalled her dark eyes, the glow of their unremitting tenderness and, very sharply, her loose, slightly rolling gait and easy movement. We always referred to her affectionately as the French sailor. Was she another? I could not say. All I know is that, again at Bassenthwaite, I felt her presence after years in a visionary experience. She came from an arid and bare-toothed region, a country relentless in the drought of summer. When I saw her last she was looking at the sea.*

For nearly forty years I have been haunted by the name of Mistral. Now I am led to him by Braïda and Graham and their earthly envoys. I see now that Ford's book did more for me than I had ever imagined. For me the atmosphere of autumn and twilight hovers above its pages. He was careless and sometimes disdainful of fact. He was far less instructed than he seemed. He was, to me, a light falling on a rock. There was a tremor in the air and with its passing I saw an old country and knew it was mine. I had regarded this book as an early and uncertain finger pointing vaguely towards Catharism. I wondered now if it had also evoked for me the memory of Mistral.

Mistral was born in 1830. He devoted his life to preserving the language and poetry of Provence and to sharpening the concept of it as an ancient and classical civilisation. He was surrounded by a handful of men similarly dedicated. He was the father of the Felibrige, the concourse of regional and often working-class poets who shared his idea that poetry is the food of natural man and that its essence impregnates that country of harsh rocks, old vines and aromatic shrubs. Did I know Mistral in my previous life? So far as I can estimate I was over seventy when Mistral was twenty. I can only go by the evidence of those who are more authoritative on the subject both of time and being emancipated from it. I know that time stood still for me three years ago when I visited Mistral's house at Maillane. The sun was at anchor and

* In 1974 I learnt from Mr. Mills that Martine had served as a sailor under his command when he functioned as Captain X in the Napoleonic incarnation.

the house was silent. The plain outside was flooded with the calm of centuries. I came to Maillane from Carpentras. In that town we stayed in a house tunnelled in the shadows and away from the main boulevard. The days we spent there were stolen from time. We drove through Provence in the heat of the day and returned in the evening to the quiet courtyard. The day in the square at Vaison la Romaine is more than unforgettable. It is inscribed in light on the scrolls of memory.

When Marion rang me a fortnight later I told her what I had heard of Mistral from Clare and Braïda. I described also how I had received from Martine the copy of *Mireille*. "I found it quite delightful," she said.

I was stunned that she had read it. I wondered how many people in England had even heard of *Mireille*.

"How did you come to read it?"

"I suppose it was through my grandmother. When my grandfather died she returned to Carpentras to end her days there. When I was a child I stayed with her often."

"Can you speak Provençal?"

"No, but I am sure that if I were back in Provence and the people speaking Provençal, in a day or two I would understand what was being said." The few spontaneous statements she made were always uncompromising and positive. I never doubted for a moment that what she said was right.

"In the last incarnation you came from Provence?"

"That is something I am sure of," she said.

"Where were you born?"

"I cannot say. When I first saw a certain square in a small town it was so familiar that I felt I was born there."

I saw the square in the midsummer heat, the road with the trees and the Roman excavations. "That was Vaison la Romaine," I said. In Cumberland Marion's mother and I walked in each other's footsteps. Had I done the same with Marion in Provence? "Yes, Vaison la Romaine." She made no other comment.

"Do you think your grandmother had any Dualist ideas?"

"She spoke of a wheel of life to which we returned till the circle was complete. After that we qualified for something like higher education. She believed implicitly in a force of evil and

221

that life was a constant battle between the forces of good and evil. She spoke a great deal about poetry and poets. Even when I was a little girl she said that poetry was not merely a form of inspiration. She explained that it was a secret method of communication between like-minded people. Readers on the same wavelength picked up the hidden meanings."

"So that in a certain sense great poetry, even if it isn't avowedly metaphysical, is essentially esoteric?"

"That would seem to be true."

It was fascinating to think of this ageing Frenchwoman instructing Marion in the principles of Dualism. Certainly her grandmother was a great influence on her but as well as the old lady and the house at Carpentras there was also the Provençal countryside for which, in her middle years, Marion yearns as she does for no other place. She loves Hampshire and especially the country around Winchester. Here she worked when on parole from Portchester. Dutifully she regards Cumbria as her home because both her parents were born there. In Hampshire she is reaching back with heartache and full consciousness to a lost experience. In the marrow of her bones she belongs to Provence.

It was strange that the same places in Cumberland and Provence should have the same magnetism for Marion, her mother and myself. I had learnt by now that the same group can be drawn together in different incarnations. I knew also that reincarnation in the same family is possible. It never occurred to me that I should be involved in such a transaction. I had my first undeciphered clue when Marion told me that if I wished to speak of reincarnation in families I should talk to her mother. When I went to Cumberland in April 1973 I visited the hamlet I will call Fellgate. I sat in the churchyard where some of my ancestors were buried and was joined by a woman who told me of a ruined house where a family called Dacre had lived and of how, following a curse laid on them, they had been scattered to the winds of heaven. As a child I had heard my uncle speak of this family. It had stuck in my mind that we were related to them. After we returned from Cumberland Braïda told Annette that at Fellgate I had learnt that I was related to another member of the group. Mrs. Dacre told me later that her husband had spoken of a ruined house at Fellgate. When he visited the village

222

he wished for nothing better than to sit on a seat at the back of the church and gaze across the meadows to the mountains. This was where I had sat when the woman told me the story of the ruined house. Even the reflective and undemanding Marion admitted finally that she and I were related.

In all these diverse and many-coloured experiences nothing moves me more than the loyalty shared with the Dacres for Cumberland, Portchester and the districts to which we were directed from it, and the other world of Provence. When I think of Mrs. Dacre I return always to time suspended on a summer day, in a cool dark room looking out on a garden. I am back in the house at Haslemere. With Marion it is always Portchester in those rigorous but happy days before we drifted apart. My mind oscillates from them to another country and a village with plane trees and a dusty square.

As with the other characters in this book I made several attempts to meet Mrs. Dacre. We were constantly prevented by illness or other more exasperating impediments. On one occasion she telephoned me to say she was going to lunch with a friend in the New Forest en route for Bournemouth. My heart leapt with joy. Then I recalled that I had on that day a clinic I could not postpone. I worked out that it would still be possible for me to meet her for a short time before she left for Bournemouth. She forbade me to do so. She said I was far too tired to drive so far and so fast for such a short meeting. She was tender but firm. It never occurred to me to override her decision. I was a man, I was years younger, I was used to making decisions and taking responsibilities. She belonged to an age when women were sheltered and decisions were made for them. I simply accepted what she said. I was back in my skin as Raymond, the Balbus of Haslemere. She had reverted to her rôle of considerate employer. It was merely a change of status. There was no need for her to amend her character. She remained as in her last incarnation, tender, wise and at times imperious.

As it turned out it was my last chance. The day came when Clare appeared with her eyes lightless and the resonance gone from her voice. It appeared that something dreadful was going to happen. I dreaded these occasions. I could not accept with equanimity that some disaster was impending and that there

223

was nothing one could do to protect the victim. We heard the same day that Mrs. Dacre had suffered a severe stroke. She never recovered the power of speech and full consciousness though Marion knew that there were moments when her mother recognised her. She died holding her daughter's hand.

I see no purpose in analysing my feelings for a woman I never met in this life, who was a father to me in a previous incarnation and something like a mother in this. What I learnt from all this was that we can love people we have never met and without sentimentality or feverish romanticism. These latter attitudes are indeed impediments. There is nothing mawkish in a love born out time.

Chapter Twenty Three

The story of our French incarnation falls into three sections, before Portchester, the period of captivity and working on parole and, thirdly, our return to France. The tale cannot be told chronologically. Portchester was the first dramatic revelation of our Napoleonic incarnation and has to be treated as such. What happened before and after was filled in later. For a long time I could not understand why Shere, a village in Surrey, meant so much to me and was so associated in my mind with French prisoners. This and much else was revealed to me later.

On my last visit to Portchester I had been preoccupied with the graffiti and assumed that I would find something directly and strikingly relevant to my own physical identity. What I had seen was interesting in all conscience but I was not satisfied. Before our next visit in the height of summer I read what I could find about French prisoners of war at Portchester. It was clear that what had been said about Masonry by Braïda, Graham, Clare, Marion and her mother was borne out by the recorded facts. In no case did the latter indicate that this was a special kind of Masonry tainted with Dualism. This could hardly be expected. At the time the books and pamphlets were written Dualism was, in Britain, even less of an issue than it is now.

Before our next visit to Portchester attention was concentrated on it from two worlds. First all Graham appeared to Clare and told her that Marion and I had been captured in the autumn. Clare had herself made it clear that we were not taken prisoner at the same time as she and Betty. We had also made an escape in the same season. The leaves were always gold in my recurrent dream. Graham said also that there had been a sea battle on July 22nd. In 1973 the stoical Marion appeared unheralded on my doorstep that day. She felt that this was the anniversary of some horrible event connected with Portchester. I traced later that this was the day on which she had been desperately

225

sick with smallpox. I wondered whether she had also been involved the same day in another year in Graham's sea battle. At this time the anniversary phenomenon was very much in evidence. Graham stressed also the year 1804. I can only think that he was telling Clare the date we were captured. He emphasised most of all that we had made three attempts to escape.

By 1973 I had developed the capacity to talk directly to the revenants, though for the most part I needed Clare's presence as an intermediary. Betty spoke to me of Portchester and of how many of the sailors imprisoned there were Provençaux. It was difficult to conceive of these conscripted rustics as anti-clerical intellectuals. Because of their Masonic activities and anti-Catholic bias I had often wondered what religion they had been nurtured in. Betty said that the vast majority were Protestants. To this day the reformed religion flourishes in Provence. She told me that I myself originated in the Luberon. It was in this area that I became violently sick after passing a small Protestant chapel. My stomach was not upset, neither was I suffering from a touch of the sun. It occurred while my wife and I were staying at Carpentras. I wondered whether the recollection of persecution after the return of the Bourbons or at any other time was stirring in my memory.

What interested me most was Betty's description of the prayer meetings which Marion had mentioned. She said the simple talks given on those occasions were partially concerned with analogies from nature. She remembered how the oak tree had been quoted as an illustration of honesty and reliability. I recalled how Graham had given the same description of the sermons delivered in the Celtic incarnation. He had also said that oak leaves were particularly revered by the Provençal sailors in Portchester. Now this was one of the modest items relayed by the revenants which fascinated more than other more dramatic revelations. Was it possible that the French prisoners of war in Hampshire had received substantially the same guidance from their spiritual mentors as the natives of Cumberland 1200 years previously?

I received further information at this time from the living. One day I returned with Marion to the question of the pompoms worn by the sailors at Portchester. At that time the head-

226

gear itself was varied. Only a small proportion wore berets and some had no hats or caps of any description. Marion had said originally that I wore a red pom-pom on a kind of beret. Her memory had sharpened since our first encounter. It was clear that she, her mother and I had acted as catalysts to each other in provoking more detail of far memory. When I returned to the question of pom-poms she said that many of the sailors wore reddish pom-poms but the red was by no means bright and she described it as a kind of dull magenta. I raised the subject with Annette. I knew by this time that she, too, had been at Portchester. Braïda had indicated this but had added that it was not one of Annette's principal incarnations. She remembered the pom-poms which she described as "A kind of reddish purple". I wrote to Jean Fortin, a retired senior officer in the French Navy, and asked him how long red pom-poms had been worn. He said that their use was officialised in 1870 but that before that date French sailors had worn pom-poms which he described as either blue or *garance*. Marion's dull magenta and Annette's reddish purple are satisfying interpretations of the French word *garance*.

On our next visit to Portchester the main feature we studied was the Masons' marks. We found these in the church, on the walls of the buildings near the keep and most of all in the keep itself. There were rough designs of compasses, scales, tridents, groups of slanting parallel lines and, what struck me most of all, what appeared at first sight to be reproductions of the letter "M" but which, on closer examination, proved to be interlocking triangles. I had been warned of the existence of these by Annette who had heard from Braïda that these signs, of especial importance to us, had been "made by cavemen and had something to do with Mithras". Translated from Annette's free diction this means that, as well as being at Portchester, they had been found on the walls of caves used by the adherents of the cult of Mithras. Braïda made it clear later that she was referring specifically to the caves in the Ariège used also by the Cathars.

Most of these signs were crudely made. It was evident that the vast majority were amateur efforts. When we were examining a particular cloud of graffiti Graham intervened and told Clare to look at the opposite wall. We saw a line of letter M's fabricated from interlocking triangles. They were far better

227

carved than the other signs. Clare gave away so little by her facial expression that it never occurred to me that she had done these herself. It needed Graham to tell us. The dramatic changes in Clare's appearance came when she was actually living as distinct from remembering the past or when she was tuning in in the present to the pains of others. So far as her own emotions were concerned her features were almost always a total mask.

Inside the keep, as well as the designs I have described, there were others which were not specifically Masonic. There were a number of circles enclosing equal-armed crosses similar to those I had seen in Cumberland and the Languedoc. They were Dualist in any age or culture. There were also stylised roses in patterns which I had seen reproduced in many different periods. Most of all I was fascinated by a hotch-potch of designs in faded and half-obliterated colours which covered a large space on one of the walls. Its components were too confused to be encouraging. Clare was interested in it but I was not prepared to linger over it. For once I was following my own instinctive choice. When I came to this mass of colour on a later occasion I was more capable of reading its mysteries. By not urging me to examine it Clare was adopting her usual policy of waiting until my inner eye had opened.

In one or two places on the inner walls of the keep I saw the outline of oak leaves. It was interesting that I should see in faint outlines what Graham and Betty had spoken of as of special interest to Provençal sailors. What I saw outside the keep was more interesting. Near a date 1806 I discovered two obvious examples of intertwining such as I had seen on the crosses in Cumberland and Clare on those in the Isle of Man. Near these eloquent patterns was the outline of a rose which resembled that I had seen in the W—— cross. What was still more significant was that, in Assheton's Tower, I saw quite clearly the simple flower and leaf design of which Marion had spoken with such conviction and which was traced faintly on the cross at W——. What was most informative of all was that Clare held my arm as she entered the tower. I noticed that her face was ashen. She described the little chamber inside the tower as dark and horrible. In its ruined state it is partly open to the light and does not merit this adverse description.

228

All this was distressing but a distinct advance on what had happened on her last visit when she had not even entered the precincts. It is surprising to me that I did not notice the flower and leaf design on my earlier visit. When I saw it on this particular day its outlines were unmistakable. It can only be that the presence of Clare heightens my ordinary as well as my extra-sensory perception.

When she flinched on entering the tower I was of course aware that she was reliving the past. I did not question her about it. I had by now fallen into a certain rhythm in these matters. I waited for others, either living or dead, to supply the missing pieces to the jigsaw. All I gathered was that she was intensely aware of Graham's presence. He had spoken to her in the keep when he had directed her to the line of M's but now she was more aware of him than ever and I knew that the support of my arm and my presence were less help than his. Nor did we need evidence that she was reliving and enduring the pains of the last century. When we were walking past the site of the hutments she said. "My ear is burning."

"Why is that?"

"We are going past the hospital."

She recalled how she had been struck on the ear by an English sailor before being brought to Portchester and how she had developed later an ear abscess. I cannot discuss here the medical implications of the two attacks of acute middle ear infection she suffered in this life and which stemmed directly from this, and another, blow received in the nineteenth century. I looked at her right ear. It was violently red, felt hot to the touch and was obviously inflamed. She asked me if any of the sailors had knowledge of healing. I mentioned Jane Butler who had practised in Portchester as an unqualified doctor. She denied that Jane was involved. I said that many of the Provençal sailors had the rudiments of medical folklore. They had a knowledge of herbs which grew prolifically in Provence and also a semi-occult belief in the healing powers provided by nature. I recalled that once, when my Haslemere employer had had an obstinate cough, I had treated her with some concoction I had brewed from herbs growing in the vicinity. Clare recalled that it was some time after admission to the hospital at Portchester before anything was done for her ear. At the end of the day Clare was unusually silent. When I asked her what she was thinking about she said that she had been wondering what her father had been in the Napoleonic incarnation.

Marion rang next morning. When I spoke of the flower pattern on the wall of Assheton's Tower she said emphatically that it had been carved by Clare. She did not mention the line of M's. It became clear later why Assheton's Tower was important for her. In our earlier encounter Marion had remembered quite clearly that the cabin boy Pierre was punished rather than his elders. She had emphasised that he was regarded as a more actively subversive proposition and had suggested that this was because he was young, more virile and to outward appearances a tougher proposition. What she did not know was that Pierre had been involved in an earlier attempt to escape which had failed when the roof of the tunnel caved in and engulfed him. This later episode was relived by Clare and will be recorded in a later work concerned with the origin of diseases in previous incarnations. Following the collapse of the tunnel Pierre became delirious. Jane Butler, in her capacity as unqualified medical assistant, described his condition as marsh fever, a diagnosis accepted by the English doctor and only doubted when the latter saw a wound on the patient's chest caused by a fall of stone during the collapse of the tunnel. Pierre was not completely recovered from his experience when, a month later, he swam out with the sketches. It was for this reason that he had hesitated at the water's edge and had been pushed in by me, an episode Clare remembered in this life in the form of an obsessional impulse to jump into the water when walking with me. There were more immediate consequences for Pierre following his dummy-run escape. It alerted the authorities as to his subversive potentialities. The aim of the torture he suffered in Assheton's Tower following his recapture was to see if he were one of the links in an intractable escapist network. Pierre held out and his British guards obtained no information from him.

As to the escape with the plans, Marion's attitude to our behaviour was more interesting to me as a psychiatrist than the facts she recounted. When she first described our escape I had been struck by the way she dissociated herself from the fate of the cabin boy. She had implied that we had successfully and patriotically accomplished our mission, that Pierre was expendable and there was nothing we could do about it. Now with the greater insight she had recently acquired, she was contrite and self-accusing. (I remembered that it was only three months since she had relived the massacre at Avignonet and felt guilty because of the part she had played in it.) Now she described herself and me as unpleasant characters. We had completely detached ourselves from Pierre. She was quite definite that it was her duty to atone to Clare in this incarnation. Though I had never felt particularly happy about the rôle I had played 170 years ago I pointed out that guilt for what had happened in a previous incarnation was a little excessive and that our detachment was probably justified because it was our duty, to those who employed us, to keep our activities secret. She was obviously unmoved by my pleading.

The next day I had my most comprehensive flashback to Portchester. Annette rang from Canada in a state of agitation. This was touched off by her concern for Clare. The previous night she had had horrific visions of her being tortured in a dark tower. Clare appeared to her as a boy of sixteen. He was not very tall and rather broadly built. He had a rugged, broad face with a russet-coloured complexion and brown hair. Only the eyes were unchanged. They were as light blue and luminous as Clare's.

When Annette saw Pierre he was unconscious. She believed he had nearly died. Annette spoke scathingly of two men who ought to have helped Pierre and did nothing for him. Graham, who was taller and darker than the unfortunate cabin boy, had done all he could for him but the other two were selfish and coldhearted. Annette's experience had been terrifying. While it lasted she had received the support of Braïda, Mr. Mills and Graham.

After I had reassured her that Clare was no worse for this experience in the last century I asked her how much she remembered of her own life at Portchester. She said very little and added tartly that I had asked her that before. Then, with no start of surprise and without any alteration of voice, she poured out a mass of information. All I noticed was that she was speaking a little more rapidly than usual. It was not until the next day that I realised fully what had happened.

Though she had said to me a minute before that she remembered little of her life at Portchester she now went into great detail about her arrival there. It should be mentioned that she had never visited Portchester in this life. After capture she was transferred from a big ship to a crowded small boat. The English sailors were a rough lot and unnecessarily brutal. She sang the same tune as Clare. She described, as the latter had done, how she went in at the gate opening on the sea and how two people stationed there took the names and other particulars. She said there was a church near the gate. I asked her which side. She said, correctly, the left and described with complete accuracy the short squat tower. She remembered also where the hospital was sited. She was taken there immediately, deloused and put in a hot bath. All she remembered of her attire was that at one time she wore a blue and white striped vest.

What Annette remembered more vividly and painfully than anything was her separation from the captain of her ship. She cannot remember much about his appearance except that he was tallish and had very blue eyes. She had hoped to be allowed to stay with him. She had obviously been some kind of batman. Annette remembered that he was sent to a building "split up by different floors". The keep had been converted into dormitories in order to accommodate the prisoners. She herself was deposited in a kind of hut. She spent a great deal of her time gambling. She was particularly addicted to games with dice. She regarded this as extremely manly and sophisticated. One day Captain X, who still exercised a paternal interest in his crew, visited her in her quarters and asked her if she could not find anything better to do. He actually arranged for her to be taught lace-making. She told me that she regarded this as extremely cissy but that she stuck to it in order to please the captain.

It is recorded in the history of Portchester, of which Annette knew not a word, that lace-making was so common among the prisoners that at one time there were three thousand people engaged in it. This consolation was later cruelly denied the prisoners after agitation among local tradesmen and workers.

Annette recalls that even at her worst she could not compete

232

with the more ferocious addicts of gambling. These lived on the top storey of the keep. They would literally gamble the clothes off their backs. Brawls, stabbings and duels with knives occurred frequently. During their confinement their deterioration was appalling. Their fellow prisoners were as terrified of them as the English guards. In describing their behaviour and relegating them to the top storey Annette is in full accordance with what is said of them in the histories of Portchester. I noticed in visiting the keep how the inscriptions on the walls diminish dramatically in number and content as one approaches the top floor. The denizens of the highest dormitory had not even sufficient interest to scratch crude symbols on the walls.

These deteriorated ruffians were referred to by their comrades as *les raffales*. This name is still quoted in some of the histories of Portchester. We know one of their number. Kathleen remembers her good-for-nothing existence. She spent her days gambling with dice. She was especially addicted to what she described as a combination of liar dice and poker. The dice were made out of bones, particularly large mutton bones. Debts incurred at this game were marked in scratches on the wall. This appears to have been the top limit of the creative ability of Kathleen and her associates. She remembers that the food consisted largely of mutton stew. She wore what she called a sloppy joe jersey and rope-soled sandals. At times she gambled away all her resources until she possessed nothing, not even her clothes.

Kathleen remembers to this day being involved in frequent brawls some of which were highly dangerous. Her worst episode was when, following a dispute over the payment of debts, her wrist was stabbed with a knife by another infuriated competitor. On the anniversary in 1974 of the day on which this happened Kathleen cut her wrist falling against a plate-glass window which broke with the impact of her hand. Hundreds of miles away Clare tuned in both to Kathleen's present accident and to the one she had sustained nearly 170 years previously. The damage to the tendons of the wrist sustained by Kathleen in 1974 duplicated exactly what she had suffered in the brawl in the keep. She emphasises that in this life she has a puritanical horror of gambling.

I was to hear also from Braïda, Betty and Jane Butler a good deal about Kathleen's character in the previous incarnation. It bore out what Annette had mentioned in her phone call. At sea Kathleen had been a good enough sailor under the supervision of the blue-eyed captain. Separated from his steadying influence and submerged by the *raffales* she went to the dogs. As a final appeal to her better nature Captain X visited her in her noisome quarters. He failed in his evangelism and was rewarded by an attack of smallpox which was getting under way at Portchester. Kathleen had been incubating the infection and soon afterwards revealed the characteristic symptoms. The fact that she had infected the captain, who was beloved by all ranks, detracted from her already negligible popularity. She survived the smallpox and was no better for it. While she remained at Portchester she was among the dregs of its society. Shortly after repatriation in 1814 she pulled herself together. She was obviously a type reduced to frenzy by being enclosed within four walls. (In this life she refuses to enter lifts.) On her return to France, when the wars were over, she worked as a general labourer. She never married. Her contribution to life appears to have been minimal but she always went out of her way to meet her old shipmates and fellow prisoners. They must have been thankful that she was more presentable than when existing on the top floor at Portchester. She occupies a high place in my pantheon of characters. She went so whole-heartedly to the dogs that it was a form of sincerity.

While all Annette said about Portchester was fascinating there was nothing so gripping to me as her account of the tall captain's missionising activities. She said, "It was funny that the captain used to teach us." The substance of what he taught was still stranger. He said that in the world there were two forces of good and evil. At the moment his hearers were subjected to the latter but a better time would come. In a way they had to see themselves as in hell at the moment. This was a neat introduction to the Dualist theme that the world was created by the Devil. The forces of good and evil did not exist only in man. They extended throughout the animal kingdom. There were even plants with good and evil thoughts.

The subject of the captain's discourses may seem to have been strange in a fighting man but he took pains to make them comprehensive to his audience. He expressed himself in simple terms

234

and there was little he said which could not be understood by uneducated sailors. This was because to a large extent he instructed by analogies from nature. Most of his listeners were country-bred and chiefly from Provence. They had been drafted into the service by conscription. I find it fascinating that the captain, addressing his audience at Portchester, should have expressed opinions identical with those I hold in this life about the indivisibility of consciousness throughout all the different aspects of nature. As Annette continued I marvelled still more that he was repeating what Graham, Guy, Clare and I had preached in the Celtic incarnation and that he had used also the methods of exposition I had employed as a Cathar Parfait when I took simple objects like tables and endowed them with spiritual significance by suitable analogies.

Captain X also read to his men extracts from the Bible. It is tempting to see in this improving picture the traditional model of the sailor eccentric, stunned by the immensity of the sea and the sweep of the planets, taking to religion and seeking to infect his crew with his enthusiasm. The captain at Portchester was not like this. His Bible reading was essentially the complement of his philosophy of nature. He abhorred the Old Testament. His particular speciality was St. John's Gospel. It would be unfair to say that he got stuck in the first chapter but he expended a great deal of time on it. The sailors accepted the captain's analogies from nature and understood him remarkably well but the Gospel of St. John was a harder pill to swallow. They were muddled by the first sentence, "The Word was made flesh". Captain X's solution was that the passage would be more easily comprehensible if it was amended to "The Truth was made flesh". This is a by no means startling innovation but it contributes to my particular picture of the captain.

The main bone of contention was his statement that all life was sacred and that men should not take life. This was the only point over which the sailors showed any appreciable resistance to the captain's teachings. Their argument was that they were members of the French Navy engaged in a war with Britain. It did not make sense that they should abstain from taking life, all the more so as a fair number had been conscripted unwillingly for this very purpose. The lecturer sidestepped this by saying that he and his audience were passing through an evil time but that they would be afforded a chance of living better. This not particularly striking explanation was welcomed by the sailors who revered the captain, who did not wish to find themselves in opposition to him and were only too anxious to bail him out of his theological predicament.

Annette revealed that her mother in her present life had been her elder brother in the Napoleonic incarnation. She had also been in the French Navy. It is highly probable that both were conscripted from the same area. Annette's brother was also a prisoner of war. He was incarcerated somewhere in the vicinity of Portchester. I wondered if he was in the shore prison at Forton but Annette did not recognise the name. I hope he escaped the hulks.

Annette said that her brother, unlike herself, had been given parole from Portchester. He had worked as a builder for a gentleman farmer, she did not know in what vicinity. She said that her brother spoke often of his employer's exceptional kindness. There was another French prisoner working at the same place. Annette's brother was subsequently repatriated but the other prisoner did not wish to return to France and continued in his employment. Mrs. Dacre had already told me that, at one time, she had employed another French prisoner as well as me. The former had left but I had hung on for some time after his departure. She could not be specific but it was a matter of years. The revenants confirmed afterwards that Annette's memory was accurate, and that Braïda and I had worked together for the same employer.

Annette was positive that when the war was over Pierre and the cabin boy Henri, that is to say Clare and Betty, returned directly to Provence. This accorded with Clare's own recollection. It was later confirmed by the revenants, in particular by Betty and Jane Butler.

At the end of the phone call Annette reverted to the two men who had done so little for Pierre when he was incarcerated in Assheton's Tower. I admitted that Marion and I were the malefactors. This did not appreciably diminish Annette's resentment. I tried again to explain that we were probably only following the rules of espionage as dictated by our superiors. I said that in the last war it was necessary for members of resistance groups to detach themselves completely from those of their comrades who fell into the enemy's hands. She was completely unconvinced and in no forgiving mood. She said that for some time Marion and I were ostracised by the other sailors, with whom Pierre was extremely popular. General opinion was that we had let him down badly. She informed me that Graham, perturbed by Pierre's condition, approached Captain X who in turn badgered the prison authorities to such good effect that Pierre was transferred to the hospital. Here he was visited regularly by Graham who has looked after Clare in one way or another through five incarnations. In the last two years of his life in this incarnation he arranged to be with her on the anniversary of the day, in the Napoleonic incarnation, on which she reecived the blow on the ear which resulted in otitis media in two consecutive centuries.

The captain also contrived to reconcile Marion and me to the rest of the community. He insisted that there was something to be said for the way we had behaved. Annette did not go into detail about what he had said for the sufficient reason that the good captain himself was not over-informative. It was obvious that he knew more about Marion and me than he was prepared to disclose to the rest of the community.

Annette beat her own record in this close-packed phone call which lasted fifty minutes. I have said she talked a little faster than usual. She was also more unswervingly informative. She never once wandered from the point. Other than this her conversation was as usual. It was utterly rational, only more so. I had, however, an inkling that there was something unusual about it. This was confirmed when she rang next morning to apologise for having spoken to me so briefly the previous evening and for having rung off so abruptly. I asked her how long she thought she had spoken. She estimated her chat at an absolute maximum of ten minutes. She could not credit that our conversation had lasted fifty. It was clear that her own memory of it had ceased when she had finished describing Clare's sufferings in the tower and the way she had been abandoned by Marion and me. It was obvious that, for ten minutes, she had described a horrifying vision which came to her directly by far memory. Following the point at which she said she remembered little of her Napoleonic incarnation another entity took over. I knew that Braïda, Graham and Mr. Mills had been present while she was enduring the spectacle of Clare being tortured in the tower. I knew the identity of Graham and Braïda in the nineteenth century. It seemed clear to me that it was Mr. Mills who had taken over the conversation and that he had supplied her with the details of his own life as Captain X.

It was obvious that Annette had again relayed accurate information in a state of amended consciousness. She was repeating her interview with Guilhabert de Castres after which she had been unable to remember with certainty that she had spoken to me. Annette said that her mother had appeared again and had confirmed what the blue-eyed captain had said about life in Portchester. She had particularly emphasised his discussions on Dualism. It was clear that Braïda was concerned that Annette should recall, in ordinary waking consciousness, what had been relayed to her the previous evening.

All the regular revenants, Braïda, Mr. Mills, Betty, Graham, as well as Jane Butler, confirmed what Annette had said the previous evening and added that Graham, as well as Mr. Mills, had taken over from her. They described this as an example of benign possession.

The same day as Annette's second telephone call, that is to say the day following her recall of her life at Portchester, Marion was expected to visit Clare in Bath. It was another of these encounters which at this time I anticipated with such eagerness. Once again I was disappointed. Marion rang to say she had been involved in an accident. This was another of her eloquent under-statements. She had actually broken a leg when a car ran into her from behind. How her recovery was painless and how Clare took her pains and exhibited the signs and symptoms of fracture is beyond the scope of this book. When Marion spoke to me a second time that day she told me not only that she was without pain and that she had endured the resetting of her fractured tibia without the slightest discomfort, but that she still felt guilty for the way she had behaved towards Clare at Portchester.

That same day, when in Clare's company, I had a number of visionary experiences in which I saw Braïda against a background

238

of St. Andrew's crosses. Then I saw the rose and the simple flower-leaf pattern I had seen on the cross at W—— and carved on the wall at Portchester. The next day she appeared again but accompanied by Graham. I saw the same symbols but this time the display ended with Graham holding the flower pattern in his raised right hand. Braïda said that the aim of the operation was twofold. I was being shown once again the continuity of the same symbols through several incarnations. This implied that the Masonry practised at Portchester was indubitably a form of Dualism. That Graham held the flower pattern was also a sign that Clare had made the carving on the wall while incarcerated in Assheton's Tower. Marion was completely justified in insisting that he had done so.

Chapter Twenty Four

At the end of the summer of 1973 I was deluged with detail
about our life at Portchester. This came from all the living members of the group and from all the revenants. It was odd that
Guilhabert de Castres participated in these revelations even
though he had not lived in the Napoleonic incarnation. This was
because he was concerned that I should accept fully our devotion
to Dualism throughout five incarnations and also to dispel any
doubts that, odd though it may seem, I was preaching Dualism
as a French sailor and after I had left the service right up to the
middle years of the last century.

While all the revenants and the living members of the group
combined to enlighten me, the major contribution from the next
world came from Jane Butler while, among the living, Marion
moved up to second place to Clare who could not be dislodged
from the rôle as main informant. It was perfectly logical that
Jane Butler should act as one of our main news sources about
Portchester. She had shown her mettle in response to the adver-
sities of imprisonment. She was the son of a doctor at Grignan, a
little town in the Drôme honoured as the home for some years of
Madame de Sévigné. When she came to me from the next world
my mind flashed back to the view from the balcony of the Hôtel
Sévigné. You looked across the square through the trees to the
road which leads across the valley to the mountains. The foothills
of Les Lances are sprinkled with gold with the broom in flower.
The plain is patched with purple with the lavender in bloom. I
knew at once where Jane Butler had lived. It is where the street
curves upwards and to the left beyond the hotel. She told me that
she was born in that house and that her father was a doctor. She
had been interested in his work and had gathered the crumbs of
medical knowledge from watching him in his surgery and on his
rounds. Nevertheless the doctor's son had not followed in his
father's vocation. He had a passion for the sea and had joined the

French Navy. Among the rest of us were those who were mere conscripts or, like Marion and myself, had entered the Navy as a sideline. When she was taken prisoner Jane Butler reached back to her other interests and by persuasion and persistence was taken on as an unqualified assistant by the English surgeon in charge of the prisoners. She had considerable skill. She was as well able to handle the traditional remedies as a qualified doctor and had a natural intuitive sympathy. She was also incredibly conscientious. During the years of her incarceration, I don't know exactly how many, she never went on parole beyond the village of Portchester. She reckoned she could not spare more time than that from her patients. How she treated me for an iritis at the height of which it was considered possible I would end near-blind and how she coped with an epidemic of smallpox will be recorded elsewhere. She used other medicines than those supplied by the hospital pharmacy. Some of these were herbal remedies which she bought out of her own pocket.

Jane materialised one day to Clare and myself and suggested that on my next visit to Portchester I could, if I wished, see something which had been of interest to me. Once, while I was laid up with gastro-enteritis, I had drawn the outline of a rose on an adjacent wall. I recalled that the illness was a minor affair of a few days' duration. For some obscure reason I remembered also that it had occurred in October. Jane did not tell me the form of the rose but she indicated that it would be of specific importance to me.

Marion Dacre followed this recommendation with two of her own. She said that I would find a name by the Water Gate which would be to me of absolutely primary importance. I was surprised by this reversion to the question of names on walls. I had assumed that my earlier interest in names was a semi-false trail and that for me the graffiti of overwhelming importance were those related to the Masonic signs. Marion said also that there was something drawn on a wall in the keep which had also a deep significance for me. I knew better than to question her further about the objects to which she was referring.

Just before our next visit to Portchester the revenants concerned themselves rather intensively with the question of watermarks. They had previously devoted some time to the Troubadours as carriers of news and as disguised purveyors of Dualism. Now, returning to the main theme, they spoke of an interlude in which court jesters took on the rôle of the Troubadours and continued to peddle a clandestine version of Dualism. I learnt, particularly from Braïda, Mr. Mills and Guilhabert de Castres, that certain watermarks were of particular interest. There was the jester's cap with the bells attached. They pointed out that the cap was often of Phrygian type. This referred us once again to the cult of Mithras. They referred also to the design of vertical and horizontal interlocking triangles. The latter we have encountered previously as constituting what looked at first like the letter M on the walls at Portchester. I gathered that this was not only a Masonic sign but, more rarely, a Cathar symbol celebrating the Virgin Mary. A proportion of Cathars believed that Mary herself, like Jesus, was not truly incarnate but had a specially spiritualised kind of body. The revenants added that this M sign was also more ancient than Catharism.

They spoke also of a rose with triangular spines between five evenly indented petals which I saw reflected on the wall. I could not help being excited to see what has been my favourite doodle for at least four decades. Anyone changing the paper on my blotting pad or looking at the backs of envelopes on which I have scribbled can testify that this is the favourite form taken by my intentionless scrawl. I learnt from the revenants that the spines had nothing to do, as I previously assumed, with the thorns of a rose. This, in the first place, was not a particularly valid assumption, seeing that thorns do not habitually grow between the petals of roses. I was informed that the spines represented the rays of the sun and that the symbol was immensely old and certainly in use in the cult of Mithras. They said that this stylised rose had been used at a watermark centuries after the fall of Catharism. I had no idea that the Dualist tradition in watermarks had continued so late in history. The revenants told me that the interlocking triangles forming an M had been used on the paper on which pamphlets written by me on Dualism had been printed in my nineteenth-century incarnation.

On our next visit to Portchester the first thing I did was to visit the Water Gate as Marion had suggested. I was surprised that once again I had been directed there. I had thought I had already exhausted its possibilities. It was, for the prisoners, the main entrance to the castle. It was not logical to look for inscriptions and significant signs at the point of entry of the harassed captives. I noticed that a section of wall had been repaired. Brick, now mellowed, had been used in place of the original stone. I saw a stone gnarled like the branch of an ancient tree which resembled for me an oak. Clare said that this was not what we were looking for. Going up a few crude and curving steps I saw the names Raymond and Guird more clearly inscribed in a stone than the writings recorded in the keep. I had no doubt that this was the signature of Mrs. Dacre's employee. Clare reminded me again that this was additional evidence of my long addiction to walls. The revenants confirmed that I had worked at the Water Gate and that I had recorded my efforts in stone.

It was evident that Marion had made a big point when she redirected my attention to the gate. I was all the more eager to follow her further instructions. I did not realise until I worked out the import of her broad, unspecific directions that she was leading me to the large confused pattern of faded colours I had observed on one of the walls during my earlier visits. On these previous occasions I had observed briefly some of the details of this pattern. I had not examined it carefully because the Masonic signs in other places were more clearly defined and the fact that the area was coloured and that the colours had faded made the outlines less distinct. I noticed, as I had before, a number of circles with equal-armed crosses. Now that I had seen so many clearer M's on the other walls I recognised four or five at the top of the painted area. Clare also pointed out to me the simple flower-leaf patterns which she had first seen when she recalled the mandala she had made in the thirteenth century and which was to be observed faintly outlined on the W—— cross. What was new to me or, perhaps more accurate, what I noticed more obviously were the outlines, rather crudely executed, of several roses. I pointed out to Clare and my wife the one I had painted. It was a crude and faded replica of my doodle. Marion told me later that the rose which she remembered me painting had been part of the crude-coloured mural. Braïda, Graham and Jane Butler confirmed later that the rose of which I have spoken was my contribution to this mysterious and inelegant canvas.

243

I noticed a number of J's, some of them inverted, which I had not seen previously and which I took to be another variety of Masonic symbol.

It came to me, while I was looking at this shadowy confluence of colours, that it had been used to instruct an audience. I saw Captain X lecturing to his flock. He, Braïda and Graham told me later that what I had thought was correct. The aim had been to offer his sailor audience a crude and unmistakable alphabet of Dualism. It was fascinating to think that here, a hundred and seventy years ago, I had listened to the man I first met in the room looking out at the square in Bath. In this life, because of his age and occasional confusion, he had little to say to me though he recognised me as he had seen me in the thirteenth century. He returned, after his death in this life, to be my mentor and particularly in the last year, but I had also listened to him with respect and veneration in the keep at Portchester. Some of the details he told me have persisted in memory with an undiminished and obdurate glow. I thought that my doodle of the stylised rose with the rays of the sun between the petals was purely and simply a flashback to Portchester. I was to find later that I was looking still further back.

Underneath this fuddled but eloquent mural is the number 1806. The 'o' is obscure and deformed into a kind of cirlicue. Is it a deliberate perversion made to resemble the letter J? I feel that my contribution towards the Portchester mural was made towards the end of my stay there. Graham said that we were picked up in September 1804. It has always been in my mind that I did not stay at the castle much more than eighteen months. I think I bade goodbye to Portchester in 1806 and that my contribution to the painting on the wall and my excursion into self-advertisement on the curved steps by the Water Gate were achieved early that year and before the mural was finished. Towards the end of my stay I was regarded as a more reliable subject. I was qualifying for release on parole. In the first year of my imprisonment I was classified by the authorities as difficult, intransigent and one of the hard cases. This was an excusable misjudgement. It was a matter of honour and conscience with me that I should try to escape. This tension was determined by the need to dispose of the sketches I had made of the coast

244

defences. It was part of my duty to see them into the hands of their proper recipients. It was for this reason that I had to escape in order to supervise the activities of Pierre and others. My superiors in the espionage network were rigid bureaucrats who did not allow one a great deal of latitude in these matters.

It was low tide on an afternoon in September 1973 when we left the castle. We walked along the shore towards the point which I now saw as the place where the boat had stood off to receive the papers. I had walked on ahead of the others. When I stopped the memories of more than a century and a half caught up with me. I sat down on some kind of bank. Braïda materialised and laid her hand on my arm. She said quite simply that I was sitting at the spot where I had been recaptured that night in April. The boat to which Pierre swam was a hundred yards out to sea. I felt that her hand on my arm was simply intended to console me. My energy was expended and I assumed I was too tired to be perceptive. Suddenly I asked myself how we came to Portchester. I had never really given much consideration to the scope of the expedition which landed us into captivity. I had thought it was too much to expect that anything circumstantial could be added to what had been first outlined in a dream. I found myself recalling with Braïda how Marion and I had landed at Brighton. We had worked our way westwards charting the coast defences as we went. We had investigated those of Portsmouth harbour including the Martello towers. The whole operation had taken two months. I had been captured in September at the spot where I was now sitting and where I was recaptured again after Pierre had succeeded in delivering the papers. Marion was not picked up with me when we were seized for the first time. She was captured at the same time but not in my immediate vicinity.

Before we leave Portchester there are other points to be made. In those days I was well acquainted with Graham. Until the end of 1973 I did not know how well I had known him. At the time of my late September visit to Portchester I learnt that he had been, like me, strongly tainted with Masonry and totally anti-Bourbon. He had also been a member of a band of enthusiasts who had visited England at the end of the eighteenth century to bring it to a right way of thinking.

Graham came of a more cultured and educated milieu than I

did. In his family the nature and basic principles of Dualism were well understood. Graham was interested in this philosophy but, in the seventeen-nineties, not yet so converted as to accept its full implications. It was only under my tuition during our captivity at Portchester that he became a convinced Dualist. I, too, in those last years of the century of enlightenment was a good Mason and Republican but not what could be called an absolute Dualist.

Betty, who meant so much to me as Hélis in the Cathar incarnation, was less obtrusively devoted in our life at Portchester. At that time she was a chubby-faced, red-cheeked boy of sixteen or thereabouts with darkish hair and deep-brown, softly glowing, rather bovine eyes. She was a gentle, submissive creature. She was detailed by Jane Butler to look after me when I was ill with iritis after erysipelas. I was, with some reason, a difficult and frightened patient. It was on the cards that my sight would at least be considerably impaired and I did not support the prospect with any particular equanimity. At this time Betty endured my vapours without complaint.

She was also invited to share in Pierre's preliminary attempt to escape by way of the tunnel in the March preceding the full-scale evasion in April. She and Pierre were inseparable and in actual fact were to remain devoted to each other all their lives. Pierre endeavoured unsuccessfully to persuade Betty to share his hazardous performance at the tunnel. Though genuinely devoted to Pierre she was not made for such escapades. She endured an agony of apprehension after he had disappeared into the mouth of the tunnel and rushed to his aid the moment she heard the sound of the shot fired by the sentry. It was she who extracted Pierre from the débris brought down by the reverberation of the shot. She dragged him out of the tunnel and managed to smuggle him to the hutments before the full night watch had assembled.

One of the most astonishing aspects of my incarceration at Portchester was my relationship with Eugene. The latter, my closest male friend in this life, was killed mine-laying from a plane at St. Nazaire in 1943.

It was only in later years that I discovered that all, or at any rate the vast majority, of my circle of friends had been in some way psychic. I described Eugene in *Silent Union* and expressed

246

my belief that he had been aware of his impending death. I wondered whether he, too, was of the same make-up as my other friends. I had thought this all the more in the last two years when I had become more aware of presences about me. Of all the people I have known since my memory of my Cathar incarnation began none has exceeded Eugene in emanatory capacity. (He died twenty years before my Cathar existence was revealed.) It seemed to me that when he was present the air vibrated. After his death there have been many occasions when I have looked over my shoulder as though I felt him behind me, and this before the days when I became easily and regularly aware of presences.

In September 1973 I was astonished when Guilhabert de Castres said that I had know Eugene at Portchester. In this life we had been drawn to each other not only by mutual liking but because we had been friends in another incarnation. I had made more than one attempt to escape from Portchester. Eugene was on guard duty on one of these occasions. I was apprehended without much difficulty when emerging from still another tunnel. It was immediately obvious that the game was up. I celebrated this discovery by an outburst of vile language of which he took not the slightest notice. After this episode for some reason he became interested in me. Our converse was limited to odd occasions when he was on duty and not particularly occupied. If the reader thinks it surprising that a British officer of those days should exhibit an interest in a non-commissioned French sailor I can only say that our guards were on the whole a humane lot, in marked contrast to the British sailors, who were the most uncouth and brutal specimens I ever encountered. Admittedly the treatment exhibited to Pierre was abominable but Clare herself bears no grudge and says the English had need of information and that she was obstinately determined to give nothing away.

While I was at Portchester my contact with Eugene was limited. We only became friends after I had left. It was he who was instrumental in persuading me to accept parole. A certain truculent pride had made me persist in my attempts to escape but in actual fact I was tired of incarceration and, under his influence, I opted for parole. It was he who found me the job with Mrs. Dacre. I cannot repay him for this and for his friendship with me in this life. In the Napoleonic incarnation he came

247

frequently to Mrs. Dacre's house. On such occasions I was treated as an equal and he and I had long talks together. I was in those days an inveterate idea-monger and it is difficult to think of me engaged willingly in anything like casual conversation. I was less socially inclined than I had been as a young man but was in no sense an acidulous intellectual. I was made of tougher fibre but obviously addicted to the search for truth. I had changed a good deal from the young man who had deliberately set out to charm at the end of the eighteenth century.

By the time I left Portchester I was an out-and-out Dualist. I discussed my philosophy with Eugene and he was fascinated by it. He was, in that incarnation as in this, a devotee of field sports as well as a fine athlete. I remember how in this life, walking by the Avon at Bath, he told me that hunting, shooting and fishing were indefensible but that if we are born with the hunter's instinct it cannot be eradicated. His pattern of leisure was similar in the nineteenth century to what it was in this.

His virile nature had been directed in those days to the Army. In his last incarnation he qualified both as a doctor and a test pilot. He joined the regular Air Force in Poland before the Second World War. He became involved in a research project designed to choose by a series of behaviourist tests the perfect pilot. He discovered that most of the best pilots were recruited from those who had been classified by the test system as unsuitable and potentially neurotic. Those who, according to research methods, were ideal material were in actual practice slow-witted, imperceptive and unsuited to war conditions. He described the whole structure and intention of this important organisation as stupid and resigned from it forthwith and from the Air Force. This was a characteristic gesture. Eugene had little tolerance for any kind of stupidity, particularly in high places. It was fascinating that Guilhabert de Castres, in discussing him, said that one of the bonds between us was our resentment of authority. Perhaps my truculence at our first meeting in the Napoleonic incarnation endeared me to him. In this life he returned to the Air Force at the outbreak of the Second World War. He refused to serve as a doctor, had an incredible number of flying hours to his credit as a fighter pilot, transferred later to bombers and was killed at St. Nazaire.

In the Napoleonic incarnation he accepted eagerly the Dualist belief that there were two primary forces of good and evil. He discussed reincarnation without prejudice but did not accept it. He was uninterested in the concept that the world was created by the Devil. In one matter of primary importance he was influenced by Dualist convictions. He decided it would be impossible for him to take human life in any circumstances and retired from the Army at an early age. His reluctance to take life did not extend to the animal kingdom. He continued his sporting pursuits in the Napoleonic incarnation into his life in the twentieth century. Perhaps he was harking back to his former pursuits when he told me, going along the road at Bathampton, that field sports were ethically indefensible but that he could not desist from them.

I had been told by the revenants that, at the time we met at Portchester, Eugene lived somewhere in the neighbourhood of Haslemere. After he retired from the Army he contracted a disastrous marriage, had two children, moved house and lived somewhere near Portchester. He was stationed at Eastleigh when he came to England in 1940. Perhaps it was somewhere near his previous home.

I have written at some length about Eugene because it fascinates me that Guilhabert de Castres should have spoken of him. Eugene was not a member of our group but a kind of fringe associate. It was evident that the revenants, and particular Betty, were deeply concerned with my personal relationships past and present. It was significant how, beyond this life, they retained what is called humanity. It surprises me that the communication came from Guilhabert de Castres because as a rule he only appears at the crucial signposts of experience or when there is some especially difficult philosophical problem requiring solution. I feel that his intervention was made to draw attention to Eugene's extraordinary capacity to emanate. Though he was not of the group he was among the first of the messengers.

My friendship with Eugene ripened after I had left Portchester. While within its precincts I was closer to Marion than to anyone. Our deep friendship continued after we had left Portchester. Marion and I met sometimes near where she worked in Winchester. There is a memory of a day in the meadows of St.

Cross. Once again it is autumn. It is cloudless but the deep blue of summer has gone from the sky. I do not know if this was our last meeting. What I am certain of is that we were very close to each other at Portchester and afterwards our paths diverged. When I talk to her in this life I have a feeling of a close bond trying to reassert itself and being impeded by a mutual reticence. When she was finally repatriated she did not go directly to Provence. She was shipped to a port elsewhere in France. It is possible that she stopped off at Brest. She and Clare remembered that she spent some time in Paris. She did what she could to spread the principles of Dualism and Masonry as practised at Portchester. I do not know what she did after she left Paris.

I cannot close my description of Portchester without reverting to the atmosphere of happiness which lingers about it. This is nothing to do with the glow imparted by the patina of age. It is emphasised by all who were captive there. Even Kathleen blames herself rather than the place for anything she suffered. Clare, who was tortured in Assheton's Tower, loves Portchester and is always happy to return to it provided she avoids the proximity to the cell in which she was incarcerated. I think our happiness is attributable to the remarkable officers who organised the life of the prisoners. Something is owing to the English guards, who were on the whole reasonable and humane men with elastic standards in accepting bribes. But on the whole it was our fellow countrymen who nursed us through what could have been an appalling experience. Remember that the treatment of our fellow countrymen in the hulks rotting in the harbours was criminal by any standards. What I say of our happiness at Portchester is borne out by those who have written the history of the French prisoners. It is generally agreed that so many of them left better men than they came in. This is not usually claimed for a prison. It is emphasised that those who entered illiterate could read and write when they left and that the formerly penniless had money in their pockets and a trade at their fingertips.

From the standpoint of the group it was Captain X to whom we owed most. On a morning in June 1974 I was walking in the park at Bath and reflecting how much he had done for us but doubting, quite reasonably, that the Portchester achievement could be attributed to one man. Graham appeared and answered my question. He said that two French members of the group had been enormously helpful. One is a woman I have mentioned in two previous books, whom I know to have been an acquaintance in ancient Rome but who I had not credited with playing any rôle in any of the intervening incarnations. At Portchester she was a short, stocky officer with a broad head to match. Though Provençal born she had fair hair, blue eyes and a pale complexion. She frequently gave us lectures. One of her main themes was that peasants with very small holdings should pour their resources into some kind of co-operative organisation. What she worked for has been realised by the vignerons of the Languedoc and Provence. The other officer was one who, in this life by her recurrent nightmares of being tortured, was among the first to lead me firmly on the road to Dualism. In the Napoleonic incarnation she was tall, sallow, dark-haired, dark-eyed and more typically Provençal than her colleague. She specialised in interpreting the Dualist symbols and often lectured in the keep, using the confused mass of coloured designs by way of illustration.

I have by now ceased to be amazed that so many I have met in this life have been known to me in previous incarnations. I am still astounded that so many should have been concentrated together within the same narrow precincts in the nineteenth century.

Chapter Twenty Five

It was an unforgettable moment in my life when Braïda told me by the shore at Portchester that it was at this point I had been captured after my sketch of the shore defences had been passed on to the waiting boat. It was important not merely because it explained my long-standing dream about waiting for a boat and proved once and for all that in my dream I had been concerned with my recapture after escape from the prison and not with my original incarceration. What was still more important was the advice Braïda gave me on this particular occasion. She said I ought to visit Waggoners Wells. I have mentioned this previously as the place in which I got lost during my walk in the early thirties. It was obvious to me that Waggoners Wells was connected with my last incarnation. It was in the vicinity of Haslemere that, as a French prisoner, I had worked for Mrs. Dacre. It was surely significant that, as Guilhabert de Castres had said, Eugene had also lived in that locality. Now Braïda said positively that I had lived there years before the visit on which Marion and I had investigated the shore defences. This baffled me considerably.

I have said that in this life it was at Haslemere that I first became absolutely convinced that I had been a French prisoner of war in England. The revelations from the revenants and from Mrs. Dacre, Marion and Clare provided me with the confirmatory detail. But what puzzled me more was my attachment to the country round Shere, Gomshall, Holmbury St. Mary, Peaslake and Abinger Hammer which is some distance from Haslemere and which was nevertheless also associated in my mind with the Napoleonic wars. I loved above all the village of Shere. At the time of my first visit in 1928 it became magical to me. It was a strangely domesticated taste for one reared in the more dramatic background of Cumberland. From the first moment I saw it this cosy, secluded country with little glimpses of the wilderness was both home and magic. How many times in the last forty-five years have I seen, with memories so sharp that I seemed to be living rather than recalling, the line of houses by the stream at Shere. The stream winds behind the willows past an avenue of limes to small fields with high hedges which, in their secrecy and silence, are a miniature of all the world's pasture. Beside the stream is a half-timbered house with an overhanging gable. I remember this most of all. Had I lived in this area as well as under Mrs. Dacre's roof?

I learnt from the revenants, particularly Braïda, Graham and Betty, about my first contacts with England. Sometimes the information came through Clare but I received a good deal directly. It seemed that I had been in this country long before the visit on which I investigated the coast defences. It all came about like this. I was of modest but not of peasant origin, the son of a small merchant or small professional man. I had received a good education. Among my accomplishments was a knowledge of English. I was an idealistic and dedicated young man. I was given to all manner of fertile ideas and fine sentiments. At this stage I looked to see their fulfilment in this vale of tears. I reached my twenties in the last decade of the eighteenth century. I must have been well able to appreciate the fall of the Bastille. "Bliss was it in that dawn to be alive, But to be young was very heaven!" I had swallowed hook, line and sinker the principles of the Revolution. I believed sincerely in liberty, equality and fraternity. I was a more sophisticated and articulate version of the sailors at Portchester. In my late teens I had joined a semi-secret republican club. From the evidence provided at Portchester I know this to have been Masonic but I persist that it was slanted away from the continental and British Masonry practised at that period. It was frankly if not totally Dualist. There is no question that at this time it had undoubted political leanings. It was wholeheartedly against the Bourbons. Was it because of the repressive Catholicism to which this dynasty was addicted? Did my society believe with the Cathars that all earthly hierarchies were evil and this one especially so? Was it opposed to the dark, ritualistic occultism practised under the Bourbons? It is clear to me that this particular variety of Masonry was especially strong in the Midi.

I came to England in the last decade of the eighteenth century. I came with the approval of the reigning political authorities but I was actually subsidised by the Masonic organisation to which I belonged. I have no idea how much liaison there was between the prevailing politicians and my immediate employers. All this adds fuel to the fire kindled by those for whom the Grand Orient Lodge in France has concerned itself constantly with the spread of revolution. In this life I am completely out of sympathy with both the Grand Orient Lodge and its detractors. I insist also that the Masonry in which I was interested was unrelated to any kind of modern Masonry and had affinities with medieval Dualism. This may seem illogical because I cannot escape from the fact that it was politically slanted. How otherwise could I have found myself as a spy in England?

The aim of my mission was to ferment revolution through the Masonic lodges. History recalls that a good deal of subversive activity in Britain was ascribed to French agents during the Directory, the Consulate and Empire. There came a time when Napoleon himself reverted to the theme that the English people had nothing to lose but their chains and that, were he to appear on their shores, the masses would arise and welcome the liberator. Like others he underestimated the tenacity and above all the insularity of the island race.

After Braïda came to me by the shore at Portchester at the spot where I was recaptured my memory of my life in England intensified. I began to understand my emotional response to Shere in this life and my feeling of personal identity with it which has lasted nearly half a century. During this intensification of memory I became aware that I had been associated with Shere for a specific purpose. This recollection was accompanied by a deepening glow of happiness and by an accepted sense of failure. I have never been able to explain to my satisfaction the happiness I feel when I think of Shere. Happiness is not usually associated with failure nor is it to be guaranteed when one is risking life and liberty in a hostile country. Inevitably I thought of some particularly tender and evocative affair of the heart but Braïda and Graham said I was never deeply involved. They told me that I was a very good actor and that, because of this, two or three women believed I felt more deeply for them than was actually the case and that some hearts were broken when I left the country. I am convinced that in this I had no intention of exploiting other people's feelings for me. I had a natural sympathy for women and a capacity to express it and show it. I expect that the fact that I was so different from their fellow countrymen made me both a help and a problem to them. My recollection of myself is that of a young man who loved company, good conversation and beautiful women, above all when they were elegantly turned out, but I was embarrassed by intimacies and lost my savoir faire if I were the recipient of any deep affection. I was essentially good-natured and deep down felt a considerable concern for others. Nevertheless I could give an impression of hostility and truculence if anyone made inroads on my privacy.

There was one particularly obsessive connection with Shere which I found hard to explain. In addition to lurking Frenchmen it was always associated in my mind with smuggling and, rather absurdly, with Kipling's poem which begins, "If you wake at midnight and hear a horse's feet". I have often pondered how, when people are asked what literature has influenced them most, they should so inevitably and untruthfully quote only the first-rate. This child's poem with its jingling refrain, "Five and twenty ponies trotting through the dark, Brandy for the Parson, Baccy for the Clerk", awakens in me the feelings usually associated with great poetry. The tightening of the scalp, the tingling of the spine, and the hair standing up at the back of the neck, the indefinable drawing up of the substance of the solar plexus, all these manifestations, which are best reserved for the "Ode to a Nightingale", fragments of Ronsard and Verlaine and a few Housman lyrics were, and still are, felt by me when I read the lines, "Them that asks no questions isn't told a lie, Watch the wall my darling when the gentlemen go by". I could not begin to explain the association between smuggling, Kipling's poem, Shere and my last life on this planet. I have known for some years that the neighbourhood of Shere had been a resort of smugglers. I had not known how far the village itself had been involved. I did not know that it had to do with me. I knew that I was far too upright to be concerned with contraband. It did not mix with my laboriously ethical republican principles.

I knew that on my first visit to England I had never concealed the fact that I was a Frenchman. It was reasonable to suppose that I passed myself off as an émigré, as a victim of the Revolution rather than an exponent of its principles. All these matters were to be clarified on my visit to Haslemere in November 1973. The circumstances resembled those which preceded the visit to Cumberland during which we were led to the stone at W——. Clare and I were bombarded with advice from this world and the next that we must go to Haslemere. Braïda was the most insistent and Annette in her calls from Canada reinforced her opinions and added that before we went to Haslemere we had to be charged up for the experience. Braïda also impressed on Annette that what Clare told me these days came from her own far memory and was not dependent on prompting from Braïda. Where necessary she could confirm what Clare said but the latter had the power of recall in her own right. She was also passing from the pains of far memory to the atrocious agony of full reliving.

Braïda was present while we were walking between the stones at Avebury. When I returned home that evening she materialised again. She said that it had been especially important for me to go to Avebury because I was capable of drawing strength from stone. She reminded me of my preoccupation with stone through my years, and lives, as a wall-builder and stone-mason.

Before we went to Surrey in the last days of November 1973 Braïda was as precise as she had been over the stone at W——. She outlined clearly for me the time gap between my two visits to England. My first visit had been about ten years before my incarceration at Portchester. I stayed first with a Frenchman near Haslemere. My sojourn lasted only a month, during which time he told me what contacts I should make in Shere, which was to be regarded as my centre of operations. I was delighted by Braïda's reference to Shere and my affection for it was sensibly heightened. I hoped that the mystery of my attachment to it would be at last revealed.

A few days later Braïda appeared to Clare and repeated that Waggoners Wells was very important to us. She spoke of three ponds, two together and one more apart. I had forgotten the exact layout of the ponds. Braïda said that one of them was very
256

important. I had an instant vision of the end of the far lake with a steep bank ascending it towards the woods. Braïda said it was necessary for us to walk again in the forests by the Wells. We should approach the heath and woodland by a lane leading through Bramshott. Clare said that Braïda had been particularly insistent about this lane. We would also see my house at Shere. In the latter particular I needed no direction. I could visualise at any time its half timber and gable. I should go back to G——, where I had built the wall.

Nature and the weather were kind to us on our journey to Surrey. Never have I seen so many golden leaves so late on the trees. It was almost as if, in my recurrent dreams coloured with the beauty of autumn, I had been looking forward as well as backwards, as though I were foreseeing the glory of my return as well as the poignancy of the still day in autumn on which I was captured. I saw the open space, now half asphalt, half grass, where I had stood the day I received the overcoat from Mrs. Dacre. The house consisted of two dissimilar sections built into each other. One was long and low and much older than the other. It was this part of the house Mrs. Dacre had recalled when she was menaced with pneumonia and a high temperature and which I had seen when I almost wept in the street at Bath. I saw the wall near which, eighteen months previously, I had become finally and unmistakably convinced of my previous incarnation as a French prisoner in the Napoleonic war. Near by was a small secluded alley with brick walls. That also was now familiar and intensely personal. Clare told me that I had also built the walls of this alley.

It was curious, but I could have sworn that on my last visit, at the far limits of the garden, I had seen a variegated wall which included in its composition brick, flint and rubble. When I wandered in that direction I saw a newer, more uniform wall, which I was assured had been erected in recent years. There was no particular reason why I should imagine, on my previous visit when I was still unaware of my activities as a builder, the presence of a non-existent wall. What, in any case, was the purpose of visualising a wall which, at that time, had no particular history attached to it? The cardinal point is that I saw this wall after I had spoken to Mrs. Butler, the first of the group to reveal to me that she had a previous incarnation other than her life as a

257

Cathar and the first to tell me that she had been a sailor in the French Navy. I saw this wall as it was some time after 1806, or as I had built it myself, on the same morning as, agitated by Jane Butler's forecasts of her impending death, I knew for the first time with blinding certainty that I had been a French prisoner of war in the locality.*

We went to Bramshott on a still afternoon with little sunshine but the air was flooded with light from the trees. The trees in the forest were clouds of gold. It was the most florid autumn I had ever seen. Clare steered us to Bramshott church. When I had lain down to rest the previous evening I had seen the same interlocking triangles as those inscribed on the walls at Portchester but enclosed in a glowing circle of amethyst. Whenever I see this deep glow of amethyst, and above all when it is in the form of a jewel, it is either a sign that Betty is present or that I am reaching far back in time. After we had visited the church Clare led me outside and we walked to the house Eugene had lived in. I had no acute photographic stab of memory when I saw the house. I can only say that I was moved by the atmosphere and felt myself to be walking out of time in a limitless world where the trees and houses were merely deteriorating symbols of a greater reality. Then we came to a road called Rectory Lane. Clare said that now she understood what Braïda had meant when she said that we must go by the lane to Waggoners Wells. She was not referring just to any lane but this particularly named road.

Though I had not recognised the house in which Eugene had lived I came to a stop at the opening of a silent avenue with part of the façade of the house visible at its far extremity. The trees in the avenue were gold with the autumn and leaning with age and I knew that they were especially familiar to me. I remembered how for years I had recalled this woodland path, the drive with its shaggy shrubs, its ancient, weary, slightly tilted trees, and the house which had seemed to me to hold a deeper mystery than that imposed by the darkness of the trees and the shade of the encroaching forest.

When I went past the house by the steep path descending to

* In July 1974 Mrs. Dacre returned from the dead and told me the wall had been there in the first years of the nineteenth century.

the ponds I knew I had lived there but I did not know how long and in what capacity. We walked past the first lake and came to a patch of white flowers, palely suffused with pink, which I had noted especially on my last visit six or seven years ago. In certain features they resembled both stitchwort and wood sorrel. I had made fumbling and unscientific attempts to identify them. I made them out to be some rare kind of wintergreen. I had been interested in them when I last saw them. Now I was positively fascinated. Though I have had an absorbing interest in plant life throughout four incarnations I could not understand my intense preoccupation with these modest and seclusive flowers.

My step and heart were light and I had a sudden access of energy. Braïda and Graham kept step beside me. Suddenly, between the middle and the last lake, I crumpled completely. It was not any kind of physical faintness, like a hypoglycaemic disturbance caused by a fall in blood sugar. Something like an iron curtain descended behind me and cut me off from the way I had come. I was hit by a curious sharp-edged depression which seemed to make an incision in time and to define me absolutely from the man I had been two paces before. Leaden with misery I raised my eyes to a sloping bank. Then it all came back. I was looking at the spot which had been my ruin.

I remembered that I had lived no more than a month in the house I had passed some minutes previously. It was my first assignment. The man living in the house at that time was a French émigré, married, with two children. Graham was also staying in the house. I do not know if he was acting as a tutor to the children. I was originally invited as an expert on trees. This was extraordinary because I was not yet twenty. My designation as a tree expert was merely a blind, nevertheless it is evident that I was regarded as some kind of authority on the subject. Some of the ancient trees in the avenue were planted under my direction. I have referred so often to my passion for trees in this life that it is pointless to repeat it. All I will say is that my contributions to newspapers and local authorities on this subject will be well known to my friends.

I was very happy in this house from which I practised for the first time in England the arts in which I had been trained. The overall strategy was simple. I described myself as an émigré from

259

the French Revolution. I was as charming as possible to the families who received me. This inclined them all the more to believe that I was a worthy object of sympathy. Having established a rapport with them I began to insert here and there items of propaganda in favour of the Revolution. My favourite line was that, while from some points of view the revolutionaries were monsters, one had to be fair and allow that they had done this and that. I would then throw in, coolly and with apparent detachment, some evident virtue which would hardly fail to appeal to my hosts. The whole thing seems crude in the extreme and indeed it was. Graham tells me that we were amateurish, at times laughably so. The whole thing was organised by a collection of bureaucrats toxic with ideas and with a rigid spinsterish attitude towards life. Nevertheless, I did not come to grief because the crudeness of my propaganda attracted the attention of my host's English friends. The cause of the disaster was more concrete and local. The secret lay in the segment of the bank I was now regarding with such indescribably intense depression.

It was here we had arranged a sort of postbox. It was either in the hollow of a tree or beneath a fallen trunk. Agents from different districts were accustomed to leave reports and information in what they hoped was a secret depository. Someone had informed the authorities. It was unfortunate for me that others had been observed using this postbox. I had myself left there an indiscreet note. My host was warned that the authorities were on the track of the whole network. I had to leave in a hurry. In order to conceal my departure I kept to the woods, leaving Waggoners Wells by scrambling up a slope at the end of the furthest lake. Braïda had warned me before that the furthest pond was important to me. It was obvious why she had insisted on our approaching the ponds by the path leading from Rectory Lane. Had we taken other routes I would not have recalled the feeling of being struck by a physical weight of depression at the end of the second pond where we had the postbox. I would not have relived the feeling of desolation when, in this life, I reached the end of the furthest point where, in my last incarnation, I had left Waggoners Wells for the forest and the road to my next dwelling.

This day Braïda was with me as I walked through the woods.

I myself recalled what had happened and she confirmed that what I remember was true.

Next day we went to Shere. I walked down the path by the stream past the weeping willows. I stopped by the house I had recalled with affection for so many years, deluding myself as a young man that I loved it because of its mellow red brick, the murmur of water outside its door and because it was hidden in the domesticated but secret country which moved me strangely. Now I knew that its lines were incised deeply in my memory because I had lived there. When I saw it that morning I told Clare that in those days there were more willows by the water. Braïda confirmed that this was true. We walked past the house to the bridge which crosses the stream below the manor house. At this point I was happy. I was bathed in an unvibrating and tranquil beauty. I was out of the zone of extreme magnetism. There was no stab of recollection and no heartache from the past. Between the avenue of lime trees I felt nothing deeper than the poignancy of autumn. Then my wife, who had lived a good deal of her life in Surrey, pointed to the manor and said she had heard that far back in the last century the cellars of the house had been used for smuggling. After she had spoken I seemed to awaken to an acuter life. When we returned from the bridge and came again to the house in which I had lived I had watched what you could call a somatic memory. I felt weak and faint. My stomach heaved and I felt I would vomit. Clare commented on my appearance, "It's only remembering but the memory is deep."

Now there was another house by the river which spoke to me but less clearly than the house with overhanging gables. Clare said that in those days it was a great meeting place for the men of the village and especially for those the wrong side of the law. She said that the village had been a great centre of the contraband trade. I recalled what my wife said previously about the cellars of the manor. I had not felt any emanation from this other house when we passed it on our way to the wooden bridge below the manor. I suppose what my wife had said about contraband being hidden in the cellars had set up a resonance in the chords of memory.

Braïda told me that when I lived at Shere the contraband trade

261

had been very active. It had links with the Channel ports and across the water with France itself. I had sent messages across the Channel with the help of the smugglers. Kipling's poem recurred in my thoughts with increased insistence. Another couplet resounded more clearly above the level of consciousness.

Laces for a lady, letters for a spy,
Watch the wall, my darling, while the gentlemen go by.

In retrospect the rest of the day was dreamlike. I swear it was not so at the time and that I was precise, clear-headed and registering what went on around me with more than average acuity. The dreamlike quality comes with hindsight. I see that what was revealed that day was so clear that it was above the level of ordinary consciousness, a kind of quintessence of experience compressed in a day.

During lunch Clare spoke of some swampy land near Gomshall which was very important to us. She admitted that Braïda had spoken of this today and on previous occasions. I thought that to visit this place would be an easy matter. I knew that there were watercress beds down the road and I assumed the swampy land must have been in their vicinity. The place was more difficult to find than I imagined. It was not merely a matter of geography. It was a question of a couple of false starts abandoned because Clare and I knew that the atmosphere was not living and evocative. Then we crossed a bridge over a stream and came to what in these days was not wholly marshland but boggy earth with coarse tussocks of grass, with the earth more sodden as it neared the stream. The wasteland was backed with a light screen of willows. I picked my way between the clumps of grass and moved towards an arched tunnel built above the stream. The air was positively alive. To me it was more vibrant than anywhere else we had visited. I had also a sense of disaster, "It was here," I said. "There was another post office here."

It was at this point that Graham took over from Braïda. After he had told me I was right I was able to recall that we had loosened a brick in the arch of the tunnel. We had left messages behind the dislodged brick. Granted that in those days the population was small and the roads less frequented, it seemed to me a hazardous proceeding. Suddenly it occurred to me that once again the network had been pierced. "We had to hide here," I said. "There were horsemen on the road."

We had hidden in the deep grass of the marshland and in the tunnel itself. The troop of cavalry clattered up the road. They gave a cursory glance across the stretch of wasteland. Had they left the road they could not have failed to find us. All this took place one mid-afternoon in autumn.

I may have been right in my criticism of our faulty system of communications but I was wrong in assuming that this was what had betrayed us. At this stage I failed to comprehend what Graham was saying. The chart of my understanding of the revenants sometimes pursued an irregular course. It seemed that we had been betrayed by another Frenchman who was what I suppose you would call nowadays a double agent. He lived in the vicinity, described himself as an émigré, had worked with Graham some time as an agent in revolutionary France and was now prepared to dispose of Graham for a consideration from the English authorities.

Once again my conscious memory returned quickly. I drove the car to the house where this unsavoury character had lived. It is a small, half-timbered black and white affair. Its contemporary appearance is attractive and altogether innocuous. When I say that my conscious memory returned very quickly this is not to say that I had not remembered clearly at another level. I rarely visited Shere without walking down the road to look at this house which in those days seemed so pleasantly attractive and where so much evil was generated.

After that we set out for Peaslake. I do not know why I was so insistent that we should go there. I realised that Graham had come for a purpose but I had no idea what was to follow. When he first came into my story I had regarded him as a minor figure. On this still day in November 1973 he occupied the stage fully because of the rôle he and I had played together more than 170 years previously.

We went first up the steep road which I wished to see again because of my long and tender memories of it. The road was narrow. I do not think I had ever before mounted it in a car. I decided to back down and take another road up. Some dumb but demanding instinct compelled me to continue. The still air,

263

hushed with the coming of winter, was light with the glow of the golden bracken. I stopped the car by a small clearing. There was not a tremor in the air when we alighted from the car. It was here, Graham said, we had had still another postbox. There was an oak tree in the centre of the clearing. It was the replacement of one which had been there in our time. All this was very fitting in view of Graham's feeling about oaks. After I had received news from France I came over from Shere and left messages for other agents who called at set times to gather information. Once again it made me shiver, to recall the insecurity of our arrangements. I think I did not allow for the fact that in those days this was wild heath country. Even then a regular traveller on a lonely road, and above all a person of foreign extraction, would surely attract attention.

As we drove to Ewhurst I did not know that we were approaching the climax. This place is almost as dear to me as Shere. I stayed there more than once in the early days after I qualified. I had scarcely alighted from the car when I walked across the green and, pointing to a house, said that Graham had lived there. He replied that he had done so and that I remembered it because I had often gone over to visit him. I wondered if the house where I myself had stayed as a young man had any connection with my previous incarnation and if, for that reason, I had been led to it. In this life I have so often returned to what, at the time, I did not consciously recognise as places I had known in past incarnations. What I remember most of the interior of this cottage is the picture of Napoleon.

Once again, guided by instinct, I did not take the direct route to Gomshall. We returned by the Ockley road, turning off through Holmsbury. As we turned down to Ockley the country was more open. Very soon we passed a field much larger than those we had seen around Shere and Gomshall. I said, "This is the biggest open field we have seen this afternoon." It was not an intelligent, interesting or even a necessary remark but it had its significance. I had drifted away and was searching the débris of decades for an old memory. I had moved away from the revenants. My mind was acting on its own account.

When we were well on the road to Haslemere Clare said, "Did anything happen at Ewhurst?"

"Not that I know. Just that Graham lived there. Why do you ask?"

"Can you hear what Graham is saying?"

What he told us was that after we had hidden from the cavalry he had returned to the house of the French renegade and had challenged him to a duel. The latter had accepted. He was an expert swordsman and thought Graham easy game. He had no wish to be discredited in France and thought it desirable that he dispose of his traducer. Graham said that he would have been perfectly happy to have continued drawing funds from the revolutionary government. The duel was fought in a field near Ewhurst off the Ockley road. Small wonder that I made both the detour in my car and my seemingly superfluous reference to the big open field.

The course of the duel went against the book. Graham's adversary was left for dead though he subsequently recovered. I myself cannot remember the duel or what followed immediately afterwards as clearly as I recall my hiding in the marshes. Graham described how, that same evening, we fled the country. I went back from Ewhurst to Shere, seized a few possessions and departed without any unnecessary adieus. I said how, just before lunch that day, I had felt faint and sick when I passed the house at Shere for the second time. Was I recalling the horror of the duel and the misery of my precipitate departure from the house in the village I had loved so much?

Certainly I can well understand how the road from Ewhurst to Shere has had for me for decades an aching beauty. When I walked it as a medical student its beauty was not only a nourishment to my senses but a pang in my heart. I have never changed in my attitude towards it.

I asked Graham if my sudden and unheralded departure had not aroused inconvenient interest. He said that its effect was far less dramatic compared with what one would anticipate by hindsight. Respected residents regularly disappeared without warning from the neighbourhood of Shere and Peaslake. A number were deeply involved in smuggling and found it not only convenient but healthy to disappear from time to time from the locality. When I left it was assumed in the neighbourhood that I was another involved in the contraband trade. One did not lose

265

face because of one's vocation. It was not generally suspected that I was an enemy agent.

We crossed the Weald and Romney Marsh and escaped by way of Winchelsea. The latter is not just another place I know and love in this incarnation. When I think of it it has the particularly stabbing image evoked when I look on places I have lived in past incarnations.

I have no satisfactory explanation for the love I have for Shere and its neighbourhood. It is reasonable to be moved by places we have lived in in past incarnations, especially if one has suffered there. But why should my memories of Shere be so happy? I was a spy in hostile country and perpetually on my guard. Were these factors, not conducive to happiness, offset by some unforgettably tender personal association? All the evidence is to the contrary. In spite of my social graces I was fundamentally an austere young man. Later I became still more austere and less amiable. Graham emphasises how much I loved the countryside and its flora. I was a keen botanist and especially interested in fungi. I have a muddled recollection of finding a rare variety of wild St. John's wort in a field near the wooden bridge at the end of the village. I believe there was a playback of this episode when I was a medical student or young doctor but I did not recognise it as such. Graham and Braïda told me that I loved the people. All this is well enough but to me there is some hidden component, as yet unrevealed, which acted as a catalyst in inducing happiness. There is no point in thinking of these matters. In this world they will be revealed in due course or not at all. In the next we shall see simultaneously past, present and future and the eternal moment.

What I am sure of is that I was at my best in England. As a propagandist for Republicanism and Masonry my methods were unsophisticated and crude and I achieved little. Was the soft air and the empiricism of England better suited to my nature than the fierce sunlight of Provence and the sharp-edged ideas of the Republicans? After we returned to France Graham abandoned espionage. I had years of training in intelligence work before I joined the Navy and was a greater success as a common spy than I had been as an agent-cum-propagandist. I think this training in clandestinity had an adverse effect on my character. I was by nature open enough and able to establish contact quickly with others. Though I was never deeply involved with anyone I was by no means a shut-in character. I believe that the constant need for secrecy established a dichotomy in my nature which was ultimately unfortunate. The sailor at Portchester, seen several times by Marion and once by myself, was a particular mixture of good nature and truculence, of innate friendliness and acquired hostility.

When I left Portchester I was closer to Marion than to anyone else I had known. Even then I had become a rather buttoned-up personality regarded with respect by my fellows but without undue affection. My life with Mrs. Dacre was my Indian summer. She thawed out the stiffness which was the particular expression of my resentment of authority. The latter reaction had developed during my years of training in France for naval intelligence. It had intensified when I was forced to submit to the authorities at Portchester. (The fault was more mine than theirs. All the evidence is that in spite of everything I was surprisingly happy at Portchester.) When I worked for Mrs. Dacre's nineteenth-century precursor I could reveal by hard work and loyalty the love and veneration I felt for him. I do not know how I tore myself away from Haslemere. My life took on a distinct second course after I left Mrs. Dacre's service. I think I was infected by the plague of duty. I did not get a great deal of happiness from it.

I do not know exactly when I returned to France after my first visit to England. At one time I had thought that I would learn no more of this interlude between my two visits to England. In this I was in error. I learnt from the revenants and also from Clare how I came to join the French Navy. I cannot recall what time elapsed between my return from England and my enlistment. There was a traditional drift of Provençaux towards the sea and I was no different from the others. I was offered a commission in the French Navy. At that time they were crucially short of officers and any man of education had a chance of commissioned rank. It was at this stage that my previous experience determined my destiny. In spite of my personal sense of failure after my first visit to England I cannot have been totally futile in the art of espionage, otherwise I would not have been taken on for what is now called naval intelligence. It was arranged that I should enter the Navy without commissioned rank. It was thought that in this way my activities would be less conspicuous. I rather fancy this suggestion came from me because I had other fish to fry. I wished to continue also my Masonic activities and to missionise as many others as possible. It was perfectly reasonable that I would attract less attention as an ordinary seaman in addition to which, in joining on such a basis, I provided myself with a bigger audience. It should be understood that the Navy, officially at any rate, were unaware of my missionary intentions when I made my arrangements. It is possible that they connived from the beginning at my twofold rôle but it is not necessary to assume this. Napoleonic fighting forces were less politically orientated than those of the preceding revolutionary armies. Certainly I was to learn at Portchester that the Navy was packed with Freemasons and that a number had worn Masonic symbols at sea before their capture. It may have been that Masonry showed itself more openly in captivity than freedom. I cannot imagine Captain X, at sea in wartime, directing operations from the bridge and throwing in a dash of Dualism in his spare moments. Certainly after we were taken prisoner there was no attempt on anybody's part to hide their Masonic addictions. It was also clear that some of the sailors must have known a good deal about the other activities of Marion and myself. The former said early in our acquaintanceship in this life that I was respected because the prisoners knew I had a special mission.

Chapter Twenty Six

For what happened after I returned to France I am most indebted to what Betty, Graham and Jane Butler told me over a period of several months, but my own memory of certain scenes is sharp enough. An immense contribution was made by Betty with the aid of Braïda on a single occasion by the lake at Orchardleigh.

I returned to France after Waterloo. I must have been among the most unwilling repatriates ever recorded. No man could have accepted his freedom with greater repugnance. I returned immediately to my native Provence. I lived in a village within ten miles of Nimes. I have a few ideas as to its location. The background against which I lived was unsympathetic and dangerous. The Bourbons were back on the throne and Bonapartists were unpopular and even hated in parts of Provence. The Catholic mob, rejoicing in the restoration of legitimacy, resumed the persecution of Protestants in the neighbourhood of Nimes. Though in dreams I have tuned in directly to this barbarism I do not believe I myself was a victim. In the past I have ascribed the blinding depression which afflicted me when I first visited Nimes to these persecutions. This is partly true but there is also a more personal explanation for my dejection.

In those days I had to lie low and not speak openly of my beliefs and past record. That I had been a Bonapartist sailor did me no good with the authorities. I was never much disturbed by the fact that I was born a Protestant. I felt deeply for my persecuted compatriots and particularly for those who had served in the Navy but I had separated myself for too long from the practice of the Reformed Church to feel myself personally involved.

There were two things to be said on the credit side. Firstly I was not short of money. I received a microscopic pension from the Navy. It was so small as to be equivalent to an insult. In this I was no worse off than the majority of others who had served the Empire and survived to endure the Bourbons. This injustice was offset by a yearly allowance from the Masonic authorities for the work I had done in disseminating their cause. What I received was enough to enable me to exist without working with the standard of living of a small professional man.

Secondly, I was well looked after. Clare and Betty were glad of employment. They had been conscripted as cabin boys at the age of fourteen. They had been more than ten years in captivity and had no particular hope of any better job. I was glad enough to take Pierre into my service. I had always told myself that I was right to keep silent when he was suffering in the tower at Portchester. In spite of this I had always had a conscience about him but I never cared to reveal this to anyone, above all when I was being ostracised for my attitude. Betty, as the ex-cabin boy Henri, chubby, kind, bovine but meltingly sensitive and with something of the woman in his composition, was also an acquisition.

Though technically I was on pension I was in no sense retired. I travelled the country addressing Masonic meetings. The aim of my lectures was threefold. I disseminated and explained the principles of our particular form of Masonry. Secondly, I went beyond my terms of reference and preached absolute Dualism. My temerity was to cost me dear. Thirdly, I flogged the theme of Republicanism and never failed to indict the evil of Bourbon rule. In those days there was no region of France which I did not visit. I know this is so because early this year* Braïda, Betty and Graham warned me that I should not visit France in 1974. They said that my Napoleonic incarnation was too near the surface and that if I returned to places I had visited in my last life I would be liable to illness. I argued desperately that surely this would not apply to Brittany. I was irked by my separation from France where to me the skies seem wider and the air more invigorating. They replied that I had visited Brittany along with the other regions of France and that this year at least I would be best at home.

My lectures meant less to me than my writing. This is because in the latter I was able to devote myself exclusively to Dualism. I wrote numerous pamphlets and also poetry. All these were

* 1974.

completely anonymous. I did not even use a pseudonym. I am amazed at my mole-like, secretive industry. I had come, or retreated, a long way from the young man with the surface gaiety who left, to his own dismay, one or two broken hearts in the neighbourhood of Shere.

Annette and Braïda insisted that the poetry I wrote was full of hidden Dualistic illusions. I cannot remember what I wrote. I know that my friend Simon* was also a poet in the Napoleonic incarnation. He was younger than I was and more intimately connected with a group of regional poets gathered around the great Mistral. Simon's name was Philippe. I cannot remember his surname except that it began with "R".

When Graham was repatriated he returned to Provence. He set up as a printer and was responsible for the issue of the majority of my manuscripts. I wish to heaven I could lay hands on one. While I cannot remember anything about my poetry I am sure that in my prose writings I was constantly preoccupied with the nature of time. If any charitable person discovers a pamphlet with no mention of the author, printed in the Midi on paper with a watermark with interlocking triangles looking at first sight like a letter M, I would be grateful if he would preserve it for me. I am not interested in the merit of what I wrote. It seems pretty clear that the world thought little of it. In my twentieth-century self I am sory for the dogged, studious individual who, in a dark silent room in a Provencal village, contributed his widow's mite in secret without acclaim. My compassion for my nine-teenth-century precursor is misguided. He believed passionately in what he was doing and passion, especially when it is without hope of reward, is one of the beautiful virtues.

Mine was necessarily a secretive existence until 1830. After the advent of Louis Philippe things became easier in that I could move more freely and speak more openly but by this time I was round about sixty and in other ways life was darker for me.

* See *We Are One Another.*

Chapter Twenty Seven

Nine members of the group, Braïda, Annette, Clare, Mr. Mills, Mrs. Butler, Betty, Kathleen, Graham and myself, have been together through five incarnations. Marion may also have done the full stint and is clearly evident in four. It is staggering that all ten of us came back as men and sailors in the Napoleonic incarnation. What is more astonishing is that not one of us married. Among the minor characters there is the same addiction to the sea—my wife and Jack were both sailors—and the same avoidance of matrimony. Jack married Penelope, the only woman in our Napoleonic circle. He had lived with her in the Cathar incarnation and found the relationship so satisfying that he repeated it in the twentieth century. There cannot be any better testimony to temperamental compatibility.

Though my experience as a doctor should lead us to beware of the more facile assumptions of psychiatry, the record of the group in the Napoleonic incarnation presupposes a marked degree of ascetism among its members. It is indeed curious that, in the Cathar epoch, when members of the group accepted the disadvantages of imprisonment in matter, they should nevertheless have produced more marriages among their number than the single example provided by the French sailors in an age and country where morals were not puritanical. If there was any ascetic streak in my contemporaries in Provence in the first half of the nineteenth century they were not worried by it. None of the group was homosexual. They were different from the self-analysing individuals I have encountered so often in my present incarnation, for whom life is a tortured attempt to achieve full self-expression, a state they are unable to define. My confrères in Provence were differently constituted. They accepted themselves as they were. Unfortunately I was less wise than they. I was close to nature but not close enough. In my late sixties I passed

272

for two or three years into a state of depression in which I was without hope.

In a conversation with Betty in 1973 I learnt that my illness was a result of a fanatical misreading of the meaning of Dualism. Before the onset of my depression I had come to regard life as a prolonged combat between the flesh and the spirit. I recognised that we develop by emancipation from the clutch of matter. I was not content to wait for the higher states which supervene after death but drifted into a state of silent turmoil in which, instead of accepting the good and evil in my own nature, I tried by aceticism and self-denial to eradicate my appetite for simple pleasures. I was in fact the embodiment of what its detractors say when they claim that Dualism was a pessimistic and arid religion. In those days, in my house in the village near Nimes, I endured the puritanical hell which can afflict equally the extremist Presbyterian and the ascetic and monkish Catholic. I could not accept simply and peacefully that I was born a *mélange* of good and evil, that I was a background of the two forces and a reproduction in miniature of the confrontation in the universe between the same two energies. Certainly I knew that I was a battleground but what I strove for was to win, in the few years remaining to me, what could only be achieved in several incarnations and in the more perceptive and educative pauses between our lives on this planet. Graham told me that at this time I was extremely self-neglectful. I went round in rags and looked like a tramp. I resisted all the attempts of Pierre to restore me to my former maritime neatness.

I was deeply shocked when it leapt to my mind that the man I had seen behind the sailor years ago in the mirror was myself as I had become in the same incarnation. I had always believed that the second man was me but it had never occurred to me that it was myself in the same lifetime. It was almost impossible to believe that the creature with the parched, pallid face, the imploring eyes, and the shrunken posture was all that was left of the good-natured but combative sailor with his easy gait and watchful eyes. Watchfulness was, I think, one of the factors contributory to my breakdown. As a secret agent I had looked too long at the menace from others and from the environment. At Haslemere and Shere I had played my rôle with a certain elegance.

The iron had not entered my soul. I think something hardened in me, in the long years of training in France after my first visit to England. I became more efficient and Marion and I certainly made a good job of the shore defences. I also became more self-contained and uncommunicative except on subjects like Dualism and Masonry which were the passions of my life. As I grew older in Provence I withdrew more into myself. The results were lamentable.

The emanation of my former misery struck me a hammer blow when I went back to Nimes for the first time in this life. It began when I walked on some country road a few miles from the city. I have said previously that I remember a quarry in which the persecuted took refuge and which may have opened me to the depression which struck me that day. This is all the more possible now that I know from Betty that, as well as the persecuted taking refuge in the quarry, I myself had held meetings there and spoken on Dualism, Masonry and against the Bourbons. But the chief cause of my blind depression in the 1930s was my memory of a similar but more prolonged affliction a century previously. Betty told me that the fact that my second daughter was conceived in Nimes was a reaction to my old misery but did not explain why this should be so. She said that, with time, I would understand. It was another lesson to be learnt more by revelation than by the gyrations of intellect.

It was painful to learn also from Betty that she had abandoned my service when I was about to plunge into the abyss of depression. Before I became too miserable to criticise I had become extremely meticulous and demanding. I was exhibiting those obsessional features which so often precede prolonged attacks of depression. Pierre, more rugged in nature and appearance, could endure my acid perfectionism. Betty crumpled under my criticism. Sometimes she was almost reduced to tears. She found suitable and more congenial employment with Mrs. Butler's Napoleonic antecedent. The latter, qualified as a doctor at Montpellier after his return from Portchester, practised at Nimes and gave Betty a job as a resident servant. The good doctor drove out to see me once a month. He sat with me for an hour and did his best to comfort and reassure me. He showed towards me the same devotion,

274

intuition and skill he had employed in the prison hospital at Portchester. I remember that he never prescribed any medicines. On his visits to me he was often accompanied by Betty. The latter retained her respect for me and her gratitude that I had given her a job. She could not bear to contemplate the distortion of my personality by my illness. It is clear that love, in the broadest and most finite sense of the word, endures through several incarnations. In our life as Cathars we were brother and sister, she was devoted to me and I had a great influence over her. It would be pleasant to think that our love for each other remained at the same high level but there is no evidence that in Provence she felt more liking for me than was customary in a conscientious servant towards his or her master.

This depression which hit me in my late sixties in Provence was an acceleration of traits which had been developing for years in my character. I was already drifting into melancholia when a precipitating factor greatly intensified my depression. I addressed a meeting in a hall somewhere in the vicinity of Nimes. The régime had become more liberal since the accession of Louis Philippe. We were no longer reduced to secret meeting places. Things did not go well for me on this particular occasion which was recalled by Clare in an episode in which she lost ordinary consciousness, fell on the floor and returned to the twentieth century on her hands and knees.

At this particular meeting I had preached, with the determination and clarity I always exhibited on these occasions, the third principle of absolute Dualism, that the world was created by the Devil. My persistence in this matter had resulted in my expulsion from Lindisfarne in the seventh century. In the thirteenth it was part of the bread and butter of my Cathar beliefs. I returned to the attack in the nineteenth century. On this occasion the audience could not accept it. By this time repression was less, people had become more prosperous and the idea of a world created by the Devil was unacceptable to them. There was an ugly scene in which, while no physical violence was offered, I was shouted down and a great deal of abuse was hurled at my head. The faithful Pierre managed to extract me from my critics. He himself had come to believe with me that the world was created by the Devil, but even had he not done so he

275

would have protected me because of his natural rugged devotion.

I was in poor health at the time and this incident intensified my repression. For many months afterwards I was ostracised by my old associates. This upset me still further and contributed liberally to my deterioration. It is odd how, in more than one incarnation, I have suffered because of my refusal to compromise on this matter. Today I hold more firmly than ever to the truth that the world was created by the Devil. Some of my friends are upset by my conviction. I am equally disturbed that people with so much heart and head could ever be able to think otherwise.

I have to admit that in my present life I used to wonder whether, as I grew older, I would sink into an intractable melancholia. I had been subject to two- or three-day bouts of depression which I was able to hide from the world and which, on many occasions, were attributable to the echo of old sorrows from past lives. I have no doubt that when I feared I might drift into melancholia I was perceiving the reverberations of the lightless years of my life in Provence.

Ultimately I emerged from my depression. Towards the end of my life I had a few peaceable years. During my last lap I was more addicted than ever to poetry but I wrote and printed less of my own. I do not suppose that I will ever be able to verify Annette's statement and Marion's implication that what I wrote was full of Dualist allusions. I know that I had contact with Mistral and his group. I find it hard to believe that I was an important member. It does not matter now. I am satisfied that I lived against an antique and classical background and that I picked up from it a poetical concept of living which was an experience of reality. Wherever I live or die, in no matter what green country, my heart turns always to dusty squares and houses blind with shutters, to silent afternoons in the shadow of plane trees. In my more perceptive moods I lean always to the Languedoc or Provence. The life I lived in the former was, with all its horror, the peak of my development. The memory of my days in Provence is nearer and more conscious. My home is where my heart is.

I lived to be a good age for those days. I died somewhere in my late seventies. I never regained my appetite for life but my last years were supportable. Oddly enough I did not read much. When I ceased to put pen to paper I was at a loss for employment. I was always better when the sun was shining. I have memories of the village street, quiet, white with the dust and broadening to a square. In the corner of the square is a clump of plane trees. I am sitting on a bench a hundred yards or so away from my home. Pierre leaves me while he buys what is necessary for our simple needs. I had lived so quietly that my death made little impact in the village. Betty said there were not many people at the funeral but she herself came over from Nimes. I wonder how many people who saw me in the last years could see, behind the hollow-cheeked old man, the young idealist so happy at Shere and the tough, square-faced sailor who went his own way and kept his own counsel.

I have no doubt that if I went with Clare I would find where I was buried in the village near Nimes. It is possible that, even without her, in certain moods I would find the place. But since belonging is not a function either of the living body or of dead bones, I see no point in wandering to where I am said to be resting. That I am writing this in a garden in Somerset is proof that I have moved on. That at times Provence is more real to me than Somerset is merely a sign that the indestructible I varies in perception across the millennia.

I do not know much of what happened to Clare after my death. She had the house and enough to live on. She lived on alone, self-reliant, tough and cheerful to the end.

Of the other prisoners at Portchester Annette and Braïda, who were brothers in that incarnation, returned also to Provence. Braïda was repatriated before her younger brother. They settled down on their parents' farm in the modern department of the Drome. I cannot give the name of the farm or the adjacent village but I could locate its site within a couple of hundred yards. It is on a road which swings off from the route leading to Col de la Pertie. My wife and I picnicked in the vicinity two years ago. It is part of my destiny to follow the tracks I have used in previous incarnations. Annette and Braïda worked hard at the lavender farm they had inherited from their parents. They distilled scent and oil of lavender from their own harvest. They sold their products in all the markets in the vicinity and in shops in Vaison la

Romaine and Valreas. They had both learned to read and write at Portchester. Though neither was of academic disposition they were able to keep their account books accurately, legibly and even with a show of elegance. They worked seven days a week and never took a holiday. They had a few hours' leisure on Sunday afternoons and evenings. These they devoted to reading a weekly local newspaper of mildly liberal tendencies. They regarded it as literally inspired. In their inarticulate and unpretentious way they were very happy. It didn't trouble them that there were wider horizons than their own. After so many years of captivity they regarded themselves as fortunate to inherit their parents' farm. They were better equipped for life than the majority of those I have met in the twentieth century.

Jack, who appeared in *We Are One Another* and who was revealed as Brasillac in the Cathar incarnation, played a minor rôle in our last appearance. In my former book I tell how he hated the sea and even loathed to walk by the shore. He was sure that he had suffered some horrible fate at sea. Braïda and Betty told me that he rose from the ranks in the Revolutionary Navy. He never really liked the sea but knew he could not do as well in any other calling. Unlike the rest of the group he returned to the Navy after his repatriation. He later became a privateer. My wife was engaged by him as a first or second mate. They had been together as prisoners at Portchester, my wife having previously been a petty officer. She was not a Provençal but came from somewhere in the centre of France. In this life her preference has always been for green country, for the Loire rather than the harsh hills of the Corbières, for the Dordogne rather than the incandescent Provençal uplands. Their ship went down in a tempest off Hyères. In this life Jack was left with a horror of the sea. My wife's love of it remains unimpaired but she prefers swimming in it to sailing on it and was for many years a bad sailor. Was she able to swim when she went down at Hyères? Her bequest from this disaster is a total inability to look at any kind of picture of a ship sinking. This gets worse rather than better as she gets older. Those who know her would find it incredible that she turns her head away or closes her eyes if, on television, she sees a ship in distress or in the process of sinking.

Jane Butler, the doctor at Nimes, played a bigger rôle in
278

society after the access of Louis Philippe. In the nineteenth-century incarnation she was never a Dualist. The doctor, who started life in the Revolutionary Navy, lived to see the introduction of the top hat which he himself wore frequently. Medicine remained his abiding passion and his attention to his patients never flagged.

It is interesting that in our French maritime incarnation none of us remembered our previous lives. Clare and Betty, as Pierre and Henri, believed in reincarnation and that they had met previously and would meet again. Those among us who had Dualist beliefs, like Marion, Graham, Mr. Mills and myself, naturally believed in reincarnation, but none of us remembered any details of past lives. On the other hand, as the revenants have emphasised more than once, all who lived in the Cathar incarnation remembered their Celtic and Roman lives. It seems that, in terms of our ultimate destiny, our incarnation as French sailors was less important than that which preceded it. It is clear also that our present existence ranks higher, though it does not feel like it, in the pattern of evolution. We are, after all, looking back in considerable detail to four previous incarnations. Though the Napoleonic episode counts for less according to certain scales of values it is dear enough to me. Certainly it was a disturbed period but all the incarnations we remember have been in their different degrees tragic and through all we have been the quarry rather than the pack. I think my heart is moved by the memory of it because I was surrounded by better people. They were harder, more uncompromising but more honest and intelligent. They had not been debilitated by an outbreak of universities. Those for whom life was harshest were more able to externalise themselves than the contemporary majority. That human nature never changes is a mere cliché. It is amusing that the people who utter it with most confidence know only one life.

In spite of my love for Betty I recognise Braïda as the dominant figure among the discarnates. Now I understand why, when I heard them for the first time, so many members of this group spoke with the same voice. In October 1974 it occurred to me that a single entity had spoken through them all and that this could only be Braïda. The latter explained that this was so and that her motive in so doing was to enable me to identify

279

them as members of the group. This had never occurred to me when I was first confronted with this phenomenon. The voice factor had been emphasised for me because while Clare had known Braïda in this life as Jocelyn I had never met her in her twentieth-century incarnation. As time went on I was able to recognise the separate voices of different members of this group but there can be no doubt about their remarkable identity at the beginning of the experience. My wife shared my confusion as to who was who.

BOOK THREE

The Amethyst

Chapter Twenty Eight

Until the late summer of 1973 I had depended on Clare, Annette and Kathleen for my contacts with the dead. This is the story of how I met them directly and of how, in so doing, I recalled another incarnation.

It was strange that when I was steered towards direct communication with the revenants I felt I was approaching a single entity rather than a group of witnesses. It began quite simply. For years I had abandoned prayer. Man created God at a distance. We cannot hear Him across the gulf of our own creation. But when I was weary and had need of comfort I asked help of some entity I felt to be near me. Though it worked far better than prayer I did not accept it as a real experience. I preferred to regard it as self-delusion.

The invisible companion to whom I addressed myself was a woman. Those who read into this confession a Freudian significance are being more mechanised than usual. I myself, with equal error, thought in more Jungian terms. I regarded myself as venerating the Mother Goddess or addressing myself to the Eternal Feminine.

I had no clue as to the identity of this female spirit. At the same time my sense of her presence was accompanied by an inexplicable compulsive thought. For two or three years, in the dark months, especially in the grey metallic mornings of January, my mind had been invaded by the idea that the greatest loves of our lives exist out of this world either in the long past or the unrealised future. This was not an ivy-entangled sentiment left over from the Gothic revival. I felt, with an intense and stinging reality, that, even in this life, we feel loves which are old reflections in a mirror or opening windows. Some dearest to us lie beneath stones sprinkled with thyme where the lizards flicker on deserted hilltops in Italy. Others are as yet unborn in some raw town with festering suburbs in Latin America. I was not thinking of love in any transcendental sense but as we know it here. I had no one living or dead in mind, that is to say that no name was written in the upper levels of consciousness.

Ten years ago, when I lay down to sleep or awoke from it, I saw waves of dark green and purple. At first they moved slowly under my eyelids but afterwards there was a silent tempest and a tumult of dark colours moving towards me and breaking on the shores of consciousness. They were always purple and green. The colours were dark and glowing and it was as though they were reflected upwards from deep water.

When I saw these colours it was a sign that my psyche was especially active. At such times I shared my thoughts and pains with others and had many precognitive experiences. There were also days of relentless hunger when someone distant from me but on the same wavelength was sick or in agony and had not informed me. My incoming night tide of dark colours was to me a sign of life in another dimension.

In the early nineteen-sixties I also saw symbols. One remains printed indelibly on my memory. This was a St. Andrew's imposed on a St. George's cross. At the point of intersection of the cross was a pinhead of light which expanded to a circle. It glowed with the pulsating radiance of a planet. I saw later in my vision that there were several circles inside each other. The edge of each circle was not an unbroken curve but evenly indented. I was looking at the petals of a rose. When I looked at it intently, concentrating on its details and wishing it to stay, it receded behind a smudged curtain which was all that remained of the millrace of purple and green which so often preceded the appearance of the rose. Normally when I concentrated on such visionary symbols they disappeared quickly. This rose was different. As I watched it it diminished to a pinpoint and expanded again in the form of a rose. It never lost its indescribable radiance. As I watched its pulsation I thought of the beating of an illumined heart.

I accepted this symbol as arising in the past but as something shared with others, as part of the collective unconscious. It was the common heritage of a certain kind of man. I dwelt often, and erroneously, on its significance. I was looking back beyond my own life to the youth of the world, to the dawn of perception

284

and to the blurred inscriptions on the first parchments of history. What I had seen I shared with those whose eyes were turned to the more shadowy corners of consciousness. None of my experiences was unique, individualised or with a direct message for me. Such thoughts never crossed my mind.

In those days I never associated the green and the purple and the glowing cross with the presence of revenants. I first became aware of the latter by other sensations. I smelt different perfumes associated with individual presences. But in the late summer of 1973 there were times when there was an unaccountable and indescribable glow in the atmosphere. It was as though a light had been drawn across the room and the air vibrated with its passage. The atmosphere was charged with an invisible current and seemed to be throbbing slightly. On these occasions the green and purple waves were intensified. The colours were alive and vibrating. I understood later that they resemble those seen by the dead on waking in the first zone of higher awareness. Then the green faded from the picture. In the course of weeks the purple changed to an amethyst glow. Then the latter was concentrated in the form of jewels. Because of the smallness of the facets and the intricate angles at which they were set the light within the jewels was alive and swirling. It seemed to flow in innumerable bright rivers. The air around the jewels was equally living. It was as if a transilluminated liquid poured from the interior of the jewels and glowed and palpitated in the air around them.

Then one night there was only one jewel suspended, it seemed, from the sky and drifting forwards and backwards. This dark amethyst was glowing, alive and unattainably beautiful. The air of the room was suffused with the light transmitted by it.

I did not know that I was seeing my first sight of something which had for me an intense personal significance. It must be understood that I still thought of these things as symbols. The jewel could represent an abstract quality like truth or alternatively a degree of enlightenment or a phase in evolution. It was part of a language of symbolism addressed, if not to all men, at least to many. I did not know that this jewel floating below the ceiling like a planet descended from the sky had a special message for me. Certainly I learnt from Clare the day following that

285

Braïda had been with me the previous evening. It was inevitable that for some time afterwards I associated the appearance of the jewel with the coming of Braïda. This was an attempt on my part to personalise the experience. My assumption was false. From the very beginning Braïda told Clare that this jewel represented the pursuit of truth. She did not say that there were other messages to come and that the final message was for me alone.

The revenants were coming nearer. Clare and Annette said that soon I would see Braïda. I did not believe it. In my scepticism I was half right and half wrong. I did not know there were different kinds of seeing. For me there was no air of expectancy yet, morning after morning, I awoke depressed. I learnt later that this was because the spirits were hovering over me and my contact with them was thwarted.

One evening I was tired and resting on the couch. Clare laid her hands on my forehead. She was inducing relaxation by the Cathar method taught her by Braïda. Her spaniel lay inert at the foot of the couch. He started up suddenly and stared at the door. It was standing half-open and I felt afraid. In my solar plexus there was a sensation of tension, mobility and heat. I saw no one coming through the door.

The air in the room felt tighter and stretched like a taut string. The dog turned his head away from the door and couch. The vibration in the air increased. It resembled the twanging, heard at a distance, of telephone wires on a night of sharp frost. It was as though the tension in the air was localised and that it was drawing towards me. I followed the direction of the dog's gaze as it turned to where my left arm rested on the edge of the couch. Though I saw nothing my other senses were alive. I felt a sudden, throbbing pulsation in my left hand and arm. Then the word "Queille" flashed through my mind and with it the vision of a stream, dark under the trees, the walls of a sixteenth-century château and the face of a farmer who had left his work and was coming towards me. He had said, "There is nothing left of the old château but nobody will mind if you go on further." That was four years ago. I had thought it strange that he knew what I was looking for. Braïda had lived here and her husband died here in 1235.

With the thought of Queille the throbbing in my hand and

arm intensified. I felt a light pressure on my thumb. I turned to Clare. "I feel something to my left. Is this Braïda?"

"She is holding your thumb."

It is part of the Cathar laying on of hands to hold another person's thumb. "I don't see her," I said.

"You're trying too hard. Don't think about her."

I could not help thinking about her because my hopes had been raised by Annette's phone call from Canada. It irritated me that she had rung beforehand because it increased my desire to see Braïda. In these matters I had always found my own will an impediment.

I cannot say that I immediately felt peaceful with the coming of Braïda. It was as if the outlines of the world had been sharpened with the promise of peace and that my heart and mind were on tiptoe. Quite suddenly I felt intensely happy. The spaniel on the floor sat up and raised his head. He moved it slowly to one side. Clare said, "She always bends down and strokes him when she goes."

Now, for me, there was a sudden lurching descent into peace. The objects round the room were less real. They had lost individuality. The fire inside them had gone out. The room had its ordinary proportions and its everyday content. "She has gone," I said.

"Do you feel peaceful?" Clare asked.

"I feel peaceful and that things are ordinary again. I am back in the world and the world is half-real."

One evening I was suffering from sensory migraine which involved an insupportable light tingling at the tip of my nose, a fine, creeping irritation as though ants were walking under my skin, the feeling that one side of my face was enmeshed in a highly irritating cobweb and the perception of spots and whirling commas in front of my eyes. (I had thought for some time that migraine could be precipitated by the proximity of discarnate entities.) Clare put one hand on my forehead and the other on the nape of my neck. The tormenting cobwebs were brushed from my face. The insect torture was abandoned. All this was accomplished in minutes by the effect of her hands on my head. But why the deep, comforting heat between the left knee and the ankle? Why also the feelings in the solar plexus? It was as if the

287

skin and muscles in the latter area were drawn up by hot magnetic needles. I wondered if this sensation resembled that felt by
people when being cupped in the old days. There was also the
feeling of heat penetrating deeply. It seemed to follow the lines
of deep incisions. I turned to Clare. "Someone else is touching me
just inside the left knee."

"Anywhere else?"

"My solar plexus. I suppose it's Graham." I recognised him by
the heavy pressure of his hand which I have described previously.

"Yes," she said.

While I had felt the first signs of his presence in the intolerable
itching and the stutter of ants in and under my skin she had seen
him with the same visual clarity as she saw me.

A few days later I learnt a further important lesson. I was sitting alone with Clare when I became aware that someone else
was present. I knew this by the usual raised tension in the atmosphere and the feeling of horizontal sheets of air oscillating
abruptly between the floor and the ceiling. Clare insisted on putting her hands on my head. This was the first time I realised consciously the crucial importance of touch in my evolution. In the
past, when she had given me treatment, it was for some specific
reason, a troublesome cough, a patch of fibrositis or a bout of
exhaustion. On this particular day I had an acute pain at the
base of the right thumb and in the right elbow due to the fact
that I had recently done an excessive amount of writing.

Clare's hands were on my neck and forehead. The pain in my
thumb intensified acutely. It was followed by a deep, boring
warmth and a feeling of pressure in the affected area. An invisible hand folded and held in its palm the swollen eminence at the
base of my thumb. I knew it was Graham because his touch was
heavier than Braïda's. He placed his other hand on my solar
plexus. Once again I had the feeling of the tissues being drawn
up as by the sharp hot rim of a cup.

Then Braïda came. I did not see her outline. I knew she was
there and I felt her touch my unaffected thumb. Almost immediately it was warm and tingling. Braïda had come to reinforce
the efforts of Graham. It was the first time I had been treated by
two revenants. In touching my head Clare had acted as their
288

intermediary. I learnt later that they had treated me because they did not wish the function of my writing hand to be impaired.

Clare asked me if there was any question I wanted to ask Braïda. This was more than I had bargained for. In my heart of hearts I doubt really whether I had desired such intimate contact with the revenants. To see them, yes, because, to me, there is something irresistibly compelling about visual evidence. Also the most intense pleasures of my life have been derived from what I have seen. I think I have always evaluated my visual faculties at the expense of the others. That is why I have been denied so long and so often the sight of many people on the same wavelength and why I had to be content with the sound of their voices heard often across continents. I felt self-conscious about talking to Braïda.

"Try putting the question silently," Clare said.

I was too uncertain and diffident to speak of what was nearest to my heart, the health of my wife. Also I did not wish to talk about the future. I had no desire to treat Braïda like a woman on a fair-ground. I had a sudden impulse to speak about Rome. Had I had an incarnation there? I longed to know why, though the Vatican and its surroundings meant nothing to me but elephantine majesty and airless oppression, I came alive and felt happy and peaceful on the Palatine Hill and in the Forum. In our first conversation I could not talk of these things to Braïda. I saw myself as a tremulous acolyte approaching the mother of mystery. I did not fancy myself in this rôle. There is a part of me which is always prepared to laugh at what is sacred. I approach the threshold of a mystery and find it necessary to make a joke. Braïda told me later that this trait derives from the fear of my own intuitive capacity and will never be eradicated from me.

So when I put my silent question to Braïda I spoke of a commonplace, immediate problem. I was bogged down in something I was writing. She said that what I wrote should be a direct testimony of my own experience, and that I should not contaminate phenomena with theory. Certainly there was interpretation to be done but this should be minimal. It is characteristic that the first advice I received from her was concerned with a technical point. Over the years she had spoken to Clare it was clear that, divested of her body, she retained her pragmatic nature and sober realism. She was always concerned with the hard outlines of truth, with how things worked and with the gnawing minutiae of everyday living.

On this first occasion when I spoke with Braïda I did not hear her voice in the same way as Clare, who heard her as clearly as the voices of the living. At this opening session our speech was certainly not wordless but the words were inaudible. What happened was that a stream of thoughts was in some way injected into my mind. Then there was an immeasurable pause and a second stream followed it. The contents of the second stream provided the answer. This mechanism was used during my earliest sessions with Braïda and the other revenants.

I have no doubt that on these occasions I heard correctly. I checked what they said with Clare, and often Annette from Canada could give the substance of our conversations. For two years they had given me a mass of minute and verifiable information which was invariably accurate. I did not see why they should fail me now. In any case this inaudible conversation was merely a preliminary. The day came, quite suddenly and without warning, when I could hear the voices of Braïda and others as clearly as I could my wife's. Their voices sounded ordinary, human and unrefined by their higher habitat. Braïda spoke to me in English. She told me frankly that I would never be able to achieve Clare's capacity to understand Occitan. When I heard the revenants speak I understood better than ever why I, and my wife, had considered that Kathleen, Annette, Mrs. Butler and others had such similar voices. It is one thing to relearn, as I knew already, that this was because Braïda was speaking through them. It was much more telling to have the indisputable proof of hearing her voice myself. It should be noted that Dr. Charles' transatlantic tones were clearer and louder than when he rang me from Canada.

I recognised the departure of the revenants by a lowering in the strange, indefinable pressure in the atmosphere. When I have previously used the word tension I have not done so to indicate anxiety. There was some fear at first but that died quickly. It was more a question of a soul on tiptoe before the unknown.

At this time I persisted that my gifts were exaggerated and

that Clare and others on the same wavelength had subtler perceptions than I had. These assessments were sincerely meant and I had an ingrained conviction that I was inadequate for the experience. It may be that the depths of my mind were turgid and I had to wait for the detritus to settle. What I thought my honest assessment of myself was blown away by the tempestuous confidence of Annette in Canada. "You talk such nonsense about blunt perceptions. Would you have been given these experiences if you couldn't register them?"

"I tell you I see nothing."

"That's what you say."

I still could not understand the intensive intervention of Graham. I could not regard him as as important among the revenants as Braïda, Bertrand Marty and Raymond Agulher. I could not see why he was especially qualified to play a leading rôle in the task of facilitating my contact with the dead. I overlooked the fact that for each member of the group one particular incarnation is of special importance. There was one more incarnation to come.

Chapter Twenty Nine

I always noticed that Graham charged the atmosphere more than others. It was a question of dosage, of something equivalent to electricity. I was to learn that the male revenants had this capacity more than the women. Certainly I was more at ease with the women. Braïda knew that I was made like this and arranged things accordingly. But I do not think this greater fluidity and reduced tension in the air when the female revenants were present was due to my subjective reaction. The wavelengths of the female emanations were of lesser amplitude and more subtle. They had on me a relaxing and invigorating effect. In the case of the male revenants you could put the adjectives in the reverse order.

My introduction to the next world was intensifying. One day with Clare's hands on my head I was aware of deep heat and light pressure on my shoulders. I was puzzled because the position of the invisible hands did not correspond to any technique in the Cathar system of healing. "Is this Braïda?" I said.

"It is."

"Is she giving me treatment?"

"No. She's just standing with her hands on your shoulders. She wants you to know that she is here."

Clare encouraged me to ask questions. Once again all I could utter were a few supplicating fragments about the difficulty in writing. I do not find it difficult to adapt to the living. Though at times I long for solitude I can easily meet a diversity of men on equal terms and adapt to what others require of me. I found it difficult to converse with those from the next world. I was unimpressed by what I had heard of such experiences. There were those who spoke with incandescent prophets, with beautiful but always penetrating eyes, who intoned from hilltops in old English set to music. There were others who discussed the details of the domestic life in the beyond with such gluttonous interest that it seemed very like this world on a wet Sunday but with even greater welfare facilities.

The revenants realised better than I did that I was getting little from the interview. Clare asked me, "Has someone else come?"

I picked up the second presence with whatever tangle of perceptive antennae I was employing at that moment. "Yes," I said. "Your father is beside me."

"Where?"

"To the right and in front."

I had taken a step forward by seeing Clare's father. So far I had recognised the discarnates by their touch. I had only known their position after they had touched me. This time, without such contact, I had picked up accurately the identity and position of Mr. Mills. For the first time I understood clearly that there is a form of perception not based on sensation. I was still feeling without seeing in the ordinary visual sense of the word but from that day onwards I always knew the identity and position of the revenants even when there were as many as four present.

"Why don't you empty your mind?" Clare said. "If you just let go you might see something."

What I saw was the wood in the silence of autumn and the clearing at its centre. There was a ring of stones outside the clearing in the shadow of the trees. Below the wood the meadow shelved down past the church of St. Bega to the silver and silence of the windless lake. Then I saw a group of people in dark-purple robes. Suddenly they were engulfed by a shouting mob. The men and women in purple ran northwards towards the mountains. I knew I was looking back at myself and that I was one of the fugitives.

I could not understand why I had at this stage looked back so clearly to the Celtic incarnation, but, because I had done so, I felt more confident and said to Braïda how much I regretted that I had not seen her. She answered quickly, "You will see one of us very soon."

"That means you," I said, with all the confidence of error.

The day following I was sitting with Clare in my writing room. I was aware that its limited space was crowded with entities. I was still in the state when I felt the atmosphere to be charged and the air to be vibrating. I had a feeling of heat in the solar plexus. It resembled the stabbing of fine needles and penetrated deeply. The pricking feeling in my right thumb was followed by a mounting sensation of heat.

"Is this Graham?" I said.

"Yes. Who else is here?"

"Braïda is kneeling on my left. Graham is to the right and in front. Someone else is behind my left shoulder. My God, it's Betty."

It was years since I had known such peace. Braïda had always been calming but the atmosphere brought by Betty was unmistakable. There was an invisible glow and an impalpable warmth in the atmosphere. I was ridiculously happy and utterly relaxed. I had no feeling of being with someone from the next world. I was as happy in her company as I would have been with a charming, beautiful and unexpected visitor outlined in twilight with the day's work done. That was what she was, seen through the frustrating elegance of metaphor. I had never met her in this life. The only picture I ever saw of her showed a scraggy, overgrown child recuperating from a chest condition by an ocean of mud and tarnished sea. She had a large, generous mouth and mild eyes and that is all I remember of her portrait.

"Is she happy to be here?" I said excitably to Clare. It never occurred to me to address Betty directly.

"She is very happy."

I do not know how long we sat in silence looking through the window. It was one of the lost measures of eternity. I was not in a mood for talking. I had no wish to ask questions except to know that Betty and Braïda were happy. In this my thoughts were natural and human. There was nothing elevated about them. More than anything else I wanted Betty to be happy. I had a feeling of guilt about Braïda. I owed her much, in a way, a world. I owed her many of my own ideas. Not all originated with her but certainly they were transmitted through her. I could not exclude from my mind the thought that, however much Braïda had done for me, in these moments at least Betty was my main consideration.

I remembered how Betty's mother had spoken of her daughter's devotion to me in the thirteenth century, of how Mrs. Smith, the central figure in *The Cathars and Reincarnation*, had recalled so clearly the grave, gentle woman who had consoled her after my death in the thirteenth century. I could not believe that the love I felt for Betty at that moment was merely a re-echo of our familial affection seven centuries before. Was my present feeling for her due to the reinforcing alchemy of nostalgia? I had failed to meet her in this world, I was prepared to love her in the next. The cynic could say with reason that this was a safe and comfortable prescription for love. But I could not exclude from my mind that there was some stronger, deeper connection between us. Years ago a friend of mine interested in reincarnation had asked why the events in *The Cathars and Reincarnation* could not be explained by the fact that a voice was addressing me from the past through the more sensitive ears of Mrs. Smith. My friend insisted that there was a kind of love which had the power to leap the gulf of centuries. I had listened with respect. From time to time it seemed to me that the voice which had spoken through Mrs. Smith was that of Hélis de Mazerolles.

Other thoughts filtered through from some reservoir deeper than consciousness. I thought of how, in the April of that year, Clare had seen Betty behind my shoulder at Bassenthwaite. Then my mind was emptied of all thoughts by the peace of her presence. I was to find later that Betty was more than all others a solvent for tension.

When my thoughts furled their wings and returned to the cage of my narrow room I found that Braïda, Betty and Graham had left us. My arms and hands lay relaxed upon the arm-rests. The palms of my hands were touching the chair. The backs of my hands faced upwards. My eyes wandered round the room as I familiarised myself with what had been living and intense while the revenants were here and were now domestic objects. Then I looked down at my left arm posed easily at the side of the chair. I noticed a red curved mark on the back of my hand. When I looked more closely I saw an unmistakable groove extending in an arc five inches long. The groove was a quarter of an inch wide and half as deep. There could be no doubt whatever that it was an effect of pressure. The redness could not have been caused by inflammation or allergy because of the perfect artificial curve and

295

the even groove which stretched across my hand. There was nothing in the room which could have exerted such a pressure.

"What has been pressing on my hand?" I said.

"The mark of Braïda's chain." She was speaking of the loop descending at the left hip from her girdle. On this evening the loop carrying the Maltese-type cross with the Tau crosses had fallen across my hand.

This was among the most astounding of the phenomena presented by Braïda and her colleagues. I knew it had been sent as a sign. I had few illusions about my own shortcomings. I had never hidden from Clare, I could not hide from Braïda, that I was one of those who must see the spear and the wound in the side. What I did not understand was what the red arc on my hand was intended to prove. I accepted completely the reality of the presences around me. I acknowledged my capacity to recognise their comings and goings and the positions they occupied in the room. I regretted that I could not see them but it was no tragedy to me. I was happy to record their activities. I said to Clare, "Is it because they know my desire for visual evidence?"

"That comes into it a little but not much now. It is more because you tend to evade issues. You underestimate your capacity to make contact with them. That is why Braïda left this sign."

The red, grooved curve was present in my hand when I went to bed six hours later. It was less red next morning but still indisputably present. It persisted during the train journey from Bath to Paddington and only died away during lunch-time in London.

It seemed to me significant that Betty had appeared to me for the first time on the same evening as Braïda had imprinted her message in my flesh. Was it that Braïda was drawing attention to the fact that Betty had a new and important rôle to play? I wondered if I was exaggerating Betty's celestial potentialities. I accepted that I had for her a positive and human affection. Was she the living, that is to say the living after death, exemplification of what I had thought recently, that we can love those we have not yet encountered or whom we have known in past lives and relinquished in varying degrees of forgetfulness? Yet in spite of the peace and inner glow I felt when I thought of Betty I accepted that Braïda was my supreme director. She had been first

296

on the stage and, in view of the sign she had written in my flesh, it seemed foolish to think that anyone could supplant her as my mentor. This was all the more so because at this time I had all sorts of direct and practical advice from Braïda. She told me how and what I should write. At this stage she had even taken charge of my handwriting. I was writing at great speed. Graham told Clare that this for me was the only sound method. How otherwise could I keep up with the current of dictated thoughts? This was reasonable enough. What was unmistakable was the effect on my handwriting. It dwindled to microscopic proportions. It was sometimes completely illegible to me. It is not necessarily quicker to write small and whatever is gained by the diminution in size is lost by the time taken to read it and the damage it inflicted on my eyesight. I mentioned this one day to Clare. She asked to see the latest version of my handwriting. "But it's absolutely identical with Jocelyn's. One literally needed a magnifying glass to read it." All in all I could not think that Betty could replace Braïda as my chief mentor.

A few days after the groove experience Betty visited Clare and told her that these days she was often with me. She said that I would see her soon. Two days later I went to see Clare. At first I was unaware that there were other visitors. There was no dramatic change in the atmosphere, and tensed-up feeling of the air being charged. There was a slow, drifting movement of air, an echo of a wind which had already fallen. I had a few silver-grey spots and whirling commas in front of my eyes but only when I looked intently at the ceiling. I said to Clare, "Is anyone there?" I asked without confidence because the visual signs were diminished and because of the vast, unaccustomed quietness in the atmosphere. I hesitated to accept the peace which was enveloping.

"Yes."

"It is Betty, isn't it?"

"Yes."

"I can't see her but she is standing to the left and behind me."

"She has just moved in front of you. Surely you can see her?"

"No."

"But she is standing right in front of you. Can't you see what she looks like?"

I did not hesitate a moment. Once again my inner vision took over from my eyes. "Dark eyes and a thin face. Her forehead is broad. The hairline dips down at one point. She is rather sallow. She has a very gentle air about her. As I see her today she is much more as she was as a young than a middle-aged woman. She was spindly as a child and chubby as a woman." (In this life I had never seen her as either.) "Am I seeing her like this because I saw a snapshot taken of her when she was about ten? I only saw it for about a minute. No, I can't be. She is wearing a dark-blue robe and a silver girdle. I'm seeing her as a Cathar Parfaite. He features are quite like what they were in this life but she is thinner and shorter."

"That's what she looks like when she comes back to me," Clare said. "She always comes back as a Cathar."

"She doesn't have a medallion like Braïda." I was describing Betty accurately but without the visual act of seeing.

"You're right, she hasn't a medallion."

"That's because she never specialised in healing in the Cathar incarnation."

"Have you anything to say to her?" Clare said.

"Everything and nothing." It was as good an answer as any. I wished to preserve, in silence, the feeling of being especially close to her.

"She wants you to tell her what's troubling you."

I accepted now that, however illogical and immature it may seem, she meant to me more than the others. But all the time I felt there was an undispersed shadow behind her. I had felt this off and on for years. I knew she had appeared before the Inquisition in April 1243. There was no record of any sentence being passed on her. What I feared was that she had recanted and denied being a Cathar. It was only human nature that some should wilt under interrogation but there was a childish something in me which wished her to have resisted.

One of the statements she made to the Inquisitors is clumsily reported. It does not make clear whether I died of a certain illness in 1235 or whether in that year I was suffering from a disease which subsequently killed me. Now by this time I had learnt from many sources, discarnate and otherwise, that I had been alive until December the 25th, 1243. I said to Betty, "Was I alive in 1243?"

298

"Yes. I made my peace with the Inquisition because that year you were in prison in Carcassonne and I still hoped to get you out of it."

"Wasn't that rather a hopeless proposition?"

"Not entirely. Our brother Isarn Bernard was a confidant of the Count of Toulouse, who at this time was collaborating with the Catholic French. In any case, whatever I did it was because I loved you."

I failed to pick up the rest of the conversation. I was intensely relieved. I had never really judged her in terms of ethics. The possibility that she had truly ceased to believe in Catharism had been aesthetically disfiguring. I had never expected her to be without flaw through five incarnations. I may be misguided but I am not insane. But I had found it hard to believe that she had in her heart denied Dualism which was our *raison d'être* through all our incarnations.

What I wanted to know from her was not the details of her life in the thirteenth century but whether, in her twentieth-century existence, she had recognised me as her brother in the thirteenth century. I yearned to know what in this life she had felt towards me. I was ready to speak of what was nearest my heart and then, suddenly, there was a great ebbing of force from the atmosphere. I felt myself depleted. I was stranded on the shore with the tide gone out. Betty had gone, the room seemed unnaturally empty and my surroundings depressingly ordinary like a faded print.

Chapter Thirty

On a sunless and suffocating day in mid-August I had a series of visions induced by the presence and touch of the revenants. For some days I had been suffering from a recurrent cough. In 1972 Braïda had said with accuracy that when I was tired or depressed I would be subject to bronchitis. This stemmed from the fact that in my thirteenth-century incarnation I had died of pneumonia supervening on pulmonary tuberculosis. Once again the cough and expectoration had reappeared.

I was sitting in my room with Clare when Graham and Braïda materialised. Once again I felt their presence and knew where they were standing. Graham placed his hands on the apices of my lungs. The heat in his hands was intense. As a priest in the Celtic incarnation he had practised as a healer before the Church became Romanised. To me he always acted as a great battery of power, as a generator rather than a transmitter of healing. This accounted for the deep, penetrating sensation I experienced when he gave me treatment. The heat overflowed to the apices of my lungs across my shoulders and down my arms.

I felt Braïda move closer behind me. She put one hand on my forehead and one hand on my neck. With the two working together it was as though I had received a stimulating injection. I was then aware of a third visitor. This was Clare's father in the robes he had worn as Bertrand Marty in the thirteenth century. He was thinner and sharper-featured than he had been in this life. Without prompting from Clare I knew his features and out-lines and the point at which he had entered the room. I had no feeling of apprehension or that I was on the brink of a revelation. All I knew was that the air in the room was tingling and con-gested and that I had lost my diffidence in the presence of the discarnates.

Perhaps I was not troubled by their presence because my atten-tion was immediately diverted from them. I began to see outlines on the opposite wall. There were first circles enclosing equal-armed crosses. They were of Celtic design and primitive type. Then the wall changed colour. There was a translucent shimmer less bright than silver and also infused with dull gold.

Then I saw a St. Andrew's cross clearly imposed on a cross of St. George. I was excited by the intersecting crosses and asked Clare what they signified. She said that she could not see them and that what was presented to us was surely the cross at W——. I could not see it at all and assumed I was wrong because of Clare's greater experience in these matters. In spite of what she said I continued to see the two kinds of crosses. At their point of inter-section I saw again the glowing rose I had first seen ten years previously and which pulsated like the beating heart of a planet. It was quite unmistakable. In the early 1960s I had seen it on falling asleep or on walking. Now I saw it magnified on the wall opposite, amplified as though it had been projected on the screen for my benefit.

As well as intersecting crosses and the glowing rose there was a design of a simple lily, with a single leaf attached. This was the emblem which had meant so much to the French sailors who, as prisoners in the castle at Portchester, had practised a medieval form of masonry. I believed that the revenants were showing me the basic symbols of Dualism as they had persisted down the centuries. I did not need to be convinced of the truth of Dualism. It lurked in the marrow of my bones. The figures on the wall were simply to be translated as a sign of my development. I felt a little self-conscious about it.

Then I saw something which sharpened my perceptions and made me doubt my modest conclusion. The symbols on the walls disappeared and I saw instead a whole cluster of roses. They were arranged in a formal pattern and resembled an ingenious Edwardian wallpaper. What gripped my attention was that between the highly stylised petals of each rose there were long spines. I was seeing again what was painted on the wall at Port-chester and what had been the main subject of my doodlings since my schooldays. The average reasonable man with a modi-cum of culture and a smattering of psychiatry would regard it as of interest in relation to what Jung has said of archetypes and symbols. I knew immediately that for me the significance of this

301

pattern was much more personal but I did not realise its full, intimate and breathtaking intimacy.

Now, between me and the wall was a palpitating haze of blue. The colour was quite unmistakable in this north room with its air of perpetual twilight. The blue was the colour called French navy but there was a shimmer of amethyst at its edges. Then the waving mist of colour concentrated and darkened. It formed up in a kind of robe and for the moment I could see the outline of a short, broad figure with wide shoulders. There was later the outline of a big, round face. Then there was nothing but the blue haze with the shimmer of amethyst at its margins. "I saw a figure," I said to Clare. "I could not see his features but I saw his outline."

"Who was it?"

"Obviously a Cathar and a Parfait." This was no great feat of deduction. For three years the visions and dreams of those on the same wavelength had been filled with Cathars in dark-blue robes. "Stop," I added. "Was it Guilhabert de Castres? You've always spoken of his big, round face."

Then Braïda spoke. "It was Guilhabert. He came to tell you that what you saw on the wall was the mandala you completed in the thirteenth century. You see you were right when you said you saw a different pattern from Clare."

On the road from Foix, which leads through a frowning defile to Ax-les-Thermes, you can look towards the caves where the Cathars practised their initiation ceremonies and advanced studies. Among these latter was the completion of mandalas. This practice is of ancient eastern origin. What is not known is that they were used by the Cathars as personality tests to determine the particular vocation of those training as Parfaits. After her test Clare was trained to be a healer. Annette, who seems to have displayed in the thirteenth century the same open-heartedness and glittering inconsequentiality she has so often manifested in this, failed altogether to satisfy the examiners and abandoned the attempt to become a Parfaite.

The mandala constructed by me seven centuries ago and projected on the wall on a grey evening in the late summer of 1973 was for me of intense significance. I had seen it ten years previously on awaking from sleep. I accepted at that time that this

302

vision was in some way related to my psychic life. It was an immense step to know that what I saw on the wall opposite was what I had myself produced seven centuries before. Over years, in my casual doodlings, I had remembered, at the near conscious level, what I had achieved in the caves of the Ariège in the Middle Ages. I had to admit that my vision was broadening and deepening. In seeing my mandala I had discovered something for myself and had resisted Clare who had been responsible for so many of my previous experiences. While I had seen what was vital to me she, looking at the same wall, had seen what was equally important to her. As her thirteenth-century mandala she had drawn the symbols on the cross at W—— with which she had been familiar in her Celtic incarnation.

I was astonished that the first of the revenants whose outlines I should see should be Guilhabert de Castres. I knew already that I had been his favourite pupil in the thirteenth century but in the three-year period of intense revelation my contact with him had been minimal compared with my relations with Braïda. I realised that a good deal of the philosophical material she relayed did not originate with her. In the course of time I learnt to recognise the touch of Guilhabert de Castres. Nevertheless the main flood of material passed on to me by Clare had been unmistakably stamped with the imprint of Braïda's pragmatic nature. I had always assumed that my contacts with Braïda were warmer and more personal because she and I had been friends in the thirteenth century. It was in my brother Isarn Bernard's house in Limoux that she was nursed during a long illness (she told me later it was a gastric ulcer), following which she became a Parfaite. I realised that she was the kind of revenant who functions nearer to the margins of human consciousness. After her Cathar incarnation she had returned of her own choice to this earth and had incarnations in both the nineteenth and twentieth centuries. Guilhabert de Castres has never reincarnated after the thirteenth century. He is more immune to the magnetic pull of matter and to the fluctuating joys and sorrows of this world. I realised that, as I was regarded by the revenants as one of the twentieth-century instruments of Dualism, I had had to deal directly with the revenants most qualified to speak of its philosophical nature. Nevertheless it was a surprise and a thrill to talk to Guilhabert de Castres.

I did not realise that years ago I had already established contact with Guilhabert. Some time later Braïda recalled for me the days when I had a tingling of the left side of the tongue, with a persisting sweet taste and an overpowering odour of cedarwood. I have described already how these signs were preludes to periods of intense psychic activity and how I learnt later that they pointed more specifically to the perception of presences. First Annette rang from Canada to tell me that Braïda had an important message for me about the nature of touch. When Braïda materialised she told me that the sensations I had felt ten years ago were signs that Guilhabert was touching me. It was staggering to learn that what I had experienced and regarded as the symptoms of a kind of migraine had resulted from a rare, impalpable form of touch and that even in those days, far off in terms of my evolution, fingers not only of the past but of Guilhabert de Castres himself had drawn themselves lightly across my forehead.

I did not realise until later when I studied my journal what an important rôle touch played in my contact with the revenants. This applied to the present as well as past lives. When I first made contact with them in 1973 I never felt their presences or could converse with them unless Clare touched me. Later there were times when she withdrew her hands when they and I were talking together. Sometimes the flow of words was uninterrupted and I continued to look back on the receding plain of the past and sometimes walked the dark valleys of the future. Sometimes, with her hands withdrawn, the conversation flagged and I lost the drift of what the revenants were saying. On such occasions it was as though a soft, yielding but impermeable layer insulated me from my own thoughts. It was as though my psyche had been excluded from myself and that for the moment I was separated from it. I noticed that at such times, surreptitiously and gently, Clare resumed physical contact and held my wrist lightly with her fingers. In these moments it was as though a previously interrupted current had been switched on again. Immediately, easily, the words came back.

In this matter of touch the revenants acted with or as a substitute for Clare. Sometimes they touched me at the same time as she did. On other occasions they alone laid their hands upon me.

Without the contact of either worldly or astral fingers I was at first unable to look into the past and talk to those described as departed but separated from us only by an impalpable curtain. Braïda's statement that Guilhabert had touched me years ago was the first evidence I received of astral touch in the past.

The same day as that on which I learnt that Guilhabert had touched me ten years ago Annette rang me from Canada. Her intonation was warm and caressing and there was nothing self-consciously or emetically spiritual about it. This was the anniversary of the day on which she had the year previously lost her husband. She spoke, as she had done often, of how she and he had induced the timeless experience by merely touching each other.

She spoke of the alchemy of this something more than common touch and of how it was a mystery. Then, suddenly, she asked me if I remembered how, recently, Clare had rested her chin on my scalp when laying her hands on my forehead and neck. Braïda had told her that this habit was a repetition of what Clare had done regularly when she and I lived together in Cumberland 1300 years previously. The resumption of this physical contact between us had summoned up the presence of Graham.

Chapter Thirty One

With my physical eyes I was still not seeing the faces in detail. What I saw first was a royal-blue haze which intensified and acquired an amethyst aura. I thought a great deal about the significance of the latter. All the conjectures I made about it were erroneous.

One day I was sitting in my room with Clare. By the chest of drawers I saw the outlines of a figure in a dark-blue robe. I knew it was Braïda. Quite definitely I saw her, but not with my eyes. In saying this I am allowing for the fact that she had been described to me so often by Clare. I knew she was small, thin, white-haired, dark-eyed and with cheeks criss-crossed by a thousand wrinkles, and wearing a Juliet-type cap. But how was I able to add that her small triangular face was broader at the forehead than I had at first thought? Still more by what process was I able to say that her left lower eyelid was disfigured by a yellowish, pallid and bloodless scar? When I asked Braïda about it she told me that in the thirteenth century she had suffered from an ulcer on this eyelid. I had applied to it a concoction created from herbs I had gathered. The grey-yellow lifeless tissue was the result of the scarring of the ulcer. It strikes me now that the adjective lifeless is inappropriate when applied to Braïda.

In the last week of August I had another session in which both Braïda and Graham were present. I could not see the outlines of Graham. Again I recognised him by the solidity and power of his touch and by the heat generated from his hands laid at the top of my chest. My recognition of Braïda was visual. The outlines of her body were engulfed and overlapped by a haze of royal blue.* Then the colour changed to a rich dark purple that

* The blue of the Cathar robes was lighter than I had previously imagined. Clare had always described it as either a dark French navy or a dark royal blue. It seems clear that dark royal blue was lighter than I had imagined.

was almost black. I wondered where I had seen this colour before. It was not the same as the purple I had seen in the days when the darkness under my eyelids was illuminated by waves of purple and dark green. Then I recalled that it had been worn by the fugitives running from the wood and whom I had seen recently when visited by Mr. Mills.

Then I saw the outline of Braïda's shoulders. She was wearing what first seemed a shawl and which I realised later was a cape. It appeared that the lines of her head were altered because she was wearing a new kind of circular and corrugated head-dress rather like that worn by nurses in some hospitals. She raised her right hand and the cape fell sideways. She was carrying a St. Andrew's cross. It seemed she was changing incarnations.

Graham had retreated to a corner of the room in the shadow of the chest of drawers. First the corner was infused with royal blue. Then the glow intensified, darkened and took shape in the figure of a man in rich, dark purple. Braïda told me that in the Celtic Church in seventh-century Cumberland and in the south-west of Scotland the cross of St. Andrew had been especially venerated. The priest's robes were dark purple. The colour necessary for dyeing the cloth was obtained from bilberries. This evoked for me childhood memories of summer in the farm by Melbreak, the incessant chattering of the brook, its sharper accents diminished by the trees, and, under the sharp, clean-cut geometric leaves, the biggest bilberries I had ever seen. I recalled also the country going over to Ennerdale, so austere that I seemed to see it always in a winter twilight.

Looking through my window at the mild colours of Somerset I was almost haunted by the cold, unrelenting beauty of Ennerdale. I raised my eyes and saw on the wall opposite the cross at W——. Though it carried, in its brooding enigmatic outlines, the mystery of centuries, at that moment it represented for me seventh-century Cumberland. There was no doubt that we had moved into the Celtic incarnation.

Suddenly the enigmatic cross at W—— which recorded all our incarnations was wiped from the wall and I saw, through a dark, purple haze, a single Celtic cross followed and overlaid by a profusion of St. Andrew's crosses. Then the crosses faded and the purple haze and, in the corner, was a lightless brown shadow but

307

still the outlines of a man. Then the shadows were displaced by a brownish glow. "It's Graham," Clare said. "He is wearing a long, brownish jacket with strips of leather." He had moved out of the Celtic incarnation and we were seeing him as a sergeant-at-arms in the Cathar incarnation.

Then I saw the glowing rose at the intersection of the crosses, described as a symbol of the light having gone underground, and which beyond any doubt I myself drew in the caves of the Ariège seven centuries ago. Then the picture simplified and I saw the rose alone, with the thorns between its petals, which I had drawn for decades on the back of innumerable envelopes, which Graham had said was Mithraic and from ancient Rome. It was clear to me now that when, in the dream in April, he had told Clare of the Mithraic stone in the squat and inconspicuous church at Torpenhow, he was pointing directly to a Roman incarnation.

In one evening we had seen the revenants in the dress of two incarnations. We had received a broad hint of another to come. It seemed I was making progress. To some extent I could see the revenants. I saw their outlines, the colour of their clothes, some details of their dress and a glimpse of their features. I saw that in her Celtic incarnation Braïda's face was smaller and her features sharper than when she lived in the Languedoc. I still regretted that, though I could locate their positions and feel their presence with complete accuracy, I could only see the outlines of their bodies and a sketch of their features. I longed to see a face as clearly as a portrait on a wall. This to me was more important than any kind of inner vision. The attitude of the revenants was different.

Chapter Thirty Two

On a day in August I wandered through the Royal Crescent. I relaxed in the warm embrace of the curve of golden stone and looked across the green to the trees in the park. I went on to the Botanical Gardens. I stayed there a long while because, with its tangible, earthly beauty, the garden was an antidote to the violently living world of my small room with the vibrations of centuries directed at its heart by the burning glass of cosmic memory.

I went to see Clare. It started up again when she laid her hands on my forehead. Stretched high across the wall I saw what at first sight looked to be a child's scrawled copy of irregular ramparts. I regarded what I saw as what doctors call the fortification spectra of migraine. I had had no trace of this condition while in the park.

The pattern on the wall changed to block-like letters joined together by a curling scrawl. To me it unmistakably spelt out the word Camplong. I was at first surprised that to Clare it was merely a Celtic intertwining. Then I saw that, though in the past I had always submitted to her judgement except when I saw my own mandala, I was now beginning to see things in my own right and becoming psychically independent of her. The word Camplong was to me unforgettable. As I have described in *We Are One Another,* Betty had written it in the sketch-book she filled as a child of seven when convalescing from scarlet fever when she was looking back seven centuries to the massacre at Avignonet in 1242. Camplong is a small village in the Corbières. It has a dilapidated lost beauty in a region which is still arid, with bare hills scrawled over with traces of rosemary and myrtle. Mir de Camplong was an obscure *chevalier* remembered by Mrs. Smith and whom I described in *The Cathars and Reincarnation.*

Then Betty materialised. She came as an incoming tide of peace. I knew that she was standing directly before me. She said that the word Camplong had been a sign that she was coming. Before the word evaporated from the wall I saw it was stretched across my field of vision as it had been across the double page of her wide-open sketch-book. Betty told me that the scrawl spelled out Camplong for me with such clarity because she and I had loved each other so much in our thirteenth-century incarnation that she spoke to me in the language of that time. For Clare the pattern on the wall was a Celtic intertwining because she and Betty had been closer in their Celtic than their Cathar incarnation.

When I was with Betty I always felt a combination of peace and yearning. You could say that the two are incompatible but, if you do, you have never listened to a Chopin nocturne. "Why can't I see you?"

"You try too hard," she said.

"And this recurring pain?" I was referring to the recrudescence of my colonic symptoms.

"It comes because you still resist seeing."

I did not discuss the mechanics of my resistance. It did not interest me. Repression is neither a willed process nor intellectually definable. It is an aspect of cosmic weather. It is part of the climate of the heart.

One day I was sitting in the room with Clare when someone else entered. There was no solar plexus awareness and no throbbing in the atmosphere. Whoever had entered was anonymous even for a spectre. "Who is it?" I said.

"Look at her and tell me."

"I can't see."

"It's Betty," she said. "Can't you tell me what she looks like?"

"I tell you I can't see. Also I can't understand why I didn't recognise her."

"You can, just describe her."

I answered promptly, with confidence, as though I were giving a description of a painting of a landscape in order to impress a board of examiners. "Well of course the most striking thing is the hair and the eyes. You don't often see such fair hair and such dark eyes together. The hair is more than flaxen. Is there an expression spun gold? The eyes are almost black."

"That is exactly how she is. You see as well as I do."

"No, I do not *see* her at all. She is taller than she was in her Cathar incarnation and in this life. I am seeing her in her Celtic incarnation."

"Why do you say you can't see her?"

"Because I can't."

"Then how can you describe her?"

"I don't know."

"I don't believe you don't try to think it out."

"I do, as far as I can go. This is obviously another kind of perception. All I can say is that I don't understand it."

At this time I was thinking things out less than ever before. I still exercised my critical faculties. There was no need for anyone to exhort me to do so because of my natural cynicism. But at this time the gaps in my knowledge were being filled quickly and accurately by the revenants and by those with whom they were in contact in this world. I assumed that sooner or later I would learn why I was able to see Betty. In the meantime I was happy and completely satisfied that I had seen her without using my eyes.

In the early autumn of 1973 Betty began to insert herself more into the picture. Whenever she came there was a drop in the atmospheric pressure and the feeling that the wind had fallen. She remained invisible to me in the ordinary sense of the term, that is to say that I could not see her in the same way as I see trees through the window. I saw her by some mysterious process of inner perception. I was compensated for not seeing her in the ordinary sense of the word by a flood of colours. When she first appeared there was usually a dark-blue haze changing to dark purple as she moved from her Cathar to her Celtic incarnation. This was followed by a deep-toned shimmer of amethyst easily distinguished from the near-black of her Celtic robes. One day when the amethyst glow appeared she told me that once she had been called Camillia. She did not enlarge on this statement. She was leaving me to infer that she had had a Roman incarnation. I was now satisfied that the amethyst, either as a glow in the atmosphere or shaped like a jewel, was especially associated with Betty and not Braïda. Sometimes it heralded her coming and sometimes it acted as a substitute for her outline.

In the last few years I have had several sudden heavy falls not

311

preceded by giddiness or indeed by any symptoms whatever. I have long since ceased to regard them as accidents. At one time I had diagnosed them as instantaneous manifestations of Menière's syndrome, as abrupt excursions through time and space determined by psychic factors. I had now reluctantly come to accept that these were possibly manifestations of the force of evil. I had known that the latter could induce accidents in other people but had been slow to accept that this could apply in my own case. I was particularly prone to these unpleasant experiences in the last months of 1973. Both Guilhabert de Castres and Braïda confirmed that I was correct in my inference that the more my psyche evolved under their direction the more I was vulnerable to the force of evil.

In the autumn of that year I was due to give a lecture. The surroundings were beautiful. That year the autumn colours were more prodigal and varied than I had ever seen them. I fell heavily and without warning on an asphalt path on my way to the lecture hall. I hit the ground with a thud and the spectators were obviously disquieted. The thought which instantly transfixed my mind was ludicrous. "Braïda and Betty will need to do their best to get me fit for this lecture."

I had no signs of shock or injury. When I gave my lecture I seemed to sail away on a gale of energy transfused into my veins. When I lay down to rest in the afternoon I was engulfed in an intense glow of amethyst. This deepened in colour and became more compact in form until it assumed the outlines of the jewel within which a living light was poured through a thousand tiny rivers. The jewel had never before seemed so bright nor its light so living. Shortly afterwards Braïda appeared and said that she and Betty had been present at this lecture, had restored my strength and fed me with ideas. (I gave my talk almost extempore from minimal notes.) She said how important it was for me to continue to disseminate the truth verbally and in writing. I told her that at times I found giving lectures excessively fatiguing. I could manage the talk itself and the questions addressed to me while I was still on the platform. It was when I mixed with people afterwards that sometimes I felt quite suddenly blank and unaccountably terrified. An opaque block seemed interposed between me and those who had something special to ask of me. I had assumed that this was merely a sudden draining away of the last lees of energy from the bottom of the reservoir. Braïda told me that this was not so. The exhaustion was engendered by the energy I had given out but the split-second desperation had another explanation. She said that at such times there was often in the vicinity some hostile human transmitter syphoning off the last relics of one's vitality. Such people were always hidden among those searching after truth. This had been so since the world began and would continue to be manifest as part of the protracted Armageddon between light and darkness. She added that people of this type could also be responsible for my falls but that the latter could also be attributed to the generalised power of evil.

I was not afraid when Braïda spoke in this way. The fear came afterwards when I reflected on it. Were there moments when one was naked to the lance thrusts of the principalities and powers of darkness? Before my next lecture Braïda visited and told me that she, Betty and Graham would be constantly present on such occasions. Those who know me well say that in the last year or two I speak with greater clarity, with less asides, and that I finish fresher than when I started.

By the glow in the atmosphere and the indescribable peace I felt Betty was very near me before I gave another lecture. Then the jewel appeared. I saw, what I had not noticed before, that it was oval in shape and less wide at its lower than its upper extremity. It was almost as though I was looking at a particular piece of jewellery rather than a visual symbol.

Betty's support on such occasions was illustrated still more dramatically when I had a prolonged and arduous interview with a journalist on the manner in which the truths of Dualism had been manifested to me. When the interview was over the journalist showed me a photo he had taken of me. My face was obliterated by an oscillating circle of amethyst, pale at first but quickly deepening in tone. The living and vibrating colours were surrounded by a golden circle. I had no idea what the latter signified because the rim of bright gold looked regular and artificial.

Guilhabert de Castres spoke to me later on the question of colours. He repeated that for me the green and purple bands had indicated from the beginning that the revenants were in the offing. He confirmed that the deep and liquid amethyst glow and the jewel itself revealed the presence of Betty. He then emphasised to me that I had had these experiences of colour before I became aware of the shapes of the revenants. I had seen the latter outlined in silver, which colour was essentially associated with the first rudiments of form and was also the colour of the waking psyche. It was vital to realise that one sensation could give rise to another, that in this case colour could give birth to form. Silver was the colour of the waking psyche because it provided the outline for the revenants when they first assumed form before the people to whom they disclosed themselves. The more pulsating the envelope of silver the higher the psychic experience.

What was more significant still was the transmutation of silver into gold. I was positively thrilled when I understood that Guilhabert was interpreting the basic concepts of alchemy. His translation of hermetic science was nothing to do with transmutation of metals or, on a different plane, with the exchange of such abstractions as higher and lower selves. He was concerned to point out the recognisable visual reality of an alchemy in which a perceptive experience recorded in silver was followed by another expressed in gold. This lesson was driven home the night Clare saw a male figure standing beside her. The outline was not silver but formed from a flood of golden light. Even after he had appeared as a clearly recognisable figure he had a halo of gold about him. He was certainly not the ordinary discarnate to which she had become accustomed. He put his hand on her forehead. She was flooded by a sensation of indescribable peace and of utter timelessness. For days afterwards she felt an inward serenity which was reflected outwardly in her expression and demeanour. It was fascinating to recall that another woman who, years previously, had had an identical experience, had also anticipated Clare in receiving instructions to read the Pauline writings and in particular the First Epistle to the Corinthians.

This was what Clare had called a Christ figure but Guilhabert told us that the term was unjustified and that it was almost impossible to conceive of Christ appearing to people on this earth in this age. There could be no doubt about the appearances at Emmaus and elsewhere but in the intervening centuries the emanations of Christ had been replaced by a hierarchy of entities extending from the revenants like Braïda, who came to us regularly with factual information and practical advice, and to those like Guilhabert who had not reincarnated since the thirteenth century but who were still available to us through the agency of entities like Braïda or directly because of our own acute need of them. There were also angels and archangels in the higher strata of consciousness beyond even Guilhabert. I learnt from him that there is an order and a hierarchy in the worlds beyond us and in fact in the entire universe.

The next time I saw Guilhabert I was sitting with Clare. I saw my mandala again more clearly than ever before. The straight equal-armed cross was studded with amethysts. The superimposed St. Andrew's cross was encrusted with topaz. The rose was silver. Clare touched my arm. She asked if I saw anything else on the mandala. At first I proffered nothing, then I saw a bird.

After that everything was clear to me. What I saw was not only immediate vision but memory. It was wisdom and true knowing. I was reliving what I had experienced before. The bird perched on the top of the mandala was a silver dove. There was movement in the darkness and in my brain the light of memory. I was back in the Ariège in the thirteenth century. I was passing from a small cave through an aperture in a rock to a larger cave. There was light in the bigger cave. It came not only from the aperture but from other fissures high up in the roof. Then I felt some crucial and cosmic change in the atmosphere. I did not know whether it occurred in the past or the present. It had all the marks and at the same time the divine mystery of the timeless experience. I felt a vibration in the air. It turned to a kind of high-pitched music which was soundless and toneless but nevertheless a continuing harmony. I had heard this sound in early childhood. At the heart of this sound there was a vibrationless world where time was halted and where the endlessness of eternity was congealed in a pang too brief to be recorded as time. In that less than an instant I knew that the bird crossed from the top of the mandala to the crown of my head and that what I had heard was not only the pulse of eternity but the beating of its wings.

As the bird crossed from the mandala to my head the silver of its wings turned to gold. I had passed from the level of psychic to that of spiritual experience.

Now I was back in myself and remembering acutely. I knew that for once I had relived an experience. It is one thing to feel, "I have been here before, I have done this before", and another to return in the totality of being to the coils and meshes of time past. Sitting in my room in Bath I had, remembering the cave, been out of my body and out of time. I had had the same timeless experience seven centuries previously. It differed from what I had known in Bath in that in the Middle Ages it had been contrived and worked for. Guilhabert de Castres posed the crucial question, "What happened after you had the timeless experience in the cave in the Ariège?"

"I knelt and touched the ground with my forehead."

I did not need Guilhabert to tell me why I had done so. Touching the ground thrice with the forehead was part of a simple ceremony in which one paid one's respects not to the Parfait but to the Spirit with which he was impregnated. What was more fascinating was the revelation that nineteen years previously I had recalled this initiation ceremony. In 1954, after I had heard the music of the spheres and the first rustle of the dove's wings, these intimations of reality had been malformed into symptoms by my own resistance to enlightenment. I had suffered from the full battery of Menière's syndrome, attacks of acute giddiness, swimminess in the head, the feeling of being off-balance and of walking on a wide base like a sailor on a heaving deck, together with tinnitus and nausea. This had been compensated for by two short experiences of inexpressible joy which, in books on mysticism, are usually inadequitely referred to by the word bliss. In these moments beyond the conception of duration I felt myself to be beyond time and in a world of indivisible consciousness and harmony before its fragmentation into good and evil.

I could not forget that these experiences in 1954 followed the performance of what at that time was to me a peculiar and inexplicable rite. Turning in my bed I had rested on my knees and touched the mattress with my forehead. In the twentieth century I repeated the genuflections I had made in the Middle Ages.

316

Guilhabert told me that the initiation I had experienced in the thirteenth century and which I had recalled partially in 1954 and more totally in 1973 was part of the instruction of a small proportion of those already ordained as Parfaits. The aim of this final initiation was to enable those receiving it to withstand torture and death by burning and other methods. By this process the recipient was able to achieve, and in practice repeat, a dissociation from the body which lessened his sufferings from fire and water and other tortures.

A Parfait was received through the Consolamentum. This was the only sacrament recognised by the Cathars. It has often been held that the Consolamentum conferred immense spiritual benefits on those who received it. It is claimed that it endowed them with the powers of resistance mentioned above. This had always seemed to me impossible. I could not believe that a single ceremony could have such powers. I had believed in the existence of the later training of a specially selected minority of Parfaits. On that day in 1973 I was permitted to look back on the training I had myself received.

Because I have had these experiences I cannot regard myself as superior to anyone else. People say that in some ways I must be more evolved. I can only say that it is none of my doing as far as this incarnation is concerned. If I have arrived at a certain level it is because I am reaping the harvest of what I learnt and trained for in my Cathar incarnation. I have no feeling of belonging to a minority élite and am constantly irritated by people who adopt such attitudes. I have noticed that such outlooks often coincide with a paucity of experience.

What I heard from Guilhabert de Castres on such subjects as alchemy and my cave initiation was of interest to me through all the levels of consciousness, but what returned to my everyday mind with nagging persistence was his preoccupation with colours and jewels. It seemed strange that he, a practitioner of a faith regarded as ascetic, should be so concerned with these matters. I learnt later that my surprise was the result of my own ignorance. Above all, he seemed anxious that I should comprehend fully the significance of the amethyst and of the light transmitted by it. He, reinforced at times by Graham, told me of the formation of the first minerals in the world and how light created

317

life which either moved on the surface of the waters or was contained and seemingly immobile but still potent in minerals and especially semi-precious stones. I learnt that the first individualisation of the consciousness that was to become me took place within an amethyst. He gave me a glimpse of my ultimate beginnings beyond my incarnation as a man. He repeated that amethyst was the colour of the search for truth.

The details of what I learnt are too esoteric and too deeply philosophical to fit into this work. I will always be fascinated by what I learnt but I have to admit that, at the time all this was received by me, I was more concerned with my conviction that the amethyst's special significance for me was in some way tied up with Betty. This conclusion seemed all the more valid on the day when Guilhabert reappeared and spoke more of the healing and creative properties of jewels, of their identification with different kinds of flowers and above all with different areas of the body. Suddenly, irrelevantly, I saw in a vision a small model of a dove. Then I saw a leather pouch suspended by some kind of thread. I knew that I had worn the model of the dove hidden in the pouch and suspended round my neck. I knew also that Betty had possessed and worn a similar medal. I could now understand fully why years ago I had been so moved, in René Nelli's drawing-room at Carcassonne, when he had shown me the small lead model of a dove claimed to be indubitably of the thirteenth century. I knew beyond doubt that, at that time, I had worn such an object round my neck. Nevertheless, in matters such as these, I am torn between, on the one hand, perception and feeling and, on the other, my natural scepticism. I made myself ask, "But isn't this bordering on superstition?"

"It depends how you look at it," he said. "If you can feel by some system of vibration my presence in your room after seven centuries, is there anything particularly right or wrong about feeling the emanation of something which was worn close to me during my life on earth? I gave you the dove and you wore it round your neck." He did not add that it had been beneficial to me to absorb from the dove what it had gained by contact with his body. I thought of the emanation from two or three of the stones at Avebury and how I had been charged by them and my perceptions increased, so that when I went to Surrey I saw with

318

piercing clarity some of the scenes from my life as a French agent in the Napoleonic era. If we accept that seemingly inanimate stones can radiate to us healing strength and enhanced perception after centuries, it is surely permissible to infer that the same effect can be obtained by wearing next to our skin what has been previously in contact with the body of someone like Guilhabert de Castres. Surely what had emanated from him was of considerable force due to the degree of emancipation from matter he had achieved in his last incarnation and which was still manifested in his visiting me seven centuries later.

Suddenly I thought of Betty. I asked Guilhabert whether he had given her the little metal dove she had worn in the thirteenth century. He said that this was not so and added the incredible information that, in November 1971, she had rediscovered it in the garden of the house at Fanjeaux in which she and I had been almost certainly born. It is clear that Betty was guided to the garden and the little model. Guilhabert said that it was her fingers touching the dove which stimulated her power of recall so that she remembered for the first time that Roger de Fanjeaux had been her brother. Until that moment she had not connected him with the Roger scrawled over her sketch-books during her convalescence from scarlet fever in the early 1930s. She was stabbed to further recollection at St. Papoul, the place where I, as Roger, had been apprehended by the Inquisition in February 1253. It was only on returning to England and after she had read *The Cathars and Reincarnation* that she recognised that it was I who had been her brother seven centuries previously.

Chapter Thirty Three

The day came when we switched from the unchangeable truths of the universe to the creation of the world and from the properties of jewels and in particular those of the amethyst. It began with a remarkably positive and concrete piece of instruction from Braïda. One evening she visited Clare and told her that she should not be alone on the day following. It was quite unlike Clare to ask for shelter or to relay disquieting information about herself. I felt apprehensive and invited her to supper.

After supper we were sitting together looking at the view when I felt her glance change direction. She was looking at the rather swollen tissues at the base of my right thumb. It was some accentuation of trouble in my osteo-arthritic joint and the surrounding muscles were swollen. "Do you get any pain there?" she said.

"Not worth talking about."

She stretched out her hand and touched the base of my thumb. She clasped it so that for a few seconds it was enclosed in the palm of her hand. I smiled as I recalled how Graham had said that in the Celtic incarnation, when she and I had lived together, she had loved to sit at my feet clasping the base of my thumb. I turned to make some reference to this when I saw that she had slumped forward with engorged cheeks and was not listening to my conversation. Then she covered her face with her hands. I was alarmed by what for her was a melodramatic gesture. When I asked her what was the matter she seemed not to hear me. Then she cried out, "It's horrible, horrible. Do something to stop them."

"Stop whom?"

She was past hearing my questions. "They are killing her," she moaned. "They are killing her with stones. Now they are cutting her."

"Cutting whom?" I had no doubt at all that she spoke about Betty. I was too agitated to work out why I was so sure.

"They are cutting off her fingers. They are trampling on her."

Behind the agony in her face, and through the thin-voiced high-pitched cries which differed so much from her own vibrating tones, I saw the setting of the horror. There was the small hill surmounted by trees and, the time being autumn, the thin golden pennants streamed back from the birches. Betty lay with the mob around her in the marshland between the hillock and the lake. The waters of the lake were still and behind it to the north the slopes of Skiddaw were purple in the autumn twilight.

Clare was reliving in detail the murder of Betty which I have already mentioned in writing of Bassenthwaite. She remained with her head buried in her hands until her shoulders stopped heaving and her quick shallow respirations dropped back to normal. The story she told was this. Betty was stoned to death at the foot of Castle How. On this knoll, in the spring of the year, Clare had been aware of Betty's presence with such intensity that she could not understand that I could not see her. She was killed by a mob of superstitious louts inflamed by the pallid priest with the sharp face, triangular seen from the front, like a vulture in profile, who instigated the attacks, described already, on Annette and Clare.

I did not see the horror at Castle How so clearly as Clare but I was aware that, when the last reflex quiver of agony was still in Betty's mutilated body, they cut off her fingers because they had been employed in healing. In the first decades after Christ the Christians practised his injunction to heal the sick as well as preach the word. This was continued until the seventh century in Cumberland. Betty, dead by the lake with her fingers amputated, was the incisive melodrama through which the Church played out its negation of the act of healing. Betty died, too, because she believed in the immediate and consoling company of the old gods with their inevitable limitations but as comforting to man as the sun and the rain. "But I the Lord thy God am a jealous God." "Thou shalt have none other Gods but Me." Betty lay dead because the lower elements of society comprehended better the tribal god of Judo-Christian demonology which the Cathars were later to recognise as Satanic.

I had never in my life seen anything like Clare's emotion. In my career as a psychiatrist I had seen people disintegrating in culminating agonies which burst like a tide through what had been eroded by long-standing tension. In such cases one had seen the water rising and the breakwater crumbling. But what I had witnessed with Clare was a sudden terrifying scene from the past projected without warning against the background of the present. To me it was far memory at its most acute. I had never realised that the process could be so agonising.

When the tumult had ceased Clare sat quietly beside me. I was grateful to return again to the uneventful mediocrity of the present. There was something more dramatic to come. When I raised my eyes I saw traced on the wall a circle of deep amethyst surrounded again by a golden rim. Then I saw, some distance away from the amethyst, an irregular and slanting shaft of silver light. "What is the shaft of silver?" I said.

"The torch we carried when we buried her."

Now I was seeing as clearly into the past as Clare herself. I saw the lake at Bassenthwaite and the reed-thatched roof of the first church of St. Bega on its far shore. We buried Betty by the light of a single torch under a stone near what is now the entrance to the churchyard. I remembered how in the previous April Clare had wandered away from us and stood at that point gazing over the lake. She was not lost in contemplation because she was seeing beyond time to the night when we had buried Betty.

The ring of amethyst on the wall opposite kept fading and returning but then it came back with overwhelming intensity and with the richness of light reflected from a jewel. I turned to Clare. "You, Guilhabert and Braïda all say that amethyst is the colour of the search for truth but to me it's always identified with Betty. I know she is about when I see this colour."

"The amethyst you are seeing on the wall is the jewel we laid on Betty's coffin."

This clinched the issue for me. In recent weeks while the amethyst glow and the sight of the jewel had been intensifying my feeling of identification with Betty had correspondingly deepened. This, to me, was the end of the story. Guilhabert de Castres had spoken of jewels to prepare me for the amethyst which was laid on Betty's coffin the night she was buried. It seemed a neat enough conclusion of a fascinating experience. But what I thought was the end of the story was only the completion of a chapter.

When we had returned to this life from the horror perpetrated at Castle How, Braïda materialised. She told Clare that that day was the anniversary of Betty's death in her Celtic incarnation. It was one more example of Clare's capacity to reverberate in one way or another to these tragic anniversaries. It seemed that her capacity to react was intensifying. I did not yet know that I was doomed to march in her footsteps a little way behind her and that my capacity for this in some ways disastrous gift of far memory would develop further still.

Chapter Thirty Four

On Guilhabert de Castres' next visit we returned to my mandala. Once again the glow of the rose was intense at the intersection of the crosses. As I watched I saw the outline of a dove forming behind the rose. It moved upwards with squared-back wings going beyond the mandala through a golden glow. It crossed the ceiling in a track of gold and settled on my head.

This time a new experience was added. Where the dove had passed I saw on the wall the outline of a chalice. When it first formed it had the inverted triangle shape of wine-glasses in vogue four decades ago. Then it became more goblet-shaped. The container itself was relatively wide and the stem short. It resembled one kind of champagne glass with the stem fore-shortened.

At first the chalice was gold. I understood this well enough in the light of what Guilhabert had said previously about gold being the colour of spiritual experience. What was difficult to comprehend was the change of colour to amethyst. Guilhabert repeated that amethyst was the colour of the search for truth. The importance of the chalice was what it contained. It took its colour from what was within it. It was essentially the receptacle of truth. Guilhabert said that the chalice was a very primitive type. It had appeared often during the Cathar initiations and it was for this reason that Catharism was often associated with the Grail legend. There was no historical association between Catharism and the Court of Arthur. The chalice was older than Christianity and the dove was of similar antiquity.

What Guilhabert wished made clear was that the rose, the dove and the chalice as seen in my visions were real materialised entities. Certainly they were symbols in the sense that each conveyed a property. For instance the chalice was the receptacle of truth. But they were not symbols in the modern sense of the word which implies that such phenomena represent only the signs and symptoms of different states of mind. They were more than milestones in the individual's psychiatric history. They were as real as the late primrose blooming in the garden. To see them one had to be for the time being at another level of consciousness but this did not in any sense detract from their essential reality.

As well as being signs that one had reached a certain level of psychic development these symbols constituted an alphabet of Dualism. In the course of millennia those who had had these experiences had inscribed them in stone or recorded them in drawings. They constituted a sign language through which searchers for truth had been able to recognise each other for centuries. If I saw in a cave in the Ariège a chalice similar to what I had perceived in my recent visionary experience this meant that whoever had carved its outlines in rock had seen what had been manifested to me in my room in Somerset in 1973. It was not merely a question of seeing a certain sign from centuries before and saying, "A Dualist passed by here." I was sharing the identical experiences of many long dead. Guilhabert emphasised that the symbols we had discussed dated from epochs before man had acquired facility in the expression of verbal concepts and when he had best expressed himself in images. In listening to Guilhabert I realised the primordial nature of Dualism, and how the most pragmatic as well as the most mystical of philosophies arose from man's reaction to the first light and the menace of the first shadows.

After he had convinced me of the immemorial antiquity of these visionary symbols Guilhabert emphasised also the great age of the more concrete signs and symbols which have been associated with Dualism for millennia. He explained to me that the St. Andrew's cross which had acted as the herald of my Celtic revelations was a simplification of the ancient sign for Pisces. The latter had been recognised by Mrs. Smith, my sweetheart Puerilia in the thirteenth century, as the emblem appearing on the buckle of the belt I had worn as Roger de Grisolles. It had also appeared in the drawings of Betty who had lamented Roger in the designs made in her sketch-book in the early 1930s.

Guilhabert told me that the curves of the sign below represent the surfaces of the sun and moon approaching each other. The horizontal bar represents the earth which joins them. This is a

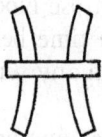

simple schematic emblem of Dualism, the sun representing the light of the good, the moon the darkness of evil, and the earth which joins them symbolising the balance between the two powers achieved in our own hearts in the passage through this world. This, said Guilhabert, was a very ancient sign. It pre-dated even the cult of Mithras. The cross of St. Andrew, affected by the Celtic Church, had the same significance as the Piscean sign of which it was a simplified version. The intersection of the diagonal lines represented the earth and its compromise between good and evil.

I learnt also that the simple cross with the long vertical arm which we describe as Latin is a very old symbol for truth and that there is nothing specifically Christian about it. It was taken up by the followers of Christ because he died on a cross of this shape. The equal-armed cross with the circle round it, known commonly as the Celtic cross, is very much older than its Latin equivalent. The circle derives from the days when Dualism was associated with sun worship. The circle representing the sun was in many areas dropped in the course of time but the cross sur-rounded by the circle is still common enough in the Languedoc, Yugoslavia, Wales and north-west Britain.

It was clear to me that my attention was being directed to something earlier than the Celtic incarnation. The main theme at this time was the antiquity of the visions and symbols I had seen and there was special reference to the cult of Mithras and to the ages antecedent to its appearance. Another sign was added to the Celtic and St. Andrew's crosses I was frequently seeing pro-jected on the wall. This appeared at first to be an M but which later I recognised as the interlocking triangles I had seen on the wall at Portchester. Graham intervened dramatically to explain this phenomenon. It was significant that his mode of intervention was different. For some time I had been able to detect his presence but now I was able to describe him for the first time. Once again it was a question of seeing him with the inner eye. He was long-headed with dark hair and dark-brown eyes. He was tallish and though wide-shouldered was in no way thickset. His expression was naturally solemn but his sudden brief smile was charming and infectious. He gave the general impression of a rangy and quick-moving Highlander. This was certainly not Graham as he had been in the thirteenth century when he was altogether a more rugged type with his features blunted by a heavier bone structure. I was obviously seeing him as he was in an earlier incarnation. I wondered if this was Celtic but his immediate contribution made me amend my ideas. He dealt immediately with the M sign. When we had been concerned with Portchester we had learnt from the revenants and their agents in this world that this particular symbol derived from a medieval masonic cult but Graham insisted that its origins were much earlier. Two days afterwards Annette rang from Canada and reported that Guy had returned to her the previous evening and said that the M signs I had seen recently were common in the cult of Mithras and were to be found on the walls of certain caves. Annette could not give me the location. The situation was clarified in a day or two's time when Braïda and Guilhabert materialised and confirmed that the caves referred to were those of the Ariège and had been used in turn by the Druids, the adherents of Mithras, the Cathars and the Templars.

Annette came forward with a message from Guy that five members of the group had kept together through five incarnations. This meant there was another to come. Annette had also been informed that equal-armed crosses enclosed in circles with, in each of their four compartments, either three dots or three trefoils arranged in the form of triangles, were very ancient signs. They recall the coins remembered by Mrs. Smith in *The Cathars and Reincarnation*. We were now told that these designs, and others allied to them, were not merely Cathar but also extant in the cult of Mithras in the Roman Empire. Guy was still more specific. He added that in our Roman incarnation a number

327

of the group had lived in and around the city but had spent some time in Ostia. I had known for some time that when Clare had visited an underground chamber in the excavations at Ostia she had vomited and left it in a state of collapse. The stage was set for our Roman incarnation.

Chapter Thirty Five

It was curious that, amid so many transcendental experiences, I felt that something like a personal tie between Betty and myself was intensifying. If it seems absurd that I should feel this about a dead woman I had never seen I can only record faithfully my impressions. When Clare told me to call on Betty when I needed her presence I was afraid to do so. I recalled that it was accounted evil to call up spirits. Nevertheless I allowed myself to be persuaded and Betty appeared. She soothed me immediately. "Why would I be near waiting if it were wicked to ask me to come? Why don't you call on me when you need me?"

I cannot say that my doubts were immediately resolved by Betty's words. I had always insisted on being passive in these matters and had been happy that the revenants had always sought me and that I had taken no steps to make contact with them. Later Betty and the other revenants made it clear to me that the operation in which we were engaged was unusual and dictated by the crucial hours we were living. It had been necessary for beings from the next of the worlds to contact those still willing to listen and residing on a planet bent on destroying itself.

At this stage she was more than concerned for me. She showed her consideration in a direct manner and was always quick to draw attention to people hard pressed and weary in my own family and especially needing my support. She was always concerned to save me fatigue and warned me not to become involved in different matters which could well have caused me increased tension and needless exhaustion. She told me that from now on she would be with me a great deal and always in the mornings when I awoke early. When this occurred I was often depressed because during sleep I had been in contact with the revenants and principally Betty. My depression on waking was due to the fact that I could not remember what we had said to each other in the hours of sleep. Betty said that I would not always be aware of her beside me in the early hours but that at such times I would have her support. Since that time, whenever I have woken early and in a state of depression, it is only rarely that I have failed to go to sleep after a short interval. She said also that whenever I needed her I should call upon her. She said she would not always be able to visit me but she would come whenever it was possible. This promise to help me when I needed her was soon translated into action.

One autumn day I drove my car down the narrow street which widens into the sweeping bay of the crescent. It has always an air of the open sea. To turn the corner is to face the sea wind. I left my car just round the corner and walked on the path below the sloping green. The leaves were thick on the trees that autumn. The gold poured down from the tops of the trees and was spilled in the light from the lower branches. Suddenly it was as though Betty walked beside me. I saw her with the instantaneous paralysing intensity of inner vision. What does it mean when I say I saw her? Did it mean that I saw her like the falling leaves and the branches bending in the south-west wind? The feeling was deeper than that. I did not see her with my visual eye. The image was richer and more real than the act of perception.

Then I remembered that two years before, while still alive, she had walked from the wide curve of great houses looking over the green to the trees and the city. The leaves were drifting down. Between the light clouds the sky was pallid with the breath of winter. She turned from the incurved bosom of the great crescent to the narrow street. Going down the street she stopped at Clare's house and left a message and a present for me. Then she walked through the silence of autumn and out of my life as we understand it.

But how did I know all this? All I had been told by Clare was that in October 1971 Betty had called at her house with a present for me. How did I know what route she had taken or that she had left her car in the crescent? Was I indulging in a capacity to visualise and a taste for romantic nostalgia?

I walked from the gold of the leaves in the park to the shadows of the narrow street. Clare was standing at her doorway and it
330

seemed that she was waiting for me. I said immediately, "Where did Betty leave her car the last day you saw her?"

"Just round the corner where the crescent begins. I remember I walked there with her before she started back to go to her mother's. Why do you ask?"

"I've left my car in the same place and ever since I left it I've been thinking of her."

"Do you know that it is two years to a day since she came?"

"You mean for the last time and with a present for me?"

"Yes."

This occurred at a time when we were being constantly visited by the revenants on the anniversaries of painful events and dramatic experiences in previous incarnations. I knew she would come that night. I asked for her not verbally nor even with whatever in my brain canalises the torrent of thoughts into the channels of speech. I asked through the cry of my heart and tissues. Of all those who came from the dead she was the nearest to me. Was she not the undisputed object of my unspoken prayer of the last few years, "You who are near me, help me."

On the wall opposite I saw vividly the rose, with the indented petals and the spines between, which had been a vital component of my mandala and which I knew was as old as Mithras. The colour was something between silver and gold, like the moment after dawn when the rim of the sun moves above the horizon. Then once more I saw the intensely glowing amethyst ringed with bright gold. Then the whole wall and the figure with a pulsating outline projected on it was golden also. The figure had a band of brighter gold light on her forehead. I did not realise at first that I was seeing a halo. Then the figure faded and in its place was a circle of deep amethyst which moved up and down in the middle of the wall. Two rays of intenser light projected from the heart of the amethyst. They moved towards me. After that there was a flash of a star being shattered. I knew that Betty was moving towards me. I had seen the flash because at that moment she was passing from one zone of contact to another in which I could see her. When I had seen the flash of the star I had been for an instant beyond my psyche and in my astral body. This is a rare experience and can only be supported momentarily.

331

As Betty drew near there was around her an uneven and pulsating silver fringe. It resembled the foam from the last flattened waves on sand corrugated by the sea wind. I saw her as I had seen her in the Celtic incarnation because this was how I already knew her but I realised I was very close to knowing her as never before.

When the figure with the golden halo had left the wall and moved towards me she had moved from the spiritual to the psychic plane. To comfort me she had achieved an alchemy in reverse. She had reflected to me the world of the Christ figures and had then quitted it for that of the revenants. By means of the reverse transmutation from gold to silver through a phase of amethyst she had returned to a world which was nearest my own. The truth itself had been reflected through light in the form of Betty.

I was satisfied not only that she and I were a closer nucleus within our circle but that these days she was visiting me for a special purpose. In stepping from the wall she had crystallised in her psychic form from a zone of impalpable spirituality. She had done this because she felt the unique particularity of human love.

She sat on the floor on my right side. These days she always appeared on that side because it was a symbol that she had become my right hand. She kissed my forehead. The sensation was indescribably cool and delicate and somehow impregnated with the sensation of mobility. It felt like drifting feathers with an exhilarating cold impact. I felt so near to her that she replaced for me the invisible forms of the summit of the hierarchy.

I knew also that I was drawing nearer to another incarnation. One morning I awoke with my right eye swollen, inflamed and painful and with the eyelids adhering to each other. My other eye refused to focus newsprint or distance. My visual field was covered by a palpitating cobweb. I could not read, I could not see features at a distance of more than five yards and outside my window the covert was a rumpled curtain. This condition persisted for hours. (I was to learn later that I was reliving the trauma received in another incarnation.)

Half-way through the morning I felt down my left arm an intense and flooding coldness. It was as though a thin film of

332

ice had become mobile. At the same time there was nothing deeply chilling about it. It was strange and exhilarating like an intensely cold and finely pointed shower directed on my arm. With my inner eye I saw Betty with her fair hair and dark eyes as she had been in her Celtic incarnation. It should be remembered that this was, at the moment, the most distant part of my far memory. I felt the gentleness and comfort which flowed from her touch.

Later that morning I saw Clare. She laid a hand above my eye. To my surprise she covered the relatively unaffected eye and left me to make do with the right which was practically non-functional. Suddenly things began to happen. It was a fine morning and in spite of my impaired vision I could see that the sun was shining above the rooftops. As I watched it it began to shrink. Its circumference and diameter diminished progressively. It retained its circular form but sank into a kind of radiant pool. From the latter emerged a thousand fine rays of light. The rays were innumerable, many times more than those usually depicted as arising from the head of Minerva. The fine bright filaments changed as I watched. Some showed all the colours of the solar spectrum. Others were a beautiful and intensely glowing rose such as I had seen before, and rarely, in sunsets. Many of the rays illumined by all the colours of the spectrum changed as I watched them to this rose-pink glow. Below the sun was a great bar of gold so radiant that my eyes were stinging as I watched it.

Then this symbol faded and I saw in its place very fleetingly the azure cell with the intensely glowing nucleus of amethyst I had seen off and on for years and more frequently in recent months, and which Guilhabert de Castres had told me indicated that one was undergoing more than a psychic experience. This was then replaced by a huge and intense amethyst glow with a golden band around it.

In a short time the light became so blinding that I could not look directly into it. This is not so say that the colour on the wall was visually dazzling. What happened was that what I was seeing with my inner eye was affecting my ordinary vision. Betty materialised with Graham. They explained that in people constituted like myself demonstrable ophthalmic impairment of vision very often accompanied an increasing capacity for inner perception. They added that the innumerable rays issuing from the sun were a Mithraic symbol. A little later I had another visionary experience. I saw once again the deep amethyst glow cohering to the form of a jewel with many facets and with rivers of light in its interstices. What was different was that this time the golden haze surrounding it was moulded, beyond any doubt, into a golden frame. Whatever its psychic significance I was looking at a jewel with a perfectly orthodox mounting. It had appeared shortly after the Mithraic sun image. I knew that it indicated my closeness to Betty. Did this close succession of visions mean that she had, in the past, been an adherent of Mithras?

The issue moved more towards a climax in the next few days. I began to see projected on the walls, and coinciding with symbols of great significance like the dove and the chalice, a diamond-shaped pattern broken by small squares. It resembled that of some varieties of oilcloth laid down in Edwardian bathrooms. I recognised that it could also be a Roman mosaic and this was confirmed by Betty and Graham. There came a day when Betty appeared again dressed as a Celtic priestess with her crinkled head-dress and dark-purple robe. The Roman mosaic was projected on the wall behind her. I indulged in a few justifiable speculations about Roman mosaics persisting in Celtic times. This was reasonable enough because after all one can see them in mass-produced materials to this day. My logical inferences were time wasted. Betty explained that the dress in which the revenants appeared depended on the immediate needs of the observer. She often appeared to Clare in her Celtic robes when Clare was reliving the worst agonies of her Celtic incarnation.

The Roman mosaic had been projected on the wall for my special benefit because at this time the question of a Roman incarnation was uppermost in my mind and because, in it, my love for Betty had been at its most intense and had been most consciously felt.

Chapter Thirty Six

My Roman experience had clamoured for long enough in the underwaters of consciousness. It began clearly and consciously one evening when I was looking through the window at the valley and the hills opposite. Braïda and Betty appeared almost immediately. It was rare for the latter to appear so quickly. She usually materialised relatively late in the proceedings. As always she drained all tension from the atmosphere. It was as though, when she came, the wind dropped and I was looking at silent country. This evening the silence intensified and the country changed. I saw a house half-open to the elements because of the wide climbing staircase at one extremity. There were rooms opening from the staircase and from the balustrade on its far side you could look between pillars directly at the garden. Somewhere in the house was a hall with a high white cupola. "I am seeing your home in your Roman incarnation."

"Do you see me too?"

"No," I said promptly, and added immediately, switching to my inner vision, "that is to say your eyes are still darker than in the Celtic incarnation. They are an indescribable colour. Black rather than brown but there are flecks of hazel in them. Your hair is fair, but not strikingly like gold as when you lived in Cumberland. It's a very light auburn with a few reddish strands in it."

I continued to describe Betty's appearance. Her face was broader than in the Celtic incarnation and her mouth as big and generous as it was in her life in the twentieth century. One could say that there was something sensual but not unpleasantly so about her face. As I write this it seems odd and significant that, on this first clear day of the Roman revelation, I could have spoken about her to her face like this. This was because fourteen years previously I had seen, behind the head of a timid, conscientious little woman in whose house I was staying, a face with intent burning eyes and an animal beauty. This face had recurred to me many times in the intervening years and I always thought of it as that of a person in whom desire was consumed by its own intensity. I had known that in seeing that face I was looking back to antiquity. I could not get out of my head the faces of certain Greek and Roman goddesses, ardent, amoral but somehow serene in the fulfilment of their own sensuality. It was strange to associate this face with the gentle and unassertive creature who, in this life, had loved her husband and occupied herself unobtrusively with works of charity. This Roman beauty was a far cry from the bereaved widow of 1971 who discovered her second loss when she called for Roger after her visit to Fanjeaux but who, conscientious and diffident, made no attempt to make direct contact with me. Nevertheless I persisted that this face I had seen for years was Betty. I did not realise till later that it derived from an epoch earlier still than her Roman incarnation.

My own case was easier. Betty's mother Jane Butler had materialised one day and told me, among other things, that I was a fetching creature in my Roman incarnation. When Betty said simply that I was beautiful this acted as a touchstone. (Was this a compensation for my present appearance?) I described myself without hesitation as having very thick, wiry, intensely dark hair, deep blue eyes and a long oval face. "Yes, that's how you looked," said Betty.

What I have to say of my life in Rome with Betty is the harvest of many interviews with her in Somerset in the twentieth century. What was disclosed to me did not arrange itself in any exact chronological order because in some of the interviews Betty was accompanied by Braïda and Guy who are more concerned with the Cathar and Celtic incarnations respectively. On other occasions the course of the conversation was directed by the subjects I raised myself. For the convenience of the reader I am arranging the facts as accurately as I can in the order in which they occurred in Rome rather than according to the pattern in which they were revealed to me.

I was picked up by Betty and her husband somewhere in the mountains in north-western Italy. I do not know exactly where it was. It may even have been what is now French territory in the Savoie. All I know is that I came out of a hovel in a high,

336

gaunt village cool in the shadow of the mountains. I saw her standing before me. She had descended from her chariot and walked a few steps towards me. Her husband remained seated. The meeting had been prearranged and all I expected of it was that I would exchange one form of servitude for another. I had no hope other than to pass from the imprisonment of poverty to perhaps better-fed but more protracted slavery. My father had served as a soldier under Betty's husband. He had recently died. I was living in great poverty but was respectably dressed. I was sixteen at the time. Betty (her name was Camillia in those days) was in her early twenties and much younger than her husband. To me she seemed older than her age because of the stillness of her gaze and the dignity of her carriage. She had a way of looking at you intently that I have never encountered in anyone else in any of my incarnations. She had a level, tranquil, not consciously pitying glance and there was nothing possessive or dominating about it.

Betty's husband does not come much into this chronicle. He was a senior soldier, distinguished in his profession, who spent a good deal of his time away from Rome. At home he appeared rather colourless and insignificant but Betty herself was in no sense domineering. Her husband was devoted to her. He allowed her to do exactly as she wished. He was not in the least jealous of the men who visited her. He assumed, and rightly, that many of them shared her philosophic interests. This was one of the traits which endured throughout her five incarnations though it was never exhibited in a pedantic manner. Her husband had no idea of her degree of intimacy with some of her visitors. He was a kindly, quiet kind of man. Working in the house was extremely easy. He left all the management to Camillia who asked very little of us.

I became a slave in the household. It is difficult to convey exactly what this meant. To say that I was a slave involves a reflex shock of recoil in these unenlightened days. Certainly I wore a bracelet round my left wrist which was an insignia of my status. The progressives of this age may liken this to a collar put round the neck of a dog but it is well to remember that some people are fond of their dogs and the latter can be devoted to their owners. There are some dog-owners who buy expensive

337

collars for their pets and are careful to see that the metal is always burnished. I remember by direct memory, and not only with the aid of Braïda and others, the pride with which I regarded the thin bracelet of silver round my wrist. I feel its echo to this day and my gratitude that my mistress chose it herself. This is not sentiment but actuality. Perhaps I am not of the stuff of which good socialists are made.

I have an impression of a hive of vociferous fellow slaves who were opinionated and not especially endowed with the virtues of co-operation. Two stand out quite clearly. Clare's name in this incarnation was Cressi or at least that is what it sounds like. She herself remembers this name and Betty, Braïda and Graham, the revenants most concerned with the Roman incarnation, confirm that this is what she was called. I had an idea that her full name was Cressida which was later confirmed by Betty. One thing is certain, her face is as clear to me in its features and expressions as that of a woman I passed yesterday when I went through the market. For a start she was a glowing redhead. She had a broad forehead and cheek-bones but the lower part of her face was triangular and tapered down sharply to a pointed chin. She had very luminous eyes (this quality Clare has manifested through all her incarnations known to us) which were sometimes blue and sometimes greenish. I did not think they really changed colour but they looked green if one's eyes had first alighted on her mane of red hair. She had a biscuit-coloured complexion with a rather brick red flush over the cheek-bones.

As I see her in the fourth century in Rome Cressi always wears a quizzical expression. There is an impish look in her eyes and it is clear she is out to extract the maximum possible humour from any given situation.

On the same evening on which I first saw Cressi in Somerset in the twentieth century, Kathleen rang from Switzerland and gave me an identical description of her. Its only variant was that she insisted that her complexion was normally pale and that the flush on her cheekbones was only present when she was excited about something. Kathleen added that Cressi had a genius for sorting things out and keeping morale high. She had a knack of getting the best out of people particularly when they were rebellious or dejected.

338

At this time Annette rang from Canada with an identical description of Cressi's appearance, painting her as a kind of domestic statesman.

The only other fellow slave I remember with accuracy is Blodena. She was a thick-set peasant with strong legs, bulging shoulders, a round, heavy-boned face, dark wiry hair and eyes aflame with a sense of grievance. She was a bustling, determined, rather insightless character in whom truculence was never very far below the surface. Clare remembered her as an obstinate and vituperative peasant but managed her better than I did. For reasons which will be clear later Blodena was not exactly enamoured of me. She appears as Kathleen in this incarnation. Her soft voice and well-chosen sentences are a sharp contrast to her mode of expression in her Roman incarnation but she has retained her gift for vituperation.

To deal with first things first, what contemporary psychiatrists call my affective life was awakened and fulfilled the first day I met Camillia. When, emerging from my hovel, I saw her standing like morning on the sea, beautiful, elegant, unattainable and in her beauty immediately welcoming, the course of my heart was charted for ever. I loved her not from the first moment I saw her but the instant I realised she was smiling at me. (I was to find later that she smiled rarely and spoke little. She was an intent listener and hearing the sorrows of others while she regarded them with her extraordinary, all-seeing eyes was her expression of the gift of compassion.) She represented another world from the grinding apprenticeship of poverty. To me, from the first moment, she was kind and beautiful and that was the end of the matter. This seeming naïvete was a flash of wisdom. I never once faltered in my love for her. She was never for an instant unworthy of it. My first impression of her was a moment of revelation. I have said earlier that when, in this life, I first saw her against her Roman background, I realised that she was in some strange, non-indictable way, not particularly moral, but this aspect of her character was only clear to me some time after I met her in my Roman life and was not manifest that grey morning when she came in warmth and light to the village cold in the shadow of the mountains.

I do not remember what my duties were when I first arrived in

339

the house in Rome. Perhaps I was too bewildered by the wide, light rooms, the coolness of the external staircase looking out on the aching blue sky and the glittering air, to recall the nature of my first responsibilities. All I know is that promotion was rapid. I do not think the opposition was considerable. The place was over-staffed. It resembled some of our contemporary state-controlled industries in being a kind of unrecognised charity. The difference was that the recipients were on the whole grateful. Clare, as Cressi, had some sort of seniority among those who had the more menial household tasks. I escaped from the not very energetic competition of my voluble and squabbling colleagues when Camillia made me her personal maid. I took care of her clothes and helped her to dress. Looking back on those days is like recalling a perpetual April. To help her dress was the gateway to heaven.

One day, speaking to her in 1973, in Somerset, it came to me suddenly, sharply, without emotion and with the incisiveness of truth that Camillia mostly wore dark purple and dark green. This was her favourite combination of colours. I saw clearly that the advancing waves of green and purple I had seen from 1964 onwards were not merely indications of psychic activity or the imminence of presences but that there was a personal inevitability about them. I had seen them for years because she had loved them most. I was satisfied that, by means of this sudden stab of memory, I had explained why I was haunted by these colours but Betty sharpened my memory still further when she asked me whether I remembered how, when she asked me to choose among clothes she had finished with, I invariably selected the green and purple robes she herself preferred. We recalled together how, even when I had acquired money of my own, I rarely bought new clothes but preferred to adapt her cast-offs. It is incredible to think that this combination of colours, which I had always thought of, and rightly, as of great occult and philosophical significance, should have made their first impact on me when I was indulging in egotistical caperings in front of a mirror in ancient Rome.

I passed rapidly from personal maid to being the head of the household. In spite of my rather childish vanity (nothing pleased me better than to go out with my ringlets carefully arranged, dripping with jewels and my bangles clashing) I was by no means stupid. I had good practical intelligence and was a reliable judge of character. I had an unerring nose for bad-hats and as such was some protection for my employer. I could pick up a bad atmosphere very quickly but my interpretation of it deteriorated often into superstition. I had not an enquiring mind. Had I been so possessed I might not have had such an unswerving and all-consuming devotion to my mistress. I had no interest whatever in the abstract and no comprehension of religion. I affected an interest in the cult of Mithras when I learnt that my mistress was intensely occupied with it. In my first Dualist incarnation my sole relevant equipment was a firm belief in the power of evil.

My rapid promotion did not fail to arouse comment. The leader of the disgruntled was Blodena. This sharp-tongued and quarrelsome Gaul was devoted to Cressi and took the view that the latter did all the work in the house while I took all the credit. This opinion was based on the fact that I ended functioning as a housekeeper while Blodena continued noisily and coarsely at more menial occupations. Kathleen, in recalling her life as Blodena, regards me as a designing minx who wormed my way for my own benefit into my mistress's affections. In so doing I left the dirty work to Cressi. This attitude is quite unjustified. I suppose the older servants found it hard to bear that Camillia had such an affection for me but nobody could accuse her of being demonstrative in her manifestation of it. The fact remains that Cressi and those directed by her had different duties to me but once Blodena had got an idea into her head it could not be extirpated by anything less than a trepanning operation. She also had little use for Camillia herself. She could not accept that she was beautiful and to this day, as Kathleen, she restricts herself to describing her as "good-looking in a way but blowzy".

When I became housekeeper I did all the buying in for the establishment. Camillia provided me with the necessary money which was always markedly in excess of what I needed, all the more so because, brought up among mountain peasants, I could batter the sellers down to something below the market prices. When I returned home after making my purchases I told Camillia very scrupulously and carefully what I had bought and what

341

I had paid for it. I handed her the change which she refused to accept. This went on for some time at the end of which she bought me a casket shaped like a rather wide urn. She told me that I need not bother counting out the change to her but that I could put it directly in the casket. When the time came to empty the latter she told me the money was mine. For the rest of my life it went on like that. It was her way of making me save. Even though still a slave I was quite well off when I died.*

Though I had enough money I would not buy clothes of my own. It mattered intensely to me that I wore what had hung round her body. This can be translated how you will. I know that there was absolutely no trace of homosexuality in my relation with her. I confess that even to this day the suggestion disgusts me. I had for her a kind of impersonal and sexless love which by modern standards is unclassifiable. I have said that while my academic and cultural attributes were nil I had a sense of atmosphere. I think I can go further than this. She was more than beautiful and I saw in her a kind of total harmony, a living principle of beauty which was beyond good and evil and which haunts me to this day. I think I was right in my attitude to Camillia because a lot of people, observing her mode of life, could say that she behaved as though she were beyond good and evil.

At one time it was a sore trouble to me that she entertained so many male guests in her husband's absence. Sometimes they hung about a long time by day. There was nothing unusual in this because we were living in a leisured society. People talked a great deal for hours. I kept my ears open to what they were talking about. At first they were discreet but afterwards they would continue their conversations in my presence. (I was more in attendance on Camillia than the other servants.) Most of them sensed that, in spite of my over-colourful appearance, I was a responsible individual and had become my mistress's confidante. It was obvious to me they were talking about the membership of a semi-secret sect which proliferated in Rome at that time and was, at the beginning of my career, on the whole well tolerated

* I have learnt since that this habit of providing some kind of pension for slaves was traditional in the better Roman families. The nest egg was called a peculum.

342

and not taken seriously by the authorities. It seemed to me that what they discussed was non-political. This was all I bothered about because I hated to think of my mistress embroiled with the authorities. What they discussed was for the most part well above my head and I had little use for it. I pricked up my ears when they talked about light and darkness because I was frightened at night and particularly of the evil spirits abroad then. My perceptive gifts tapered off into superstition. When they passed from light and darkness to the need for self-purification I was not interested. They mentioned the names of too many philosophers. I could not understand why my mistress, who was so beautiful reclining on her couch with her head on her hand, should be reduced to discussing such dull subjects. In my first years with her such subjects as the cult of Mithras were to me of secondary importance.

Not all the men who came to see her were thinkers and philosophers. A number were men about town. They aped an interest in philosophy to qualify for her company. She was the principal hostess in that particular quarter and one of the most sought after in the whole of Rome. She drew people towards her by her beauty and by a particular glow which seemed to emanate from her. For a hospitable person she spoke and smiled very little. I think she concentrated her energies in bringing other people together and in stimulating them to talk by the magnetism of her own receptive silence.

Among her male visitors there was a third group which interested me more than the others and at first roused my hatred. These were people frightened by some secret, or not so secret, worry, a sick wife, an erring child or the fact that they were crossed in love. Sometimes she was visited by men who had passed their prime and were sinking into an inevitable melancholy. It was the sombre and agonised members of this third group who stayed on late at night. It seemed to me that this was because they had nowhere to go, or that the homes they returned to were comfortless, cold or saturated with misery. At first I pitied these people but the day came when it became obvious to me that sometimes one or two of their number would spend the night with her.

There is no point in dwelling on the agony I felt when I made

343

this discovery. There is enough pain in any single life without raking the embers of old hates and rages felt in previous incarnations. What is extraordinary is that I recovered so quickly. Here was the one and only love of my life and I had discovered that she could spend the night with a haggard counterfeit of masculinity when, if she needed, she had the whole of Rome to choose from. (I did not tell myself that if she made her selection from the whole of the city I would have taken it equally badly.) But I cannot say that my agony was anything more than a few days' duration. Of course I wished her lovers dead but there was about her something which disarmed criticism. Though she had shared her bed with them, though she may even have invited them to it, in some way she was unsullied by it, it was not her responsibility. What was extraordinary was that when I first discovered her infidelities she made no attempt to explain them. She merely asked me if I would keep her secret. She never played on my feelings. She looked at me absolutely intently. I can still see and feel the fixity of her eyes and the unsmiling immobility of her in no sense rigid features. She never told me she loved me. It was not even implicit in her glance. She looked through my soul and beyond it. I said I would keep her secret. When she said she did not wish to hurt her husband I knew that this must have been said several million times in the history of Rome. This, the oldest gambit in the world, exonerated her in my eyes and, believe it or not, I forgive her everything. Why? Because it never occurred to me I could love anyone else of either age or sex in the same way as I loved Camillia. Mine was one of the rare cases of a single love lasting a lifetime. I imagine that at our first meeting there was an intense psychic contact between us. I cannot otherwise explain how I could have been throughout my life so undeviating and so wholly absorbed in a single reaction. Perhaps I was at my best in my earlier incarnation as a woman. Perhaps it is simply that only a woman can love in this way.

Because she knew I would keep her secret she began to speak more freely to me. When I reacted badly to a twitching apparition who shared her bed she said it was the only means she knew which diminished his anguish. It is easy to say that I believed her because I was besotted with her. I do not think this is true. I believe that even at that moment, which was very painful for

344

me, there was within me a core of peasant wisdom which knew that some kind of physical contact was the only way of easing the agonies of those people who repeated in age what they had experienced when their mothers passed a hand over their foreheads in hours of fever.

Very early in her concentrated pilgrimage to me in the late summer and early autumn of 1973 Betty raised the question of her intimate life in the house in Rome. In this life I felt no pain when she spoke of what others would call her marital infidelities. This was not only because she introduced the subject so subtly, allowing me to see in an almost impersonal way how perfectly the component parts fitted into the pattern, but also because I had been prepared for such revelations by thoughts which had traversed my mind in the last decade and which I now know to have been implanted by Braïda and Guilhabert de Castres and which Betty was now to recall for me in the course of her visits in 1973.

If it was not painful it was eerie and moving to hear from the revenant Betty the details of her life as Camillia. One day when she was talking of my love of jewellery there was a sudden stillness in my mind and I listened no more to what she was saying. It was strange to feel this blankness in the presence of one whom I had loved so much in a past life and who had come from the next world to talk to me. I knew that in that moment I was looking back on her life with her lovers, and that the void in my brain was imposed by my disinclination to talk about it. When I thought of her as she had been in this life it was of a quiet, modest, middle-class woman desolated by the loss of her husband, or as an etiolated schoolgirl with candid eyes, wide mouth and not especially good-looking. It was an awkward feat of mental gymnastics to shift from this picture to that of a dreamlike version of a Roman lady of easy virtue. She made it easy for me by saying that what she had to say harked back to something I had written three years ago about a girl called Julia who slept with an outcast to convince him that he was not a homosexual. I understood at that moment that her activities in her Roman incarnation had been motivated by compassion but I was confused by what she told me. I was incapable of realising that, in what she had been in Rome, she differed not at all from the girl

345

of whom her schoolfriends Clare and Kathleen had said that even in her teens peace seemed to flow from her.

It may seem strange, but often when I was talking to Betty I was carried away elsewhere by my own thoughts. It took me a little time before I realised that this was another way of saying that she led me to other scenes and subjects to prevent me thinking of her too personally. She wished to make the process of recall as painless as possible. I had suffered enough in those few days in Rome when I sat up in the dark knowing that she was entwined with another. It was in this way that I thought suddenly of the temple women of the Hindus who gave men peace by certain techniques in loving. I had pondered this subject on several occasions in the last few years. I suppose this was inevitable because the function of the psyche had become of such importance in my approach to psychiatry that I could not help considering the psychic and transcendental possibilities of physical love. Then, talking to Betty, I recalled how an amiable, chaste woman with no knowledge of Eastern religions had suddenly and abruptly spoken of passivity in love and had described sex as we know it as a form of violence. Betty told me that this woman had had, in this life, no practical experience of what she discussed but had had two Eastern incarnations in her last five lives. In one she had been a Buddhist priest and in the other "something not quite like a priest in a Hindu incarnation". In both these lives she had been a man. I could not help remembering that once, when I was greeted by this woman, I had passed her by, not recognising, in the features of the handsome young Indian imposed on her own, the woman well known to me.

I noticed that at this time, whenever I spoke to Betty about her lovers, our talk was always preceded by a discussion about touch with Braïda and Graham, with Betty appearing when the flow of conversation was well established. I had at first no idea that this subject was particularly related to Betty. I thought that, like all the revenants, the subject of touch was of especial importance to her. It was only later that I realised that Braïda and Graham were wrapping up the intimacies of Betty's life in general references to the subject of touch. I had to saturate myself in the contemplation of this question to provide a suitable background for the proper consideration of Betty's so-called infidelities in the Roman incarnation. Even early in our discussions of these matters I was able to ask her whether, in her love-making in her Roman days, she was seeking some philosophical intention beyond passion. When I asked her if she had hoped to kill desire by expressing it she answered in the affirmative but it was obvious that mine was a crude simplification and that she had more to say.

Gently, as time went on, she persisted more and more in talking of her philosophical interests in relation to touch and sexual experience. At this time she was visiting me often because I had particular need of her, but in general she came to see me less than the others because she was studying philosophy with my deceased friend Simon. She and he were more concerned with Guilhabert de Castres' transcendental philosophy. It was odd that this should be connected with the physical intimacies of her Roman incarnation.

I told her that I found it strange that she had never exhibited any interest in philosophy until the end of her life in the twentieth century. In the last months before her death all her Cathar past had returned to her and she had recalled the basic principles of the philosophy she had then practised. Not a complete rebirth but sometimes a kind of renaissance begins before the act of dying. It was like this with Betty. In the last weeks left to her in 1972 she had pondered more than in her whole lifetime the purpose and meaning of existence. She had not been aware until after her death of the details of her Roman incarnation but now, in her visits to me, she wished me to understand something of the life she had led in those days and how her actions, which must have seemed inexplicable and at times painful to me, were strung on the thread of a philosophic purpose, though, while alive in Rome, she had never succeeded in expressing in words or even conscious thoughts this motive of destroying desire by amending its course and nature.

Betty tried to educate me rather by fact than by persuasion. She relied more on her record through her five incarnations than on any reaction in a single life. She told me the main motives joining together her five lives on a mild winter day when I walked in the country. For some days previously Graham, Braïda and Guilhabert de Castres had been preoccupied with touch in relation to, and as a substitute for, sexual experience. The ideally happy marriage of Annette and Guy had never been consummated. By lying together with their bodies in contact they had been enabled to go out of time and to lose all sense of their separate identities. This was one way in which the body, aided by the psyche, could achieve a sense of its own dissolution. Betty said that in such an experience as Annette's and Guy's the first feelings aroused were perhaps erotic but the active induction of psychic union was in no sense sexual.

Walking in the quiet country at the hour of sunset, with the last rooks flying to the dark plantations, I knew Betty had something more to tell me and that it was an intimate communication. I simply was not anxious to hear anything of a physical nature from her. What I felt for her was quite literally outside this world. Was it logical to wish to hear the facts of life or any embroidery or distortion of them, from a woman I had never met in this life and who came to me like a benediction when I was depressed and tired?

She told me that never in her five lives had she felt the fever of sexual passion. In her Roman incarnation she lay with the sick and dejected as Annette had lain with Guy. She calmed and sometimes cured them by unmoving contact with her body. Where there was any greater intimacy it was accompanied by immobility. If those she comforted insisted on the turbulence of physical passion she ceased to receive them.

I asked her if what she had done in Rome was analogous to what had been practised in Hindu communities by the temple women and to certain rituals in Tantric Buddhism. She agreed but was not greatly interested in these Oriental practices. What concerned her more was that what she had practised was part of the Troubadour concept of love. The latter in its highest development was completely aphysical, a kind of mystic devotion to a female Holy Spirit. Only a small proportion of the Troubadours were capable of such refinement. The basis of their concept of love was that physical contact should be minimal, that love should be maintained by the tension of its own longing and that, where the lady granted her favours, she did so piecemeal and over a long period of time. The processes involved were unrelated to sublimation. It was fascinating to learn, by direct revelation,

348

that one of the rarer practices of the Troubadours was the passive and prolonged intercourse described by Camillia.

I was astonished when she spoke in this way of the Troubadours. What she said was identical with the views I had expressed verbally and in writing for several years. Years ago, before the stream of impressions had begun to pour in on me directly from the past, I had written a novel called *The Gibbet and the Cross*. Certainly at this time I had met Mrs. Smith, portrayed in *The Cathars and Reincarnation*. I had acquired some knowledge of Catharism and of the civilisation of the medieval Languedoc, but this did not extend to the knowledge of the love techniques practised by the Troubadours. Nevertheless in this novel I depicted a woman granting favours piecemeal to a young man whom I depicted as a Troubadour. What was still more striking was that the lady in my novel was called Berenice, my own name in my Roman incarnation. At the time I was writing this novel I was having my first experiences of the bands of dark green and purple produced by the touch of Betty and Guilhabert de Castres. In the same book I attributed to the heroine Andrée attributes manifested by Annette as Aurelia in her Celtic incarnation as well as anticipating the damage done to the latter's left ankle in Celtic Cumberland.

Betty pointed out that since her Roman incarnation she had had small experience of the flesh. In the Celtic incarnation she had been a priestess but had never lived with a man even though in that age this was permissible. In her Cathar incarnation her sexual life was minimal. She had married and had three children. She and her husband were not suited to each other. Her passivity during the sexual act led him to stray to more enlivening pastures. In her early twenties she had devoted herself to Catharism. When she became a Parfaite before the age of thirty she had parted from her husband for some years. With his departure her sexual life was over. She never ceased to be interested in the welfare of her children, one of whom, Pierre de Mazerolles, was an avaricious scoundrel. She was never able to detach herself from him. She continued all her life to be hurt and ashamed at his lack of virtue. In the Napoleonic incarnation she came back as a man and remained chaste and unmarried throughout her life.

349

With her previous minimal sexual record it seemed in a way a step back that she had married in this life. She had had no children. The reasonable assumption was that she had submitted to her husband because it was required of her. I was astonished to learn from her that once again, in the twentieth century, she had returned, in her married life, to the passive love she had practised in the Roman incarnation.

It was interesting to contemplate the sudden leap from Betty's seeming promiscuousness in Roman days to her dedicated and sexless life as a Celtic priestess. Certainly she had been seeking for something inexpressible and beyond the body in the house in Rome which I think of always as still and with its garden silent in the numbing heat. Its site was somewhere near the Villa Borghesi but Betty would not answer when I asked her. Nevertheless her career in Rome seemed a fragile and perverse foundation for a succession of lives in which the meditative aspects seemed to predominate and certainly in relation to the basic physical urges. I did not leap on her transformation, from the sophisticated Roman lady to the Celtic priestess looking over the lake at Bassenthwaite, as a manifestation of Karma. The latter doctrine plays no part in Dualism. In our group of reincarnating Dualists destiny is not so computerised. It seems that our basic purpose is that each of us must develop to the full the predominating creative urge in his make-up.

What interested me about Betty's career through her five lives was its zigzag course. Certainly the philosophic streak was present throughout, it was even revealed later in the Napoleonic incarnation, but it was intertwined with her matrimonial responsibilities in the Cathar and twentieth-century incarnations. This cannot be ascribed to a to and fro submission to the flesh in the midst of her philosophical evolutions. With her there was never any question of battles between the flesh and the spirit. She simply was not made that way. Her gentleness and timidity were natural and not imposed by repression. All through her known incarnations sex was never more than an instrument of a philosophical intention. She never tried to justify herself. She had no guilt for the past. She told me that one day, when her twentieth-century husband formed an innocent attachment for another woman, she was completely undisturbed. She realised there was no question of her waiting for his return because, in truth, she had never lost him. After all, she added, he had been her husband in her Roman incarnation. Neither could she blame him because she herself had had other attachments in her life in Rome.

I told her of a peculiar stabbing sensation I had felt recently in my solar plexus, which was quite indefinable and which I had never experienced before. It was not like the pang of communication I had sometimes felt when I had established psychic contact with another. It was accompanied by a feeling of intense yearning. I knew that she accepted that there was a special bond between us but I was astonished when she said that this new feeling was due to my growing recognition of my attachment to her. She laughed with me at the idea that I was falling in love with a wraith. She said I was simply reliving the feelings I had had for her in my Roman incarnation. I have said before that sometimes, adding peasant superstition to a genuine perception of atmospheres, I feared that evil spirits were after me at night. When I had the horrors particularly badly she took me into her bed and put her arms around me. Sometimes she kissed me but only rarely. In short, she nursed me in the same way as she did the other casualties though there cannot be any doubt of her affection for me.

I said that, in the modern world, there were those who would consider our Roman relationship to be tinged with homosexuality. She said this was in accordance with contemporary thought and was manifestly idiotic. She realised she was offering evidence which could be used against her by contemporary psychiatrists with mechanised brains when she admitted that, deep down, she had in her Roman days preferred her own sex, but this was because of their greater capacity for intuition and compassion. If, as Camillia, she had at times a certain disdain for men it was only because she shrank from the aggression and dominating will expressed by the male ego. This attitude was reflected physically in her refusal to indulge in the, to her, violent manifestations of sexual passion.

She told me that the embraces we had exchanged were unforgettable to me because, through them, I had been borne, like Annette and Guy in this life, like her so-called lovers in her

351

Roman incarnation, to a world of harmony and obliterated self. She added that the stab of yearning I felt in my solar plexus was a sensation especially adapted to suit my nature. It had a healing function. By what it induced in me I could bring greater comfort to others I touched.

Camillia never told me that she loved me. She reserved her expression of affection till after her death in the twentieth century. In Rome she was simply not made that way. This was not from any inhibition on her part but because she regarded love as an emanation. You either felt it or you didn't. Once or twice, impulsively, in my early days as a slave, I told her what I felt for her. This is not surprising. It must be remembered that I was only sixteen when I entered her service and my attachment to her began the first day I saw her. She did not repulse me but merely stroked my forehead. The other members of the household saw nothing pathological in our relationship however much a proportion led by Blodena resented it and regarded me as a calculating hussy who had used her sharp wits and beguiling manner to jump the promotion queue.

During my life with Camillia I thrust from my mind the thought that other members of the household might be aware of her technical infidelities. The latter were better known than I had imagined. Kathleen tells me that she remembers how, as Blodena, she did not hesitate to give, to a chosen circle, her opinion of Camillia's morals. That she does not agree that Camillia was beautiful affects me more than any criticism of her character. Kathleen allows that she was striking but the adjective blowzy jars my sensibilities. I suppose it is part of my conviction that beauty represents an image of harmony beyond good and evil.

Betty told me that while the Roman incarnation, with her addiction to the cult of Mithras, saw the beginnings of her interest in philosophy, she never in those days practised any form of meditation. She said that she had done so for many hours at a time as a Celtic priestess overlooking the lake at Bassenthwaite. She had done so sitting down and had not adopted any special posture. It was clear that her philosophy and what meditation she practised were rooted in her European origins and not derived from Oriental sources. She added the fascinating item

352

that among Dualists it was usual for one's experience of meditation to be concentrated in a single incarnation.

From time to time, from autumn 1973 to well into 1974, the revenants were particularly concerned with the function of jewels. I had by now recovered from the shock of finding that ascetics like Guilhabert de Castres should have such interests because I realised that their preoccupation with this subject was related to such cosmic considerations as the creation of life and the nature of healing. When Betty and, to a lesser extent, Graham returned to discuss with me the properties of different jewels I knew that we were concerned with scientific and philosophical matters and not with the trivialities of self-adornment. Nevertheless, in view of my repeated vision of an amethyst, I obstinately persisted in my belief that some jewel or jewels had, in the Roman incarnation, a personal significance for me. I was therefore very happy when, in communicating this belief to Betty, she told me that in my life in Rome it had made her happy if I dressed up in her jewels. When she told me that quite often she made me presents of her jewellery I asked her to stop while I described to her three examples which had just been flashed on the screen of consciousness. One was a circle of silver with a St. Andrew's cross inside it. The cross was picked out in deep-blue stones. Betty told me I was right and that the stones were in fact sapphires. Because in recent weeks the St. Andrew's cross had appeared to me so often I asked Betty if she had given me this present for any particular reason. She answered no and said that she had given it to me simply because I liked it. She said I remembered it in the present because of the love there had been between us.

Another gift I remembered was a swastika on a silver chain. Betty reminded me that the swastika was only three-legged. I did not remember this detail myself. When she spoke of this particular object I recalled the Triskele stone with the three-legged swastika in the church at Isel. So far as I know nobody has explained the design on this stone or accurately pin-pointed its date.

I remembered also the present brought to Camillia from Alexandria by Graham. In his Roman incarnation he had been a distinguished lawyer and had shared her philosophic interests.

353

While in Alexandria he had studied at some school which carried on the teachings of the Therapeutics who had, centuries previously, practised a system of truly psychosomatic medicine. In our age this latter term is misapplied and used loosely to express the influence of emotional conflicts in general on physical or seemingly physical symptoms. The true interpretation of psychosomatic implies the direct influence of the soul in inducing physical diseases. Graham had been particularly anxious to obtain this jewel for Camillia because her health was indifferent. She had suffered from no recognisable condition but was easily tired and often rested in the afternoons. This was not a polite manifestation of neurosis exhibited by a member of the Roman upper classes. It was merely that she was a perceptive type and emanated beyond her capacity.

I saw the stone quite clearly in all its details when Betty was talking to me. It was an equal-armed silver cross with deep-blue sapphires set in each arm. Once again it was suspended on a chain. I do not know why but Camillia never gave me anything but pendants except for the thin silver bracelet. This was obligatory as an insignia of my status as a slave. I have no recollection of having received a ring or any other variety of jewellery from her and Betty herself confirms that this was so.

Graham had hoped that the equal-armed cross with the sapphires would help to abolish Camillia's fatigue. In my many interviews with the revenants, but especially in those in which I talked to Guilhabert de Castres, Graham and Braïda, it was clear that they believed in the healing power of jewels. They saw the light in them or reflected by them as a substitute for the natural radiations and colours of the earth. For those susceptible to their vibrations they acted as storage batteries for the beneficent rays of the cosmos. For example amber in autumn was cheering to melancholics. It restored to them the richer radiations of the midsummer sun.

Graham took endless pains to secure the right ornament for Camillia. I regret that its effect was negligible.

Chapter Thirty Seven

In all the revelations I have received during the last two or three years there have been several continuous but intertwining themes presenting themselves at the same time. It has sometimes been a sore problem to record experiences in which three or four related but clearly demarcated subjects have been discussed at a single interview with the revenants. My progress from ignorance to perhaps a little knowledge resembles the growth of a thick-set hedge in which the twisting strands of bryony, convolvulus and traveller's joy are inseparable from each other. There came a time when the theme of the cult of Mithras predominated. My informants were chiefly Betty and Braïda. This is very important because it has been so frequently urged against the cult of Mithras that it was an exclusively male religion.

All those who came back from the dead told us that in our Roman incarnation they had belonged to or been involved with the cult of Mithras. The latter was well established in the Roman Empire and perhaps particularly in the days of its decline. It was Dualist in that it believed that there were two active principal forces of good and evil in the universe and that the battle between them in the heart of man was a reflection on a small scale of the struggle between light and darkness in the cosmos. Reincarnation was also one of its basic tenets. It is said that in the last years of the Empire the cult was strong in the army among officers and men who lived austerely and ethically, possibly with the hope that in so doing they would help to arrest the final decline.

The cult of Mithras has been criticised because of the allegations that it was exclusively male and indulged in animal sacrifices. What I learnt from Braïda, Betty and the others refuted these firmly held convictions. Describing her life as Camillia Betty said that the idea that women played a minor rôle, or none at all, in the cult was nonsense. She herself was a devotee and her house was a secret rallying place for believers. The years I spent in her service coincided with the rapidly increasing expansion of Christianity and its political influence. At the time of which I am speaking the cult of Mithras was regarded with great venom by the Christians. Mithras was born at midnight on December 24/25th. It was therefore assumed that the practitioners of the cult had stolen Christ's birthday. The fact that Mithras had been born centuries earlier was seemingly irrelevant. The Christians accused the followers of Mithras of having also appropriated the Eucharist. The simple meal of bread and wine had been common in the cult before the birth of Christ. Christianity was in my life-time the official religion of the Roman Empire. The Christians were therefore able to hurl these charges with palpitating irrelevance. At first the secular authorities took no action and the Christians had to be satisfied with a few private beatings up, an insufficient diet for such a band of fanatics. The Roman authorities were not actively interested in the numerous religions practised in Rome unless they could be proved to be subversive. Under the influence of the Christians this tradition of tolerance was rapidly eroded.

Betty told me that the erroneous idea that Mithraism was for men only arose from the fact that for the most part men and women worshipped separately. Six carefully chosen representatives of each sex met twice a year, on March 21st and September 21st, for special services. This association with the equinox characterises many forms of Dualism. In the Celtic Church before its Romanisation the same spring and autumn rituals were observed. In the last months of 1973, when we were hearing much of the cult of Mithras, Mr. Mills, attired as Bertrand Marty, recalled how in his Celtic incarnation he and I had regularly visited together the summit of Skiddaw at dawn on the above-mentioned dates, and that we had stayed there until the sun had descended into the Solway. This preoccupation with certain dates in the calendar has always been a feature of Dualism and is manifested to this day.

I never believed that, at any rate in its later days, the cult had practised the sacrifice of animals. I accepted that the slaying of the bull, regarded as the centrepiece of Mithraic ritual, was an

356

allegory for the control of the brutish aggression insecurely locked within our personality. It was fascinating to hear Braïda's version of the animal sacrifices. She herself had served in the Roman army and had achieved minor commissioned rank. She had been married with two children and had been stationed for a period of years at Autun. It is extraordinary how, in my ramblings on holiday, I have so regularly visited and stayed in places which, though I did not know it at the time, were familiar to me or to other members of the group in previous incarnations. I remember with great affection my night and day in Autun. It is unnecessary to say that the Roman remains meant more to me than anything else in the town.

Braïda told me that in her day there were no animal sacrifices except of cocks which were sometimes decapitated. The fact that the bird continued to walk after it had lost its head was taken to represent the separate directive energy of the psyche. I talked also with Braïda of the Emperor Julian the Apostate. He was favourable to the cult of Mithras and also addicted to the examination of animal entrails. The latter occupation has always been explained as evidence of Julian's desire to see into the future. This was apparently a misinterpretation of his intentions. He was searching for the point at which the soul entered the body. Braïda commented that the Emperor had sound ideas but as far as their verification was concerned he "often went about it in the wrong way". If her description of Julian's preoccupation seems far-fetched I can only record that as a medical student our textbooks still stated that the pineal gland was a vestigial organ of no importance—a view almost certainly wrong—and that it had been regarded by the ancients as the point at which the soul entered the body.

Through Betty, Graham and Braïda I learnt a great deal about the cult of Mithras in our Roman incarnation. I had always understood that the Mithraic manuscripts had been very completely destroyed during the persecution. I wondered whether any unmistakably Mithraic teachings were still to be found. Annette rang from Canada to say that Braïda had visited her the evening previously and had passed on the word "veda". I wondered if this meant that there were analogies to Mithraic teaching in certain Hindu scriptures but I leave this to the scholars to

357

comment on. What was more positive was that, stimulated by Graham's presence, I saw the celebration of a Mithraic Communion. This involved the communicants sitting on long low benches before a still lower table. A flat slab of bread, a jug of wine and a wash-jug were on the table. This simple Communion was celebrated twice a year at the times of the equinox. The first celebration was designed to thank God for the coming of the light and sun, and the second to prepare for the advent of winter. Graham was as emphatic as Betty in saying that both sexes attended these celebrations.

Graham visited Camillia's house constantly. His name was Cornelius. He was a distinguished lawyer and a devotee of Mithras. He was emphatically not one of her lovers though he admired her greatly. Another visitor was a young man called Claudius. As soon as Betty had described him I was able to put a name to him. Months previously Annette had told me that her name in her Roman incarnation was Claudia. She had no knowledge of Latin and did not realise that Claudia was a girl's name and Claudius its masculine equivalent.

Betty described Claudius as a rich, well-read young man who was especially interested in herbs and rare plants. He had a garden in which he grew all manner of choice specimens. He never practised medicine, it seems he had no need to work at anything, but he distributed to his friends potions of his own concoction. There is no evidence that any of his circle came to any harm from his ministrations. Equally there is nothing to tell us that they did much good. His special interest in healing herbs is significant because, when she next returned to this world in her Celtic incarnation, Annette blossomed out into a competent healer of independent views.

Betty, with Braïda and Graham present, reminded me of something I had forgotten and which I recalled again when they raised the question. As a young man Claudius fell madly in love with me. Perhaps he was captivated by my ringlets which were not the fashion but something of my own concoction. I was a few years older than he was. I did not respond to him at all. I was not even flattered that he should pay his attentions to a slave. His intentions were sincere enough. There was no question of his desiring to seduce and enjoy a pretty girl. I regarded the whole affair as ludicrous and treated him with as much disdain as I could risk. He was so broken-hearted that he did not resume for years his visits to Camillia's house because he could not bear to be reminded of his abortive passion. My attitude towards him was completely unfeeling and I regarded him as a bizarre and even comical figure. If I believed in Karma I would say that the desolation I felt when Annette went to Canada restored the balance of my ancient contempt. Perhaps when she left for the New World without seeing me I relived a little what she as Claudius had endured in the Roman incarnation.

A few weeks after I had learnt from Betty and the others of the existence of the boy Claudius in the Roman incarnation Annette provided me with further details of his life at that epoch. Her memories were quite independent of those recalled by Betty, myself and the others because I had not told her about them. Annette's description of herself fitted in well enough with the attitude I exhibited towards her during my life as Berenice. Speaking of herself she was brief and derisive. She said, "I was a frightful pansy. I spent a fortune dressing myself up and trying to make myself look beautiful. I had very fancy sandals which fastened with a kind of thong affair wound round the ankles. I did not do anything much except drench myself with perfume."*

I had hoped that Annette, because of her interest in plants, might remember a red rose that Betty recalled as growing in her garden. This had sounded to me like Rosa Gallica, which later came to be called the Apothecary's rose and which was used in medicine. Unfortunately Annette could not provide me with any useful description.

Claudius, who was rich and belonged to a privileged class in a leisured civilisation, had another alibi for his unproductive existence. Most of his life he suffered from attacks of acute abdominal pain accompanied by vomiting. These were attributed to all

---

* Clare recalled that as a small child in this life Annette had retained her love of perfumes. On one occasion, when aged no more than seven or eight, she bought surreptitiously several phials of cheap perfume and sprinkled Clare and her mother with them to such a degree that when they got into the car to drive home the atmosphere was insupportable.

kinds of infections and humours. The treatment applied was never efficacious. They were usually of a few days' duration but got worse as he grew older.

In the last quarter of 1973 and through the following year Clare was subject to attacks in which her face became engorged and her eyes at first distant and then ultimately fixed. In some of these attacks she lost completely what we commonly call consciousness and passed into a state of amended awareness in which she whimpered and moaned while she was reliving tragedies which had happened and horrors which had been inflicted on her in previous incarnations. Where she was completely reliving old sorrows and reflecting their pains in her body the loss of ordinary consciousness was complete, but on other occasions she merely slipped out, without too much pain, into her old surroundings in previous incarnations and was not entirely unconscious. In one of these latter episodes she saw the setting of a Mithraic celebration and the objects used in its performance. She spoke of an urn of similar shape to a flower vase in my possession. The urn had two lateral handles. There was an intertwined cable pattern flung from the top of the handle on one side to the bottom of the handle on the other. The intertwined pattern was similar to that I have described in our Celtic and Cathar incarnations. There was a pattern of vine leaves stuck at right angles on the handles rather like ears on a skull. The urn was a greyish-green olive colour.

One room in the house in Rome was set apart for the Mithraic celebrations but was only equipped for these on rare occasions in order to avoid attracting the attention of the authorities. The walls were of greenish marble. The table and its supporting pedestal at one end of the room were of the same material. On ceremonial occasions a small statue rested on the table. It rested on a square plinth with two triangles above. The latter met at their apices producing an effect like an hour-glass. Inside this structure was a figure of a young man with two rays emanating from the sides of his head.

On the right of this stood the urn already described. On the left side was a circle with a central nucleus and rays issuing from it, the whole producing the effect of something like a daisy. It was almost identical with what Clare and I had seen at Torpen-
360

how in 1973 when Graham had told us to look out for the Mithric stone. (See below.)

Behind the statue was a white niche on a wall. It contained the figure of a girl holding her hands behind her head, with her elbows partly bent and clasping a diamond-shaped amethyst in her fingers.

All the above-mentioned articles were only used during meetings. The room was only made ready a short time before the celebrations were due to start and the objects described above were cleared away as soon as possible. The figure of the girl was removed from the niche which was filled with a vase of flowers. On both sides of the room were long, low benches below which were similar but much lower ones no more than a foot from the ground. These last were for people to kneel on.

Clare made great play of a golden spoon which was used in the course of the ceremony. It was dipped in the urn which contained some form of potion and put on the forehead of each of the worshippers. The action had a double function. It was part of the ritual and also held to have a curative effect.

Clare remembers also a manuscript with a dark-purple cover. After she mentioned it I recalled that it had on this cover a golden circle enclosing a sunray pattern in the same colour. The name of the book was something like "meda". It was certainly not "veda", the name picked up by Annette from Braïda when the latter was discussing lost Mithraic manuscripts.

Once when I was looking back with Clare to the room in Rome I saw the sea from an outer staircase on the left side of the house, but Clare insisted that this was not Rome but the house in Ostia which belonged to Betty and where also there was a room set aside for the cult of Mithras. In the room at Ostia there was an urn and a circle as in Rome but no statue with the male figure.

361

Both in Rome and Ostia our houses were liberally supplied with the household gods then in favour in the Empire. This was a precaution to hide the fact that Camillia was an adherent of Mithras. Her husband did not share her views but supported her in this, as in all things, because of his love of her and his feeling that everything she did was right. He was one of those colourless, admirable people who tend to be overlooked in more striking company. He connived with Camillia in hiding at Ostia people in trouble with the Roman authorities and hoping to escape to Gaul. In those days ships sailed from Ostia in this direction. Some of these clandestine supporters of Mithras came from as far as Greece and the Levant and saw Camillia surreptitiously. Clare and I remember particularly one blond man with a fair skin, pointed face, particularly pointed chin, small, triangular beard and clear blue eyes. He stands out because, though he came from the East, he was far from Levantine in appearance.

All these years were a time of great happiness. Except for my first possessive agonies when I learnt about Camillia's bedfellows I knew no greater pains than those inseparable from the frictions of a congested household. It is hard but typical and inevitable that one should have a fuller memory of the fears and miseries of the bad years. Our period of agony was much shorter than the long springtime which enveloped us before we attracted the attention of the Christians.

Chapter Thirty Eight

One day when I was sitting with Clare I saw on the wall opposite a simple diamond-shaped pattern which could have been found in a bathroom fifty years ago. I knew by now that this was a Roman mosaic. A little later Graham appeared and we talked of such absorbing and soothing subjects as the creation of plants and of how each has a kind of soul. Suddenly Clare went off into what looked like a standing sleep. She shuddered and twitched and did not answer my questions. I was disturbed by this terrifying mutism. I knew from past experience that she was reliving some shattering experience. Her features were sharpened and her face seemed shrunken. I did not realise that her expression of agony, her silence and the twitching she manifested as though she were flinching reflexly from a shower of blows were an accurate reproduction of what she was reliving.

When Clare came to and was able to talk two other phenomena occurred. Firstly, I myself was able to supply a good deal of what she had suffered because I had been stimulated to recall by sharing her agonies. Secondly, at this stage Betty came into the picture. She was dressed in her Celtic dark purple. Her hair, which reached to her shoulders, was puffed out under her small crinkled cap. I could not understand why I should see her dressed in the clothes of her Celtic incarnation when I had already seen the Roman mosaic and when I presumed we were dealing with our lives in the latter period.

When Clare recovered consciousness she described how she relived being beaten by an unofficial investigating body consisting of a rabble of Christians inflamed by a fanatical priest. The latter resembled the other ecclesiastic who in the Celtic incarnation had been responsible for Clare being attacked by the mob at Loweswater and for Betty being lynched beside the shores of Bassenthwaite. This second priest was another dark-haired, pale fellow but had fuller features than his Celtic counterpart and looked less schizophrenic. These Christian guardians of the public conscience were already satisfied that Camillia's house was a centre for the cult of Mithras. Their immediate aim was twofold, to obtain the names of as many adherents as possible and to find out what happened in the course of the ceremonies. They had a nose for dirt and black magic. To them the secret or semi-secret must necessarily be orgiastic. Black magic meant anything outside the occultism of the Christian sacrament. Above all they wished to find out if the cult of Mithras had any political aspirations and could possibly be described as subversive.

Clare was beaten systematically and with relish. She remained obstinately silent. Her persecutors learnt no names of the adherents and no details of the ceremony. Had she wished she could have supplied the desired information because she herself had attended the meetings. She had more brains and was more perceptive than I was and was capable of a positive interest in the proceedings. She was intensely grateful to Camillia that she, a slave, had been allowed to share in the ceremonies. The idea of my doing so never came into the picture. Much as I loved Camillia I was not prepared to be bored by attending meetings or philosophical discussions. That was for others. I had no need to compete with them. In a way I had her to myself.

Clare's staring silence on an autumn evening in Somerset in 1973 symbolised admirably the mute stoicism she had shown sixteen centuries before. When in her Roman incarnation she had recovered consciousness she managed to crawl from the room into which she had been dragged and beaten. She collapsed after rising to her feet and making a few paces in the fresh air. I found her lying in the road and managed somehow, half supporting, half dragging her, to get her to Graham. I cannot remember the details of the journey. What stands out clearly is that under no circumstances would I take her back to Camillia. It is typical of me that my main interest was to divert all suspicion from my mistress.

Graham kept her in his house until she was fit to return to Camillia. I do not know how long she stayed with him but it was for both of them the beginning of a devotion which was to last the best part of two millennia. On this particular evening on which, in Bath, she recalled her sufferings, she admitted that

364

with time she became fond of him. I felt there was more to it than this. What is certain is that since those days in Rome he has always shown her affection and protected her in all her incarnations. He helped to care for her when she was knocked about by the mob at Loweswater in her Celtic incarnation. In his Cathar incarnation he had been very fond of her even though he was married to Arsendis, now reappeared as Kathleen. He looked after her when she was in solitary confinement at Portchester. In this life he was fond of her and looked after her for twenty years and was careful in his last years to spend in her company those days on which she had suffered particularly in her Napoleonic incarnation.

Graham told us that Clare was beaten up in an underground room not in Rome itself but in Ostia which in those days was on the coast-line and an important port. Both Camillia and Graham had houses in Ostia as well as Rome. In the early 1960s Clare had a holiday in Italy in the course of which she visited Ostia. While wandering through an excavated site she saw an opening leading to an underground chamber. She was interested and went inside. She was overcome by a feeling of indescribable anguish and promptly vomited. I have no doubt that she had every reason to do so and that she was recalling on that occasion the agony she had suffered in this room. There is a world of difference between the accurately recording human seismograph and the suggestible hysteric.

I asked Betty why she had appeared dressed as a Celtic priestess when it would have been more fitting had she worn a Roman dress. She replied that she had dressed in this way to identify herself with Clare in her sufferings and to remind her that she, too, had suffered at the hands of a mob.

The day after Clare's recall of her so-called interrogation in the underground room at Ostia I had an agitated phone call from Annette in Canada. In a vision she had herself been an eye-witness of the proceedings. She said that she had also been visited by her mother and that Braïda had predicted that there was another ordeal which Clare would have to endure alone. When I next saw Clare and asked about her latest experience she said tersely that what she had suffered the previous night was worse than the re-enactment of the first interrogation which had

365

occurred in my presence. She had suffered at the hands of the same mob. Once again after she lost consciousness she was dragged into the road and once again I found her and took her to Graham's to divert suspicion from my mistress. Graham was an eminent and much respected lawyer and was certainly at this time regarded as above suspicion by the authorities.

We had other troubles with the rampaging Christians but none of the magnitude of the two episodes I have described. From now on the nature and tempo of our life were radically changed and we lived in a world of impending shadows. The Christian priest informed the secular authorities of his suspicions. Later we were to suffer from more rigorous, better-organised and more intelligent investigators. Nevertheless in spite of the menace which hung over us I cannot say that we were continuously unhappy or chronically tense. Certainly it was a bad time, with peaks of unmitigated horror, but somehow we retained still our capacity to drop our troubles and enjoy the immediate consolations of life. I think many liberal and revered historians are laughable in that they put themselves into the shoes of those who have lived centuries earlier and imagine that the reactions of their antecedents were identical with those felt by the comfortable intelligentsia of the present day. We were simply not made like that. I came from a hovel. I have no idea of Cressi's background but I think it was less humble. I think what was always at the back of our minds was that we were slaves who had landed for ourselves good berths, with generous and even loving employers, and if we were beaten up once or twice or suffered great pain this was to be weighed against the fact that we had done far better for ourselves than we could ever have imagined when we left the background of our humble homes. I think also that our attitude to our employers was simple and unqualified. We knew we had to serve but it was a luxurious addition to our life to know that our services were appreciated. We had not picked up the jargon of enlightenment and were in no sense intellectual but I think in our basic biological intelligence we were above the modern average.

Betty on a later visit spoke of the two priests who had been our persecutors in the Roman and Celtic incarnations. She said that in all our previous lives we had been tracked by a particular bloodhound who made it his business to cause trouble for us. In the Cathar incarnation it was Pierre de Mazerolles. In the Napoleonic incarnation there was also, according to Betty and Graham, a malevolent and dedicated Legitimist who did his best to inhibit the influence of my lectures and pamphlets and to paint a picture of me as dangerously subversive. Betty refused to say whether there was a specific person in this life. She emphasised that a considerable hostile force of evil was directed against us and had caused many missed rendezvous due to illness, accidents and other causes.

In the last months of 1973 it was clearer to me than ever that for years the thunder and alarms of my early incarnations had been rumbling below the surface of consciousness. Three years previously I actually wrote a story in which a girl belonged to a Mithraic cult and was martyred by a Christian mob inflamed by a priest corresponding identically to the black-avised, triangular-faced creature who had incited the mob to dispose of Betty at Bassenthwaite. One can say that in this shadow-land of half-memory I confused the incarnations a little because in my book the girl was killed in her Roman incarnation. Against this one can say that the scene of my story oscillated between Cumberland and Rome, that is to say in the two regions involved in our Celtic and Roman incarnations. In this story I insisted against the evidence that women belonged to the cult of Mithras. These premonitions of truth were proved later in the information I received from Betty, Graham and others.

Chapter Thirty Nine

For weeks I had noticed that my time sense was dislocated. This was not disorientation as it is understood by the psychiatrist. I had still what one might call a historical memory. The question of dates concerning myself or others I could have answered with my usual precision. What I had lost was my capacity to estimate duration. I could remember incidents in minute detail but I could not estimate how long it was since they happened. It was not a matter of being years out in my estimation. Where I was dealing with the revenants I did not know whether incidents I was recalling had occurred three weeks or three months previously.

Clare herself was equally affected. This was a small burden compared with the agonies of clairvoyance and wondering, when she apprehended disaster, on which of her friends the blow would fall. Nevertheless she was troubled by this blurring of the edges of chronology. Her father impressed on her the need to live from minute to minute. This was all the more difficult in a person with the capacity to see into the future. Mr. Mills found it necessary to reinforce his exhortations by a couple of practical demonstrations.

I had met Clare while she was driving through the park. She stopped and talked to me without getting out of the car. I felt the conversation was over and was preparing to depart when she began to fiddle with something on her lap. She gave no explanation of her activities and I was finally reduced to asking. She said that her watch had just disintegrated. I assumed that she meant the glass had fallen out. This had indeed happened but, in addition, the back of the watch had parted from its hinges. The dial was detached and the works exposed. The watch had not fallen nor had she banged it against anything. Quickly, undramatically, it had come apart. I did not think a great deal about this incident because in recent months I had experienced far more dramatic happenings than a mechanical instrument falling to pieces.

On the following night Clare was in her bedroom looking in the direction of the bedside table. Her clock "suddenly leapt from the table and hurled itself on the floor". Then Mr. Mills materialised. He said that what she had just seen, and the piecemeal separation of her watch the day previously, had been arranged to demonstrate the non-reality of time. He knew that she realised this already but believed she was in need of a sign of some sort of recognition that at that particular moment time was dislocated for her. He said that she and I were now moving on a plane where time did not exist. Even in this world our psyches were essentially functioning in another. We were still handicapped and impeded by the rags of our old concept of chronological time which limited the freedom of our thoughts and perceptions. He said that the purpose of the assault on Clare's watch and clock was to prepare us for another revelation.

After my meeting in the park with Clare I returned home to tea and then went to lie down. I did so not because I felt unwell but because, since my cardiac catastrophe, my doctors had told me to retire from the battle when I felt exhausted. I was not nursing myself unduly or anticipating the onset of any illness. Quite suddenly I began to feel excessively cold. It was not that I was chilled from without. The day was not excessively cold and my room was warm. There was ice in my bones. I felt literally chilled to the marrow. I heaped blankets on the bed but nothing would warm me. I was reminded of my father in one of his attacks of malaria. The attempts to thaw myself having failed I resigned myself to waiting for the appearance of the first symptom. It seemed obvious to me that I was booked for at least a sharp attack of flu and perhaps something worse. I had never felt so cold before an attack of influenza.

I had a telephone call from Clare. She said she had been speaking to her father and that he would be visiting me. I was aware immediately of his presence in the room. His outline was not clear but I knew exactly where he was standing. Today, he said, was the anniversary of an unprecedented snowfall in Rome. It was on that day that the first official investigator representing the secular authority appeared at Camillia's house. The authorities

369

had been pestered by the Christians who insisted that it was a meeting place for the adherents of Mithras whom they were careful to describe as politically subversive.

The officer who came to interview Camillia was not over-zealous and not particularly enamoured of his Christian inform-ants. She denied all knowledge of the cult and that her house was used for meetings. Her visitor was on the point of leaving, per-fectly satisfied with her answers. At this moment Clare and I returned from a walk which had been prolonged because Clare had never seen snow like this before. She came from the south and for her snow was something scattered thinly on the tops of remote mountains and not something thickly deposited in the streets.

The sight of the footprints made by the visitor in approaching the house made an eerie impression on Clare because it was such an unusual experience for her. Seeing that she, a much calmer and more courageous person than I, was obviously afraid, I lost my head and in a second was in the grip of country superstitions and obsessions which were, in me, never far from the surface of consciousness. It seemed to us both that these clean-cut footsteps leading to the house must be of ill-omen. At this moment Camillia appeared in the porch with her visitor. Clare and I behaved fatuously. With the investigator still present we clus-tered round Camillia chattering excitedly like rooks, bombarding her with questions and asking what the visitor was here for. Our conduct cannot have failed to arouse his suspicions.

Our conduct after his departure may seem even more incom-prehensible. Clare and I set out to obliterate his footsteps. I feel sure that in this I was the main instigator but we both had the primitive idea that if we erased all marks of his visit it would be as if he had never been. Psychiatrists and others will recognise this as a mixture of obsessionalism and primitive magic. We stayed for hours at our task and were chilled to the bone with cold and fear.

Back in my room in Somerset I felt relieved and had no further fear that I was booked for a serious illness. I still felt that there was ice in my spine but I was able to help entertain visitors with-out feeling that I was addressing them from within a glacier which had converged in me in all directions.

370

The investigator who visited Camillia must have been a frigidly bureaucratic type. He must have made an entry in his books to the effect that he would reopen the matter after a fixed period of time expressed in round numbers. It was analogous to a doctor seeing a patient for a check-up in so many months' time. Exactly a year after we had cleared the snow we submitted to our first interrogation by the secular authorities.

One morning I woke up in Bathford with the near and distant objects in the room all blurred. The scene outside the window was a palpitating cobweb. I wondered if there was a defect in fusion and a lack of balance between the two eyes. I closed each eye in turn but the results were no better. All I saw was something like a fall of sleet and behind it the dim outline of familiar objects. I could not help meditating such lugubrious possibilities as detached retina or retinal haemorrhage. My fears were allayed when I heard from Clare that she had woken up in the middle of the night in a state of panic. She thought she was going blind. She sleeps with her curtains open. All she could see, looking across the opacity of the room, was that the window was a slightly less dark rectangle. She switched on the light and the result was little better. When she started her day's work she admitted that she could not recognise the faces of people familiar to her until they were within three or four yards. I was well aware that I had picked up her symptoms or she mine. By this time we had had in the group innumerable examples of people acquiring each other's symptoms.

When we met later that day she laid her hand on my eyes. I felt the burning and tingling in her palms and knew that there was a recognisable lesion in my eyes otherwise the healing process would not have been initiated. This healing reaction is not provided for hysterics. She had no sooner laid her hands upon me than Graham appeared. He said that last night was the anniversary of the occasion on which she and I had been interrogated for the first time by the secular authorities. The priest and his confrères had nagged them with rabid persistence, in addition to which their suspicions had been aroused by the way Clare and I had behaved that day when the snow lay thick on the ground. In the time of which I am speaking the influence of Christianity was becoming paramount in Rome. Permeated by Christian

371

theology the Roman authoritarian tendency showed its vicious aspects. Under secular domination people had more or less worshipped as they pleased provided they did not make a public nuisance of themselves in frenzied demonstrations and provided their intentions were not subversive. With the increasing Christianisation of Rome every belief other than a carefully doctored and commentated version of Christ's teaching was regarded as dangerous. We did not know that we were seeing the beginning of Christianity as an international theocracy, as foreseen by the Emperor Julian. All we could know, as illiterate slave girls, was that these matters were beyond our comprehension and that we had to protect our mistress.

Up to now I had escaped the unorganised attack by the rabble. This time Clare and I suffered together. Once again the aim of the investigation was to find out whether our mistress was an adherent of Mithras and whether the house was used for meetings. We were beaten with whips which were even laid across our faces. I came off worse than Clare. I was so badly beaten about the face that my eyes were closed. This was not merely a question of swelling of the eyelids and adjacent tissues. On one occasion I received the whip full in the eye. It was a blessing that I had, as a natural reflex, screwed up my eyelids as the whip descended. I do not know how it came about that Graham was present when we were being interrogated. It is possible that he himself was under suspicion and that the authorities were interested to know how he reacted. Or it may have been that he was allowed to represent Camillia on this occasion since two of her servants were being interrogated. Certainly at no time were he and she subjected to personal violence. The interrogators extracted no information from us.

Sitting in my room in Somerset I did not need Betty and Graham to tell me that the eye condition from which Clare and I had suffered had its origin in our Roman incarnation. I now learnt from the revenants that these anniversary phenomena, so noticeable in the Celtic and Napoleonic incarnations, were being intensified, and that I would feel more deeply the pains and diseases from which I had suffered in past lives. It was a part of the pattern woven not into this world only but into the huge, cosmic quilt thrown over the sun, the stars and the universe itself. There was nothing we or the revenants could do to prevent it. What was in their power was to give us an understanding of the origin of our worst bouts of anguish and to help to minimise its effects by applying their own forms of healing.

This not altogether satisfying consolation was reinforced by Braïda. I was in the Botanical Gardens on a still day with the sky low and the birds silent. There was no sound but the singing of the brook beneath the overhanging branches. I was walking with half a dozen others past the thicket of fine-leaved bamboos towards the pond and the temple. I was suddenly aware of an overpowering odour of balsam poplar though it was late in the year and long past the time when the tree is perfumed. I knew that this was the smell by which Braïda announced herself to Clare. I had smelt it myself when in the latter's company. I now knew that Braïda would announce her presence directly to me when I was surrounded by people and inhibited by the pressure of personalities.

Later that day Betty appeared to me out of doors. It was late afternoon and the pearly haze which had lasted all day had sharpened to silver at twilight. At the same moment as I felt Betty's presence I visualised clearly an amber necklace. She told me that she had given me the necklace to cheer me up after I had been returned to the house after interrogation. She told me that my face was not permanently disfigured by the treatment I received but that it had remained battered and bruised for weeks. She herself had never been submitted to any great pressure. She had simply denied all knowledge of the cult. I can well imagine her confronting her questioners with her compelling candid eyes and her head set very still on her relaxed shoulders. The authorities were not yet prepared to extend the persecution to the upper classes.

Chapter Forty

One day, when Clare and I were speaking to Betty, I asked her how much, in this life, after she recalled me as I had been in the thirteenth century, she had wished to establish contact. She had longed to talk to me or meet me but was too diffident to make more than one veiled and tentative approach. She read a passage from Plato which she found so beautiful that she felt she must telephone Clare about it. Plato had said that the soul must be the most important component of being because it was always in movement. Clare range me immediately she had heard from Betty. That day I had been writing a review of a truly enormous book in which this particular quotation of Plato was buried like a nugget of fine gold. Before Clare told me what Betty had said I knew the passage to which she was referring, a matter of two or three sentences in a tome of over eight hundred pages.

Betty said, "That passage from Plato started something in me in the last weeks of my life. I was getting ready for what I had to do. Now I spend much of my time with your friend Simon."

I recalled the day on which I heard of Simon's death. In *We Are One Another* I have told how Betty, who had never heard of him in this life, returned from the grave to tell her mother that Dr. Guirdham's best friend was dead. That was before I had heard from his family of his death in Paris. I reminded Betty of this. "On the day Simon died and also the day after, I felt my body to be burning."

"That was because Simon was burnt at the stake in the thirteenth century."

"What was his name?" I asked.

"Jean de Cambiaire."

Even though I had become innured to staggering revelations I felt a shock of surprise. Jean de Cambiaire was one of the first names I had seen among the written messages which engulfed Clare in 1971. For a long time she, for no reason known to me, had suggested that this Cathar Parfait had been my friend Simon in this life. I had thought little of this suggestion because I was preoccupied with the need for confirmatory evidence and because I was slow to realise that many of our deepest friendships in this life are determined by acquaintanceship in earlier lives.

The records of the Inquisition tell us that Jean de Cambiaire, a Cathar Parfait, was burnt as a heretic in 1235.

"Are you close to Simon now?" I asked.

"We are studying together."

"Did you know him other than as a Cathar?"

She did not answer.

I remembered how Simon and his wife had stayed with us a quarter of a century ago. Like all our meetings it was written in light. It was as though the world had ceased to rotate and time was a wind which passed outside the window. There was the day we sat in the inn, remote from the down, looking through the fugitive, imploring trees to the valley sleeping in the haze of autumn. It was during that visit that I asked him to see a patient. When he listened to her he seemed to withdraw into his own gentleness. He spoke little English. It was not what he said but what he heard that mattered. Her own words, stumbling, ill-ordered, wakened richer echoes in his own heart so that he quietened her by his own unspoken pity. It had always been a pain to me that he, the complete and perfect physician, should have inexplicably decided to become a pathologist. "Why did he change?" I said to Betty.

"Ask him yourself." In the quietness drawn from her own silence and deepening with it I was aware that someone else had entered. I could not see his outlines. Once again it was a question of knowing he was there and exactly where he stood. It is no good indulging in florid prose about my first re-encounter with Simon. It would be a distortion of the truth to say that I felt transported and out of this world. How could I feel myself moving into another dimension when I had already crossed the frontier between this world and the next? I can only say that I was living more calmly in a state of immensely enhanced perception.

I spoke to him in the same way as I did to Braïda and Betty. Words and thoughts were formed together and for me the exchange was silent though Clare heard their voices as though

375

they had been living. Simon asked me if I remembered a conversation in a restauarant near a station on one of our last meetings. I remembered it well. We had eaten in an Alsation restaurant near the Gare de l'Est. I recalled that he had told me then that he had left clinical practice because he was appalled by the materialism. I had understood at that time that what he meant was the pursuit of money rather than vocation, of the slapdash stupefication of patients with drugs as a punishment for mentioning their symptoms. Now he told me that he meant also the cult of violence which has infiltrated medicine in the form of needless exploratory operations, the removal of organs designated as superfluous by surgeons with wives and children to keep, and the dragging of patients from beds after major operations to minimise the minimal risk of embolism and to ensure that they suffered for months from exhaustion.

I asked Simon if, when he first saw me, he remembered me as I had been in past lives. He said that on our first meeting he had known that I was a Cathar but that he had never spoken of it because he had not wished to condition me. Nevertheless he bought me a book about the Cathars to read on my return journey. He also gave me Giono's book about Provence. He was anticipating my recall of my Napoleonic incarnation.

He wanted especially to know if I remembered a day in a house in a forest because it was the happiest day we spent together. I had no need to remember. There was the walled town looking over the plain to the vineyards and the green, curling avenue between the towns. We left the road on a dwindling path through the darkness of the forest. From a high clearing we looked over the green, dark ocean of undulating forest to the plain, the river and the country beyond it. That was the only time I saw him against his own background. Suddenly, thawed out by the memory of the forest and its timeless whispering, I asked about my wife because at this time she was in pain, exhausted and losing weight. I remembered how, on one occasion for a fraction of a second, he had looked at her with a strange intensity. "Did you," I asked, "ever recognise my wife as she had been in any previous incarnation?"

"On one of our last meetings. I knew she had had a Celtic incarnation."

I thought of how my wife suffered from reacting to Annette's illnesses in Canada.

After Simon left me I reflected on how he had returned to me through Betty. She had restored to me the man who, after Eugene's death, spoke most clearly to me in the language of psychic communication. I felt she was guiding me but not in the direct, pragmatic manner of Braïda. She was carrying a lantern through shadowy country. I wondered where she would lead me.

At this time, as well as picking up the miseries of people hundreds or even thousands of miles distant, I was more troubled by the poor health of my normally outgoing and buoyant wife who had suffered for months from an intestinal spasm which caused her pain and other distressing symptoms, including a well-concealed depression out of line with her normal, optimistic, courageous nature. One evening she and I went to dinner with Clare. Afterwards the latter and my wife retired to another room to look at some dresses. I stayed where I was, absorbed with what I was reading to such a degree that I endured longer than I normally would the strange, humming vibration which increased as I read. The noise, which was rhythmical, sharp and in a way musical, became increasingly high-pitched. My first thought was that it was some form of mechanical aberration and that there was something ominously wrong with the electric supply. I was sufficiently concerned to go into the next room and draw Clare's attention to this by now uncomfortable and demanding noise. She returned to the sitting-room and said at once, "The glasses are vibrating." She opened the door of a cupboard where she kept her glassware. There could be no doubt that the noise issued from this quarter. It was so obviously magnified when she opened the door. Then it ceased suddenly. I had not time to see any vibration in the glasses.

"But what makes them vibrate?" I asked.

"I expect somebody is trying to get in touch with you."

At the cost of appearing naïve I have to admit that at first I did not take her seriously. In view of my experiences during the last three years I should have done so immediately. At such times I have no sensation of inhibiting my perceptions or turning on the batteries of scepticism. It is simply that something slows up

377

inside me and I do not see. "Have you heard these glasses vibrating before?" I asked.

"No."

She closed the cupboard door especially firmly so that there could be no chance of its contributing to any transmitted vibrations. She returned next door to resume with my wife their inspection of the clothes she had bought. I continued my reading. I had not time to recover my concentration before the vibration returned more loudly and imperatively. Now I was perturbed and irritated. I called Clare immediately. She returned to the sitting-room. It was obvious that she did not share my anxiety but it was clear that she was listening intently. She repeated again, "I tell you that somebody must be trying to get in touch with you."

When I opened the cupboard door the clamour was louder than ever and the note more insistent and localised. I could see that one glass in particular was vibrating. It was a new type of rather broad red wine-glass. I could watch the fine tremors which traversed its substance. Clare placed her hand on the glass and the tremor ceased. She went back immediately to the next room. She did not stay with me because what was being uttered was for me alone.

I returned to my book but the effort of concentration was unnecessary. I recognised Simon by an outlined zone of vibration in front and to the right of where I was sitting. He asked if I remembered a day he, my wife and I had spent together in the month after Munich before the old world died. In his presence it was as sharp as pain to recall the wide fields, the clear light, the sharp-etched steeples and the oceanic sky, its blue frosted slightly with the breath of autumn. I had known that autumn that we were living a reprieve. To me the silence of our small hotel was hallowed. It was a backwater in which I felt, in the still air, the long memory of Paris and the lament of its old sorrows. There was nothing like the day going down between the poplars, leaves yellowed with the autumn, spinning down between the trees, to Blois silent and lost in the contemplation of its own history, to Beaugency and the sweep of the river and back through Orleans when the lamps were lit. Now, years later, sitting in a room in Somerset, I could not think of this living and immortal day as in

378

the past. It lived always for me in a state of eternal reverberation, leaves falling, fallen, on the *quais* of Paris, still drifting down in late October, still dead and insistently alive. The sharpness and beauty of what I remembered served as a solvent for time.

How many times in past years had I looked back on that imperishable day? I had never imagined it had meant so much to Simon even though he was made to share the happiness of others. Now he told me that this was a remarkable day in his own life. I listened to him as though these were the first words spoken, as though there was a great silence over the world, because it reflected the stillness in my own heart. He said I must tell my wife how much he had loved that day. He added that she was more depressed than I imagined.

Simon had ideas about my wife's régime. He was of homoeopathic inclination and shared her dislike of heroic medicines. He suggested that I give her a little whisky at night to help her sleep. I took the whisky suggestion all the more seriously because in the last years of his life he had touched no alcohol.

When he had gone I could not return to my book. I was recalling the past so acutely that I was living intensely in the present. If this seems a paradox I cannot help it. The great experiences of life all occur out of time. Blois in 1938 and Somerset in 1974 were all a vibrating instant echoing with maximum intensity in a room with a corner cupboard containing wine-glasses.

My wife and I were preparing to leave when the glass sounded again. This time there was no slow and constantly increasing hum but a perceptible clanging. I got my wife out of the room on some pretext and listened to what Simon had to say. The message was short. "I should put her on an anti-depressant."

My wife's spirits were raised appreciably by Simon's message about our day at Blois. The prescription of whisky at night worked well and immediately. She began to improve after she took a very small dose of an anti-depressant. Then she hung fire a little. Simon returned again at the instigation of Betty. He told me to double the evening dose. It was interesting that he had never used these drugs in his lifetime because he had changed his speciality and ended his days as a pathologist. Following the régime he had suggested was the turning point in my wife's illness.

379

Simon is another example of the fact that all my oldest and deepest friends were of psychic constitution though, when I met them, I had no idea that they were so made because in those days I had no interest in such matters. When I met Simon in 1938 and Eugene in 1940 the idea that I had known them in previous incarnations would have appeared to me fantastic because at this time I was not remotely preoccupied with the subject of reincarnation. It is interesting and significant that both died on April 21st. I had learnt by now that certain days and periods in the year are ominous for members of the group and those attached to them.

I failed totally to see that Simon's intervention through the medium of the wine-glasses was not merely to draw attention to my wife's condition and to clarify my own ideas about it but to announce his own increasing intervention in our story. This began when Clare was receiving dental treatment because four of her front teeth had become increasingly loose in the previous year in spite of the fact that there was no severe tooth or gum condition to account for it. I was at a loss to understand why anybody who made so little fuss about her troubles could be so shattered by the manipulation of her teeth. One evening, after treatment, she had one of her attacks in which her face became engorged and her eyes fixed and distant. She sagged sideways in her chair and dropped her arms with a bang on the table as though she were relinquishing two heavy weights. Then her head fell between her arms and she stayed in this state with her pulse reduced in volume for two or three minutes. When she came to she was dazed for an approximately equal period of time following which she told me what she had seen and relived.

For a week previously she, and I too for that matter, had exhibited symptoms involving weakness, particularly of the legs, general malaise and low fever with a feeling of heat punctuated by bouts of shivering. The revenants had told us that at this date in the Roman incarnation there had been some sort of epidemic. I am sure that in my case the infection was grafted on a substratum of malaria to which I was addicted and which was still rife in the flat country not far from Rome. Whatever the diagnosis the secular authorities thought it a God-given opportunity to interrogate us once again on the old theme as to whether

380

Camillia's house was a centre for the cult of Mithras and if so, who were involved. Clare recalled that she and I were both interrogated at the same time. Neither of us admitted anything. My denial was less heroic than hers because I had neither knowledge of, nor interest in, Dualism, though I could have given the names of some of the more constant visitors to Camillia's house. Clare, who had attended the meetings, was a different case. It may be that the interrogators realised that her knowledge of these matters was more intimate than mine. In any case she fared worse that I did.

While she was telling me of her experiences Braïda, Graham and Mr. Mills appeared and later, to my astonishment, Simon. It was reasonable enough that he should have announced himself by shaking the wine-glasses when my wife was in the vicinity because he had been very attached to us both. I could not imagine that he had any specific interest in the present proceedings and could only assume that he was more incorporated in the group than I had previously imagined and might become later a regular though possibly infrequent visitor.

The interrogation described by Clare was semi-private. There was nothing really formal about it. She was hurled on the floor and her four front teeth were loosened. Those supervising the proceedings were obtaining information to be reported later to more formal and dignified authorities.

Braïda and Graham told us that that particular day, on which Clare had paid a visit to the dentist, was the anniversary of the day on which she had been knocked about in Rome. What was fascinating was that the recent and seemingly unaccountable loosening of her teeth which she had experienced in this life had taken place over the last few months. In other words it coincided exactly with the reliving of her Roman experiences over the past year.

Now, in her room in Somerset, she remembered that Camillia brought a doctor to her after she was returned from the interrogation. He was dressed in a russet-coloured robe with a golden girdle suspended from the centre of which was a medallion. The latter was decorated with a design of the sun with numerous rays issuing from it and also a simple flower and leaf design similar to what she had seen on the cross at W—— in Cumberland and which had also been affected by the members of the group serving in the French Navy and living as prisoners at Portchester during the Napoleonic wars. She could not remember if the doctor had done anything specific for her teeth. She remembers that he saw her alone, that he put one hand on her forehead and the other on the back of her neck, a procedure familiar to her from her Cathar memories, and told her to tell nobody that he had given her such treatment. He had thick brown hands with a rather coarse skin. Now, back in Clare's room in Somerset, Simon intervened to say that his skin was coarse and his hands brown because he worked a great deal in his garden growing his own herbs. He said that as a doctor in the Roman incarnation he had used belladonna, opium, foxglove (to produce digitalis, the classical heart remedy), and some other plant the name of which I could not distinguish.

Without prompting from him Clare remembered how he had sometimes given her massage with one hand on a fixed point and the other moving about. He was, in fact, practising the same amended technique as that in which she herself had been instructed by Braïda in the early months of their association in this life as discarnate teacher and incarnate pupil. This was to avoid attracting attention. To keep one hand moving was less noticeable, less occult, than if both were kept immobile. Clare recalled how, while treating her, he had spoken of forces of good and evil and explained that what she was undergoing at that time was attributable to the latter.

Simon told me that in those days he had given me no instruction. He had not been called in to treat me because after this particular interrogation I had not come off too badly and in any case my interest in Dualism was non-existent and my capacity to absorb its principles strictly limited.

Next day when I visited Clare her right foot was bandaged. She had a swelling, half the size of a hen's egg containing fluid, just lateral to one of the main tendons on the top of the foot. It was extremely painful. That morning she had tripped down some stairs and caught her right foot underneath her. She had put out her left hand to save herself and had hurt her thumb in so doing. When she picked herself up she knew that this was a replay of an accident in her Roman incarnation. While I was

382

examining her foot the revenants appeared to say that she had incurred the identical damage in the same way when being thrown downstairs in the course of the interrogation which had taken place on the same day of the year sixteen centuries previously.

In the presence of the revenants Clare relived the end of this particularly concentrated and vicious period of interrogation. She remembered how she and I were escorted by four men from Camillia's house. She was only able to hobble because of her bad foot and was helped along by the four guards. Some distance down the street we turned to the right and then to the left up some stairs to a long room at the end of which was a dais on which five men were sitting round a table.

Clare and I were examined separately as to the beliefs held by the cult of Mithras. I can remember on my own account that they were especially concerned at the beginning of the interrogation with the forces of good and evil. I recalled that they were wondering if the adherents of Mithras believed in a god of evil. They were obviously keen to prove that members of the cult were engaged in devil worship. They were also anxious to know if the cult included belief in a third god. Did believers regard Mithras himself as God or a Son of God? With the revenants round me I remembered attempts to drag from me the confession that Mithras was at least the Son of God and therefore a subversive rival to the Christ presiding over the destinies of the Roman Empire. I think I satisfied the interrogators that I knew less about the subject than they did.

It was obvious that the theological subtleties were not the main purpose of this interrogation. I think the grim-faced, silent but not actually bullying investigators were not really concerned with the respective merits of Christ or Mithras. What was more important to them was that Christ, in their eyes, was an acquisition of the Roman Empire whereas Mithras was, in being opposed to him, a potential destroyer. At any rate they changed tack abruptly. Having found that I was no help at all on the question of gods of evil or third gods they fired questions at me designed to elucidate whether Camillia's house was the centre of a military conspiracy. I was so obviously bewildered and taken completely offguard that my very confusion convinced them that

383

I at any rate knew nothing about any such possibility. When it came to Clare's turn I think on this particular matter she was as amazed as I was. Certainly she had been admitted to the ceremonies but I think the question of a military revolt instigated by the adherents of Mithras had never crossed her mind.

Sitting with her in Somerset sixteen centuries afterwards I was astonished to learn that the inquisitors' suspicions were actually justified. There was some kind of conspiracy among the soldiery dedicated to Mithras. Betty's husband was in no way implicated but some of his colleagues who were also friends of Camillia's were deeply involved. Some of them spoke of the Emperor Julian who had been favourably disposed to Mithras and who opposed Christianity, among other things because he saw its potential menace as an international theological system concerned with the maintenance of temporal power.

At the end of this session Simon divulged some information of great interest to me. He told us the treatment he had applied to Clare's foot in the Roman incarnation. It consisted in the application of a cold lotion alternating with that of a hot paste. The cold lotion was called something like plumbiacus. The name is sufficiently suggestive to enable me to say that this was a lead lotion which in my earlier days as a doctor was still in use for sprains, bruises and suchlike. At this stage my perceptive powers faded out but Clare remembered that this lotion was red. As to the hot paste the nearest she could get to its name was Coalancius Meteorith. She remembered an oil from a blue flower resembling, if not identical with, flax and having as another constituent a seed from a yellow flower.

Some days later I saw Simon's outline on the wall opposite. I could not see his features but I noted distinctly the russet-coloured robe taken in at the waist with a golden girdle. It was interesting to reflect that Clare, in this life my chief guide to the unseen world, should have received her first instruction in Dualism sixteen centuries ago from the man who, in this life, had been the closest to me for the longest time.

We had further experience of Simon as he was as Marcellus in the Roman incarnation. One day I was visiting with my wife the grounds at Stourhead. I have a great affection for this place with its mixture of a formal beauty which is never repressive and its

384

unmenacing suggestion of the infringing wilderness. I was very happy until we were walking round the last lake on our return journey. Silently in my heart I called for help from Betty. My plea was certainly apposite but scarcely logical. It was she who needed help.

When I returned to Bath I visited Clare. She said she had felt the same feeling of leaden depression and horror as I had in the middle of the afternoon. We were both convinced that this was something which had happened in the Roman incarnation. Then we both knew Betty had come to see us, Clare with the accentuation of visual perception which enabled her to see the revenants as she saw passers by, except that the outlines of the latter were more solid, and I with the inner perception which enabled me to know the second she appeared, exactly where she was standing and that she had fair hair and dark eyes. I knew at once that in the Roman incarnation Camillia had been involved in an accident. I quite clearly saw her fall from a chariot. She was dressed in a white, toga-like garment slit up the left leg and with a purple cloak bordered with gold worn over it. The two horses shied at some object in the road and Camillia was thrown out and I saw her lying unconscious. Sitting in the room in Bath I knew for certain that she had fractured the right side of her skull. I could name the bone (parietal) which was actually involved. I knew also, what Simon, or Marcellus, did not know at the time, that she had also sustained another fracture of one of the lower vertebrae in the neck and that there was some displacement of the bone fragments and pressure on the ulnar nerve. Because of this second fracture and its pressure effects her left arm was partially paralysed but this was not discovered for days, due to no fault of the doctor, because the patient was unconscious. I can only think that I saw this calamity in such detail because Betty and I were especially close to each other.

The man driving the chariot was cut about the face and had some broken ribs.

Clare and I were in the house when we heard about Camillia. I went for the doctor while Clare went to look for Graham who was already in love with her.

Later, in this life, Clare passed into a condition in which her voice thickened and slowed up and in which she did not

385

comprehend the questions I addressed to her. After some minutes, though still dazed, she understood the gist of what I was saying. She was in actual fact remembering more details of the accident. Camillia was completely unconscious and was obviously badly concussed. Then she passed through a stage of cerebral irritation in which she became very restless. She had two hard pillows placed each side of her head to control her movements. She began to wave her hands about while she was still unconscious and these had to be controlled. It was noticed that her left arm moved less than the right and it was this which enabled Simon to locate the site of the second fracture.

The external head wound was bathed with a potion made from nettles or some plant closely approximating to them. It was a jagged wound the edges of which were brought together and treated by some gluey substance the nature of which I cannot recall.

Camillia was fed on a liquid diet of honey, salt and water. This was put on her tongue literally drop by drop even before she was able to swallow. This was good medicine because the components of the potion were equivalent to those of a modern drip.

Simon also gave her massage. This in itself was not striking because the art was practised commonly in ancient Rome. What was unique was that, as he had practised with Clare when he helped her after her interrogation, he only used one hand. The Mithraic system of healing resembled that of the Cathars in that its practitioners preferred to keep both hands still. By his massage Simon was so able to relax Camillia's neck muscles that he could feel the broken bone fragments and realign them. The pressure being taken off her ulnar nerve she had free movement of her left arm and no wasting when she recovered from her fracture.

Chapter Forty One

We had known for some time that Christmas was a bad period for those who remembered their lives as Cathars at Montségur. We now learnt that at this season we had, for the time being at any rate, another burden to bear. Three days after Christmas Clare felt excessively depressed and passed into one of her half-absences. In this she went back to a further interrogation in which we were not knocked about but investigated more or less publicly while being restrained by a device which consisted of a post attached to which was a kind of collar which fitted under the arms. The aim was to keep us standing rigidly upright. While Clare was reliving this experience she was visited by one of the revenants who said, "Look under your arms." On each side a wart had formed a little below the armpit at the point of contact with the wooden collar.

It was perfectly logical that the authorities' attention to Camillia and her friends should be accentuated over Christmas because the date of the latter was also a Mithraic festival and had been celebrated as such for centuries. The more fanatical among the Christians nagged the authorities for greater activity round about the season of peace and goodwill and repeated their accusation that the cult of Mithras was subversive.

Three days after her first recall of the wooden device Clare passed out completely. When she came round she gave me the details. Once again she and I had been made to stand in our respective collars. On the previous occasion we had seen this together. The purpose of her second attack was to ensure a deeper vision of the interrogative procedure. The room in which we were questioned was panelled with slabs of brownish marble. There was a long table with six people sitting round it. Another interrogator was sitting apart from the others on something shaped like a piano stool. What was unique was that Camillia as well as Graham was present while we were being interrogated.

The latter had been a witness on a previous occasion when we had been knocked about. So far as I know this was Camillia's first appearance. Graham and Camillia were not encased in the wooden device which was, I think, something reserved for slaves or for those regarded with maximum suspicion.

Matters were coming to a head. In the first days of the New Year there was yet another playback in which Clare and I, once again with Camillia and Graham present, were investigated not only for information about the cult of Mithras but to discover whether there was some still more esoteric and mysterious organisation operating behind it. This time there was another room with a long low table. It was different from any room in which we had been investigated previously because Clare remembered that it was above a shop in which they sold pepper. While Clare was remembering the room above the shop I saw the seashore and knew we were at Ostia and that Camillia had lost something on the beach. This was a tiny model of a dolphin. I remembered that in those days we regarded this animal as another symbol of light and darkness and therefore of good and evil. Its Dualist symbolism was attributable to its being in the sun one moment and plunged the next below the surface of the water. The curve it describes when jumping from the water tends to complete a circle and thus represents immortality. I remembered also that this dolphin was worn by some French sailors belonging to the Masonic group at Portchester. It was combined with the simple flower and leaf pattern described previously.

Whatever the dolphin had become in the Napoleonic incarnation its esoteric significance was undoubted in Camillia's lifetime. Clare saw, in her return to the past, that it was a central figure in a mystery cult infinitely older than that of Mithras. I recalled that in the days when she was receiving written messages from Braïda the word Eleusian mysteries had been recorded along with that of Mithras* and when I suggested that this was what we were dealing with now the revenants indicated their approval.

Clare was able to give us details of the actual ceremony. The dolphin was made of some transparent material and was placed with a light inside it at the centre of a table. The light was in

---

* See *We Are One Another* (Neville Spearman, London, 1974).

some way intensified and then diminished. It continued to wax and wane. I felt that there was some concentration of mirrors round the room to produce this alternation of light. After the light had achieved its maximum intensity the dolphin was transformed in some way into an ear of wheat. Whether another symbol was introduced for the dolphin at this juncture I cannot say but the effect produced was that of a straight transmutation from the tail of the dolphin to the ear of wheat.

It came to me that this mystery cult with which we were dealing was more of a psychological and esoteric system and something equivalent to a fourth-century yoga. Its aim was to enhance sensitivity and perception and it was from her practice of the techniques embodied in these mysteries that Camillia had acquired a capacity to give peace to people and had built something into her nature which had persisted throughout five incarnations.

The investigators were less concerned with a possible rapport between the cult of Mithras and the Eleusian mysteries than with the possibility of Camillia being an active participant in the latter. I do not think they had much evidence to go on. Somebody had picked up the dolphin which she had lost. It was found not far from her house but there was no positive evidence to connect her with it. In investigating membership of the mystery cult they were not concerned with subversive religion or mutiny but with the simple and bracing issues of perverted sexuality. The mysteries were associated in their minds with communal sex orgies. They had no hope whatever of finding evidence of such practices in Camillia's circle but any stick was good enough to beat the suspects, particularly in the atmosphere of goodwill engendered by Christmas.

If I say I cannot describe my feelings during the evening after this latest revelation I risk being boring. For months I had suffered the pains and depressions inseparable from reliving rather than merely remembering the worst episodes of previous incarnations. There were times when for short periods one's sufferings were intolerable. This night in particular was one of them. In the presence of Clare and my wife I felt appallingly agitated. I could not keep still and went to another room to open the window to get air. This had nothing to do with my history of cardiac disease. It was just as though there was no air in the world and I was stifling from lack of it.

I awoke early next morning. It is pointless to try to define the extremes of horror I felt on waking. When I saw Clare later she said that she had had a terrible night in which the earth was shaking, followed by an earthquake. She had the feeling of being engulfed and of somebody with her who had suffered the same experiences with worse consequences.

In quick succession I had a call from Annette in Canada and Kathleen in Switzerland. The former said that Braïda had told her she had been with Clare a great deal last night, that the latter had been ill and had some trouble in her chest. Kathleen said that the night previously she had had the feeling of being involved in an earthquake. She felt it was somewhere in the eastern Mediterranean. She said that Clare had been engulfed in the earthquake and somebody close to her had been killed.

Kathleen's most striking statement was that she felt that what she and Clare had experienced the previous night went back to an incarnation before our life in Rome. I had this impression myself. One might say that this was reasonable enough and obtained by deduction because the Eleusian mysteries originated in Greece.

Later that day Clare, in my company, went off not into one of her trances but into a self-absorbed state in which her eyes were fixed on infinity and she answered questions slowly with a dragging intonation. At this stage she amplified what she had experienced the previous night. She heard a great noise, the sea rose and the earth opened. The latter calamity had impressed her most. All the houses in the neighbourhood had been destroyed. She (at this time she was a woman) had been engulfed by débris. Someone else close to her, a man, had been killed. She knew this man was me. The huge weight of débris had rested on her chest. She admitted that the latter felt tight and that it was painful to breathe and I noticed that her voice was croaking. I remembered what Annette had said in her telephone call about Clare having trouble with her chest. I looked at the latter and found that she had a distinct and painful bony swelling about the third left rib near the breastbone. This swelling occupied the same site as that sustained when she had relived being buried by débris in trying

390

to escape from a tunnel at Portchester in her Napoleonic incarnation.

I felt convinced, but for no reason that would satisfy my demanding brain, that in this disaster we were dealing with an incarnation still earlier than the Roman. At this stage Braïda and Graham appeared. I asked them if Clare had relived the earthquake because this was an inevitable tie-up with the Eleusian mysteries. Was the earthquake, I asked, a demonstration of the power of evil inherent in nature? Were we back before Pythagoras at the very beginnings of Dualism? They said that this was so. I asked next if some of the oldest myths were not in fact illustrations of Dualism. Was the story of Pluto and Persephone a symbolism of the light being engulfed in the darkness of the earth? Was Persephone's disappearance a representation of the night and evil and was light and goodness associated with her return? Was the grain of wheat in the Eleusian mysteries an indication of Persephone returning to the light and bringing with her the advent of spring?

We spoke also of spring feasts to celebrate the return of the light and of how goodness itself was contained in light because through it the fields were fertile again. We spoke of the spring rites which had been celebrated in places in ancient Greece and which were frankly sexual and orgiastic. The revenants said that these excesses were to be regarded as neither good or evil but as a natural, reflex consequence of disaster. They had first occurred among the survivors of the great earthquake. The darkness had passed, the light had returned and they knew they had escaped being engulfed in the great hole which had appeared in the earth. The whole point of reliving the earthquake was to see that this was the cause from which the Eleusian mysteries began. The great cataclysm had been a positive proof of the power of evil inherent in nature. The return of spring with the renewal of crops over what had been devastated was a sign of the resilience of nature and of the power of good inherent in it. The reflex orgiastic celebrations were important because it was from these indisciplined excesses that the refined and creative intercourse practised by Camillia had been developed in the course of centuries. The revenants reminded us that modern man had behaved in this gregarious and uninhibited fashion after the Messina earthquake. They emphasised that the earthquake Clare had relived was to illustrate the birth of the Eleusian mysteries and was not related to the Atlantis myth.

The revenants confirmed that I had been killed in the earthquake and that Clare had been badly crushed. There was further evidence of the latter disaster. On the following day, in addition to the swelling near the breastbone, she had great pain over the coccyx, the lowest section of the spinal column. There was discoloration, particularly on the right side, and in the course of days this spread like a V-shaped bruise covering the whole area. In addition there was pain, swelling and increased tension of the tendons in the nape of the neck. The neck symptoms cleared up in three days but the pain and discoloration of the coccygeal area, with the consequent restriction of movement, lasted well over a week.

In the course of the next few days, while recovering from the shock of the earthquake, Clare described in greater detail the vessels used in the Eleusian mysteries. These were often tri-coloured. They were usually amethyst, gold and silver. The amethyst indicated the search for truth and gold the realisation of the search and the attainment of absolute truth, whereas the silver represented the emergence at the mouth of the tunnel at the time of the great cataclysm. The mysteries were essentially concerned with alchemy. The transmutation of amethyst to gold was one of the significant changes to be observed in personal evolution.

Graham said that it was important for people constituted like Clare to wear gold and amethyst in the month of January before the return of Persephone in February. In the Demeter legend the return of the lost daughter occurred in that month.

To return to our life in Rome. The authorities were unable to extract from Clare and me any information about the cult of Mithras. The bad time lasted during the last three or four years of Camillia's life. She was always fatiguable from having given so much in a quiet way and I wondered how much the tension of the last few years contributed to her early end. The accident occurred when she was about thirty-two. She had still two years to go. I do not look on the years during which we were under surveillance as an unrelieved horror. If I put myself in the skin

392

of my Roman predecessor I consider I lived through a nightmare. I am quite sure that this is an exaggeration. Of course we were afraid in between interrogations but I do not think we were paralysed by our apprehension. I think we accepted fear and pain as a part of life to a degree it is difficult for people in this age to understand. The idea that we were less sensitive than modern man and responded less to the brutalities which were inflicted on us is nonsense. I think we were more prepared to pay in pain and fear for the undoubted benefits we got from working for such a mistress as Camillia. I do not think the thought of betraying her or of buckling up under pressure ever entered either of our heads.

Before the final disaster there are isolated memories, some painful some pleasant. Among the former was another interrogation inflicted on Clare alone. After being questioned by the secular authorities she was thrown down some stairs and then dragged into a dark underground chamber. The latter was almost pitch black except for a chink of light which entered from some place she cannot recall. What terrified her more than the darkness and the loneliness was the feeling of huge spiders crawling over her. Apparently the place was infested with them. In this life she has a phobia about spiders and reacts excessively from the mere sight of one.

Kathleen's memories were more pleasant though she recalled well the animosity she had shown me sixteen centuries previously. She remembered Betty's favourite colours were purple and dark green and how I had worn her dresses. She said that my hair was very dark, that often I had worn a golden band with a yellow jewel in its centre round my forehead and that I had worn something yellow round my neck. I think the latter was an amber necklace. She was bound to admit that in those days she had not cared much for me and insisted that I was not very popular with the rest of the staff. She remembered that the family and guests had eaten at long, low tables like coffee tables and had reclined on cushions while doing so. She and others had served at these meals. She made it plain that I was too elevated to have done so. Clare recalled that we sometimes used platters instead of plates for ordinary meals and that where sauces and gravies were used they were served in separate receptacles.

Kathleen remembered that Clare had the same luminous eyes

as she has had in all her five remembered incarnations. She could not be sure of their colour. I am convinced that they were not as blue as in this life.

I have mentioned that fifteen years before I had seen the face of a modest, shy and conscientious woman change to that of a girl with a pagan, half-animal beauty, and with smouldering eyes. Betty identified this as herself as she had been in a pre-Roman, eastern Mediterranean incarnation.

Chapter Forty Two

I come to a time when, day after day, without intermission, I saw the amethyst and the golden ring around it.

One day when I rang Clare I could hear over the phone that her breathing was rapid and light and that her speech was rather uneven. I asked her what was the matter. She said that she was shivering and could not keep warm. She had closed all the windows in the house and utilised every available form of heating. It was a raw day with an east wind blowing but could not be described as arctic. She was emphatically not a cold soul. At times I have found her house excessively healthy with more fresh air than I can comfortably support. I assumed that she must be sickening for something. Even over the phone I had the idea that her shivering merged on rigors.

I had what for me was a poor night. I was restless and agitated. I asked help of Braïda and Betty. Even when I had jibbed at calling up the revenants to answer my questions I had no compunction about invoking their aid to ease my own sufferings. Next morning I rang Clare. She had slept little and laughed apologetically as she described her condition as ghastly. She said she still felt starved to the marrow and could not stop shivering. I asked her if she had taken her temperature but she was not that kind and did not possess a thermometer. She came to see me later in the day. Suddenly I was aware of Braïda on the left of the chair on which I was sitting with Betty standing on my right.

Betty spoke to me very gently of her philosophic interests diffused through five incarnations. Then suddenly I saw the amethyst nearer, clearer than ever before. It was as though I was looking through a microscope which magnified its form and showed me in exquisite detail the facets of the jewel and the light like a meshwork of communicating rivers imprisoned in it. The palpitating golden haze around it had hardened into the glittering reality of beaten gold.

One moment I was seeing the rich luminous currents flowing within the amethyst ringed in its circle of gold, and the next I was looking at a tall house with an outside staircase open to the air, the sky and a landscape hardened by the harsh glitter of the sun on the scattered houses. Camillia was dying in that house. We gathered round her bed but after the lapse of so many centuries it was like looking at a picture. She was shivering violently. Then with her eyes closed and in a state of coma her rigors continued.

"She died of a fever," I said.

"What kind of fever?" Braïda asked me.

After that I took over. I said calmly and precisely, as though I had been reading a case history, that Betty had died of cerebral malaria. She had been attacked by malignant tertian, a virulent form of the malaria parasite. She had contracted it in the Campagna, the region round Rome in which malaria persisted until the 1920s. This was her first attack. Except for the accident she had had no previous illnesses of any consequence though she had often been described as delicate and was easily tired. This was the doctor in me looking back across the lapse of sixteen centuries. When I said that even on her death-bed her face had not been jaundiced by malaria I was not merely manifesting my clinical powers but expressing a desperate pride in her unimpaired beauty.

She was aged thirty-four when she died. She passed away on the night of October 13th/14th, that is to say on the same night as that on which Clare and I had felt her passing in the twentieth century.

It was significant of the intensity with which Clare relived the past that she suffered for two days and a night from the terminal rigors which accompanied Betty's cerebral malaria. During this period she shivered constantly and sometimes violently. We had another dramatic witness of Camillia's last hours. I was sitting in my chair after Clare's departure recovering from an experience in which the inexorable fact of death was joined to the imperishable truth of continuance. Kathleen rang from Switzerland. She had been troubled for several nights by what she called a vivid dream and which I imagine is better described as a vision. She was in a house with marble floors and walls and

396

with a marvellous view over a city she knew to be Rome. There were many people in white robes gathered round a bed on which a woman was lying. She was obviously very ill. The most striking feature of her illness which Kathleen stressed several times was that she was shivering violently. I asked her what the woman looked like. She said, "You know what she looked like. She was very good-looking in a blowzy kind of way. She was always striking enough. You remember her very fair hair and very dark eyes."

"Do you remember anything else?" I asked.

"Yes, one thing very vividly. She was being sprayed with some kind of scented water. I think it was made of rose leaves."

The spray was Claudius' contribution. He had kept away from the house since I had so mockingly repelled his overtures but his respect for Camillia was such that he forgot his own pains and waited by her death-bed. I don't know what he expected of the rosewater. Perhaps he hoped it would reduce her soaring temperature.

Kathleen said that for several nights she had seen her rugger forward who came when she most needed support. She was peculiarly disturbed by her vision which was, for her, the sharpest recollection of her Roman incarnation. It is possible that her fourth-century conscience was aroused when, standing at Camillia's death-bed, she recalled all the criticisms she had made of her.

Then came what I thought was surely the culminating experience. Braïda and Betty reappeared and told me that after the latter's death I had inherited her dearest possession, a pendant from which was suspended a large dark amethyst. It was cut into many facets in the front and sides. It was flat at the back. It was fitted into a thin golden frame. It was oval-shaped with the inferior limit of the oval slightly pointed. Betty's description corresponded exactly to what I had seen so often in visions and sometimes in moments of tension before or after giving public lectures on Dualism.

Camillia had regarded the amethyst as an amulet. She had worn it to protect her against disease and the evil eye. She gave it to me because she loved me deeply but also because she remembered the nights when I clung to her for protection against the evil spirits.

This to me was that last word, and the logical conclusion of the bands of purple and dark green I had seen years ago, of the dresses I had inherited from her in my life in Rome, and of the vision of the amethyst which had intensified in recent months. The latter was something she had given me because she had loved me. There could be no doubt whatever that seeing the amethyst was to me the sign of Betty's presence and an indication not only of our love for each other through nearly two millennia but a sure sign that among all the revenants she was the closest to me and to be regarded as my mentor.

I was satisfied and happy that I now understood the purpose of the visionary experience of years and that I was confirmed in the strange, impalpable other-worldly love I felt for Betty. Two days later I went to my room to rest. Once again Braïda and Betty appeared. For some time now I had not seen the symbols basic to my visionary experience. Now the dove, the rose and the chalice appeared. They were outlined in silver which soon turned to gold. Once again the visual alchemy was in operation. Then the lozenge-shaped Roman mosaic appeared on the wall. This time the design was coloured. The lozenges were a faint green and the interstices between them pale gold. Then I saw on the walls the outlines of a figure and afterwards a face and a still head bound up in what seemed a kind of head-dress. Then I saw that what I thought was a head-dress was a kind of bandage wound firmly round the cheeks and that above her face it was splayed out slightly. I knew that I was seeing Camillia dead and prepared for burial. The mosaic was the pattern on the floor of her bedroom. I saw these things clearly with my visual eye and not with the organ of inner perception. They were not as plain as the bookcase which confronts me at the moment but I saw them the same way and through the same ocular processes. It was sad and ironic to reflect that Betty's mother, Mrs. Butler, had said years previously that I would see Betty before I saw any of the other revenants. I knew now that Betty's mother had meant that, before all the others, I would see her daughter by the ordinary processes of vision. It was sad that when I turned to the sight we use in this world I saw Betty after she had died. It was a painful paradox that I had seen her previously with her fair hair and dark eyes by the non-sensory perception

398

acquired by some in life and inherited by a few who are blind at birth.

The sight of Betty as Camillia, immobile and aloof, was intensely moving. At the same time I was compensated by feeling her presence beside me. I lived in that room in those moments not an allegory of life but its compressed substance. We had been together in four lives and been held apart from each other in the fifth by the malice of geography and circumstance. More than all this we had survived five deaths. I know she was standing to the right of my chair these days. I always regarded her as my right hand.

There is a stage in life when one takes a deep protracted breath and tells oneself one has reached a milestone. It seemed to me that when I thought of Betty it was for ever and that the amethyst was an accompaniment of our common eternity. It was in an April mood of the heart that I said to Clare, "Of course the amethyst is inextricably associated with Betty." Even as I said it I regarded my words as superfluous. I did not wish to be reassured or to be supported in my conclusion. I merely spoke because it made me happy to share my conviction with Clare.

"But it isn't," she said firmly. "The amethyst is part of you quite apart from Betty. It's a symbol of the search for truth but there's more to it than that. It is also your stone."

"What do you mean, my stone?" It seemed to me ludicrous that a concept favoured by the cheaper magazines should be weighed against all I had traced of the stone's history and all I had learnt of its intimate significance for me.

"These things were laid down long before you met Betty."

"You mean I sentimentalise the business of the amethyst and Betty?"

"You don't face the truth about it," she said. "It appeared in your own life long before Betty. The life inside it is the same as yours. The vibrations it gives off are tuned to the particular rhythm of your nervous system and because of this they are healing to you." She then recalled for me what Guilhabert de Castres and Graham had told me of the formation of the first minerals in the world, and how light created life which either moved on the surface of the waters or was crystallised and seemingly immobile but still potent in the rocks and stones.

399

Graham added that the first individualisation of consciousness which was to become my human life took place within an amethyst. The details of what he told me are too esoteric and too deeply philosophical to fit into this work. All I can say is that the beginnings of my personal sentience were contained in some primitive form of existence born of the vibrations of the amethyst. He gave me a glimpse of my ultimate beginnings beyond my incarnation as a man.

The revenants, including Betty herself, confirmed that I was right in all I had deduced about the amethyst's personal significance for me. There could be no doubt whatever that what I had seen in my visions was what Betty had worn suspended on her pendant in the Roman incarnation. They added that it was necessary for me to get beyond the personalisation of a visionary experience. I see their point but I do not think I have achieved what they suggested.

At this point Clare produced for me a block of natural amethyst she had bought for me some weeks back. She told me I should keep it beside me particularly when I was writing and that I should hold it several minutes each day. I jibbed at the suggestion. It seemed to me too analogous to the wearing of holy images and the reverence for the hypothetical bones of still more hypothetical saints. I could not see that what was wrong in a Catholic was right in a Dualist and expressed my doubts to Braïda who replied, "If you don't know the difference by now you will never know anything."

My brain sharpened a little at this and I asked if my receiving the amethyst from Clare had anything to do with the application of the principles of psychometry. It then transpired that before she gave me the amethyst Clare had handled it herself about ten minutes a day for five or six weeks. I suggested to Braïda that, because Clare had, through her psyche, the power to disperse herself through time, she was able, by emitting a system of vibrations beyond the limitations of chronology, to link up with the emanation of the amethyst and impart to it something of her capacity to heal and to see into the past. Equally she could evoke from the substance of the amethyst vibrations which, transmitted to me when I touched it, could strengthen me by taking me back to my own beginnings and
400

could also sharpen my visions of the past. Braïda told me that all these things were not only possible but operative. There can be no doubt whatever that when I touch the amethyst I feel quite characteristic and unmistakable sensations. For a start it is always icy cold as though newly excavated from the high fastnesses from which it was obtained. This chilling sensation is independent of the habitat in which it has been kept. A sensation of cold travels up from my fingers in icy channels to my upper arm and is accompanied immediately by marked pulsation in the arm itself. This accentuated arterial circulation is sometimes felt also in the trunk. It corresponds to the sensations registered when psychic healing is being conducted at full blast and is manifesting itself in arterial pulsations rather than in the more common heat and tingling.

I feel stronger and more confident if I hold the amethyst for a few minutes. There can be no doubt that as well as increasing my physical well-being it clarifies my mind to the degree that, during a particularly good session, the answer to problems flows in a clear form and without effort. Like everything else in this world my block of amethyst is not a complete cure nor does it operate at all times but its efficiency cannot be doubted because in holding it I feel the same vibrations as those associated with healing. The revenants also told me that at times, when some particular effort was demanded of me, I should recharge my batteries with it. I did this, for example, when I was called upon to give a midnight broadcast which, theoretically, is a physical ordeal beyond my capital and from which I emerged not only unscathed but untired. They also advised me to carry a piece of amethyst in my pocket for use when I was exposed to such pressures as giving lectures or answering questions at their conclusions. I remember one occasion when, in the middle of a lecture, my mind emptied with disconcerting rapidity and I lost the thread of what I was saying. Except on rare occasions I always speak from minimal notes. I was jerked back immediately to full consciousness by touching a piece of amethyst I had in my pocket.

I do not understand fully the mechanism involved in what is transmitted to me from the amethyst. There still lurks in me a reluctance to use it. Were I pressed to ask why I would be

401

reduced to the pompous argument that it is a bit against my principles. The pragmatist in me tells me that I must go by results. Because of its effects I accept now that my relationship with the amethyst is older than my love for Betty, but I persist that she, the amethyst and myself make a kind of indissoluble trinity and I know that as I write she is directing the words I utter.

Chapter Forty Three

It is quite useless trying to describe my feelings after the death of Camillia. There was an agony all the more terrible in being in a way detached. What was worst was the frozen, central core of numbness and the certain knowledge that life had stopped. The torture was so external, so irrelevant to the inner death, that when the authorities seized us for further interrogation it was difficult to distinguish the two kinds of horror from each other.

Graham took Clare and me to his house immediately after the death of Camillia. His motives for so doing were various but altogether honourable. He had a genuine veneration for Camillia and knew that my safety and to a somewhat less extent that of Clare would be very dear to her. He felt that we would be a renewed target for the authorities. By this time he was also well in love with Clare. (It is interesting that neither he nor Claudius manifested the class rigidity which characterised the privileged sections of Roman society.) On the very first day we arrived in Graham's house we were visited by the secular authorities. It is some reflection on the sickening persistence of the bureaucracy at that period that they should have seized this opportunity to harass us again when we were crushed by our loss. Clare saw, in one of her half-absences, the interrogators demanding the significance of two objects left to her by Camillia. One was the head of a young man with two prolongations from the top of the head. It resembled the figure which had been used in the Mithraic celebrations. Graham succeeded in persuading the authorities that this was merely a personal legacy to Clare. She was also questioned about another bequest. This was a cross surmounted by a circle and decorated with an intertwined pattern similar to what was to become common on Celtic crosses three hundred years later. This second gift was also a Mithraic symbol but Graham succeeded in having it passed off as *objet d'art*.

After the death of Camillia my own life was a shadow. When

403

the agony of the first months was past I was no longer depressed except on the anniversaries of days when we had had special outings together and at other moments when she came back to me like a sweet, stabbing perfume. I kept my self-respect. With my ringlets and jewels I dolled myself up as impressively and perhaps as absurdly as ever. Though to outward appearances I was a picture of rather self-conscious sophistication my heart was dead within me because the purpose had gone from my life. I had given my heart to Camillia when I came from my hovel in the mountains. It died with her and for me there would be always a cold emptiness at the core of my being. As I was of peasant stock and with a peasant's wisdom, because I knew that a branch can die of a fissure in its bark, and because I knew from nature that not to confront the world's wild weather is to write one's own death warrant, I worked as hard as ever and dressed myself with the same careful ostentation. I knew that self-respect consists often in maintaining a succession of habits.

I did my best for Graham because I was intensely grateful to him. It was not his fault that I could not regard my work as a labour of love. There were no green and purple dresses to inherit and my duties were inevitably not so interesting. Clare was in better case. What she felt for him was something deeper than gratitude. Quite soon after entering his house she became his mistress. One thing I am certain of and that is that this was not a question of a gentleman exploiting a slave girl. Graham was a grave, considerate and compassionate man. It was not in him to act as a philanderer.

I never envied Clare her improved status. This was not because my nature was particularly self-effacing or tolerant but simply because I could not see what there was to envy. I had loved once in my particular way and that others should require passion of each other was to me a meaningless external diversion. It was not that there was anything in any sense ethereal about me. I suppose I was naturally chaste but I was in no sense shrinking. I had a hard streak at times and knew which side my bread was buttered. It was just that Camillia absorbed totally and for ever all the affection I was capable of. I was fond of Clare and admired her greatly but my heart was not involved.

I lived what to me was a comfortable and featureless life. I had no need to work at all because I had saved enough money in Camillia's service but it was not in me to be unoccupied. Clare's life was certainly worth living. She was in love and grateful. She was also more elastic and sensible than I was. It was not to last. One night Clare was silent, self-absorbed and obviously depressed. Annette rang from Canada. She had picked up across the ether that Clare was depressed and exhausted. She asked me if this was the anniversary of Graham's death in either the Celtic or the Roman incarnation. I opted for the latter. Later that night Clare was visited by Graham. He said that the day which had just passed was the anniversary of his death in his Roman incarnation. Clare's misery that day was understandable seeing how she had lost someone who had protected her in five incarnations.

The day after the anniversary of Graham's death in the Roman incarnation Clare had supper with us. I noticed that her face was engorged and her eyes somewhat distant but she did not admit that she was looking back to a previous life and my opportunities to question her were inconsiderable. Some minutes after she had gone I looked out of the window and happened to see her car still standing there. It appeared she had set off for her home, had then been overcome by the giddiness which so often followed these excursions into the past, and had reparked her car as she considered herself unfit to drive. While sitting in the darkness she recalled that, on this particular day in Rome, seizing on the despair induced in us both, and in her in particular, by the death of Graham, the authorities had seen fit to call on us again. We had been interrogated further and knocked about in the process.

It is extraordinary, when one thinks of the calculated inhumanity practised on us by the authorities, that Clare can look back on the Roman incarnation without revulsion and I with positive affection. Knocking people about is bad enough in itself. To seize the opportunity to do so within twenty-four hours of their having suffered bereavements is the outside edge of human cruelty. Is it that, in regarding the past, we make the same error as we do in this life when contemplating our own youth? On looking back on it after decades we forget its agonies and only remember its ecstatic Aprils. For my own part I believe that,

405

except for the years in which I was harried because of my supposed knowledge of the cult of Mithras, I was positively happy because I knew a degree of security I was never to experience again in any of my incarnations. Happiness is always a by-product. Mine arose from the opportunity to love and serve Camillia.

Betty regarded her life in Rome as her second happiest incarnation. She said that even during the decline of the Empire and until the disturbances of the last years the life of her circle was leisurely and gracious. She regarded her life in Celtic Cumberland as her happiest incarnation.

For slaves we were extremely fortunate and indeed privileged. I do not know how many years we lived with Graham but after his death, when we were taken over by Claudius, I think I was in my late thirties. By this time his deep and self-destructive love for me was burnt out and he could support without pain the sight of my face and my pretentious ringlets. It was good of him to take us on. There was something feeble and a little pathetic in his make-up. He was undoubtedly good-hearted and after years had not forgotten his reverence for Camillia and felt a definite responsibility for Clare and me as two of her dependants.

By the time Clare and I went to serve him I don't think he was capable of any deep sensation, enclosed in his cocoon-like and hedonistic existence. At my worst I had never been as concerned about my appearance as he was and my use of perfume was far more restrained. (Once again there is no evidence that he was homosexual. He was merely effeminate and self-decorative.) Annette is referring only to these latter characteristics when she describes herself in the Roman incarnation as a "frightful pansy". One of our duties was to prepare his bath which was sprinkled with sandalwood. Annette remembered this quite clearly. She imparted this information to me in a great rush because she is still definitely, though illogically, ashamed of her make-up as a man in the Roman incarnation. I am quite sure that our washing and drying Claudius gave him no more than ordinary sensory satisfaction. His desires were not at all aroused by these proceedings which in any case were common enough at that time. He lived in the pleasures of his five senses, was basically good-natured but too inert to do much positive good and

406

certainly did no harm to anybody. He had some excuse for his aimless existence. As I have indicated previously, his health was not good and he looked grey, toxic and dull-eyed during his attacks of abdominal pain accompanied by vomiting.

Claudius was quite incapable of taking responsibility. This was brought home to us sharply sixteen hundred years later in Bath. One evening I was sitting with Clare when I was suddenly afflicted with a pain in my right side. It was a momentary stab which could have been of no significance, a few seconds' spasm of muscle induced by sitting too long in a cramped position. Still it was sharp while it lasted. There was no reason at all why any ordinary person should have noticed my momentary discomfort. Clare spotted it immediately and asked where the pain was. The latter returned so acutely that I caught my breath and wondered if I was starting pleurisy.

It was not necessary for me to think out this problem. Annette rang from Canada a little later. She said she had felt awful all day and asked me if something horrible had happened. I felt she was expressing her usual concern for Clare. She brushed this suggestion aside quite brusquely and said she was referring to something that had happened in the Roman incarnation. She then told me that she had seen the house in Rome where she had lived as Claudius. I had been ill with a pain low down on the right side. Her description corresponded exactly with the site of the pain I had just experienced. The doctor, our friend Simon, or, as she knew him then, Marcellus, had visited and had applied some kind of poultice. Annette recalled clearly and frankly how agitated she had been because I had been taken ill in her house and it was clear that she was at that moment thoroughly ashamed of her reaction of centuries ago. I can understand better after this why, in spite of his being fascinated by healing and herbs, Claudius had never given himself wholeheartedly to medicine. He had a number of attributes which go to make a doctor. He was compassionate, interested in healing and science, patient and would have been presentable if he had restricted himself to orthodox attire and not been intoxicated by the need for self-embellishment. But he lacked altogether the capacity to bear the responsibility for anybody acutely ill without getting himself into a state over it. Through all this he had the impulse to heal.

407

What was timidly exhibited in his Roman incarnation was courageously displayed at Loweswater and Bassenthwaite in the Celtic incarnation when Annette, as Aurelia, was not only a competent healer but had an independent mind and a will of her own and prepared potions fresh, on a while you wait system, rather than dishing out stock prescriptions like many of her confrères. She had the same love of medicinal herbs in her Cathar incarnation. She and I discussed this subject when I was gravely ill from tuberculosis and pneumonia at Montségur.

I wonder whether Clare and I made enough allowance for Claudius' ill health when we laughed at his weaknesses and idiosyncrasies. Was he always a little toxic from his grumbling appendix? I think that Clare was more compassionate towards him than I was. I was sorry for him in a way, but then I had hurt him grievously when he was little more than a boy and it is always harder to forgive those whom one has oneself wounded. Anyway we were all shaken enough the day Claudius suffered another of his attacks of pain low down in the right side of the abdomen, with continuous vomiting. The doctor came and could do nothing for him. He died in great agony of what I am sure was a ruptured, chronic suppurating appendix with consequent peritonitis.

As the reader may remember, in the summer of 1973 Annette was desperately ill with a ruptured appendix and a fulminating peritonitis and was given up for dead. Accidents in which she was involved were play-backs of events occurring in previous incarnations. I was sure that her almost mortal peritonitis in 1973 was a recall, at the visceral level, of her final illness and death as Claudius in the Roman incarnation.

After Claudius' death I lived alone in a house of my own. I still remained friends with Clare. I was now in my fifties and had enough to live on. After Camillia's death the rest of my life was a secret cult. I became a follower of Mithras. It meant little to me. I only did it because I thought it would be comforting to Camillia in the shades. It also helped me to fill in time. It was a comfort that in these latter days we escaped discovery and persecution. I never really cared for the cult of Mithras. I became distracted easily when I had to concentrate on anything I did not care for.

One day I was sitting in Bath with Clare when she passed into one of her semi-trances in recovering from which she said she had been reliving my death in the Roman incarnation. Sometimes, in these states of amended consciousness, Clare acted as a strong catalyst, so that I was able to see myself as I was in my last hours. It was like that on this occasion. I was sitting quietly with Clare in Rome one evening when suddenly, without pain or warning of any kind, I vomited blood. The last thing I remember before I collapsed was that the haemorrhage was copious. Clare dragged me to my bed and went for the doctor. I remember coming to while I was alone. I lay very quietly without pain or fear. Something impelled me to put my hand on my abdomen. It was as hard and resistant as a board. Though I knew no medicine I realised that I was near the end. I felt absolutely detached from myself though I was completely aware of my surroundings. I did not care one way or the other. I was not afraid. I was drained of all emotion and fear went out with the rest of my feelings. By the time Clare arrived with Marcellus I had gone.

I have no doubt that I died of one of those rare, highly acute peptic ulcers which give rise to no premonitory symptoms, which perforate and which are often accompanied by considerable haemorrhage. In these days I suppose I would have lived but, though by this time I was no longer depressed and was fulfilling my obligations in my usual methodical manner, I had really had enough. Possibly modern psychiatry would say that the ulcer was a surreptitious erosion of myself after the death of Camillia. I suppose this explanation is as good as any. I am certain that all my psyche was looking for was to resume my old job with my mistress.

It was Braïda, reinforced by Guilhabert de Castres, who first told me that I should write this book to describe in it how I first made direct contact with the revenants. It was Betty who indicated how I should write it. She said that the story should be centred round her. It surprised me that one so self-effacing should give me such advice but I see that the story comes together better in this way. In addition she felt it was good for me to express in writing my old and continuing love of her which seemed to me so frustrating and purposeless in the last years of my life in Rome. Sometimes I see her as my sister in the thirteenth century. She sits with her trunk inclined slightly forwards from the hips but the line of her backbone remains very straight. She had the same posture and the same attentive smile and soft voice in the thirteenth century as she had in her last incarnation but her features were sharper though no less gentle. But while I am writing this book I see her as stately, lovely and a little languid while the shadows fall on Rome. She is mostly unsmiling but she watches me intently.

She is still around me. When I am in trouble and call for her she comes more quickly than the others. I cannot say here what I know of the nature of time, the dissolution of form and the persistence of individualised consciousness. All I will say is that she will be with me always, that there are no ends and no beginnings, that in what we call eternity there are distinct chords which harmonise especially with each other and which at the same time echo in all directions.

In my Roman incarnation I ended my life somewhere beside the sea. I think it was Ostia but the revenants did not tell me. I am certain that it was somewhere quite near because Braïda and Mr. Mills told me that, with my life in Rome pressing so closely upon me, I should not visit there for another year. They felt that if I did so it would be too much for me.

Chapter Forty Four

The story of how I made contact with the revenants is intimately but not entirely bound up with that of my Roman incarnation. There were many occasions on which the signs given me were not only manifested in the present but referred to the present as in the episode of the groove moulded in my hand by the pressure of Braïda's chain. We have seen also how Braïda directed the minds of others for the benefit of members of the group, as when she influenced the thoughts of Dr. Charles on the subject of autumn colours, cornelians and moss agates at the beginning of his treatment of Annette. When, later, Dr. Charles became acquainted with Clare and myself he was astonished at the identity not only of our opinions about Annette but of the very words we used to express them. On one occasion he was expressing the idea that Annette lived her life in compartments in all of which she was amazingly competent but that she seemed unable to facilitate communication between them. Talking more rapidly than usual, I told him that to me Annette was like a section of a honeycomb in which each cell was perfectly made but in which there was no communication between the individual cells. Dr. Charles interrupted to ask if I had recently discussed Annette in these terms with Clare and when I assured him that I had not done so he expressed amazement that Clare had not only expressed the same ideas about Annette but had quoted the analogy of the honeycomb in identical words. I had considered such phenomenon to be explicable by telepathy but Braïda dismissed this latter as a subsidiary mechanism. She spoke of the fusion of psyches and admitted that in what concerned Annette, she had fed those nearest to her and those attendant on her with her own ideas and it was because of this that Clare and I spoke at times not only similar but absolutely identical language to a degree which was unique in Dr. Charles' experience.

This particular activity of Braïda was revealed at its most

411

dramatic when Neville and Peggy Armstrong stayed with us for a week-end. Neville is my publisher. On Friday and Saturday we had spoken a great deal of the persistence of the group through its different incarnations. I had spoken especially of the drawings Betty made as a child of seven which proved that she was tuning in to a group of obscure characters in the thirteenth century. Apart from the general riveting interest of this child's drawings there was for me an intensely personal factor. It is not given to everyone to have written evidence that someone remembers him as he was seven hundred years before. In several places in Betty's sketch-book my thirteenth-century name Roger is scrawled across the pages.

After breakfast on Sunday morning Peggy Armstrong called my wife to the bedroom where she and Neville had slept during the week-end. A few moments later my wife asked me to come up and look through the window and Neville followed soon after. The night before there had been a heavy frost. The grass was still frozen on the lawn outside. It was silver grey and crisp except for the pattern of letters traced across it. I could not believe my eyes. Peggy and my wife asked me what I thought was written on the frosted grass. While I recovered my equilibrium I murmured something about a badger but these were not the tracks of a badger or any other beast because animals do not write letters of the alphabet. What was written was absolutely clear to all three of us. There was first a letter "A". Following that, written in huge letters, was the word Roger. As astonishing as the existence of the name was the fact that the letters were formed as in Betty's sketch-book. This was shown in three ways. Firstly, Betty made her Rs in a special way. Secondly, the whole name Roger, as traced on the lawn, was swung in the same kind of curve as in Betty's notebooks. Thirdly, the final "R" tapered off below the level of the rest of the name in the same scrawl as that employed by Betty in her childish drawings.

The lawn on which we were looking belongs to our neighbours. We drew their attention to its state that morning. In order not to condition them in any way I repeated my piece about badgers. Our neighbour looked at the lawn and said that this was not the work of badgers but of her grandson. She said the name Roger, which she read as easily as we did, was the effort of her grandson who had a friend of that name. Even for the rationalist the matter does not end there. Any little boy can trace a name in hoar-frost (incidentally I would not have said that this was a common occupation in these hard-boiled days), but do little boys write with the exact idiosyncrasies of little girls scrawling in notebooks forty years previously and now dead? If they do are the same little boys tuning in to the massacre at Avignonet in 1242? This really is a lot to ask. And why the capital "A" preceding the Roger? Why should my neighbour's grandson put the initial letter of my Christian name in the twentieth century before its equivalent in the thirteenth?

What was the mechanism which produced this writing? My own first thought was that this was an extraordinary example of telepathy at its most powerful. Unknown to himself, had this child next door picked up something from the heart and centre of our conversation the day previously and early that morning? I feel that Peggy Armstrong thought differently from the beginning. She was insistent that I asked Braïda.

The Armstrongs left us somewhere round about midday. Braïda appeared that evening. She confirmed that the capital "A" before Roger was the abbreviation of my current Christian name, and said that the child next door did not produce it, or the name Roger, under the influence of telepathy. She had been hovering in the wings that week-end and had herself directed the operation, the whole aim of which was to produce vital evidence, if not on my doorstep at least outside my window, of my common identity in two centuries. She admitted that she had put the idea in the child's mind and explained her motive in so doing. She knew that Neville and Peggy Armstrong were deeply interested in my work and had no doubt of the validity and importance of the phenomena I recorded. She said most firmly that they required no instruction in these matters or any further proof of their significance. But she felt that, being concerned with the publishing of my books, the Armstrongs should be aware of the full intensity of the experiences I had had in the last few years.

Even I, inured to these manifestations from another world, was amazed at the experience. There are certain high peaks which, in the last four years, stand out above the uplands of my cosmic consciousness. The groove on my hand from Braïda's chain, Betty's notebooks and Mrs. Butler's burnt legs on the anniversary of the auto-da-fé at Montségur were in their different ways unique and astonishing experiences. What distinguished them from this latest revelation was their relative privacy. It was a new and awesome experience to see the evidence of a former incarnation scrawled on the grass outside one's window. At the cosmic level I had the commonly experienced anxiety, "What will the neighbours think?"

Chapter Forty Five

My different kinds of contact with the revenants and the way I recorded them both reveal clear stages in my psychic development. In *The Cathars and Reincarnation* and *We Are One Another* I was engaged in a protracted verification of what was said and written to us from another dimension. I was, in fact, rebutting materialism with its own weapons and operating chiefly on the plane of intellect and personality. In recording my Celtic and Napoleonic incarnations the enlightenment I was given took place at the psychic level and was built for the most part on extraordinary synchronisations between the living and the dead. The history of my Roman incarnation was derived from my direct contact with the revenants, with Clare acting sometimes as a go-between. Some of my experiences at this time were beyond the psychic, as, for example, my recall of my initiation in a cave in the Ariège.

By this time a great deal of care and time had been spent by the revenants on my education. I realised that what they intended for me was important. I understood more clearly than in 1971 what they meant when they said that I should write and speak as much about Dualism as possible. They had always said that in view of the clash of materialistic systems in this world the hour was crucial. We were menaced by a return to the Dark Ages. The most solid contribution I, and other members of our group, could make was to enlighten people on the same wavelength as to the nature of Dualism, so that its truths would not become obscured during epochs of darkness. Dualism, according to Guilhabert, was the oldest European philosophy and the least amended by the erosion of time and by the necessity to live secretly in certain ages. All I envisaged for myself was a perhaps more voluble rôle as an exponent of what the revenants were ceasing to call Dualism and referring to under such simple headings as the truth about life. It seemed that I had not

415

been sufficiently pretentious in my estimation of my own rôle.

The day came when I heard something which, three years previously, would have plunged me into a fever of excitement. I should have known something was in the offing. Clare was with me that day and while I spoke to her I noticed that her face sharpened and her rather small nose became finer and longer. Her eyes remained the same. I had noticed a detail I had never seen before. The corner of her mouth was a little raised on one side. I asked her if she had ever had a Bell's palsy. This is a disease of the seventh nerve which causes paralysis of the muscles on one side of the face so that the two angles of the mouth are not on the same level. Clare replied that she had never had such a condition in her life and could not remember having been thus afflicted in a previous incarnation. Braïda materialised at this stage and said Clare had had such a palsy in the thirteenth century. It had been associated with a septic process affecting the ear which had involved the seventh nerve. Readers will recall that this vulnerability of the ear persisted through Clare's Napoleonic and twentieth-century incarnation. What all this amounted to was that I was seeing her as she had been as Esclarmonde de Perella in the thirteenth century.

The occasion was also important because, when Guilhabert de Castres appeared, I saw more clearly than before his stocky broad shoulders and heavy trunk. I could not help smiling when I reflected how many had exaggerated the ascenticism of Catharism. If Guilhabert ever practised any severe fasting it did not show in his figure. I had never before seen so clearly his chubby and good-natured face.

Our conversation began unpretentiously enough. We discussed the diet he had eaten and he said that he had never fasted excessively. He told me that the tradition that Cathars had abstained from food and drink for days and even weeks was quite without foundation. He said that he himself had eaten meat when it was provided for him by his hosts because there was no point in abstaining from so doing as the animal was already dead. He also said that he sometimes ate meat to sustain him on long journeys. He was an inveterate traveller and covered what for those days were huge distances in preaching the word.

416

After these homely details there was a sudden elevation of the spiritual temperature when I asked him if he had ever written down all the knowledge and experience he had passed on to me verbally. He said that he had done so in a book which had constituted part of the Montségur treasure. Over the years there has been a great deal of discussion as to the nature of the treasure which was smuggled out of the château during the siege. Until this particular day I had always thought that it consisted of rare and precious rather than esoteric works. It was exciting and moving to know that at one time the Cathar treasure had included what Guilhabert had told me in the caves of the Ariège and what he had repeated to Clare and me in the twentieth century. That he had written such a book had been concealed from me until I was capable of profiting from the knowledge.

I asked Guilhabert when his book had been smuggled out of Montségur and he said just before Christmas in 1243. I have described previously how all my life I have been tense and depressed just before and including Christmas. The misery experienced at this season was now shared by Clare, Kathleen and Annette who, with their awakened far memory, endured again the apprehension they had felt seven hundred years ago. Now I saw why members of our group had been particularly agitated during the disposal of the treasure. It is too much to suppose that all were so scholarly as to be tortured by the fate of some books. On the other hand it was only natural that we should have been especially concerned at the fate of the manuscript written by one who was intimately known to us and revered by us. For two years Clare, Kathleen, Annette and I had lived a black day on December 20th. It was on this date that the bearers of the treasure were refused admission at a house en route for the Château d'Usson. The treasure, said Guilhabert, had ultimately arrived at the latter place. There it had simply been lost in the course of ages. It is fascinating to reflect that when Annette was smuggled from Montségur in men's clothes on March 15th, 1244, the date on which she marched out mingled with the garrison, she proceeded to the Château d'Usson where she remained until she died at what for those days was a ripe old age. The treasure remained there in her lifetime and for decades after but Guilhabert would

417

not say at what date it ultimately disappeared and what was the manner of its disposal.

In a flash-back to the thirteenth century Clare and I saw this manuscript. It was striking because of its pale apple-green binding.

I had been moved enough to know that what I had heard from Guilhabert in Somerset was only a repetition of what he had told me before. It was personally painful to know that what had been put down in writing was lost. These reactions faded to nothing when I heard Guilhabert's next words in which he said that what he had written once must be recorded again and that the task was laid on me. He said that it was important in this present book to record how I made contact with the revenants in order, in a later book, to give the substance of those esoteric truths which dated from long before Catharism and were incorporated in the mystery cults of classical Greece.

It was a numbing prospect for a provincial doctor to be told that he was the philosophic and literary heir of a heretical bishop who had died seven centuries before. To me the implications of what Guilhabert had said were at one and the same time immense and sobering. It meant that he considered me sufficiently knowledgeable and responsible to act as another link in the long chain of transmitters of truth who, from Pythagoras onwards, have sometimes openly and sometimes in veiled words and symbols relayed to man the truth about his creation and destiny.

All this was more than I had hoped or even asked for because I had never set out to be anything more than a conscientious reporter of life as it exists outside the frontiers of matter. What followed after laid further responsibilities very squarely on my shoulders. Suddenly I saw myself standing clear of the trees on the side of a mountain which went up in sunshine, through the darkness of low scrub, to a castle at the summit. My companion was a dark, rugged-looking man with rather craggy features. He was dressed in a mid-thigh length tunic strengthened with strips of leather. I was explaining something to him slowly and carefully and he was listening intently. Then I was with him inside a room mostly in shade but with light entering from an aperture high in the wall. I was handling two manuscripts held together by a purple cover with a golden circle in its centre.

418

When the vision faded I turned to Guilhabert. "I wrote those books myself."

"Do you remember what they were about?" he asked.

"They were a commentary on your own book. I tried to amplify it in places to make it more understandable for ordinary people."

"That's why your book was longer than mine," he said. "This is also what you do nowadays in your lectures and writings, particularly your lectures. You try to put the basic teachings of Dualism in a form in which they can be comprehended by everybody. This is what is still required of you except that, in the future, you must write about the philosophy of Dualism as well as its accepted principles."

I now saw more clearly than ever the reason for the tension manifested by Clare, Annette and Kathleen in the days before Christmas. Earlier in my conversation with Guilhabert I had believed that their tension, and my own, had been heightened by the knowledge that Guilhabert's book was among those in jeopardy as the treasure was moved surreptitiously from the beleaguered fortress through hostile country. I now saw that there was a still more personal reason for the depression of my three confrères. At that time I was lying at the point of death at Montségur and suffering from pneumonia grafted on pulmonary tuberculosis. Annette, Clare and Kathleen remembered looking after me, and Annette recalled, with complete clarity, how I, a worn-out and emaciated wreck in my late sixties, had derived pleasure from her company and our talks about flowers and plants. It was only natural that she and her two friends should be interested in the fate of a manuscript produced by one so well known to them and evidently not long for this world. It should be remembered that Montségur was a relatively small château and that what happened within its crowded walls must have been of intense interest to the community. My book would be well known to them and its safe disposal a major concern.

Chapter Forty Six

One day I saw with great clarity Betty as she had been in her Celtic incarnation. The contrast between her light golden hair and dark eyes was particularly striking. That same day I spoke to Braïda of the old gods and goddesses, speaking particularly of Greece and Rome but mentioning also those still venerated in the Celtic Christian Church in Cumberland before it was Romanised. We spoke of them with regret, seeing them not only as deities but as projections of human moods and therefore as more accessible to us than the monolithic gods of the semitic religions.

I dreamt a lot that night. There was the dream of the tall beautiful woman who rode very upright on a grey hunter. I rode with her through a forest which was not dark and with light percolating between the tree trunks. For some obscure reason I knew her to be Polish. I did not know why this was so because she was long-headed and had classical features. The Polish women I had known did not answer to this description. Was it because of Eugene who was a Pole and an inveterate hunter? It was difficult to fathom because I could not think of the trees, through which the beautiful huntress was riding, as part of a Polish forest. It was more like woodland in a Mediterranean country. I felt that I had this dream because I had spoken to Braïda of the old gods and goddesses. Was it that in my sleep I had stretched out a timid and groping hand to Diana the huntress?

In my dream she and I rode on and on. It was night round my bed but in my dream it was day and sunlight until the light faded at twilight and it was cold in the forest and the shadows of evening. Our horses slowed down and she said she wished to spend her life with me but that the decision was mine. I could not make up my mind. It seemed to me that I was caught between the pagan, that is to say pre-Christian goddesses—in some odd way the gods had evaporated—and the comforting revenants who spoke my own language and shared my pains. I saw Braïda and her friends as Christian in the primitive and true sense of the word. I had to choose between them and the goddesses of antiquity. I had, above all, to accept or reject the beautiful huntress. I do not know whether I failed to make up my mind or whether she rode out of the dream before I had done so.

But if Diana the Huntress had ridden out of my dream there were echoes of her former presence. I went on dreaming of goddesses not symbolised as beautiful women in modern dress riding through earlier than primeval forests but as statuettes carved in stone. There were three of these figures with hooded faces whom I knew to be Mother Goddesses. I did not know why their faces were covered. Perhaps it was because in this life we cannot absorb the fullness of truth. We cannot infringe the law that it is only after death that we enter the second zone of enlightenment.

Next morning it was as if my dream had been continued. Clare had seen me in the small hours in my etheric body. I had spoken regretfully of the old Celtic gods we had still worshipped surreptitiously in Cumberland in the last years of the independent Celtic Church. I had said that it was better to have contact with lesser gods able to comfort us and transmit our needs to a greater entity. The old gods were kinder and more tolerant than the monolith Judeo-Christian God. I had hardly finished speaking to Clare when Annette rang to say that last night she had spoken to her mother of the old Celtic gods and goddesses in terms identical with my own even to the actual words I had used.

What all this meant was that in the space of a night I had been concerned with the old goddesses both classical and Celtic. I felt there was some message for me deeper than the need to choose between the Christian and the classical. Why, for instance, was Diana so insistently Polish?

I had to wait several months for the answer. One day when Betty appeared she told me that, when I returned to France in the early nineteenth century after being a prisoner of war at Portchester, I went on a clandestine mission to Warsaw. This was concerned with my activities as a member of the non-ritualistic school of Masonry deriving directly from the Freemasons of the Middle Ages. In Warsaw I met a Pole who, in this incarnation,

421

was my friend Wing-Commander L——. In those days the Poles were lamenting their lost independence. I was welcomed enthusiastically by the patriotic circles I frequented in Poland because my liberal ideas and antipathy to the Bourbons coincided with their own resentment of Tsarist rule. I was treated with great kindness, almost with reverence, by this group of courageous and cultivated Poles. My meetings with them were arranged by the nineteenth-century antecedent of Wing-Commander L——, whom I was to meet in 1940 when the the squadrons of the Polish Air Force flew from France to continue the defence of civilisation. Our house in Bath became known as an unofficial resting place for Poles during their leaves. I was also instrumental in the formation in Bath of an Anglo-Polish Society of which I became president. One of my dearest possessions is a letter of thanks to me signed by all the officers of a Polish aerodrome, following a letter I wrote to the press to correct some hideous misrepresentation of Polish aims engendered in the febrile brains of a section of the would-be intelligentsia. I have no doubt that, in this life, I was returning the kindness I had received a century and a half previously.

During my nineteenth-century visit to Poland I went to Vilna and Cracow as well as Warsaw. In these places as well as in others I preached with unflagging tenacity my three Dualist themes that the universe is a battleground of the forces of good and evil, that men can purify themselves by reincarnation and that the world is created by a lower entity. I delivered also my usual diatribe against the evil of Bourbon rule which went down well in a country where legitimist reaction was exemplified by the Tsar.

I seemed to be indulging only in nostalgic reminiscence as I talked with Betty in my house in Somerset, but as soon as she said that my dream was connected with an experience I had in Poland I saw a town with many medieval buildings. Though I had never been there in this life I knew it was Cracow and Betty confirmed this. I was walking through a widish street towards a cobbled alley inclining to the right and mounting slightly. I saw clearly enough the street and the alley leading from it. As I entered the alley the way was barred by a figure outlined in golden light. Betty told me that this was analogous to the illuminated shapes and outlines I had seen with an indescribable golden light diffused about them and which Clare had first described as Christ figures. Of the so-called Christ figures seen by Clare and myself there had hitherto been two varieties. The first was delicately male and the second represented an abstract principle of beauty which was essentially sexless. Betty was calmly positive that what I saw in Poland was a female figure and also non-Christian. She said that such a vision should not be described as a Christ figure but as a revelation of what she called the Mother Goddess. She said that when one described such a figure as female one was referring only to the face. It expressed the beauty and compassion of the female but the lines of the body were partly male.

Betty said that to see such a figure was the highest visual experience obtainable in this world. I repeat what she said though I find it a little hard to comprehend. I would have thought that a face representing mostly a sexless beauty would have been the ideal. But perhaps in this I am being foolish because we see visions *from* this world and they have to be expressed in terms comprehensible to us. An entirely sexless face is not easy to envisage. Where one finds it difficult to say with certainty whether a face is that of a boy or girl one is not confronted with the sexless but with a possible manifestation of bi-sexuality. I think the difficulty I experienced in accepting to the full what Betty said was due to my own capacity for self-criticism. For years I have spoken of the eternal feminine principle and of the superiority of the Mother Goddess over masculine counterfeits. Why should I shrink from what fulfilled for me all I had felt and known and hoped for?

Betty said that the dream was a signpost in my life because it was a veiled and clandestine repetition of my experience in Cracow a century and a half ago. What I had seen at the entrance to the alley in that city moved me as nothing else was to do in my Napoleonic incarnation. I had just come out into the street after addressing a meeting. I was exhausted but satisfied with my efforts. The vision I saw was in no way a comfort, a recompense, a solace for my weariness. It was a dazzling revelation which spoke its own language. I was taken out of myself into another world where there were no questions and where one

423

was engulfed in a harmony so total that the instant and eternity were identical and God and I were part of each other. Betty told me that throughout all my life in my Napoleonic incarnation I had longed for the return of what she called unequivocally the Mother Goddess. I had always believed I would see her again. When she did not return immediately I told myself that this was more than one could expect but perhaps at some crisis, perhaps in some illness, I would see her again. She was not something to be worshipped. She was too enchanting for reverence. She was something to love, to live with and to follow. I never saw her again. That was one of the reasons for my depression which struck me in my sixties in my Napoleonic incarnation. I do not know why so incomplete a person was vouchsafed a vision which seems to me to have been in excess of his inner development.

It seems that also in this life I have longed always for the Mother Goddess. It is pointless to string together the vague intimations I have felt of her presence. More than thirty years ago I was exalting what I called the woman principle at the expense of its male equivalent and indicating that all civilisations and culture stemmed from its operation. In the last several years I have not failed to write openly that to me the Mother Goddess is the only ultimate deity and that the idea of a god conceived of in any way as male is vain and preposterous. I believe also that the Mother Goddess is not the last word but that behind this too finite conception of a beloved figure there is a passive, creative and feminine influence beyond definition and analysis.

Betty told me that, in my dream of the huntress, I had seen not the Mother Goddess herself but one of her intimate messengers. I had seen Diana because she healed as well as hunted. We were together because I was very close to nature, because in my childhood I had had another experience of gods in the forest when I had seen Pan who was in part evil but also a healer. This dream of Diana came in the middle of a period during which I was making many out-of-the-body visits to Annette, Clare and Kathleen. It was also significant that I had had an out-of-the-body experience the very night I dreamt of Diana. On that occasion I had joined Graham in his astral body on a visit to Clare. Diana herself could travel out of her body by night. Perhaps this was one of her methods of healing.

424

Betty explained to me that Diana had appeared as a Polish lady to remind me that the last time I saw her was in Poland at Cracow. She also said that I had been right to associate this dream with Eugene, because he was a great hunter and because he had an immense power to emanate. The latter had enabled him, in his astral body, to act as a catalyst that night when Diana was with me not only in the forest of uncharted antiquity but in the cobbled alley off the street in Cracow.

Diana had said at the end of my dream that she would stay with me all my life if I wished it but that it was for me to make up my mind. I had not done so. Betty said this was because I was still conditioned by Christianity, above all by its obsessionally comprehensive ethical code and its insistence on the necessity for guilt.

Betty spoke to me at length about the Mother Goddess and Diana because they represented what she had sought in the Eleusian mysteries she practised in her Roman incarnation. She had believed always, unaggressively, even anonymously, that there is a hidden divinity in womanhood. It was this she had tried to utilise in all the incarnations known to us.

When I contemplate this beautiful and inconclusive dream, I see clearly another reason for being taken back to an epoch, earlier than our life in Rome, to the time of the great disaster. I have said that light and goodness came back to the world with the return of Persephone from the underworld. Persephone represents the light of goodness in this earth and Pluto a Luciferian darkness not wholly evil because, through her, he perceived a little the power of the light. But, more primordial than Persephone and Pluto, one thinks of Demeter, the earth mother, calling back her daughter from the shades and seeing the devastated earth replenished with crops and the fissures between the rocks suddenly, dramatically, aflame with flowers. Here we have a Mother Goddess more comprehensible, more merciful and more fulfilling than the masculine deity of the Old Testament. She faces the fact of the irremovable evil in this planet. She sees the cavern into which the light has been drawn in the darkness of winter. She affects a compromise with the god of the underworld to win back her daughter with the advent of spring. Note that she performs no obscene gymnastics like the masculine god of the

Old Testament who claims to be all good, to be dominant over evil, yet to have created everything including what is evil. Demeter accepts the evil in this world because this is the best she can do within the narrow compass of this planet but she knows that her blessed and rejuvenating fertility can be transformed, by a spiritual alchemy, into sharper perceptions which open the gates to new worlds of awareness and which lead ultimately to the silent, unpulsating central core of truth which is feminine in its passivity and silence.

Guilhabert de Castres wished me to write this book because he knew from past experience and present knowledge of me that I was capable of understanding the creative female core of human experience. Once the book was under way Betty took charge and told me how the theme should be handled. She was chosen to fulfill this rôle not merely because of her closeness to me through several incarnations and in the present but because, of all the characters in the group, she approximated most closely to the classical pre-Christian concepts which beckon to me from across immeasurable distance. She appears to me mostly as she was in her Roman incarnation, unsmiling, intently gazing and utterly truthful, the nearest approximation, in my conscious and unconscious experience, to one of the white goddesses of antiquity. With Betty present I no longer thirst for the Mother Goddess because I cannot aspire in this world to be nearer to her than I am now. The separation from her is less painful than it was in my Napoleonic incarnation because I understand better in this life what goes on in my own mind, and secondly, in the narcotic beauty of Somerset, I am not so haunted by her as I was in my years in Provence when, against a classical background, I could hear her footsteps but never see her before me as in the alley in Cracow.

I think it is fair to say that I have never felt sentimental about Betty. I have not elevated the thin, spindle-shanked, candidly smiling child, seen in a seaside snapshot, to the level of a Mother Goddess. When I talk with her I see her often in the green and purple she wore by day. With darkness fallen I see only the pallor of her face and her searching eyes, as, widening her arms, she swept from my mind the fear of the demons that walked by night.

I have learnt a little from my lives. The more you expect from life the less you get from it. The sun shines on the just and the unjust alike. It often seems biased in favour of the latter. Generally speaking the harder you try the less you get. There are certain consolations. Love is stronger than death and wisdom comes to all, however unteachable, however unwilling. In the course of a cycle of lives I cannot see that wisdom can be realised against the background of a single life, however much the latter is trimmed with the pretty and alluring enticements of the orthodox heaven. We acquire what sense we possess in walking down the corridors of many lives. This life which we regard, according to our constitution, either as tragedy or comedy, is in point of fact a mirage, a faint reflection in a mirror and without importance except as an image of a fuller harmony, a more living beauty and a deeper truth. All beauty in this world has a piercing and tragic quality because it is evanescent. We must regard what is given to us as the faintest reflection on the furthest shore. The very colours of this world are attenuated tones of the vibrating harmonies which await us after death. The thoughts and feelings we exchange in this world are fragmentary and interrupted, like the broken columns of temples whose proportions we can hardly realise.

I have talked with the dead and what I know from them is that the life we live here is a kind of death. What in this world I regard as beautiful is no more than the breath of a ghost on my forehead. As we ascend the next planes of consciousness we come to life. We wait, beyond the wasteland of time, in a world where Guilhabert de Castres said there are no beginnings and no endings and memory is a cloud of vibrations which moves backwards and forwards.